Samuel Johnson
and the Politics
of Hanoverian England

Samuel Johnson and the Politics of Hanoverian England

JOHN CANNON

CLARENDON PRESS · OXFORD
1994

Oxford University Press, Walton Street, Oxford OX2 6DP

Oxford New York
Athens Auckland Bangkok Bombay
Calcutta Cape Town Dar es Salaam Delhi
Florence Hong Kong Istanbul Karachi
Kuala Lumpur Madras Madrid Melbourne
Mexico City Nairobi Paris Singapore
Taipei Tokyo Toronto
and associated companies in
Berlin Ibadan

Oxford is a trade mark of Oxford University Press

Published in the United States
by Oxford University Press Inc., New York

British Library Cataloguing in Publication Data

Data available

Library of Congress Cataloging in Publication Data
Cannon, John Ashton.
Samuel Johnson and the politics of Hanoverian England / John
Cannon.
p. cm.
Includes bibliographical references.
1. Johnson, Samuel, 1709–1784—Political and social views.
2. Politics and literature—Great Britain—History—18th century.
3. Great Britain—Politics and government—18th century.
4. Johnson, Samuel, 1709–1784—Contemporary England. 5. England—
Civilization—18th century. I. Title.
PR3537.P6C36 1994 828′.609—dc20 94-9429
ISBN 0–19–820452–3

1 3 5 7 9 10 8 6 4 2

Typeset by Best-set Typesetter Ltd., Hong Kong
Printed in Great Britain
on acid-free paper by
Bookcraft Ltd.
Midsomer Norton, Nr Bath, Avon

Contents

Abbreviations

A Course of Lectures	*A Course of Lectures on the English Law, Delivered in the University of Oxford 1767–1773 by Sir Robert Chambers, Second Vinerian Professor of English Law, and Composed in Association with Samuel Johnson*, ed. T. M. Curley, 2 vols. (Oxford, 1986)
CJ	*Journals of the House of Commons*
DNB	*Dictionary of National Biography*
Fortescue	Sir John Fortescue (ed.), *The Correspondence of King George the Third from 1760 to December 1783*, 6 vols. (London, 1927–8)
Hawkins	Sir John Hawkins, *The Life of Samuel Johnson, LL.D.*, ed. B. H. Davis (London, 1962)
HMC	Reports of the Royal Commission on Historical Manuscripts
House of Commons, 1715–54	*The History of Parliament: The House of Commons, 1715–54*, ed. R. R. Sedgwick, 2 vols. (London, 1970)
House of Commons, 1754–90	*The History of Parliament: The House of Commons, 1754–90*, ed. Sir Lewis Namier and John Brooke, 3 vols. (London, 1964)
Journey to the Western Islands	Samuel Johnson, *A Journey to the Western Islands of Scotland*, ed. M. Lascelles (New Haven, Conn., 1971)
Junius	*The Letters of Junius*, ed. J. A. Cannon (Oxford, 1978)
Idler	Samuel Johnson, *The Idler and The Adventurer*, ed. W. J. Bate, J. M. Bullitt, and L. F. Powell (New Haven, Conn., 1967)

Letters, ed. Tinker	*The Letters of James Boswell*, ed. C. B. Tinker, 2 vols. (Oxford, 1924)
Letters, ed. Chapman	*The Letters of Samuel Johnson*, ed. R. W. Chapman, 3 vols. (Oxford, 1952)
Letters, ed. Redford	*The Letters of Samuel Johnson*, ed. B. Redford, 5 vols. (Oxford, 1992–4)
Life	*Boswell's Life of Johnson*, ed. G. B. Hill, rev. L. F. Powell, 6 vols. (Oxford, 1934–50)
Lives of the Poets	*Samuel Johnson, Lives of the English Poets*, ed. G. B. Hill, 3 vols. (Oxford, 1905)
Miscellanies	*Johnsonian Miscellanies*, ed. G. B. Hill, 2 vols. (Oxford, 1897)
Parl. Hist.	*Cobbett's Parliamentary History of England from the Norman Conquest in 1066 to the Year 1803*, 36 vols. (1816)
Rambler	*Samuel Johnson, The Rambler*, ed. W. J. Bate and A. B. Strauss, 3 vols. (New Haven, Conn., 1969)
Reflections	*Edmund Burke, Reflections on the Revolution in France* (Everyman ed.; London, 1910)
Sermons	*Sermons of Samuel Johnson*, ed. J. Hagstrum and J. Gray (New Haven, Conn., 1978)
Thraliana	*Thraliana: The Diary of Mrs. Hester Lynch Thrale (later Mrs. Piozzi), 1776–1809*, ed. K. C. Balderston (Oxford, 1942)
Tour	*Boswell's Journal of a Tour to the Hebrides with Samuel Johnson, LL.D.*, ed. F. A. Pottle and C. H. Bennett (London, 1936)
VCH	*Victoria County History of England*
Wyvill	*Political Papers Chiefly Respecting the Attempt . . . to Effect a Reformation of the Parliament of Great Britain*, 6 vols. (1794–1802)

Introduction

FEW reviews have been more influential than that by Macaulay of Croker's edition of Boswell's *Life of Johnson*. It appeared in the *Edinburgh Review* in the autumn of 1831. Macaulay succeeded in blasting the reputation of editor, author, and subject alike. Croker was indicted for slipshod scholarship; Boswell was impaled on the paradox that had he not been a great fool he could never have produced a masterpiece; Johnson was exhibited as a man of quaint, old-fashioned prejudice, an antediluvian eccentric.

Macaulay's motives are not hard to detect. He was a Whig, newly elected to Parliament for the borough of Calne, and in the process of establishing his political reputation. All three of his victims were avowed Tories. Each was innocent and from Macaulay they received little mercy.

John Wilson Croker had been in Parliament since 1807 and was a close associate of Sir Robert Peel. He was by far the most pertinacious and expert critic of the Reform Bill introduced by the Whigs in the spring of 1831, specializing in drawing attention to the anomalies and inconsistencies in the measure. Was it not strange that Calne, the borough for which Macaulay sat, had been accorded favourable treatment? Croker and Macaulay clashed repeatedly in the House in the course of 1831. In March, Macaulay wrote to the editor of the *Edinburgh Review* that he would write on Croker's edition when it came out, and he waited throughout the summer with his gun loaded.[1] The review commenced, 'This work has greatly disappointed us . . .' and continued, 'we cannot open any volume in any place without lighting on a blunder . . .'. In fact, Croker was, for his day, a good and careful editor. He defended himself in the 1847 edition of the work, printing Macaulay's strictures and his own explanations side by side.[2] Few people who choose to compare them will doubt that Macaulay's criticisms were spiteful, petty, and unfair.

The treatment of Boswell was equally absurd. He was, declared Macaulay majestically, 'one of the smallest men that ever lived . . . a

---

[1] Macaulay to Macvey Napier, 8 Mar. 1831, in T. Pinney (ed.), *Letters of Thomas Babington Macaulay* (Cambridge, 1974), ii. 7.

[2] Croker sent Blackwood a defence, which was passed on to John Wilson and used in no. 59 of Noctes Ambrosianae in *Quarterly Review*, Nov. 1831. See M. F. Brightfield, *John Wilson Croker* (Berkeley, Calif., 1940), 301.

man of the meanest and feeblest intellect'. He was totally devoid of those talents 'which ordinarily raise men to eminence as writers' and had blundered into success. His vacuity of mind meant that he could act as blotting-paper for Johnson's ink. Nothing could be further from the truth. Boswell could be silly and unstable, but he was gifted and intelligent, and in the *Life of Johnson* he knew exactly what he was doing. To his friend Temple he wrote in 1788 that he had devised a new method which could not fail:

I am absolutely certain that *my* mode of biography, which gives not only a *history* of Johnson's *visible* progress through the world, and of his publications, but a *view* of his mind, in his letters and conversations is the most perfect that can be conceived, and will be *more* of a *Life* than any work that has ever yet appeared.[3]

Few books could have been more carefully planned or more triumphantly executed.

The account of Johnson himself which Macaulay offered was a gross and lurid caricature. He could not forgive Johnson for being a Tory nor comprehend how he could have been proud of it. 'The characteristic peculiarity of his intellect', Macaulay assured his readers, was 'the union of great powers with low prejudices'. Johnson suffered from 'the lowest, fiercest, and most absurd extravagances of party spirit, from rants which, in everything but the diction, resembled those of Squire Western . . . his passions were violent even to slaying against all who leaned to Whiggish principles'. Johnson entertained, Macaulay declared, 'a fixed contempt' for 'all those modes of life and those studies which tend to emancipate the mind from the prejudices of a particular age or a particular nation'. That he was not himself splendidly emancipated never crossed Macaulay's mind. Johnson's comments on literature were vitiated by 'an enslaved understanding' and his opinions were already treated with ridicule.[4] Against the Americans Johnson had poured forth 'torrents of raving abuse'. His writings were fast fading and only his peculiarity of manners and vivacity of table talk would keep him before the public.

Macaulay reserved until the end his most patronizing remark. Having scattered literary corpses throughout the review, he bade a smiling farewell with effortless effrontery: 'we would fain part in good humour

---

[3] *Letters*, ed. Tinker, ii. 344.
[4] 'He could see no merit in our fine old English ballads,' added Macaulay, 'and always spoke with the most provoking contempt of Percy's fondness for them.' In fact, Johnson suggested to Percy that he should publish them and wrote the dedication for the *Reliques*. See B. H. Davis, 'Johnson's 1764 visit to Percy', in P. J. Korshin (ed.), *Johnson After Two Hundred Years* (Philadelphia, 1986).

from the hero, from the biographer, and even from the editor . . .'. He had 'beaten Croker black and blue', he told his sister exultantly; Croker was 'smashed', he wrote to Ellis.[5]

The frequent republication of Macaulay's essays, together with the article on Johnson which he wrote in 1856 for the *Encyclopaedia Britannica*, gave his views of Johnson very wide currency.[6] They were reinforced by other critics such as Carlyle and Leslie Stephen. Though Carlyle included Johnson as a hero of literature, he had nothing but contempt for the eighteenth century and his description of Johnson was little improvement on Macaulay's burlesque: 'Figure him there, with his scrofulous diseases, with his great greedy heart, and unspeakable chaos of thoughts . . . Johnson believed altogether in the old.'[7] Leslie Stephen, like Macaulay, had several bites at the question, contributing a biography in 1878 to the Men of Letters series and writing the article on Johnson for the *Dictionary of National Biography*. Stephen continued the tradition of admiring Johnson for his character, while remaining dismissive about his writings. Johnson left behind him, he told his readers, only 'scanty and inadequate remains'; much of the literary criticism was 'pretty nearly obsolete'; and the greater part of his output had 'lost its savour'. The political writings were 'grotesque', defending the 'most preposterous and tyrannical measures'. Johnson, declared Stephen, seemed like some huge mechanism, grinding out a 'ponderous tissue of verbiage'.[8] On the centenary of Johnson's death in 1884, *The Times* was very cool, declaring that the 'infatuated admiration' which Johnson had once enjoyed was 'not wholly comprehensible' to the present generation of readers.

But the recovery of Johnson's reputation in the twentieth century was dramatic. The poet Alfred Noyes wrote in 1940 that, in his observations on Shakespeare and Milton, Johnson was 'far shrewder, far truer and far more independent of authority than any later critic'.[9] T. S. Eliot, in a lecture of 1944 on Johnson as poet and critic, offered very high praise. He

[5] *Letters of Macaulay*, ii. 95, 106.

[6] Macaulay's treatment of Johnson in the article was more restrained, but he persisted with his tedious paradox on Boswell, insisting that he could not reason and had no wit, no humour, and no eloquence.

[7] *On Heroes, Hero-Worship and the Heroic in History* (London, 1841). To be rebuked by Carlyle for chaos of mind is on a par with being reproached by Stalin or Hitler for want of humanity.

[8] *Samuel Johnson* (London, 1878), 166–84. One wonders quite why Johnson was chosen to launch the Men of Letters series.

[9] 'Johnson', in *Pageant of Letters* (New York, 1940), 75–99, quoted in J. L. Clifford and D. J. Greene (eds.), *Samuel Johnson, a Survey and Bibliography of Critical Studies* (Minneapolis, 1970), 173, ref. 10/6:246.

was one of the three greatest critics of poetry in English literature, the other two being Dryden and Coleridge, and his own poetic output, though small, was first-class. 'London', his first major work, was marred by 'feigned indignation', but in 'The Vanity of Human Wishes' Johnson had found a theme perfect for his abilities and had produced a meditative poem superior to Gray's *Elegy*. Of the late lines on the death of Robert Levett, Eliot commented that they were 'unique in tenderness, piety and wisdom'.[10] After the Second World War, the output devoted to Johnson increased spectacularly, with a number of important biographies. The *Cambridge History of English Literature*, published in 1983, had James Barry's portrait of Johnson on the dust-jacket. The bicentenary, in 1984, revealed how much Johnson's reputation had soared: he would make, declared *The Times*, a better national saint for the English than St George.[11]

Meanwhile the rehabilitation of Johnson's political views had commenced. The credit for this goes largely to Donald Greene, one of the first to suggest that Johnson's political opinions were worthy of serious study and to draw attention to some markedly liberal aspects of his thinking.[12] Greene's book was an important and influential pioneering effort. But it was published as long ago as 1960, and written as a dissertation in 1954, when the influence of Sir Lewis Namier was in the ascendant. Much of the subsequent period has been devoted by historians to challenging Namier's conclusions and offering substantial modifications to the picture which he painted of Hanoverian politics. It is no longer possible to see political life solely in terms of country-house manœuvres nor to limit it to the world of Westminster. In particular, the attention now paid to the growth of an informed public opinion, which Namier had undoubtedly underestimated, is bound to change our perception of Johnson himself, since he was one of the most potent forces encouraging the growth of that

---

[10] *On Poetry and Poets* (London, 1957). See also an influential article by F. R. Leavis, 'Johnson as critic', *Scrutiny*, 12/3 (Summer 1944), which describes Johnson's as 'a powerful and distinguished mind operating at firsthand upon literature'.

[11] Quoted by P. J. Korshin, 'Preface: The Paradox of Johnsonian Studies', in *Johnson After Two Hundred Years*, ix.

[12] *The Politics of Samuel Johnson* (New Haven, Conn., 1960). A second edn. was published in 1990 by the University of Georgia Press. Greene confirms that 'the text remains essentially the same' but adds a valuable introduction, summarizing reactions to his book, discussing some recent publications, and reiterating his position on the question of Johnson's alleged Jacobitism. A perceptive early comment, defending Johnson from Macaulay's charge of being a 'bigoted Tory', was by John Sargeaunt, 'Dr. Johnson's Politics', contributed to the *Johnson Club Papers* (1899).

opinion and has been hailed as the most successful journalist of the eighteenth century.

It is not however my intention merely to try to update Greene's volume, but to use this study of Johnson as a means of registering and reassessing the changes in historical interpretation which have been made or suggested in the past three decades. The volume of work on Hanoverian England since the death of Namier has been enormous. Though it is very agreeable to see what was once a historiographical desert blossom as the rose, the results have been distinctly confusing, as revisionist elbowed revisionist to one side. Change and continuity, stability and strife, have been stressed in turn. Indeed, there is some danger of historians of the period grouping into two armed camps, exchanging fierce fire on party, Jacobitism, the Tories, Anglicanism, popular politics, and so on. My friend Professor W. A. Speck has surveyed the scene in a delightfully named review article.[13] The disagreement, he commented, is no mere 'storm in an historiographical teapot' but involves substantial issues and to some extent represents a continuation of the old conflict between Namier and Butterfield, narrow against broad, static against changing.

It should be possible to use Samuel Johnson's life and writings to reassess Hanoverian politics. Born in 1709, he takes us from Dr Sacheverell in Anne's reign to 1784, leaving the young William Pitt in office, the American colonies lost, and the French Revolution on the horizon. We start in a world of the Divine Right of Kings, with the young Johnson taken to be stroked by the queen, the last British monarch to perform that ceremony, and we finish within sight of the Rights of Man. All his life Johnson was concerned with politics, from his early years working up debates for Cave's *Gentleman's Magazine* to his endeavours in the 1770s and 1780s to help his friend Henry Thrale to retain his seat for the tumultuous borough of Southwark. He was on close terms with a number of politicians. In the 1760s he seems to have acted as backroom adviser to William Gerard Hamilton; Charles Fox, Sir Charles Bunbury, and Richard Sheridan were members of the Club; Gibbon was a close acquaintance while he sat in the Commons; William Strahan, one of Johnson's many printer friends, was a supporter of Lord North's administration; and Edmund Burke was a pallbearer at Johnson's funeral. In the 1770s Johnson produced four remarkable and influential political

[13] 'Will the Real Eighteenth Century Stand Up?', *Historical Journal*, 34/1 (1991), 203–6.

pamphlets. He met Wilkes, argued with Mrs Macauley, the radical historian, and at one time seriously considered taking a seat in the Commons himself.

I have not taken politics in the narrowest sense because I wanted to see how Johnson's ideas related to the more general development of thought in Hanoverian England. I have therefore included chapters on religion, on the Enlightenment, and on nationalism. Since the context for the latter two must be European rather than British, I have allowed myself to run slightly wider of the mark to fit the broader intellectual picture.

The view of Johnson's mind which emerges does not confirm Macaulay's portrait of him as a man of ridiculous and extreme prejudices, increasingly out of touch with the spirit of the times. In a number of instances—on education, prison reform, or slavery—he was if anything ahead of his day. But, as a general proposition, Johnson's opinions were run of the mill, though expressed with a vigour and often a wit that were all his own. This is what one might expect. He was not, after all, a trained philosopher, but a working man-of-letters and a journalist, picking up ideas as he went along. Though a failed teacher, he was a great educator, spreading knowledge and learning. He tried out his ideas and listened to those of other people in the clubs, dinner parties, and taverns that formed so important a part of his life. It would not be surprising if, under these circumstances, his views should often seem derivative, as those of most of us are. Though that means that he cannot often be credited with original thinking, it makes him an even better guide to the topics being discussed in his own day, among his friends and acquaintances.

The reputation of Johnson suffered much at the hands of liberals and Americans; where the liberals have also been Americans, the criticism has been fierce. As recently as 1986 a distinguished American scholar could refer to Johnson's pamphlet *Taxation No Tyranny* as 'infamous'.[14] But in recent years we have been frequently reminded that, in Hanoverian England, Toryism remained a popular creed. Johnson was convinced that firm government and respect for authority made for the greatest possible happiness in society. His dislike of Whiggism was that it fed on discontent and encouraged sedition. He was, like his friend Bathurst, a good hater, but what he hated was hypocrisy. To later generations his views may sound harsh, but they did not rule out compassion for the poor and unfortunate. 'A decent provision for the poor', he remarked, 'is the true

---

[14] T. W. Curley, introd. to *A Course of Lectures*. In fairness one must also acknowledge that American scholars have also been among the most devoted and informed commentators on Johnson and his work.

test of civilisation', and he filled his house with waifs and strays. He was so soft a touch for beggars that they lay in wait for him. He defended the hapless Admiral Byng, shot as a scapegoat for the loss of Minorca in 1756; he did his best to save Dr Dodd from the gallows; he wrote movingly on behalf of French prisoners of war; he left his property to his negro servant, Frank Barber, educated at his own expense. His love for his own country is not something for which many of us would wish to condemn him. 'To love their country', he wrote in *Taxation No Tyranny*, 'has been considered as virtue in men, whose love could not be otherwise than blind, because their preference was made without a comparison; but it has never been my fortune to find, either in ancient or modern writers, any honourable mention of those, who have with equal blindness hated their country.'

Far from being, as Macaulay suggested, an extreme and outlandish figure, Johnson was to be found, on most questions, putting forward a moderate case, and one which he shared with many of his fellow country-men. In his deep concern for religion, his mistrust of abstract rationality, his respect for antiquity, his strong sense of genuine patriotism, his dis-taste for the politics of envy, his belief in the benefits of order and authority, his warning that governmental mistakes should not be made the pretext for persistent disobedience, and his insistence that citizens have responsibilities as well as rights, he anticipated Edmund Burke. He deserves greater recognition than he has been accorded as one of the founding fathers of mainstream conservative thought.

I

Johnson and Religion

WE begin our survey of Johnson's views with religion, in deference to what he regarded as a proper sense of values. All civilized society, in his opinion, rested upon religious foundations, and he did not believe that an atheist could have a secure moral code. He would not, I think, have dissented from the syllogism proposed in the title of one of Dr Sacheverell's sermons in 1702: 'A Discourse, Showing the Dependence of Government on Religion in General; and of the English Monarchy on the Church of England in Particular'.

We are less concerned with Johnson's private devotions and spiritual life, which have been very fully treated in a number of works,[1] than with his attitude towards ecclesiastical organization and the relations of Church and State. It raises issues that are still with us in the 1990s—to what extent one should tolerate the intolerant, and how far religious fanaticism can endanger the stability of society.

The Glorious Revolution, which established the political context for Johnson's life, was a revolution in both Church and State. Indeed, it is arguable that the religious aspect was more important and that James II's English subjects disliked his popery even more than they disliked his autocratic behaviour. The Bill of Rights, passed in December 1689, declared that experience had demonstrated that a Catholic monarch was 'inconsistent with the safety and welfare of this protestant kingdom', and that in future no Catholic, or person married to a Catholic, could succeed to the throne.[2] This provision was reinforced in 1701 when the death of Anne's last surviving child made it necessary to set aside more than fifty Catholic heirs and offer the throne to Sophia of Hanover and her successors.

---

[1] M. J. Quinlan, *Samuel Johnson: A Layman's Religion* (Madison, Wis., 1964); C. F. Chapin, *The Religious Thought of Samuel Johnson* (Ann Arbor, Mich., 1968); C. E. Pierce, *The Religious Life of Samuel Johnson* (London, 1983); I. Grundy, *Samuel Johnson and the Scale of Greatness* (Leicester, 1986).

[2] This produced what could have been a very serious constitutional crisis in the 1790s as a result of George, Prince of Wales's secret marriage in December 1785 to Mrs Fitzherbert, a Catholic.

At the same time, the Revolution demanded a general reorganization of the ecclesiastical arrangements of the three kingdoms. In tactical terms, the crisis of 1688 had turned very much on whether the mass of the Protestant dissenters in England would resist James's insistent wooing and make common cause with the Anglicans. They did so and in 1689 were in a position to claim some reward. The fact that the new monarch, William of Orange, was himself a Calvinist made him more willing to encourage a large measure of toleration towards Protestant dissenters, some of whom were Presbyterians.

Since the restoration of Charles II, when the Church of England was re-established and its bishops reinstated, dissenters had suffered a number of serious disabilities. The breakdown of somewhat half-hearted negotiations for comprehension led to a reactivation of the Elizabethan statutes requiring attendance at church, and was followed by the Clarendon code, a series of measures aimed at curbing, or ever extirpating, dissent. By the Act of Uniformity of 1662, which required clerics to accept the Book of Common Prayer, repudiate the Covenant, and subscribe to the 39 Articles, some one thousand clergy were extruded. An Act of 1665 forbade them from living within five miles of their former parishes or within a parliamentary borough.[3] A Conventicles Act of 1664, repeated in 1670, prohibited unauthorized meetings of more than five persons. Those holding public office were, by the Corporation Act of 1661 and the Test Act of 1673, required to take the Anglican sacrament. At Oxford and Cambridge Nonconformists were excluded by the requirement that all students above the age of 16 should subscribe on matriculation to the 39 Articles. The dissenting groups—Presbyterians, Baptists, Congregationalists, and Quakers—could therefore find their meetings and services broken up, their marriages declared unlawful, their dead refused burial, their property seized to pay fines for not attending church. In addition, they were under an obligation to pay tithes to support a church establishment of which they greatly disapproved. Their inability to hold office, either as members of Parliament or as magistrates, made it hard for them to influence policy or obtain redress.

The implementation of these statutes rested mainly with the justices of the peace, sometimes urged into action by informers. Consequently, enforcement varied according to the strength of the local dissenting groups, the zeal or forbearance of individual justices, the national mood, and the

---

[3] 17 Charles II c. 2. The preamble to the Act declared that some nonconforming clerics had taken 'an opportunity to distil the poisonous principles of schism and rebellion into the hearts of His Majesty's subjects'.

vagaries of government policy. Periods of comparative peace and quiet alternated with bursts of fierce repression. The most famous of Protestant dissenters, John Bunyan, spent twelve years in Bedford gaol between 1660 and 1672; the Presbyterian Richard Baxter, who had been offered a bishopric in 1661, was sent to prison for sixteen months by Judge Jeffreys in 1685; the Quaker George Fox was in prison for five months in 1660, for nearly three years between 1664 and 1666, and again for fourteen months in 1673–5; William Penn, though a man of property, son of an admiral, and with influential friends, spent seven months in the Tower of London in 1665. One of the worst periods for the Protestant dissenters was in the last years of Charles II's reign, when the royal government, triumphant over its Whig opponents, saw no reason to dissemble or to tack.

In the course of 1689, after James had fled, there was another attempt to bring all Protestant dissenters back into the Church, but a measure of comprehension failed in the face of hostility from Convocation.[4] The Toleration Act of 1689 declared that, 'as some ease to scrupulous consciences', all who were prepared to take the oath of allegiance and to testify against transubstantiation would be relieved from the operation of the penal laws and were free to worship without hindrance in their own chapels or conventicles provided that the doors were not locked, barred, or bolted. Nonconformist clergy were exempted from the penal laws provided that they accepted most of the 39 Articles.[5] Not only did the Act fail to bring about religious uniformity, but it added yet another schism as a group of some four hundred clerics, led by William Sancroft, the archbishop of Canterbury, decided that they could not take the oath of allegiance and broke away to form the non-juring Church. They developed their own ecclesiastical organization, ordained new recruits, and remained in formal existence until 1779, when Robert Gordon, the last non-juring bishop, died. Having rather few parishioners to care for, the non-juring clergy played a prominent part in theological polemics and, in Charles Leslie, produced a formidable and persistent spokesman.

In two separate respects, the toleration granted in 1689 remained incomplete. The great majority of the Protestant dissenters were relieved from the operation of the penal laws and could worship in their own fashion. But the civic and public disabilities remained. They were still

---

[4] See N. Sykes, *From Sheldon to Secker: Aspects of English Church History, 1660–1768* (Cambridge, 1959), 44–5, 86–9; H. Horwitz, *Parliament, Policy and Politics in the Reign of William III* (Manchester, 1977).

[5] They were not required to accept the 34th, 35th, or 36th arts., nor the section of the 20th art. which gave the Church authority to decide 'in controversies of faith'.

required to pay tithes[6] and the continuation of the Test and Corporation Acts meant that they could not hold public office, unless they had accommodating consciences. Nor were they allowed into the universities, though the establishment of excellent dissenting academies helped to minimize this disadvantage. Secondly, there were important groups to whom toleration, even to this limited extent, did not apply. A substantial concession to the Quakers permitted them to make a declaration rather than take an oath,[7] but Catholics were specifically and pointedly excluded from the terms of the Act, and the clause demanding acceptance of the Trinity put toleration out of reach of Socinians, Unitarians, and atheists.[8]

It is hard to be certain what was the position of the English Catholic community in the aftermath of the Glorious Revolution. The folly of James II had unleashed upon them a new barrage of hatred and suspicion. In theory and at law, their situation was desperate, if not impossible. All the previous penal legislation remained in existence, and fresh penalties were added at moments of crisis. In 1689 they were disarmed, forbidden to own a horse worth more than five pounds, and ordered not to reside in London or Westminster, or within ten miles.[9] In 1692 a double land tax was imposed; in 1696 Catholics were forbidden to practise the law; in 1700 a statute declared that they could neither purchase nor inherit land, and stipulated that their property could be taken by Protestant relatives.[10] In 1714 archbishops and bishops were instructed to investigate 'secret trusts and fraudulent conveyances' whereby papists had retained advowsons;[11] in 1716 a special registration of land was instituted; and in 1722, after Atterbury's plot, a fine of £100,000 was imposed upon them. Their priests could be hanged, their marriages were invalid, they could be fined for not attending church, they could not send their children abroad to be educated, and they could not hold public office or exercise the right to vote.

---

[6] Art. VI of the Act.

[7] Art. XIII conceded the declaration to persons 'who scruple the taking of any oath'.

[8] There were few people who expressly declared themselves Socinians, but the accusation was freely made. Charles Leslie denounced Gilbert Burnet and John Tillotson (Sancroft's successor as Archbishop of Canterbury) as Socinians. In Scotland, Thomas Aikenhead, a youth of 19, was hanged in 1697 for blasphemy. William Whiston, Newton's successor at Cambridge as Lucasian professor, was deprived of his chair in 1710 for his views on the Trinity. Thomas Woolston lost his Fellowship at Sidney Sussex, Cambridge, in 1721 and eight years later was sent to prison for blasphemy, where he remained until he died in 1733. The most recent work on this aspect of the Glorious Revolution is O. P. Grell, J. Israel, and N. Tyacke (eds.), *From Persecution to Toleration: The Glorious Revolution and Religion in England* (Oxford, 1991), and J. R. Jones (ed.), *Liberty Secured? Britain Before and After 1688* (Stanford, Calif., 1991), esp. ch. 4 and 5, by G. J. Schochet and R. K. Webb.

[9] 1 William and Mary c. 9 and 1 William and Mary c. 15.   [10] 11 William III c. 4.

[11] 12 Anne c. 14 strengthened the provisions of 1 William and Mary c. 26.

Some of them undoubtedly suffered grievously. Bonaventure Giffard, who for a brief seven months in 1688 had been President of Magdalen College, Oxford, and was a papal vicar-apostolic, wrote that in the summer of 1714 he had changed his lodgings fourteen times to escape arrest. Thomas Blackburne, arrested in 1696 in connection with Fenwick's conspiracy, was never tried but spent fifty-three years in prison.[12] But, most of the time, the laws were not enforced. No priests were hanged, though some were imprisoned.[13] A friendly magistrate could dismiss a case; a friendly parson could make an entry that Catholic children had been duly baptized; a friendly tax commissioner could undervalue an estate; a friendly returning officer could waive the oath and allow a papist to vote. In 1710 a confidential report to Cardinal Paolucci declared that, of all the penal laws, the only ones in operation were the double land tax and the prohibition on holding public office:

> As regards the exercise of their religion itself, they enjoy complete freedom . . . As a proof that the spirit of persecuting catholics does not rule here, it is enough to say that, four miles from London, in a very public and frequented place, a kind of Convent of nuns maintains itself with its own church and chaplain, where likewise are boarded many girls having their education, without any obstacle from the government, although it is known to them and to everybody.[14]

In Scotland, the Revolution brought about a complete change in church government, but no immediate advance towards toleration. There were three main religious groups. The Episcopalians, who had been in control since the Restoration, were strongest in the east; the Presbyterians in the south; and the Catholics in the Highlands and Islands. In 1689 the Episcopalians, bewildered at the news reaching them from England, played their cards badly at the Convention in Edinburgh and stayed in allegiance to James. The result was that, when those sixty surviving Presbyterian ministers ejected in 1662 were called back and Presbyterianism re-established, there was no provision for the toleration of other groups, many of whose members were in open rebellion. The Presbyterian form of church government was confirmed by the Act of Union in 1707 and not until 1712 was a Toleration Act passed, allowing religious freedom to the Episcopalians. It was accompanied by a Patronage Act which restored to landowners most of their former rights of presentation to benefices.[15]

---

[12] M. D. R. Leys, *Catholics in England, 1559–1829* (London, 1961), quoting Catholic Record Society, vi. 160.

[13] G. Rupp, *Religion in England, 1688–1791* (Oxford, 1986), 184 n. 8.

[14] PRO 31/9/101, dated 22 June 1710, in E. N. Williams (ed.), *The Eighteenth-century Constitution, 1688–1815* (Cambridge, 1960), 340–1.

[15] W. Ferguson, *Scotland, 1689 to the Present* (Edinburgh, 1968).

In Ireland, toleration was postponed even longer than in Scotland. In 1688 the native Irish, who formed the large majority, saw in the divisions among the English another chance to shake off English supremacy, as they had attempted to do in 1641. But the Irish Catholic army that might have effected it was wasted by James II outside London, and by 1691, after the Treaty of Limerick, William III was in full control of the country. At one stage, the most probable outcome of the religious disputes seemed to be a Presbyterian supremacy, as in Scotland, since a number of the adherents of the Church of Ireland had shown themselves unreliable: four of the bishops of the Church of Ireland had responded to James II's summons to an Irish Parliament at Dublin in May 1689, though they explained subsequently that they were merely protecting the interests of their flock. But, in the end, the supremacy of the Church of Ireland was confirmed. The Presbyterian dissenters, who had fought side by side with William's troops against Catholics and French, were not even accorded formal freedom of worship, perhaps because it was assumed that their precarious situation would always keep them loyal to the English connection. In fact their position was worsened in 1704 by a statute requiring a sacramental test for public office, which excluded them from municipal corporations and was not repealed until 1780. Not until 1719 did an Irish Toleration Act pass, allowing religious freedom to Presbyterians, but continuing their political and economic inferiority.[16] Despite vague and cautious assurances to the Irish Catholics at the Treaty of Limerick,[17] they were exposed to the full battery of the penal laws, augmented, as in England, by fresh disqualifications. In 1691 a statute prevented Catholics from sitting in an Irish Parliament by demanding an oath against papal power.[18] The report to Cardinal Paolucci, which had stressed the fair treatment given Catholics in England, described the situation of Irish Catholics as one of total subjection.[19]

The religious settlement effected after the Glorious Revolution lasted almost intact throughout Johnson's lifetime. The Anglican supremacy in England survived until the repeal of the Test and Corporation Acts in 1828 and Catholic Emancipation in 1829. But it was inevitable that political developments and changes in the intellectual climate would begin the

---

[16] 6 George I c. 5.

[17] See J. G. Simms, 'The Establishment of Protestant Ascendancy, 1691–1714', in T. W. Moody and W. E. Vaughan (eds.), *Eighteenth-century Ireland, 1691–1800* (Oxford, 1986).

[18] They had not previously been ineligible. They retained the right to vote.

[19] Simms says that Catholic land was reduced to 14% but that laws against priests and religious observances were 'ineffectively and spasmodically administered' ('Protestant Ascendancy', 12, 16).

process of unravelling the complex legislation, and questions arising from the church settlement were among those frequently raised in Johnson's circle, since a great deal of the politics of Hanoverian England was religious in character.

The first problems thrown up by the 1689 settlement became apparent in the decade before Johnson's birth; despite a general trend in Europe towards scepticism and toleration, the tide in England ran in the other direction. While dissenters could hardly be satisfied with the grudging and limited treatment they had received, many Anglicans began to resent the concessions which James II's conduct had forced them to make. They were particularly alarmed at the dramatic increase in the number of dissenting chapels built after the Toleration Act and dismayed at the spread and the success of the academies, the dissenters' answer to their exclusion from Oxford and Cambridge. The animosity between High and Low Church and their allies reached great heights. John Wesley's father wrote from Lincoln gaol in 1705, where, according to his testimony, he had been confined because of his attacks upon the Nonconformists: 'I saw the growing power and insolence of the dissenters and their party, and that the Church, the clergy and the universities were every day insulted in their writings'; his adversaries, he complained, 'shouted, hazza'd, drummed and fired guns and pistols night and day under my windows'.[20] The High Church party adopted as its slogan 'The Church in Danger'.

These animosities focused on the issue of occasional conformity in Anne's reign. Dissenters could escape the prohibitions of the Test and Corporation Acts by taking communion once a year in an Anglican church, while worshipping regularly in their own chapels.[21] To dissenters it was an innocent device forced upon them by the bigotry of their opponents; to High Churchmen it was blasphemous and hypocritical mockery of the very heart of Christian worship. In a sermon at Oxford in 1702, Henry Sacheverell denounced those 'crafty, faithless and insidious persons who . . . creep to our altars and partake of our sacraments [the] more secretly and powerfully to undermine us'.[22] These religious con-

---

[20] Samuel Wesley to Wake, 5 Oct. 1705, Wake MSS, Christ Church Library, Oxford, quoted in G. Holmes and W. A. Speck (eds.), *The Divided Society: Party Conflict in England 1694–1716* (London, 1967), 53–4. Samuel Wesley's daughter Martha made an unhappy marriage to Westley Hall. In his last month, Johnson was thinking of bringing her, then a widow of 77, into his strange household.

[21] The practice was not acceptable to Baptists and Quakers but was adopted by some Presbyterians and Congregationalists. It was counter-argued that before 1688 dissenters had sometimes worshipped in Anglican churches to show Christian fellowship.

[22] Quoted in Holmes & Speck, *The Divided Society*, 118.

siderations were reinforced by political ones. The qualification of dissenters by this means would enable them, particularly in the West Country
and East Anglia, to control whole corporations, some of which were
parliamentary boroughs. This would give a considerable advantage to the
Whigs, for whom the dissenters traditionally voted, at a time when the
two great parties were nicely balanced.

Danger for the dissenters came with the accession in March 1702 of
Anne, sympathetic to the Tories and a strong supporter of the Church of
England. The first step was to summon Convocation, which had not been
allowed to meet since 1689, when the lower house had revealed strong
High Church sympathies. Three attempts to push through a bill to prohibit occasional conformity failed between 1702 and 1705, but the religious question boiled over once again in the last five years of Anne's
reign. The impeachment of Sacheverell in 1710 misfired badly and produced a Tory and High Church triumph: the general election of 1710 saw
a Tory landslide and legislation against the dissenters soon followed.
First, a qualification Act in 1711 insisted that members of Parliament
should possess landed property and was a blow against the Whig and
dissenting moneyed interest.[23] Next, an Act 'for preserving the Protestant
religion' in 1712 forbade occasional conformity, declaring that anyone
present at a conventicle after taking office would face a fine of £40 and
disqualification.[24] Lastly, the Schism Act of June 1714 stated that all
teachers of youth should subscribe to the liturgy of the Church of England
and receive a licence, thereby hitting at dissenting academies.[25] But the
impact of these measures, intended to lay the foundations for a permanent
Tory supremacy, was nullified by the death of Anne on 1 August 1714 and
the decision of George I to throw in his lot with the Whigs.

The Whig counter-attack was slow to get under way. Convocation was
suspended indefinitely from 1717 onwards. The Occasional Conformity
Act and the Schism Act were repealed in 1719,[26] but the Property Qualification Act was not, suggesting that the Whigs themselves were beginning to change and becoming more of an establishment party. Nor were

---

[23] 9 Anne c. 5. Members for the counties were required to hold estates worth £600 p.a.
and members for the boroughs £300 p.a.

[24] 10 Anne c. 2.   [25] 12 Anne c. 7.

[26] 5 George I c. 4. The delay was significant. There was great opposition to the repeal,
which was carried in the Lords only by 86–68 and in the Commons by 243–202. Fifteen
bishops (including the two archbishops) voted against repeal and only eleven in favour. The
archbishop of York described dissenters in the debate as 'open and avowed enemies of the
church . . . never to be gained by indulgence', and the earl of Nottingham agreed that they
were 'an obstinate sort of people, never to be satisfied'. *Parl. Hist.* vii. 567–89.

the concessions to the dissenters as generous as they had hoped. There was a small gesture to the Quakers in 1722,[27] but the Test and Corporation Acts remained on the statute book. The most the Whigs would grant was an annual Indemnity Act and even that was not passed with total regularity.[28] With some justice, Norman Sykes commented that relations between the Church and the dissenters had reached 'an uneasy armistice' and that the Church's position rested upon 'a makeshift compromise'.[29] Even so, sporadic skirmishing continued. When the dissenters mobilized their forces in 1736 to move for the repeal of the Test and Corporation Acts, they were defeated in the House of Commons by a slashing 251 votes to 123.[30]

There is some disagreement among historians as to the practical effect of the disabilities on dissenters, which varied from place to place and from time to time. N. C. Hunt thought that their protests were justified and that they had 'real grounds for complaint'.[31] But the most recent study suggests that for most dissenters the handicaps were venial, pointing to dissenting MPs like Sir John Barnard and Sir Henry Hoghton, dissenting peers like Lord Willoughby de Parham, and dissenting corporations like Taunton and Nottingham. The bulk of dissenters took an active part in public life:

Although the Dissenters often perceived the establishment as an oppressive force, in fact they enjoyed freedom of worship and freedom of political expression to an unusual degree; their ministers were not denied the opportunity to preach political sermons, even when they bordered on sedition. If the Dissenters wished, they were relatively free to advance in the government itself, both locally and nationally, and they did so, particularly in the local setting, in surprisingly large numbers.[32]

If Bradley is right, one has more understanding of Anglicans who argued against further concessions to the dissenters, hinting that they aimed, not at equality, but at ultimate supremacy.

---

[27] 8 George I c. 6 modified the terms of the declaration.

[28] N. C. Hunt, *Two Early Political Associations: The Quakers and the Dissenting Deputies in the Age of Sir Robert Walpole* (Oxford, 1961), 120–7.

[29] *From Sheldon to Secker*, 102, 104.

[30] *Parl. Hist.* ix. 1046–59. Of the 1736 session Lord Hervey wrote: 'all the considerable debates that passed this year in Parliament were upon church matters; and Parliament, like bulldogs, sticking close to any hold on which they have once fastened, the poor Church this winter was as much worried as Sir Robert had been any other.' J. W. Croker (ed.), *Memoirs of the Reign of George II by John Lord Hervey* (London, 1884), ii. 261.

[31] *Two Early Political Associations*, 127.

[32] J. E. Bradley, *Religion, Revolution and English Radicalism: Non-conformity in Eighteenth-century Politics and Society* (Cambridge, 1990), 36–7.

Johnson's attitude towards these questions and the others that arose during his lifetime is a little unexpected. In view of his deep religious beliefs and powerful Tory loyalties, one might expect his defence of the supremacy of the Church of England to rest either upon its apostolic descent or upon the truth of its doctrines. Of his zeal in its defence, there is no doubt. Boswell assures us that Johnson would have stood before a battery of cannon to restore Convocation to its rightful place.[33] Johnson's defence of the University of Oxford's decision to expel six students who were over-righteous could not be more emphatic: 'that expulsion was extremely just and proper . . . they were not fit to be in the University of Oxford. A cow is a very good animal in the field; but we turn her out of a garden.'[34] He had no sympathy whatever for the petition to Parliament to allow dissenters into the universities by releasing them from the need to subscribe to the 39 Articles: 'we must not supply our enemies with arms from our arsenal.'[35] But though he was clear that there must be an established religion and that the state had a duty to protect it, his justification was in wholly secular terms.

Johnson's position was that an established religion was necessary for the preservation of good order and a stable society. It was certainly not based upon any claims for the superiority of Christian revelation, since he conceded willingly that a Muslim or a Buddhist was equally under an obligation to accept the established religion in his own country.[36] Indeed, it was hardly necessary to look so far afield, since Anglicans had accepted with little difficulty the establishment of a Presbyterian church government in Scotland, largely on political grounds, and had specifically afforded it protection under the terms of the Act of Union.

Contemporaries and commentators alike have drawn attention to Johnson's uncommon zeal for subordination. But it was less subordination for its own sake than as a means of preserving public order. It is hard not to believe that Johnson's very heavy emphasis on the paramount importance of peace and order did not derive from the experience of his own

---

[33] *Life*, i. 464: 'Shall the Presbyterian *Kirk* of Scotland have its General Assembly and the Church of England be denied its Convocation?'

[34] Ibid. ii. 187. Technically the six, from St Edmund Hall, were expelled for ignorance but it is clear that their addiction to praying and preaching was the real offence.

[35] Ibid. ii. 151. Note the employment of the term 'enemies' in reference to Johnson's fellow Christians.

[36] Ibid. ii. 14: 'Then, Sir, a poor Turk must be a Mahometan?' 'Why, yes Sir, and what then . . .'. See also in *Life*, iii. 298, Johnson's exasperation with a young girl for embracing Quakerism: 'we ought not, without very strong conviction indeed, to desert the religion in which we have been educated, . . . the religion, in which it may be said, providence has placed you.'

native city. His grandparents had lived through the Civil War, in which the cathedral of Lichfield had suffered more than any other at the hands of religious fanatics, its windows broken, its library wrecked, its nave used to stable horses, the heads hacked off its statues, the lead stripped from its roof.[37] It used to be common to mock the eighteenth century for its mistrust of religious zeal and its preference for cool latitudinarianism, but there was plenty of surviving evidence of the destruction that fanaticism could produce.

These public motives were buttressed by Johnson's private anxieties and apprehensions. For many years he was haunted by a fear of madness and a sense of the meaninglessness of life. Though in 'The Vanity of Human Wishes' he provided some kind of answer, the black thoughts were never absent for long. The theme of 'Vanity' forms a running bass to his essays: how transitory is fame; how soon is a scholar's work super-seded; what a repository of lost hope is a great library; how absurd that people should expect their home town to honour them. Much of Johnson's intellectual life and many of his personal habits were attempts to hold despair at bay. Better to count the drops as they fell from his retort or tap the railings than to contemplate the void.[38] No doubt his greatest undertaking, the *Dictionary*, was primarily a commercial proposition, but it involved trying to impose order on the ever-shifting nature of language. Society needed a religious framework to hold it together, and so did Johnson.

There were other reasons why Johnson was convinced that a public moral code was essential. First, he could not see how, in practice, even the most rational man could constantly pause to work out the probable result of his decisions: simple rules and habits had to determine the vast majority of human actions. Even the strictest utilitarian might be puzzled to know where the balance would lie in pursuing the greatest happiness of the greatest number: with profound decisions it would be hard to guess what the long-term consequences would be. Secondly, the formal legal code was largely negative and needed to be fleshed out with a more positive code of ethics: after all, a man might refrain from murder, arson, armed robbery, and the more heinous crimes, yet still be mean, irritable, pomp-ous, envious, and generally disagreeable. Charity, compassion, and kind-ness, on which Johnson placed great emphasis, can scarcely be legislated

---

[37] *VCH Staffs*, iii. 174.

[38] Mrs Thrale wrote that Johnson told her that the character of Sober in *Idler*, no. 31, was intended for himself. Johnson wrote that Sober's daily amusement was chemistry: 'he draws oils and waters and essences and spirits which he knows to be of no use; sits and counts the drops as they come from his retort, and forgets that whilst a drop is falling, a moment flies away.'

for, yet they may be encouraged by sermon and example.[39] Thirdly, for many men morality would remain a mere abstract proposition unless dramatized and driven home by exhortation and ceremony. Lastly, Johnson doubted whether most people were capable of deliberating on moral choices and he was not at all sure that they should. 'The mental disease of the present generation', he wrote, in words that anticipate Burke, 'is a disposition to rely wholly upon unassisted genius and natural sagacity.'[40] Though sharing some evangelical dispositions,[41] Johnson greatly mistrusted the concept of an 'inward light'. 'How can I tell what that person may be prompted to do?', he asked.[42] Much of this went back to those terrible days of the Commonwealth 'when any unsettled innovator who could hatch a half-formed notion produced it to the publick: when every man might become a preacher, and almost every preacher could collect a congregation'.[43]

Johnson was, accordingly, not at all apologetic in his defence of a powerful established Church, prepared to put down heterodox opinions. The fullest discussion of his attitude was in a conversation of 7 May 1773, which Boswell masterminded. The dinner party was at Edward and Charles Dilly's, booksellers, themselves dissenters and of radical tendencies. The company was distinguished, though Boswell does not allow it much more than a supporting role. It included Goldsmith, Bennet Langton, and three clerics, all controversialists. Augustus Toplady held the living at Broad Hembury, near Honiton, possessed Calvinist views, and had just engaged in furious controversy with Wesley and the Methodists; William Temple, author of *An Essay Concerning the Clergy*, was Boswell's close friend and confidant; Henry Mayo was pastor to an independent congregation at Wapping. In reply to Boswell's question about toleration, Johnson offered a flat and categorical statement:

Every society has a right to preserve publick peace and order, and therefore has a good right to prohibit the propagation of opinions which have a dangerous tendency . . . The magistrate may be morally or theologically wrong in restraining the propagation of opinions which he thinks dangerous, but he is politically right.[44]

[39] *Life*, ii. 250: 'Perfect obligations, which are generally not to do something, are clear and positive; as, "thou shalt not kill". But charity, for instance, is not definable by limits. It is a duty to give to the poor, but no man can say how much another should give to the poor, or when a man has given too little to save his soul.'

[40] *Rambler*, no. 154.   [41] See Greene, *The Politics of Samuel Johnson*, 50–3.

[42] *Life*, ii. 126.   [43] *Lives of the Poets*, i. 214–15.

[44] Johnson insisted that the magistrate was acting on behalf of society. This was a good tactical move, placing the argument on a higher footing. He was not apparently challenged whether Anglican justices really represented society as a whole or merely a dominant faction. It is clear however that he is giving political considerations—i.e. the preservation of order—priority over theological truth or justice to the individual subject.

To Mayo's predictable retort that every man was entitled to liberty of conscience, Johnson replied that that was not in dispute:

People confound liberty of thinking with liberty of talking; nay, with liberty of preaching. Every man has a physical right to think as he pleases, for it cannot be discovered how he thinks . . . But no member of a society has a right to *teach* any doctrine contrary to what the society holds to be true.

Johnson comes close to arguing for the untrammelled power of the majority. The only right permitted is the right of private thought, and even then one has the feeling that, could he have got hold of it, it would not have lasted long. Indeed, it is strictly no right at all since, by Johnson's admission, it is not granted by society and society can do nothing about it.

Another member of the company then tried to open a loophole by suggesting that a magistrate might perhaps tolerate purely speculative opinions, such as preaching against the Trinity, which would not lead to overt acts. Johnson closed it at once:

I think that permitting men to preach any opinion contrary to the doctrine of the established church tends, in a certain degree, to lessen the authority of the church, and consequently to lessen the influence of religion . . . I think it is *not* politick to tolerate in such a case.

Boswell once tried to defend Johnson by telling Robertson that he always ran to extremes in debate: 'when you talk with him calmly in private, he is very liberal in his way of thinking.'[45] But there can be little doubt that the uncompromising views expressed at the dinner party represented his considered opinion. In 1766 he insisted that 'the vulgar are the children of the state and must be taught like children'; in 1780, that 'the state has a right to regulate the religion of the people, who are the children of the state . . . every man has a right to utter what he thinks truth and every other man has a right to knock him down for it. Martyrdom is the test.' Towards the end of his life, in 1783, he repeated that 'the vulgar are the children of the state. If any one attempts to teach them doctrines contrary to what the state approves, the magistrate may and ought to restrain him.'[46]

The point at which Johnson seems to have wished to make his stand was 1714, when he was 5 years old: on the throne, a queen devoted to the Church; a huge Tory majority in the House of Commons; an act against occasional conformity in force; the Schism Act to curtail the teaching

[45] *Life*, iii. 331.   [46] Ibid. ii. 14; iv. 12, 216.

power of dissent just about to come into effect. We have the paradox of an argumentative man who feared discussion. In Johnson's view, free discussion led, not to the triumph of truth as Milton and Locke had argued, but to dissension, confusion, bigotry, crankiness and, ultimately, the subversion of the social order. Of all the many causes of dissension, Johnson believed, none was as dangerous as religion: 'no malice is so fierce, so cruel and implacable, as that which is excited by religious discord.'[47] In a sermon written for 30 January—the day of Charles I's execution—Johnson wrote of the civil war in terms of class hatred:

It was a war of the rabble against their superiors; a war, in which the lowest and basest of the people were encouraged by men a little higher than themselves, to lift their hands against their ecclesiastical and civil governors, and by which those who were grown impatient of obedience, endeavoured to obtain the power of commanding. This 'strife' as we all know, ended in 'confusion'. Our laws were overruled, our rights were abolished. The soldier seized upon the property, the fanatic rushed into the church . . . Such evils surely we have too much reason to fear again, for we have no right to charge our ancestors with having provoked them by crimes greater than our own.[48]

It may seem strange that Johnson, dining well in the company of dissenting clergymen of impeccable respectability, should feel that he was sitting on a powder-keg. But, on both sides, old enmities died hard. He wished to fight intolerance with intolerance, or, perhaps more fairly, he found, like most of us, his own intolerance less offensive than that of others. But this was not merely personal to Johnson. It was a dilemma close to the heart of enlightened thinking. Few *philosophes* quite resolved the question of how to dispute freely without running the risk of others joining in, and 'not in front of the servants' was a constant message. 'Once the populace begins to reason,' wrote Voltaire, 'all is lost.' Indeed, Johnson himself was guilty of breaking the rules when, to tease Mrs Macauley, an ardent egalitarian, he begged her to invite her servant to join them at table. It is partly that, out of the corner of their eyes, they saw democracy and egalitarianism advancing apace, but more because they were acutely aware that they were surrounded by ignorance, superstition and excitability.[49] Some intellectual progress towards toleration there was, but, when Lord North brought in some very modest proposals to alleviate the lot of the Catholics, the populace took flame and pillaged London for six days.

[47] *Sermons*, no. 1.   [48] Ibid. no. 23.
[49] Johnson agreed that gentlemen might properly discuss the Trinity but not in front of children. One is tempted to read 'lower orders' for 'children'. *Life*, iv. 216.

Within the limits of his general position, Johnson showed some generosity of spirit. Since his basic stance was political, the intricate doctrinal
disputes which fascinated so many of his table companions meant little to
him. He conceded that there was not much in the Presbyterian creed to
which he took exception: it was their temper, their cast of mind, which he
found disagreeable.[50] In his life of Milton, Johnson noted that 'they who
most loudly clamour for liberty do not most liberally grant it', and in
his comment on Samuel Butler, author of the satire *Hudibras*, Johnson
referred to the 'sour solemnity, the sullen superstition, the gloomy mo-
roseness, and the stubborn scruples of the ancient Puritans'.[51] He was not
sure that the modern ones were much better and on his Scottish tour with
Boswell pointedly refused to enter a Presbyterian church.[52]

Towards Catholicism, his attitude was noticeably warmer, perhaps
because he saw in the very few English Catholics no surviving political
danger. 'I would be a papist if I could,' he confided late in life to a
surprised Boswell.[53] He defended Catholic doctrine with some vigour on
several occasions,[54] and was particularly indignant at the treatment of the
Irish Catholics. Dr Maxwell wrote that Johnson 'severely reprobated the
barbarous debilitating policy of the British government which, he said,
was the most detestable mode of persecution'. Maxwell's testimony to the
strength of Johnson's feelings on the subject is confirmed by another
outburst witnessed by Boswell, where Johnson condemned the 'monstrous injustice' of British policy: 'the Irish are in a most unnatural state;
for we see there the minority prevailing over the majority. There is no
instance, even in the ten persecutions, of such severity as that which the
Protestants of Ireland have exercised against the Catholics'.[55] It is true that
he attacked the Jesuits, condemning their maxims as 'shocking, weak,
pernicious and absurd', but this was because he believed that they encouraged political subversion: where dissenters appealed to contract against
monarchs, Jesuits appealed to papal authority.[56]

[50] 'All denominations of Christians have really little difference in point of doctrine,
though they may differ widely in external forms.' 21 Mar. 1772, *Life*, ii. 150.

[51] Ibid. i. 214–15.   [52] Ibid. v. 121, 384; iv. 289.

[53] Ibid. iv. 289: 'A good man of a timorous disposition, in great doubt of his acceptance
with God, might be glad to be of a church where there are so many helps to get to
Heaven . . . an obstinate rationality prevents me . . . I shall never be a papist, unless on the
near approach of death, of which I have a very great terror.'

[54] Ibid. ii. 103, 255; iv. 289.   [55] Ibid. ii. 121, 255.

[56] Johnson began work on a translation of Paul Sarpi's *History of the Council of Trent*, but
abandoned it when he discovered another Johnson in the field. All that was left was a short
'Life of Sarpi', printed in *Gentleman's Magazine* (Nov. 1738).

Towards the new Methodist movement, which remained in his lifetime part of the Church of England, Johnson was ambivalent. He shared with Wesley a deep affection for William Law's *Serious Call to a Devout and Holy Life* and he admired the simple, direct preaching of the Methodist ministers.[57] But the displays of enthusiasm which accompanied many of their mass meetings troubled him, and he found their attitude increasingly self-righteous: 'he owed that the Methodists had done good . . . but, he said, they had great bitterness against other Christians'.[58]

However illiberal Johnson's opinions may seem by later standards, it is not clear that they were by those of his own day. If anything, they were rather conventional and middle-of-the-road. It has been said of Burke's view that the 'indissoluble union' of Church and State was the foundation of the constitution that such opinions were 'not the preserve of a coterie of High Churchmen . . . but the commonly accepted maxims of both governors and the governed in the late eighteenth century'.[59] It is easy to see the period through enlightened spectacles, to exaggerate the triumph of reason and scepticism, and to underestimate the continuing strength of traditional religious belief.

Perhaps the best-known statement of the Anglican case was William Warburton's *The Alliance of Church and State*, published in 1736, when Johnson was aged 27. Warburton was no Tory: his political connections, which eventually gained him a bishopric, were with William Pitt, and he was defended in the nineteenth century by Macaulay.[60] His basic position was, however, almost identical with that of Johnson. He presumed that every religious group would struggle for supremacy and would encroach upon the others if it could. The only way to avoid perpetual strife was therefore to establish the religion of the majority and to keep its competitors out of Parliament and positions of power by some form of test. Warburton thought in terms of a compact or contract:

---

[57] *Life*, i. 458–60; ii. 123.

[58] Ibid. v. 392.

[59] David Hempton, 'Religion in British Society, 1740–1790', in J. Black (ed.), *British Politics and Society from Walpole to Pitt, 1742–1789* (London, 1990), 201–21.

[60] Perhaps significantly, Warburton had been brought up on stories of the Civil War related by his grandmother, and he later claimed to have read all the tracts of that period. *The Alliance of Church and State* was very influential, perhaps because it was short, and was in its fourth edn. by 1766. See R. W. Greaves, 'The Working of the Alliance: A Comment on Warburton', in G. V. Bennett and J. D. Walsh (eds.), *Essays in Modern English Church History in Memory of Norman Sykes* (London, 1966), 163–80.

If there be more than one [religion] at the time of Convention, the Alliance is made by the State with the largest of the religious societies . . . And a full toleration given to all the rest. But restrained from injuring that which is established by the guard of a Test-law . . . This alliance is perpetual but not irrevocable—i.e. it subsists so long as the Church, thereby established, maintains its superiority of extent; which, when it loses to any considerable degree, the Union is dissolved.[61]

If Warburton was the accepted authority during most of Johnson's lifetime, William Paley took over towards the end. His *Principles of Moral and Political Philosophy*, though published the year after Johnson's death, was based upon lectures Paley had given at Cambridge between 1766 and 1775. He began by arguing that the 'single view' of a church establishment was 'the preservation and communication of religious knowledge'. But he moved some distance from that objective when he discussed how some form of test (i.e. exclusion from office) could be justified.[62] The only case on which he placed any weight was when religious dissent was the best guide to potential political subversion. Papists, for example, might be Jacobites and might be excluded for that reason. 'But, even in this example, it is not to popery that the laws object, but to popery as the mark of Jacobitism.' These tests were not to exist 'one day longer than some visible danger renders them necessary to the preservation of public tranquillity'. It seems to me that Paley, though cool and moderate in tone, had not advanced at all on Johnson's position, that political, not religious, considerations justified exclusion. It is merely that Paley was muddled and Johnson not.[63]

Johnson's animosity towards dissent may have been unbecoming, but it was by no means unusual, nor did it go unreciprocated. Theological

---

[61] *The Alliance of Church and State* (London, 1736), 111. I am not sure whether Warburton's argument is quite as ingenuous as it appears to be. It begs the question of whether the established Church would not use its political power to prevent any other sect growing into numerical superiority, as the Tories had tried to do between 1710 and 1714.

[62] Paley quoted only two cases for defending a test-law. The first was self-evidently unconvincing: 'when two or more religions are contending for establishment; and where there appears no way of putting an end to the contest, but by giving to one religion such a decided superiority in the legislature and government of the country, as to secure it against danger from any other'. That would imply that dissident religions should have full equality when they were feeble but should lose it if they grew strong. It was presumably put forward by Paley as a straw man. But he agreed with Warburton that 'if the dissenters become a majority of the people, the establishment itself ought to be altered or qualified', (2nd edn. (1786), 582–3).

[63] Ibid. 555, 584–5. It is difficult to believe Paley was not being disingenuous in choosing his Jacobite example. Nobody seriously thought Jacobitism a menace in 1785. But it enabled Paley to avoid the more difficult question of the continued exclusion of Protestant dissenters. Nor did he explain who was to decide that all danger was past and the tests might go.

controversy was frequently robust. Revd Augustus Toplady, present at the discussion of 7 May 1773, thought John Wesley, a fellow Anglican minister, 'the most rancorous hater of the gospel system that ever appeared in this island'.[64] Joseph Priestley, a Presbyterian moving into Unitarianism, denounced Trinitarianism as being 'as idolatrous as transubstantiation, and Jesus as much a creature of God as a loaf of bread'.[65] Robert Robinson in his *Plan of Lectures*, published in 1778, looked forward with relish to the Day of Judgement when the bishops would be sent packing, and Gilbert Wakefield, looking in 1788 for the *Four Marks of Anti-Christ*, found them all in the Church of England. Even within the ranks of dissent, Christian charity was not always apparent. The 'Happy Union' of Presbyterians and Congregationalists, founded in March 1691, lasted four years and devoted much of its energy to internal disputation: 'popish vomit' was one Congregationalist minister's description of the views of his new Presbyterian allies.[66] By these standards, Johnson was rather free from vituperation.[67]

Further evidence which suggests that Johnson was not significantly out of touch with majority opinion during his lifetime is that very few changes were made to the 1689 settlement. The death of Stanhope at the height of the South Sea crisis removed one minister who might have been prepared to do something for the dissenters. His attempt to modify the Test and Corporation Acts in 1718 was frustrated by the disapproval of the bishops and the factious opposition of Pulteney and Walpole.[68] Walpole's own attitude towards reform was not heroic. He repeatedly advised the dissenters not to raise the question again and, when they did so in 1736, spoke and voted against it. The majority was sufficiently decisive to settle

[64] Letter of 6 Sept. 1773, *Posthumous Works of the Rev. A. M. Toplady* (London, 1805), 346.

[65] Quoted in M. Watts, *The Dissenters* (Oxford, 1978), 477.   [66] Ibid. 289–97.

[67] Another of Johnson's friends, Edmund Burke, wrote mordantly on Richard Price's famous sermon of 1788, attacking it as dissent for its own sake. Price had suggested that anyone dissatisfied with all other forms of worship should form his own congregation. Burke replied: 'It is somewhat remarkable that this reverend divine should be so earnest for setting up new churches, and so perfectly indifferent concerning the doctrine which may be taught in them. His zeal is of a curious character. It is not for the propagation of his own opinions, but of any opinions. It is not for the diffusion of truth, but for the spreading of contradiction. Let the noble teachers but dissent, it is no matter from whom or from what . . .'. *Reflections*, 10–11.

[68] A clause modifying the Test Act was included in the bill to repeal the Occasional Conformity and Schism Acts, but it ran into opposition in the Lords and Stanhope dropped it during the committee stage. *Parl. Hist.* vii. 581. Stanhope was also engaged in an attempt to alleviate the plight of the Catholics, offering to ease the penal laws if the Papacy would allow Catholics to swear allegiance to the new dynasty. The negotiation broke down.

the issue for a whole generation.[69] Two pieces of legislation in the Pelham period actually worsened the situation. Hardwicke's Marriage Act of 1753, though intended primarily against illicit Fleet marriages, insisted that only Anglican clergy could solemnize valid marriages, thus placing dissenters in a new dilemma.[70] The Jew Act of 1753 roused such fury that it had to be repealed the following year, leaving ministers under no illusions about how dangerous it was to stir up old and deep prejudices.[71]

The changed atmosphere of the first decade of George III's reign, the end of the Seven Years War, and the excitement arising from the varied activities of John Wilkes persuaded a new generation of dissenters once more to challenge their subordinate position. Theologically, they were moving towards Unitarianism and rational dissent; politically, they were less docile and more assertive than their immediate forebears. But their first move was a serious tactical error. In July 1771 a number of Anglican clerics and their sympathizers met in the Feathers' Tavern, London, and agreed to petition Parliament that they might be excused subscription to the 39 Articles and that undergraduates at the two universities should no longer have to subscribe. They approached Lord North, the first minister, and received the advice that their predecessors had received from Walpole thirty-five years earlier—that the time was not ripe. Nevertheless, in February 1772 Sir William Meredith introduced their petition, in which they asserted 'the Protestant privilege to question every human doctrine and bring it to the test of scripture'. At this, the heavens opened upon them. Sir Roger Newdigate, member for the University of Oxford, pointed out that the petitioners were themselves Anglican clergymen, had subscribed to the Articles, and stood self-condemned as hypocrites. Hans Stanley declared that the 'absolute destruction' of the Church was the real aim, and warned against raising religious mobs: 'political mobs are in comparison of them as harmless as doves.' North echoed his sentiments: 'when our civil dissensions have, thank God, in a great measure subsided, would you introduce religious quarrels?' Burke argued that it was naïve to appeal to the authority of the Bible when that book itself was notoriously open to wide interpretation.

[69] See *HMC Egmont Diary*, ii. 244. The voting was 251–123. William Plumer, proposing the motion, argued that it was unseemly to use the sacrament as a test 'to qualify a man to be adjutant to a regiment or the bailiff of a little borough'. Walpole retorted that the motion was the thin end of a campaign to disestablish the Church. A modest attempt to improve the lot of the Quakers also failed in the same parliamentary session: see Hunt, *Two Early Political Associations*.   [70] 26 George II c. 33.

[71] 26 George II c. 26 relieved Jews seeking naturalization from the need to take the sacrament. It was repealed by 27 George II c. 1.

The petition was rejected by 217 votes to 71.[72] The argument about mobs may appear strained until one remembers that the Gordon riots were a mere eight years ahead. Johnson was delighted with the outcome:

It was soon thrown out. Sir, they talk of not making boys at the University subscribe to what they do not understand; but they ought to consider, that our Universities were founded to bring up members of the Church of England . . . No. Sir the meaning of subscribing is, not that they fully understand all the articles, but that they will adhere to the Church of England. Now take it this way, and suppose that they should only subscribe their adherence to the Church of England, there would be still the same difficulty; for still the young men would be subscribing to what they do not understand. For if you should ask them, what do you mean by the Church of England? Do you know in what it differs from the Presbyterian Church? from the Romish Church? from the Greek Church? from the Coptick Church? they could not tell you. So, Sir, it comes to the same thing.[73]

The next move was more judicious—an appeal by dissenting ministers to be relieved from the need to subscribe under the terms of the Toleration Act. The debate in the House of Commons in April 1772 revealed much more sympathy and the bill went on its way by 70 votes to 9. But this spectacular conversion to broad-mindedness was not all that it seemed. The king had already made clear to Lord North his total disapproval of the measure, expressed with his inimitable briskness: 'the question is a very short one, at the Revolution the Toleration Act was established, the Dissenters have not been molested therefore why must now an alteration be made: this I think contains the sum of the argument.' North replied that some members who were dependent upon the dissenters' electoral support would be in difficulties: this was 'one of those bills which ought to be thrown out by the House of Peers and not by the commons'. The hostile majority in the Commons was merely lying in wait to ambush the bill from better terrain, and their lordships duly obliged by 102 votes to 29. The following year saw a repeat performance. Once again the campaign had stalled.[74]

As happens not infrequently, war proved a more effective agent of reform than argument. In the early 1770s the threatening situation in America made it all the more necessary to frame a permanent settlement

[72] *Parl. Hist.* xvii. 245–95. Many of the petitioners, such as Jebb, Disney, and Lindsey, subsequently left the Church. On the question of asking undergraduates to take the oath, the majority argued that the two universities could amend their own regulations if they chose.

[73] *Life*, ii. 150–1.

[74] Fortescue, ii, nos. 1048, 1049, 1061, 1062. But at the very least North's caution acknowledges the voting power of the dissenters. On the second occasion, in 1773, the bill passed the Commons by 87–34 and was defeated in the Lords by 28–86.

for Canada, acquired by the Treaty of Paris in 1763. There were some sixty to seventy thousand French Canadian Catholics, and only a few hundred Protestants, mainly in Quebec and Montreal. Lord North had therefore little alternative in his Quebec Act of 1774 but to apply the Warburtonian principle and accept Catholicism as the majority religion, especially as pledges of religious toleration had been given at the peace settlement. French Canadians were to have the unhampered exercise of their religion and were to be permitted to pay tithes to their clergy.[75] North was hotly attacked in both houses for pandering to popery, though the wisdom of his policy was demonstrated within a few years when the Canadians did not follow the thirteen colonies into rebellion. Johnson defended the Quebec Act stoutly in *The Patriot*: 'Persecution is not more virtuous in a Protestant than a Papist . . . in an age, where every mouth is open for *liberty of conscience*, it is equitable to show some regard to the conscience of a papist.'

But the concession to the French Canadians started a small avalanche. The official recognition of Catholicism in one part of the empire made the continued subjugation of the Catholics at home all the more indefensible, particularly since they were a small and inoffensive group. Moreover, ministers hoped that some relaxation of the penal laws might make it easier to recruit Catholics, especially from the Highlands of Scotland, into the armed forces. In May 1778 a group of Catholic peers and commoners offered a loyal petition, pointing to their irreproachable conduct for many years past, and including a formal panegyric on the British constitution:

We behold, with satisfaction, the felicity of our fellow subjects, and we partake of the general prosperity which results from an institution so full of wisdom.[76]

It was followed up by a bill introduced by Sir George Savile, who had strongly supported the Feathers' Tavern petition in 1772. It went through both houses without opposition and, while maintaining the Test and Corporation Acts, relieved Catholics from the fiercer proscriptions imposed by the act of 1700.[77] This, in turn, drew attention to the continuing disabilities under which Protestant dissenters suffered, and Sir Henry

---

[75] Quebec Act was 14 George III c. 83. The best commentary is still R. Coupland, *The Quebec Act: A Study in Statesmanship* (Oxford, 1925). The acrimonious debates on the measure are *Parl. Hist.* xvii. 1357–407; xix. 655–84.   [76] *Parl. Hist.* xix. 1138–9.

[77] 18 George III c. 60 relieved Catholics from most of the penalties imposed by 11 William III c. 4: namely, the prosecution of priests and teachers and the inability to purchase property. Nevertheless, a fairly severe oath was demanded whereby Catholics repudiated not only Charles III but the doctrine that the Pope had any temporal power within the realm and could depose princes.

Hoghton in 1779 carried, with little opposition, the concession to dissenting ministers which had been refused in 1772 and 1773.[78]

The response to the comparatively modest changes effected by Savile's Act revealed how little progress towards genuine toleration there had been in some quarters since Johnson was a boy. In 1710 the Sacheverell riots had been directed largely against dissenters; in 1780, towards the end of his life, the Gordon riots were against the Catholics. It started with a campaign to prevent the legislation being extended to Scotland and finished by demanding its repeal in England. There is, of course, no doubt that the great majority of the rioters, who wreaked such havoc in London for six days, were ruffians and criminals, little interested in theological dispute. But there is ample testimony that most of the crowd who accompanied Lord George Gordon to Westminster to present the monster petition were sober citizens, a number of them from the ranks of the Protestant dissenters. Of their fanaticism and intolerance there seems little doubt. Johnson had a grandstand view of the proceedings. His house at Bolt Court in Fleet Street was no more than half a mile from Moorfields, where the riots started.[79] Langdale's distillery at Holborn went up in flames on the sixth day of the riots, the mob rolling in the gutters on unrectified gin, and it was a question whether their friends would cross the river to try their hands on Henry Thrale's brewery at Southwark. A number of them did so, but John Perkins, Thrale's chief clerk, kept them happy with generous drafts of best porter, until troops arrived: 'the villains had broken in,' wrote Mrs Thrale, 'and our brewhouse would have blazed in ten minutes.' To the Thrales, then at Bath, Johnson reported:

As I went by, the protestants were plundering the Sessions house at the Old Bailey. There were not I believe a hundred, but they did their work at leisure, in full security, without Sentinels, without trepidation, as Men lawfully employed, in full day. Such is the Cowardice of a commercial place . . . the history of the last week would fill you with amazement, it is without any modern example.[80]

Though the next dissenting campaign for the repeal of the Test and Corporation Acts reached its climax after Johnson's death, it is necessary

---

[78] 19 George III c. 44. Hoghton drew attention to the concessions recently made to the Catholics. Dissenting ministers were relieved from the need to subscribe to the 39 Articles, but North carried an amendment insisting upon a simple oath 'as a Christian and a Protestant'. *Parl. Hist.* xx. 239, 305.

[79] There was a large Irish community in Moorfields, disliked as competitors who drove down wages.

[80] *Thraliana*, i. 437; Johnson to Mrs Thrale, 9 and 10 June 1780 (*Letters*, ed. Redford, iii. 267–71).

to refer to it in order to establish the point that the prospects for political
and religious reform in England were discouraging, even before the great
iron gates of the French Revolution clanged shut. Hopes were high among
the dissenters that the new prime minister, William Pitt, would be more
sympathetic towards them than his predecessors had been: he had, after
all, staked a good deal on his efforts to promote parliamentary reform, and
the support the dissenters had given him at the general election of 1784
had contributed greatly to his stunning victory over the Coalition. The
organizers were granted an interview in January 1787 and gained the
impression that Pitt was favourable. But the bishops remained hostile and,
when Beaufoy moved for repeal on 28 March 1787, Pitt spoke and voted
against. The danger to Church and State from repeal was, he declared, by
no means chimerical:

> The Church and State are united upon principles of expediency; and it concerns
> those to whom the well-being of the State is intrusted, to take care that the Church
> should not be rashly demolished . . . there is a natural desire in sectaries to extend
> the influence of their religion; the dissenters were never backward in this, and it is
> necessary for the Establishment to have an eye to them.[81]

The motion went down by 176 votes to 98, leaving the dissenters 'aston-
ished and chagrined at the part taken by Mr. Pitt'.[82]

The conservative case, to which Johnson subscribed, held that the settlement in Church and State worked out at the Glorious Revolution was
indissolubly related, that it had proved itself in practice, and that it was
acceptable to the majority of the nation. It was by no means a Tory
sentiment but one shared by most Whigs. Touch one part of the settlement and the whole would be in danger. One politician who put the case
moderately and persuasively was Lord North, who, blind and very much
the elder statesman, was led into the House of Commons in 1787 and 1789
to speak against Beaufoy's motion. He would not, he hoped, be accused of
bigotry or intolerance, since liberty of conscience and freedom of worship,
both of which he supported in their entirety, were quite different from
access to public office. All states had reserved the right to debar certain
persons. If the revolutionary settlement of 1689 could insist that the
monarch himself must be of a certain religion, surely it could say the same
thing of subjects?

---

[81] *Parl. Hist.* xxvi. 780–832.

[82] Quoted in J. Ehrman, *The Younger Pitt* (London, 1983), 68. The organizing committee
made two further attempts, in May 1789 and in Mar. 1790. The motions were lost by 124–
104, and by 294–105.

If the present motion should be agreed to, it would be going into a new system. He venerated the present system as it had stood for a century. If the question should ever be carried, the ancient maxim, that the constitution of England was to be supported by the constitution of the church, would be questioned, and supposed to have been abandoned by that house . . . it was evident from history that the cause of the church was the cause of the state . . . If they removed one stone of the bulwark, and made the first breach, no one could say how soon the whole would tumble to pieces.[83]

North's language may seem unnecessarily melodramatic, but his prophecies were, from his point of view, fulfilled. The repeal of the Test and Corporation Acts, when finally accomplished in 1828, was followed in quick succession by Catholic Emancipation, the Great Reform Act, and the Municipal Corporations Act of 1834. It was indeed a 'new system'. For the defenders of the old order, their trump-card—that the relationship of Church and State was interlocking and mutually reinforcing—had become a liability. The great advances in religious toleration throughout Europe at the time of the French Revolution made the continued exclusion of the Protestant dissenters particularly hard to defend.[84]

Johnson's attitude towards ecclesiastical organization and toleration has won him few admirers. Baretti thought that it represented a 'nasty blot on his character' and that he would have made an excellent Inquisitor.[85] Even a sympathetic and scholarly modern commentator seems to find difficulty and observes that Johnson's views on toleration were harsh, even for his own day.[86]

One can see how this impression has arisen. Johnson expressed his views pithily and trenchantly. Yet there is little doubt that he thought of himself as moderate: the degree of toleration granted at the Revolution should neither be eroded nor extended. The Church of England has often been seen as a *via media* between Catholicism and Calvinism. Johnson also thought of it as balancing between the extremes of religious fanaticism and godlessness, both of which posed a grave threat to society. After his visit

---

[83] *Parl. Hist.* xxvi. 818–23; xxviii. 16–22.

[84] In France, the Edict of Toleration in 1787 gave full civic rights to Protestants. Art. VI of the Declaration of the Rights of Man, adopted in Aug. 1789, declared that 'tous les citoyens, étant égaux à ses yeux, sont également admissibles à toutes dignités, places et emplois publics'.

[85] Baretti's comments are in notes he made to the published letters of Mrs Piozzi; *Life*, ii. 252; iii. 429 n. 2. He added 'to his shame, be it said, he always was tooth and nail against toleration'. Boswell, perhaps slightly embarrassed, recorded Johnson amazing the passengers in a coach by defending the Inquisition on the grounds that 'false doctrine should be checked on its first appearance'. *Life*, i. 465.

[86] N. Hudson, *Samuel Johnson and Eighteenth-century Thought* (Oxford, 1988), 223.

to St Andrews in 1773, where his walk among the ruins of the old cathedral on the cliffs had moved him so deeply, Johnson reflected:

The change of religion in Scotland, eager and vehement as it was, raised an epidemical enthusiasm, compounded of sullen scrupulousness and warlike ferocity, which, in a people whom idleness resigned to their own thoughts, and who, conversing only with each other, suffered no dilution of their zeal from the gradual influx of new opinions, was long transmitted in its full strength from the old to the young, but by trade and intercourse with England, is now visibly abating, and giving way too fast to that laxity of practice and indifference of opinion, in which men, not sufficiently instructed to find the middle point, too easily shelter themselves from rigour and constraint.[87]

Johnson was unfortunate that opinion on these matters was changing during his lifetime, though more slowly than has sometimes been presumed. Nevertheless, a comparative survey suggests that his views were fairly standard, save that he showed a somewhat unusual degree of sympathy for Roman Catholicism. Opinions which were broadly those of Walpole, North, Pitt, Wilberforce, Warburton, and Paley can hardly be said to be extreme.[88] The idea that there should be religious tests for public office is so obnoxious to modern minds that it is necessary to point out that a contrary view was held long after Johnson's death, and that it was advocated by some of the finest minds of the nineteenth century and often expressed with a vehemence that makes Johnson look tepid.

A late restatement of the conservative case was Robert Southey's strange book *Colloquies on the Progress and Prospects of Society*, published early in 1829. Southey had long since abandoned the radical opinions of his youth and was an agitated spectator of the changes which 'the manufacturing system' was bringing about. The privations of the poor would, he thought, very likely lead to class war or a *bellum servile*; a *laissez-faire* society could not but be heartless: 'while gain is the great object of pursuit, selfishness must be ever the uppermost feeling.' In a series of conversations with the ghost of Sir Thomas More—a curious choice of confidant for someone as hostile to Catholicism as Southey—he maintained what he clearly regarded as a self-evident proposition, that religion was the basis of all government and that the governors had the duty to direct religious opinions: the lower orders must be 'trained up in the way they should go'. Southey's book was ripped to pieces by Macaulay in a brilliant and facetious review, which denied that religion was the basis of all government,

---

[87] *Journey to the Western Islands*, 6.
[88] Wendy Hinde, *Catholic Emancipation: A Shake to Men's Minds* (Oxford, 1992), 187, agrees that the Act of 1829 was carried 'almost certainly against the wishes of a majority of the country'.

doubted whether politicians were any wiser in religious matters than the people they governed, and concluded with a famous paean to progress. But the religious arguments of the *Colloquies* had already been ripped to pieces by events. No sooner had Southey predicted that the arrangements of Church and State were sure to survive than they were dismantled, Catholic emancipation granted, and—worst of all—the perpetrator of the betrayal was a fellow Tory, the duke of Wellington.[89]

Despite the repeal of the Test and Corporation Acts in 1828 and the granting of Catholic emancipation in 1829, difficulties rumbled on. The dissenters stayed dissatisfied; they were obliged to pay church rates until 1868; they remained excluded from Oxford and Cambridge until 1871. On the other hand, Anglicans braced themselves for an all-out assault on the Establishment and the cry 'The Church in Danger' was heard as it had been in the days of Anne. In 1831 Coleridge wrote that he 'had known very few dissenters indeed, whose hatred to the Church of England was not a much more active principle of action with them than their love for Christianity'.[90] A petition from the University of Cambridge in 1834 to admit dissenters produced from him a ferocious denunciation of those dons who were fraternizing with the 'open and rancorous enemies of the church': they had joined forces with a faction 'banded together like obscene dogs and cats and serpents'.[91] Coleridge was convinced that logic not only justified but demanded persecution:

It would require stronger arguments than any which I have heard as yet, to prove that men in authority have not a right, involved in an imperative duty, to deter those under their control from teaching or countenancing doctrines which they believe to be damnable, and even to punish with death those who violate such prohibition . . . Some criterion must in any case be adopted by the state; otherwise it might be compelled to admit whatever hideous doctrine and practice any man or number of men may assert to be his or their religion.[92]

One may, if one chooses, dismiss Coleridge as an extreme figure, intoxicated by the violence of his own language. But when the young Gladstone in the 1830s tackled the problems of Church and State, he went out of his

---

[89] *Colloquies*, ii. 47–8. See also G. Carnall, *Robert Southey and his Age: The Development of a Conservative Mind* (Oxford, 1960). The timing of Southey's volumes was cruel. He had been working on them since 1820, but they came out in the spring of 1829 just as Catholic Emancipation was going through. Macaulay's review was printed in *Edinburgh Review* (Jan. 1830).

[90] *Table Talk* (Oxford, 1917), 166. He excepted the Wesleyans.   [91] Ibid. 300.

[92] Ibid. 288. Coleridge's published views are contained in 'On the Constitution of Church and State' (1830). For modern comments, see P. Allen, 'S. T. Coleridge's Church-State and the Idea of an Intellectual Establishment', *Journal History Ideas*, 46 (1985), 89–106, and subsequent ripostes.

way repeatedly to praise Coleridge for the pre-eminence of his intellectual capacity and the acuteness of his analysis.[93] Indeed, Carlyle thought that Gladstone had swallowed 'Coleridge's shovel-hattism' completely.[94] Gladstone disliked Warburton's defence as passive, secular, and inglorious:

The adoption of a national church is then with it matter of calculation, and not of conscience . . . The view of the state . . . is wholly unsatisfactory. It is represented as restricted absolutely to temporal, nay to material, ends; and is consequently stripped of all its nobler attributes . . . it is a very low theory of government.[95]

But in his zeal to propose a more positive role for the state, Gladstone opened himself to Macaulay's famous attack that he would bring back persecution:

The state . . . has a power, a mighty power, to act upon the people, as well as a liability to be acted upon by them. Inasmuch, therefore, as dissidence, taken in the whole, however the rule may be qualified or even reversed in particular cases, implies a failure in one of the conditions of full national life, it also implies a defect, be it more or be it less, of competency for public office, whose holders act on behalf of the nation. The State, therefore, in certain circumstances, may disqualify. It does not thereby persecute, because it inflicts a negative penalty, not for its own sake, but incidentally and by the way, while it is engaged in seeking the most competent men who are to be had for its instruments.[96]

Gladstone's agonized and qualified reasoning was one of the last great statements of the old position: in Macaulay's jeer, 'the strenuous effort of a very vigorous mind to keep as far in the rear of general progress as possible'. Slowly and reluctantly, the concept that the state was specifically and exclusively Anglican was pushed into retreat, to be followed, as conservatives had warned, by the abandonment of a Christian state at all. The admission of Jews to Parliament in 1858, followed by the decision in 1886 no longer to refuse admission to Charles Bradlaugh, an avowed atheist, marked the end of that theory which Johnson, along with Locke and Burke, had regarded as the very rock upon which civilized life might be built. 'We know,' Burke had written, 'and what is better, we feel

---

[93] *The State in its Relations with the Church*, 4th edn. (London, 1841), 24, 115, 167.
[94] Quoted in J. Morley, *Life of Gladstone*, i. 131 n.   [95] *The State*, i. 18–19.
[96] Ibid. i. 337. Only Gladstone would think that disqualification, if it were 'incidentally and by the way', would be more bearable. Macaulay, in the *Edinburgh Review*, retorted: 'he maintains that conformity to the religion of the state ought to be an indispensable qualification for office; and he would, unless we have greatly misunderstood him, think it his duty, if he had the power, to revive the Test Act, to enforce it rigorously, and to extend it to important classes who were formerly exempt from its operation.'

inwardly, that religion is the basis of civil society, and the source of all good and of all comfort.'[97] Most of the debate on the Bradlaugh case was of a detailed and technical nature, but R. N. Fowler, one of the members for London, made a last and, as it proved, unavailing effort to rally support for the old order:

Is a man who denies the common God of Jew and Christian to be permitted to sit in this House? . . . If a man denies God and a future state, I do not see how he can be expected to be a moral man. His language must necessarily be—'Let us eat and drink, for tomorrow we die'.[98]

It was an argument which Johnson would have found very familiar.

[97] *Reflections*, 87.
[98] *Hansard's Parliamentary Debates*, 3rd ser., ccliii. 461–3 (21 June 1880).

Johnson and Jacobitism

AN obvious retort to the suggestion that Johnson's political stance was basically moderate is that he was, on the contrary, a notorious and ardent Jacobite. It forms a kind of secret agenda which must be investigated before we can evaluate his utterances on other political questions. In addition, it will enable us to make some estimate of the importance of Jacobitism during the first half of the eighteenth century, which must have a very direct bearing upon the debate about the stability of the Hanoverian regime. If one of the two major political parties was, as has been suggested, predominantly Jacobite, the Hanoverian dynasty was far from secure.

The charge that Johnson was a fervent Jacobite was made frequently during his lifetime and has been repeated at intervals ever since. His acceptance of a grant of £300 p.a. from George III in 1762 unleashed a chorus of sarcasm from Charles Churchill and others:

> He damns the *Pension* which he takes
> And loves the STUART he forsakes.[1]

Hannah More called him, bluntly, 'Jacobite Johnson'.[2] William Hazlitt thought that Johnson went through his Highland journey in 1773 with 'lack-lustre eyes', because he had seen it all before after Culloden.[3] John Wilson Croker, normally a hard-headed editor, suggested that the paucity of information about Johnson's life in 1746 meant that he had been in hiding.[4] John Buchan wrote a somewhat unremarkable novel, *Midwinter*,

---

[1] *The Ghost*, bk. III, 819–20.   [2] *Miscellanies*, ii. 191.

[3] *Of Persons One Would Wish to Have Seen*, in *Complete Works*, ed. P. P. Howe (London, 1933), xvii. 127. If Johnson was at Culloden on 16 Apr. 1746, he managed to be back in London by 30 Apr. to finish his *Scheme for a Dictionary*, and he breakfasted on 18 June with the booksellers who contracted for it. Even for Johnson this seems remarkable composure of mind.

[4] Proponents of this theory have also tried to make something of a letter dated 3 Nov. 1746 from Gilbert Walmsley at Lichfield to David Garrick. It asks Garrick, when he sees Johnson, 'pray give my compliments and tell him I esteem him as a great genius—quite lost both to himself and the world'. It seems torturing evidence to presume that this is a reference

in which Johnson marches off to Carlisle to catch up with Prince Charles. Perhaps the most bizarre suggestion was that Johnson's unaccountable patience with his lifelong companion, the sombre Robert Levett, must have been because he was being blackmailed about his Jacobite past.[5] It has been argued that, even as late as 1784, the last year of his life, Johnson was trying to cover his tracks by recovering incriminating evidence from the widow of his former friend and amanuensis, Francis Stewart.[6]

We must accept that persons participating in treasonable activity are wise not to leave too many letters around and that the quality of surviving evidence may not be impressive. Nevertheless, many of these straws are too slight to build with. Hannah More was 6 months old at the time of the '45 and is not a good witness. The suggestion that Johnson was out in the '45 may have the merit of helping to explain why that campaign was so disastrous, but one would otherwise wonder what use a short-sighted, clumsy, and ataxic scholar would have been. If Levett was really a ruthless blackmailer, it is surprising that he could think of no better reward than living in so poor and quarrelsome a household, unless of course Frank Barber, Miss Williams, and Mrs Desmoulins were Jacobites as well; nor is it easy to understand why Johnson, released at last from nearly forty years of blackmail by Levett's sudden death in 1782, should have mourned him in one of his finest poems and written to his friends how much he missed him.[7]

In recent years, the debate has continued and, like much to do with Jacobitism, has acquired a sharp edge. Donald Greene was clearly exasperated when he wrote in 1960:

> It is hard to know what to do with the assertion 'Johnson was a Jacobite', which still continues to be made. If 'Jacobite' means one who seriously desired the restoration of the Stuart family to the British throne, there is no evidence for its application to Johnson at any time during his life.[8]

---

by an ardent Whig to a Jacobite refugee. The more natural explanation is that, after the success of 'London' in 1738, Walmsley was afraid that Johnson was drifting into Grub Street obscurity and was offering friendly encouragement.

[5] C. Petrie, *The Jacobite Movement* (London, 1959), 479.

[6] It is discussed by Croker in his 1831 edition of Boswell's *Life*. The episode is intriguing, but not even Jacobites carried round incriminating evidence involving their friends for forty years. Since Stewart had looked after Johnson's business affairs, it may have had reference to the production of the *Dictionary*.

[7] *Letters*, ed. Redford, iv. 15, 137, 160, 167, 265.

[8] *The Politics of Samuel Johnson*, 298 n. 37. See also Chapin, *The Religious Thought of Samuel Johnson*, 13: 'it is admitted on all sides today [1968] that Johnson was no Jacobite.'

Unfortunately, this rather begs the question: 'seriously' is a qualification which played havoc with Jacobite plans at the time and has haunted Jacobite scholarship ever since. A different view, from a later scholar, concludes that Johnson had 'strong Jacobite inclinations'.[9] Again, this turns on the question, how strong was strong? In the light of continuing disagreement, it seems wisest to re-examine the evidence, relying as far as possible upon what Johnson wrote rather than upon what he is reported to have said. What, in a review of Johnson's politics, we can hardly do is to leave undiscussed what some have seen as the most important loyalty of his life.

On the day Johnson was born, 18 September 1709, the Jacobite cause was far from being a forlorn hope. The death of James II at St Germain in 1701 had freed it from the incubus of his harsh and unpleasant character and his three years' disastrous reign. The 'warming-pan' Prince of Wales, whose birth in 1688 had triggered off the revolt, was not yet 'the Old Pretender' but a young man of 21. He retained the assistance of Louis XIV of France, who had recognized him as the lawful king of England on the death of his father. Though France was reeling under the hammer-blows of Marlborough's victories, Louis was still by far the most powerful monarch in Europe and his country remained pre-eminent in population and resources. The Protestant claimants to the British throne, afforded parliamentary recognition by the Act of Settlement of 1701, were the dukes of Brunswick-Luneberg, raised in 1699 to the status of electors of Hanover. Of George Lewis, next in succession to Sophia, little was known save that, from 1694 onwards, his wife had been immured in a castle in Ahlden, her lover having been murdered. It was a story upon which Jacobite propaganda could hardly fail to improve.[10]

At home, there were also encouraging signs. Queen Anne, half-sister to James Francis Edward Stuart, was believed to be torn by remorse at her usurpation of his throne, and it was rumoured that, on her deathbed, which in the course of things could not be long delayed, she would declare

---

[9] H. Erskine-Hill, 'The Political Character of Samuel Johnson', in I. Grundy (ed.), *Samuel Johnson: New Critical Essays* (London, 1984). See also H. Erskine-Hill, 'The Political Character of Samuel Johnson: The Lives of the Poets and a Further Report on the Vanity of Human Wishes', in E. Cruickshanks & J. Black (eds.), *The Jacobite Challenge* (Edinburgh, 1981).

[10] e.g. by insinuating that George Lewis's children were not his own, hence the frequent references to him in Jacobite squibs as 'the cuckold'. Richard Savage, then in his Jacobite phase, wrote: 'And what's a Riddle, that you may explain, | Gave him a Wife, but gave him ne'er a Queen; | For Prince of Wales adopted him a son, | Who like the crown he wears is not his own.' (C. R. Tracy (ed.), *The Poetical Works of Richard Savage* (Cambridge, 1962).)

in his favour.[11] The Whigs, in power since the start of the war with France and the party devoted to the Hanoverian succession, had become dangerously unpopular, and their ill-judged prosecution of Henry Sacheverell in the spring of 1710 was the prelude to their overthrow.[12] The Tory party, which swept to victory at the general election of 1710, was led by Robert Harley and Henry St John, each of whom had some sympathy for the House of Stuart. St John, created Viscount Bolingbroke in 1712, fled to France in 1715 and joined the Pretender as Secretary of State; Harley, raised to the peerage as earl of Oxford in May 1711, assured the Pretender the previous month that, if he would follow advice, his restoration could be accomplished as easily as that of Charles II, fifty years earlier.[13]

It is not easy to assess the strength of the Jacobite challenge, politically or militarily. Its fortunes fluctuated with changes in the European diplomatic situation. After the death of Louis XIV in 1715, the domestic problems of the regent d'Orléans ushered in a period of *rapprochement* between France and Britain, forcing the Jacobites to look to second-rate powers like Spain and Sweden for assistance. Since neither of them was capable of protecting its own empire, they were unlikely to be able to do much for the Jacobite cause. The more realistic Jacobites understood, however, that without foreign help a restoration would be almost impossible. The number of determined Jacobites in England seems to have been small and diminished year by year as the Hanoverians consolidated their position. Since it was in the interests of both the government and the Jacobites to exaggerate their numbers, and it is in the nature of a conspiratorial movement that it does not publish lists of supporters, it is hardly surprising that modern historians have found as much difficulty in making estimates as did contemporaries.

Although the Jacobite movement is associated with plots, risings, and invasions, it is arguable that its best chances were political. Charles II had, after all, been restored in 1660 not by invasion but at the invitation of Parliament, with few conditions and speedy negotiations. Perhaps the fatal mistake, from which the cause never recovered, was made at the outset when James fled the country and sought refuge in France. He rescued William from an extremely awkward embarrassment and, by identifying himself with the national enemy, brought into play strong

[11] For a convenient summary of the position, see E. Gregg, 'Was Queen Anne a Jacobite?', *History*, 57 (1972).

[12] Sacheverell's sermon *The Perils of False Brethren* was interpreted by his opponents as an attack upon the validity of the Glorious Revolution. His impeachment became a grand debate on the principles of 1688.   [13] B. W. Hill, *Robert Harley* (London, 1988), 174.

feelings of English nationalism. Quite simply, James's nerve failed him and the vision of his father on the scaffold swam before his eyes. To Lord Ailesbury he confided, somewhat unnecessarily, 'I retire for the safety of my person'. Had he stayed it would have been hard to avoid a Regency on behalf of his infant son, a solution which William would probably have rejected. It was most unlikely that William would have contemplated executing his father-in-law, or that he would have been allowed to do so.

The main stumbling-block to a Jacobite restoration was religion. Most of James's former subjects mistrusted his Catholicism as much as his autocratic tendencies, and he and his successors were repeatedly urged to abjure their religion as Henri IV of France had done. Halifax and Danby, two very experienced observers, agreed that, were James to change, it would be hard to hold out against him. One cannot, of course, be sure that they were right, and the rather simple proposition that James preferred a heavenly crown to an earthly one may be doubted. It is at least possible that conversion would have been denounced as yet another example of popish knavery, that he would have lost old friends without gaining new ones, and that so abrupt a change would have been no more persuasive than his sudden reversal of policy in the autumn of 1688.[14]

After James's death, negotiations began with the young Prince of Wales, now, to his followers, James III of England and VIII of Scotland. His main reliance was upon Anne, who had succeeded William in March 1702 and had pledged St Germain to make restitution. Though she could hardly be expected to admit that she was a usurper and make way for him, a declaration in favour of James would have been of great consequence. It was never forthcoming. There was however still the possibility that Harley and Bolingbroke, acting independently, could contrive a Jacobite succession. Their motive was self-preservation rather than ideology, since they had good reason to fear that the treaty of peace they had made, leaving the Hanoverians to fight on alone, had ruined their credit with the court at Herrenhausen. At Christmas 1713 Queen Anne's severe illness reminded them that time was short, and each separately made fresh overtures to St Germain. James's total refusal to consider a religious conversion—'it is for others to change their sentiments'—threw them into confusion, in which state they remained until Anne's death in 1714. The result was an extraordinary anticlimax whereby the Hanoverian

---

[14] James Francis Edward subsequently spelled out the case against conversion, arguing that it would render him an object of mistrust to every honest man. Quoted in D. Szechi, *Jacobitism and Tory Politics, 1710–1714* (Edinburgh, 1984), 186.

succession went unopposed, and each month made a political solution less probable.

Once the Hanoverians had taken possession, only military success could bring about a Jacobite restoration. The prospects were not encouraging. In 1708 a threatened invasion of Scotland had been postponed when James caught measles, and was later thwarted by adverse winds. But in 1715, after a general election under Hanoverian auspices had swept the Whigs back to power, the Jacobites launched a major rising. In Scotland, under the leadership of the earl of Mar, the rebels had some success, but in England, the main theatre of operations, support was meagre, and the government rounded up the conspirators comfortably. After the rising was almost over, James arrived in Scotland on his first and last visit to his lost dominions. It was a damp and dispiriting affair, lasting no more than five weeks, and the impression made by James, even on his supporters, was dismal.

Another rising in the Highlands is sometimes dignified as the '19 but got no further than Glenshiel. Layer's plot in 1722, which hoped to draw upon some of the discontents left by the South Sea bubble, was equally unsuccessful and served only to bring down Bishop Atterbury.[15] But the '45 was a different matter. Charles Edward succeeded in bringing Scotland temporarily under Jacobite control and his army advanced as far south as Derby. It has been suggested that the decision to retreat, taken at the famous council of war, deprived the prince of certain victory and 'might well have changed the fate of the world'.[16] This is a little over-enthusiastic. The council determined on retreat for sound military reasons and there is little evidence that victory was there for the taking. The most experienced of Charles Edward's advisers, Lord George Murray, wrote: 'had not the council determined the retreat from Derby, what a catastrophe must have followed in two or three days.'[17]

After Culloden, Jacobitism was dead. Charles Edward took to the bottle; William Pitt engaged the loyalty of the Scottish clans by using them in the Seven Years War; and the accession of George III in 1760 was the signal for most Tories to bring to an end their forty years in the wilderness. Charles Edward's brother and successor—Henry IX to an ever-dwindling band of subjects—was a cardinal in the Catholic Church.

---

[15] E. Cruickshanks, 'Lord North, Christopher Layer and the Atterbury Plot: 1720–23', in Cruickshanks and Black (eds.), *The Jacobite Challenge*, 92–106.

[16] Petrie, *The Jacobite movement*, 372.

[17] Memo to Prince Charles, 6 Jan. 1746, quoted in W. Duke, *Lord George Murray and the Forty-Five* (Aberdeen, 1927), 135–6.

When he fell upon hard times during the Napoleonic Wars, George III arranged for him to receive a small pension. The reconciliation was complete when the Prince Regent, in 1819, paid for a monument to be erected in St Peter's, Rome, to the Old Pretender and his two sons.

To establish Johnson's attitude to these dramatic events is not simple. The evidence is patchy and often ambiguous. We have to allow off something for prudence, hindsight, and occasion. Many of Johnson's later remarks are passed on to us by Boswell, who had himself strong, if vague, views on the subject. They depend upon his quality of recall, which was of a high order, and his objectivity, which was not.[18] We should not read too much into Johnson's question to a young girl, 'I hope you are a Jacobite, my dear?', save that it demonstrates his taste for teasing and provoking, as when he is reported to have offered a toast at a gathering of Oxford dons to the next slave revolt in Jamaica.[19]

Johnson came from a small cathedral city and from a county where Toryism was strong and shaded into Jacobitism. His father, Michael Johnson, was credited by Boswell with Jacobite sympathies, though he was prepared to take the oath as a magistrate.[20] Lichfield itself was a parliamentary borough with an unusually large electorate and a reputation for turbulent contests 'owing to a strong and aggressive Jacobite element in the town'.[21] At a by-election in 1718, when Johnson was 9, a mob paraded with white roses in their hats, and again in 1753 the Tory candidate was supported by voters wearing white ribbons, a symbol of the house of Stuart. There were strong contests in both county and borough at the general election of August 1747, and at the Lichfield races the following month a Tory/Jacobite mob, 'most of them in plaid waistcoats, plaid ribbons round their hats, and some with white cockades', broke the arm of an old soldier for drinking a health to George II.[22]

It is clear that Johnson could not remember much of his visit to Queen Anne when an infant, though we may presume that the occasion lost nothing in family re-telling.[23] He is also said to have 'caught the public zeal and spirit for Sacheverell' at the age of 3 and to have been carried by his father on his shoulders to see the doctor preach in the cathedral. Oxford in the late 1720s can have done little to discourage any Jacobite

---

[18] For an example see below, n. 71. G. B. Hill's contribution to the *Johnson Club Papers* (1899) on Boswell's proof-sheets gives many examples of Boswell altering his drafts and serves as a warning against regarding Boswell's printed version as uncontaminated evidence.
[19] *Life*, i. 430; iii. 200.   [20] Ibid. i. 37.   [21] *House of Commons, 1715–54*, i. 319.
[22] Ibid.   [23] *Life*, i. 42–3.

sentiments Johnson might have had. Matthew Panting, Master of Pembroke College during Johnson's residence, was a sympathizer, and Johnson later described him as a 'fine Jacobite fellow'.[24] There had been disturbances at Oxford in 1715 when the Pretender is said to have been proclaimed. When the University's Chancellor, the duke of Ormonde, fled to join the Pretender in August 1715, he was replaced by his brother, the earl of Arran. In 1749, at the opening of the Radcliffe Camera, Dr William King, Principal of St Mary's Hall, delivered his famous 'redeat' speech, and ten years later, on Arran's death, presented the earl of Westmorland as his successor. Westmorland, a military man and a strong supporter of the Hanoverians in the 1720s, had moved into opposition in the 1730s when deprived by Walpole of his regiment, and began a flirtation with Jacobitism. According to Horace Walpole, Westmorland's supporters at the installation in July 1759 were 'all be-James'd with true-blue ribbands'.[25] Johnson attended and clapped his hands until they were sore at Dr King's speech.[26] But it was Oxford Jacobitism's last gasp. In 1761 the new Chancellor, accompanied by William King, presented the University's compliments to George III on the occasion of his marriage, and caused some embarrassment by seizing the hand of Lady Sarah Lennox, the king's former sweetheart, in mistake for the new queen.[27]

From 1729, when he was forced by poverty to leave Oxford, until 1735, when he married, Johnson's main habitat was among his whiggish friends at Lichfield—the dazzling Molly Aston and the urbane Gilbert Walmsley, registrar of the ecclesiastical court and brother of the former dean. Johnson adopted a Tory posture, partly, as he later confessed, out of contrariety. Of his relations with Walmsley, twenty-eight years his senior, Johnson wrote, simply, 'I honoured him and he endured me'.[28] It is doubtful, however, whether explicitly Jacobite sentiments would have been endured in Walmsley's fine house in the Close.[29]

---

[24] *Life*, i. 73.

[25] Walpole to Montagu, 19 July 1759 (W. S. Lewis (ed.), *Correspondence of Horace Walpole*, 48 vols. (New Haven, Conn., 1937–83), ix. 240–2).

[26] This is Johnson's own account (*Letters*, ed. Redford, i. 186). According to D. Greenwood, *William King* (Oxford, 1969), 289, there is no report of the speech, so we cannot be certain what Johnson applauded but we may presume that it included some ironic references to the Hanoverians.

[27] H. Walpole to Duchess of Grafton, 12 Sep. 1761 (*Correspondence of Walpole*, xxxii. 3). It was not wasted on observers that Lady Sarah, being a descendant of Charles II by Louise de Kerouaille, had Stuart blood.

[28] The tribute is in *Lives of the Poets*, under the account of Edmund Smith.

[29] Walmsley lived in the Bishop's Palace, which he leased.

In March 1737 Johnson made his journey to London, in the company of David Garrick and with a letter of commendation from Walmsley in his pocket. There began the tedious and protracted process of finding a literary foothold. One of his most influential new friends was Richard Savage, a decayed poet and man-about-town whom Johnson regarded, at least at first, as a polished genius. Savage played the central role in Johnson's poem 'London', which brought him something of a reputation in May 1738, and was the subject of the first of Johnson's *Lives of the Poets*.[30]

In his youth, Savage had been an ardent Jacobite, publishing doggerel verses, but he soon seems to have realized that this was an unprofitable line of advance and obtained a pardon in November 1715. Thereafter his politics appear to have been dictated by his needs. On George I's death in 1727, Savage lamented him, rather unoriginally, as 'the best of kings'; but the appeal to George Bubb Dodington for patronage—'accept this po'esy, void of venal aim'—fell upon deaf ears.[31] He was then taken up by Lord Tyrconnel, whom he claimed as a nephew.[32] A panegyric upon Sir Robert Walpole in 1732 brought in a much-needed 20 guineas, and an even better investment the same year was an ode in honour of Queen Caroline, which produced a pension of £50 p.a. and induced Savage to stand forth as her 'Volunteer Laureate'.[33] But at the moment when Johnson must have made his acquaintance, Savage's prospects plummeted. The patience of most of his friends and patrons had been worn out; an appeal to Frederick, Prince of Wales, failed; and, six months after Johnson's arrival in London, Queen Caroline died, leaving Savage adrift once more. In March 1738 he produced an ode in her memory and the following month reprinted his first 'Laureate' poem, in the hope that his pension would be continued. It was not, and on 1 September 1738 he wrote to Thomas Birch that he was the only one of her pensioners whose grant had been cancelled. At the time when Johnson was writing 'London', therefore, Savage was uncommonly anxious to remain on good terms with the court, and it is unlikely that he would have paraded his former Jacobite views, even if he

[30] It was written soon after Savage's death in Aug. 1743, though the rest of the lives did not appear until the last five years of Johnson's life.

[31] 'A Poem Sacred to the Glorious Memory of . . . King George, Inscribed to the Rt. Hon. George Dodington, Esq.', in C. Tracy (ed.), *The Poetical Works of Richard Savage* (Cambridge, 1962), 82–7.

[32] For the complicated story of Savage's claim to be the son of Earl Rivers, see C. Tracy, *The Artificial Bastard* (Toronto, 1953).

[33] On the death of Laurence Eusden in Sept. 1730 Savage hoped to succeed him as poet laureate. When he was disappointed by the post going to Colley Cibber, Savage declared himself a Volunteer Laureate.

still held them. Johnson's description of how he and Savage roamed the streets of London, attacking Walpole and the court, and resolving 'to stand by their country', sounds like a reminiscence of 1737, when Savage temporarily switched his hopes to Frederick, Prince of Wales, and the patriot opposition.

It is important to establish Savage's influence on Johnson, since the greater part of 'London', a poem in imitation of Juvenal, consists of a speech by Thales, bidding farewell to a friend and expressing his detestation of the city. Boswell denied that Thales was based upon Savage, insisting that Johnson had not even met Savage by May 1738, and in this he was followed by J. W. Croker, editor of the 1831 edition of the *Life*. But it is clear that Boswell had been misinformed.[34] The prime objection to the identification of Thales with Savage is that the latter did not leave London until more than a year after the poem appeared. But to deny the identification strains coincidence to an unreasonable extent. Sir John Hawkins, who knew much at first hand about Johnson's early life in London, was sure that the portrait was based upon Savage.[35] In the poem, Thales is leaving Greenwich for Cambria: Savage, in return for a small allowance, was packed off by his friends to Swansea. There are detailed touches in the portrait which suggest that Johnson had Savage in mind. Thales is a poet and predicts that the time will come when he will re-emerge and 'once more exert his rage': Savage tired of Swansea in due course and, to his friends' dismay, left in 1742, getting as far as Bristol before his funds ran out again. Thales embarked upon his wherry, taking with him 'of dissipated wealth the small remains'—a state of affairs all too

[34] T. Kaminski, 'Was Savage "Thales"?: Johnson's *London* and Biographical Speculation', *Bulletin of Research in the Humanities*, 85 (1982), 322–35, denies that Thrales was based upon Savage, and repeats it in *The Early Career of Samuel Johnson* (Oxford, 1987), 225 n. 20. But I do not find the argument convincing. Boswell's informant was Revd John Hussey, whose claim to be remembering what Johnson had told him is printed in M. Waingrow (ed.), *Correspondence and Other Papers of James Boswell Relating to the Making of the Life of Johnson* (London, 1969), 233–4. Hussey's memory was not reliable. He wrote in his own copy of Hawkins's *Life* that Johnson had told him that 'London' was written 'many years' before he knew Savage. That was clearly impossible, since Savage left for Wales in 1739 and was dead by 1743. Hussey also noted that Boswell did not 'think proper to believe me'. Nevertheless, Boswell relied upon Hussey's testimony in the *Life*, possibly out of a desire to score points off his rival Hawkins, whom he corrects. Kaminski suggests that the parallels between Savage and Thales could be 'applied to many eighteenth-century personalities'. I do not know how many possible candidates for the Thales prototype went into voluntary exile in Wales at this time, but am inclined to believe not many. My argument at this point is merely that, if Thales was based on Savage, it weakens rather than strengthens the likelihood of finding Jacobite sentiments, since Savage was paying court at this time to George II. If Thales was not based upon Savage, the question of Jacobitism does not arise at all, unless it is found in the text. [35] Hawkins, 31–2.

familiar to Savage's acquaintances. There is a hint at Savage's self-appointed post of Volunteer Laureate in the comment on Thales:

> Who scarce forbear, tho' Britain's court he sing,
> To pluck a titled Poet's borrow'd Wing.[36]

Lastly, the lines 'dreaded as a spy', which would be a strange invention, seem to apply to Savage, who was believed to have supplied Pope with information for *The Dunciad*.[37]

It remains true that, if Thales was based upon Savage, it is necessary to believe that Savage's journey to Wales was in preparation many months before he departed. But, since it was dependent upon raising a small subscription from his friends to get rid of him, this is not difficult to credit. Indeed, there is little need for conjecture since Johnson himself tells us that the scheme was accomplished 'after many alterations and delays'.[38] The most piquant piece of evidence is a two-line Latin tribute to Savage, printed in the *Gentleman's Magazine* for April 1738—i.e. the month before 'London' appeared. It was subsequently reprinted in the *London Magazine* and attributed to Johnson, who never denied it. The couplets are an appeal for generosity towards Savage.[39] It is hard to believe that Johnson would have written on behalf of a man he had never met. But even if the author were not Johnson, the lines suggest that the collection for Savage was under way before 'London' appeared and that the exile in Wales had already been mooted.

Erskine-Hill argued that 'London' is the first of the early works of Johnson which reveal his Jacobite sympathies. But there are two difficulties to this suggestion. The first is that 'London' is an imitative poem based upon a satire by Juvenal and there is therefore unusual caution to be employed in attempting to infer the views of the second author. The next is that since the opposition to Walpole was led by Tories and dissident Whigs, and supported by the Jacobites, it is far from easy to separate the component parts.

'London' was Johnson's first breakthrough, attracted favourable comment by Pope, and was reprinted at least twenty-three times during

---

[36] ll. 69–70.

[37] These points were made by F. V. Bernard, 'The Dreaded Spy of London', *Notes and Queries* (Sept. 1958), 398–9; id., 'A New Note on Johnson's "London"', ibid. (Aug. 1964), 293–6. See also *Gentleman's Magazine* (Dec. 1840) 612.

[38] C. Tracy (ed.), *Life of Savage* (London, 1971), 114.

[39] 'Humani studium generis cui pectore fervet, | O! colat humanum Te foveatque genus.' (Devotion to mankind burns in your breast! | O! May mankind in turn cherish and protect you!)

Johnson's lifetime. Though it brought in only 10 guineas in ready money, it helped to consolidate Johnson's dealings with Edward Cave, printer of the *Gentleman's Magazine*, and prepared the way for his close association with that journal. It contains many striking lines, especially those welling up from Johnson's own experience.[40] The art-form, an imitation or paraphrase of the original, imposed severe constraints upon the author, and did not long retain its popularity with readers. 'It is a kind of middle composition,' Johnson explained, 'which pleases when the thoughts are unexpectedly applicable and the parallels lucky.'[41] Few readers today are equipped to enjoy the felicities of Johnson's paraphrasing. He runs wide of Juvenal in places but the need to refer back causes some awkward transitions, as in the reference to Orgilio's palace being struck by lightning. The sentiments, consequently, are second-hand and do not always ring true. It is strange, for example, to find Johnson, whose love of London itself was matched only by his contempt for the barrenness of Scotland, writing:

> For who would leave, unbrib'd, Hibernia's land,
> Or change the rocks of Scotland for the Strand?

Erskine-Hill suggests that 'the idea of Jacobite exile lurks within the printing of Johnson's lines'.[42] I am not sure how far we should push this. The parallel between Johnson's needy poet and the rightful king over the water seems distinctly forced. The fact of exile is dictated by Juvenal's original, where it is Umbricius who takes his leave. If it is objected that, at least, Johnson chose this poem to paraphrase, one may surely retort that he might have found to hand many better and more effective Jacobite parallels. The choice of the poem for Johnson was an opportunity to express his early and vivid impressions of a great city and he chose a subject which would permit many topical references and allusions.

Politically 'London' has the hallmarks of a fairly standard opposition critique of Walpole and his regime, and Johnson wisely peppered it with contemporary satire which can have done its sales no great harm. Overall, it may reflect something of the opinions of Savage, who, as Johnson tells us demurely, 'did not appear to have formed very elevated ideas of those

---

[40] The most celebrated, and given capital letters by Johnson, were: 'This mournful truth is ev'ry where confest, | SLOW RISES WORTH, BY POVERTY DEPREST.'

[41] Johnson was commenting on Pope's imitations in his *Lives of the Poets*. For a detailed comparison of Johnson and Juvenal, see N. Rudd, *Johnson's Juvenal* (Bristol, 1981).

[42] Erskine-Hill points out that the reference to 'one true Briton' (l. 8) reflects the title of Wharton's journal of that name in 1724. Wharton went over to the Jacobites in 1725.

to whom the administration of affairs . . . has been intrusted'.[43] The overarching figure is Orgilio, a man of vast influence and wealth and presumably intended for Sir Robert Walpole, but he is not described very closely.[44] There are gloomy references to excise, court pensioners, the ruined honour of the country, Spanish insolence, greed, French fashions, and crime. There is nothing to suggest a Jacobite stance rather than a Tory one—or, indeed, an opposition Whig one. The only reference to George II is a sharp comment on his regular visits to Hanover:

> Scarce can our fields, such Crowds at Tyburn die,
> With Hemp the Gallows and the Fleet supply.
> Propose your schemes, ye Senatorian band,
> Whose Ways and Means support the sinking Land;
> Lest Ropes by wanting in the tempting Spring,
> To rig another Convoy for the K–ng.[45]

Sir John Hawkins, our best authority for this period of Johnson's life, remarked simply that the topics of declamation were taken largely from weekly newspapers and particularly from the *Craftsman*, the organ of a 'malevolent faction' who professed themselves Whigs.[46]

Johnson followed up his first incursion into political commentary with three more pieces in quick succession: an introduction to the Lilliput debates, published in the *Gentleman's Magazine* in June 1738; *Marmor Norfolciense*, which came out in May 1739; and a *Compleat Vindication*, which appeared the same month. Not until the early 1770s was Johnson to show a comparable intensity of interest in political matters.

Edward Cave, having been warned by a fierce parliamentary resolution in the spring of 1738 to desist from publishing debates, hit upon the celebrated device of printing them as though they were the proceedings of the Senate of Lilliput. Speakers were given anagramatic names. His June 1738 number contained an introduction which explained the device and offered a short résumé of the affairs of the state of Lilliput, reported by the grandson of Lemuel Gulliver. It was an opportunity to follow Swift in ironic political allusion. The introduction observed sweetly that 'the late resolution of the House of Commons, whereby we are forbidden to insert any account of the proceedings of the *British Parliament*, gives us an opportunity of communicating in their room'.

---

[43] Tracy (ed.), *Life of Savage*, 65.
[44] Juvenal's original was Verres, chosen as an archetypal rapacious administrator.
[45] ll. 242–7.   [46] Hawkins, 34–5.

The introduction to the debates has been attributed to Johnson on internal evidence, and, since we know that he played an important part in the later production of the reports, it must be a possibility.[47] It certainly contains sentiments close to his own. It begins with a strong attack upon Lilliputian colonialism, imposed by 'rapine, bloodshed and desolation', draining the population of the mother country, and to little end save the acquisition of 'vast tracts of land . . . too spacious to be constantly garrisoned, and too remote to be occasionally and duly supplied'. Nevertheless, Lilliput contends for supremacy with its petty rivals and war is brewing with Iberia (Spain), which has urged its claims with 'insatiable ambition'. As a result of a *coup* since Captain Gulliver left, the Emperor of Lilliput has been overthrown and a new constitution adopted which is an 'exact account' of the British one. Unfortunately, the Lilliputian constitution has degenerated as a result of the introduction of septennial parliaments, which have encouraged 'venality and dependency' to such an extent that the electors of Lilliput show little interest in the character or abilities of a parliamentary candidate unless he 'solicits voices with gold in his hand'. The introduction concludes with another nicely ironic touch. Gulliver's grandson is intrigued to try to discover 'by what means the government of Lilliput, which had been once established on so excellent a plan, became so miserably degenerate; while the government of Britain, its original, maintained inviolate the purity and vigour of its primitive constitution'.

Though unmistakably written from an opposition point of view, the satire is gentle and not easy to categorize. Attacks upon the septennial act and bribery were staple fare. But Greene has remarked that the description of the *coup* was hair-raisingly seditious.[48] It is certainly violent:

The People . . . demanded the heads of the Man-Mountain's accusers. The Ministers, according to custom, ran for shelter to the royal authority, but far from appeasing the people by that artifice, they involved their master in the common destruction . . . the People (set) fire to the Palace and buried the whole royal family in its ruins.

But, in the context of the piece, the *coup* was followed by the remodelling of the Lilliputian government as a copy of the British constitution. Readers might see it as a rough paraphrase of the Glorious Revolution

[47] It is discussed in B. B. Hoover, *Samuel Johnson's Parliamentary Reporting: Debates in the Senate of Lilliput* (Berkeley, Calif., 1953), who follows G. B. Hill in attributing it to Johnson. It has also been attributed to William Guthrie, a collaborator on the *Gentleman's Magazine*. Kaminski, *Early Career of Johnson*, 42–3, suggests a joint production.

[48] *The Politics of Samuel Johnson*, 94.

rather than an immediate incitement to rebellion and murder. Cave was, after all, a cautious man, already in trouble with the authorities, and unlikely to allow avowedly Jacobite propaganda into the pages of his magazine.

Johnson's next political venture was *Marmor Norfolciense*, an elaborate piece of spoof scholarship.[49] An ancient stone is dug up (by chance, in Norfolk, Sir Robert Walpole's county), with a Latin inscription which appears to be a prophecy. A commentator then attempts, with a considerable parade of mock learning, to decipher the message, but, retiring baffled, proposes a standing committee of scholars to examine and report on it.[50] The usual opposition strictures are worked in, with varying degrees of subtlety. Much attention is devoted to a plague of 'scarlet reptiles': the commentator is inclined to think that they must be ladybirds, but at length confesses that he is 'not able to determine anything on this question'.[51] In comparison with the introduction to the debates of Lilliput, the satire is sharper, and Johnson seems to have extended his disapproval to kings in general, who come in for heavy sarcasm.[52] The commentator cannot agree with his friends, who feel certain that the prophecy must be the work of some ancient king: kings do not normally show the regard for posterity that the author of the stone clearly possessed, nor are speeches from the throne much concerned with anything 'other than for the current year':

Nothing indeed can be more unreasonable and absurd than to require that a monarch, distracted with cares and surrounded with enemies, should involve himself in superfluous anxieties by an unnecessary concern about future generations. Are not pretenders, mock-patriots, masquerades, operas, birth-nights,

---

[49] It was published anonymously, but Pope attributed it to Johnson in a letter to Jonathan Richardson (G. Sherburn (ed.), *Correspondence of Alexander Pope* (Oxford, 1956), iv. 194); a copy of the 1739 edn., with corrections in Johnson's own hand, is in Manchester Central Library.

[50] Johnson suggested that Greenwich Hospital could be handed over to the commission: all that would be necessary would be 'the expulsion of such of the seamen as have no pretensions to their settlement there, but fractur'd limbs, loss of eyes, or decay'd constitutions'.

[51] The technique produces an inner tension, whereby the reader is reduced to a kind of silent chorus, longing to shout out: 'It means red-coats, a standing army.' It is a dramatic device of the 'look-behind-you' variety, used in Punch and Judy shows.

[52] Sometimes, of course, the comments are directed at George II. Had previous rulers possessed the gift of prophecy, remarks the commentator, it would surely have been pointed out. In our own day, 'no princely virtue can shine in vain. Our monarchs are surrounded with refined spirits, so penetrating that they frequently discover in their masters great qualities invisible to vulgar eyes, and which, did they not publish them to mankind, would be unobserved for ever.'

treaties, conventions, reviews, drawing-rooms, the birth of heirs, and the death of queens, sufficient to overwhelm any capacity but that of a king?

The British lion is, of course, feeble and degenerate:

> His tortur'd sons shall die before his face,
> While he lies melting in a lewd embrace.[53]

Johnson exploits to good effect his device of the baffled commentator, who professes not to understand the passage. 'In what place can the English be said to be trampled or tortured? Where are they treated with injustice or contempt? What nation is there from pole to pole that does not reverence the nod of the British king?' The Hanoverian connection, which was extremely unpopular, came in for predictable attack:

> And, yet more strange! his veins a horse shall drain,
> Nor shall the passive coward once complain.[54]

After the plague of reptiles comes anarchy:

> Then o'er the world shall Discord stretch her wings,
> Kings change their laws, and kingdoms change their kings.

With *Marmor Norfolciense*, we come closest to a Jacobite Johnson. Hawkins tell us that after its publication Johnson was obliged to go into hiding for a while.[55] Erskine-Hill is emphatic: 'this is Jacobite sedition', he writes; *Marmor* is 'a Jacobite tract if ever there was one'.[56] Nevertheless, the impression is slightly blurred. The general contempt for kings sits rather awkwardly with the suggestion that James III's return will save the nation: if kings are really that bad, why bother to change? It is rather odd to insult George II as a passive coward for not standing up for Britain against Hanover, when, presumably, he represents Hanover.

The line between Tory or even dissident-Whig opposition and Jacobitism is, as we have said, difficult to establish. Disrespect was not confined to Jacobites. Few people could have surpassed William Pitt in his contempt for that 'despicable electorate', but nobody has suggested that

[53] The tortured sons are victims of Spanish atrocities, like Captain Robert Jenkins, whose ear had been cut off in 1731. The lewd embrace refers to Madame Walmoden, brought over to England by George II after Caroline's death and created Countess of Yarmouth.

[54] The Saxon horse was a symbol for Hanover.

[55] Hawkins, 41. Kaminski, *Early Career of Johnson*, 229 n. 66, doubts whether Johnson was forced into hiding, pointing out that the printer, John Brett, does not seem to have been threatened on this occasion.

[56] 'The Political Character of Johnson', 121; 'The Political Character of Johnson: The Lives of the Poets', 161.

he was a concealed Jacobite. 'And kingdoms change their kings' may sound like a pointed incitement to rebellion, but in the context of the 1730s it may not have seemed remarkably bold. Lord Hervey, a great supporter of the Hanoverian dynasty, wrote that George II was frequently reminded, 'both in Parliament and in print, that his crown had been the gift of the people; that it was given on conditions; and that it behoved him to observe those conditions, as it would be both as easy and as lawful, in case he broke any of them, for the people to resume that gift, as it had been for them to bestow it.'[57]

Johnson's own commentator raised the question of the underlying meaning of the piece when he professed vast difficulty in understanding the prophecy that the horse would suck the lion's blood. He notes that the meaning might concern Hanover, but is reluctant to come to 'such shocking conclusions', which could occur to 'none but a virulent republican or bloody Jacobite'. But before we rush to the conclusion that here Johnson confesses the Jacobite tendency of the piece, we should note that, by that argument, he also confesses himself a virulent republican, which he was certainly not. Indeed, since it is manifestly difficult to be both a bloody Jacobite and a virulent republican at one and the same time, perhaps we should take it as a warning against trying to read too much from the text. The most one can say is that Johnson enjoyed skating on thin ice. It was not necessary, particularly in an anonymous publication, to spell out one's exact position.

The Jacobite issue arises again in Johnson's next piece, *A Compleat Vindication of the Licensers of the Stage*, which appeared only a fortnight after *Marmor Norfolciense*.[58] In 1737 Sir Robert Walpole had carried legislation to give power of licensing plays to the Lord Chamberlain and his deputies. Early in 1739 the deputy-licenser, William Chetwynd, refused a licence to Henry Brooke's play *Gustavus Vasa, the Deliverer of his Country*.[59] The play dealt with the rescue of Sweden from Danish

[57] R. R. Sedgwick (ed.), *Memoirs of Lord Hervey* (London, 1931), ii. 280–1. See also Hervey's description of the unpopularity of the regime in Croker edn. of *Life*, iii. 21.

[58] The attribution to Johnson is rather thin. It was published anonymously and not acknowledged during Johnson's lifetime. 'An Account of the Writings of Dr Samuel Johnson', *European Magazine* (Jan. 1785), gave it to him 'on the authority of an old bookseller'. It was reprinted in the 1787 edn. of Johnson's collected works and has not subsequently been challenged.

[59] Johnson's attention might have been drawn to the issue by the fact that William Chetwynd had contested Lichfield in 1731 in an attempt to take over his brother Walter's seat. He had been forced to withdraw by a Tory, George Venables Vernon. The play was published by subscription. Professor Speck remarks that the subscribers read like a roll-call of the opposition to Walpole (*Society and Literature in England, 1700–60* (Dublin, 1983), 192).

domination by the revolt of 1521. Johnson's intervention was a satire at the expense of the licensing authorities and a sturdy defence of freedom of opinion. Donald Greene points out that rescuing one's country from a usurper 'might also be regarded as Jacobite propaganda'.[60] But it seems more likely that it was Brooke's portrait of a corrupt first minister which irritated Walpole and brought the Lord Chamberlain's men into action. Henry Brooke was at this time closely associated with Pitt and Lyttelton, and under the patronage of Frederick, Prince of Wales: it would be a delicate operation to put out avowedly Jacobite propaganda under the banner of a Hanoverian prince.[61] Moreover, Brooke subsequently returned to Ireland, where he was awarded a lucrative place for producing in 1745 a tract calling upon all Irishmen to resist any Jacobite landing: if this was Jacobite intrigue, it was uncommonly devious.[62] Hence, Johnson's piece may be taken as a straightforward defence of the press and the general tone that of the 'patriot' opposition.[63]

The zeal for politics which Johnson seems to have exhibited during his early years in London was not sustained. In 1739 Savage was finally packed off to exile, removing one input. It has been suggested that Johnson's opinions were changing fast even before the fall of Walpole. Giddings has argued that, in his editing of the debates, Johnson, far from making sure that the Whigs did not have the better of it, showed respect and admiration for Walpole.[64] I am not quite convinced, though it would be scarcely surprising. Shippen's respect for Walpole is well documented, and many of the Tories were reluctant to pull down Sir Robert in order to replace him with Pulteney. Later on, Johnson paid some handsome tributes to Walpole as a statesman.

A significant shift seems to be discernible as early as March 1742, when Johnson contributed to the *Gentleman's Magazine* an essay on 'An Account of the Conduct of the Duchess of Marlborough', prepared by Nathaniel Hooke.[65] It contained some good Johnson touches: 'Distrust is a necessary qualification for a student of history'; Queen Anne was 'born

---

[60] *Yale Edition of the Works of Samuel Johnson*, x: *Political Writings*, ed. D. J. Greene (New Haven, Conn., 1977), 52.

[61] Pope to Hill, 22 Jan. 1739 (*Correspondence of Pope*, iv. 159), makes it clear that Brooke had access to the prince's court. [62] *Farmer's Letters*.

[63] The play was subsequently performed in Dublin under the title *The Patriot*.

[64] 'The Fall of Orgilio: Samuel Johnson as Parliamentary Reporter', in Grundy (ed.), *New Critical Essays*, 86–106. There is a good discussion of the debates in Kaminski, *Early Career of Johnson*, 132–9. He suggests that Johnson did not depart from the neutrality practised by Cave.

[65] pp. 128–31. This essay was attributed to Johnson by Boswell. Its authenticity is discussed by J. Leed, 'Samuel Johnson and the *Gentleman's Magazine*: an adjustment of the canon', *Notes and Queries* (May 1957), 210–13.

for friendship, not for government'. But Johnson went out of his way to discuss Sarah Churchill's savage portrait of William III, in whom she saw scarcely any redeeming qualities, contrasting him with the affable and engaging Charles II. Johnson was sardonic:

Charles II by his ability and politeness made himself the idol of the nation, which he betrayed and sold; William III was for his insolence and brutality hated by that people, whom he protected and enriched.

It was a strange comment from one credited with tenderness for the house of Stuart.

But the main factor was probably the growing disillusion with the Patriots which Johnson shared with many others in the early 1740s. On the fall of Walpole, the opposition broke into factions, showed as much zest in pursuing place and profit as the old gang they had ousted, and abandoned most of their pledges. Sir Robert Walpole was not brought to justice, the Septennial Act was not repealed, the property qualification remained intact, Hanover was not cut adrift, and the only Place Act to root out corruption and restore the independence of Parliament was a very tepid measure disqualifying Commissioners of the Navy and Victualling Office from sitting in the Commons.[66] The note of dismay and betrayal was caught by Johnson in the preface he wrote for the *Gentleman's Magazine* in 1743:

It has been for many years lamented . . . that the struggles of opposite parties have engrossed the attention of the publick, and that all subjects of conversation and all kinds of learning have given way to Politicks . . . it must be owned, that Life requires many other considerations, and that Politicks may be said to usurp the Mind, when they leave no room for any other subject.[67]

The *Gentleman's Magazine* would, in future, diversify its offerings.

The retreat from Patriotism gathered pace. William Pulteney, the charismatic leader of the opposition to Sir Robert Walpole, transformed in 1742 into the first earl of Bath, Johnson dismissed as 'as paltry a fellow as could be'.[68] Walpole himself, once removed from office, grew in stature, his sins forgiven, his amiability remembered: he had been, declared Johnson, 'a fine fellow . . . his very enemies deemed him so before his death'.[69] The last straw seems to have been the defection of Lord Gower, who joined the 'Broad-Bottom' administration in December 1744 as

[66] 15 George II c. 22.   [67] p. 1.   [68] *Life*, v. 339.

[69] Hawkins, 227. Johnson also referred to Walpole in the 1753 preface to the index of the *Gentleman's Magazine* as 'a statesman as able perhaps as any that ever existed'.

Lord Privy Seal.[70] The fact that Gower was a Staffordshire man, Lord-Lieutenant of the county and Recorder of Lichfield made his apostasy all the more painful to Johnson. A decade later, working on the *Dictionary*, Johnson still wished to commemorate the betrayal with his definition of 'renegado': 'one who deserts to the enemy—sometimes we say a GOWER.' From this studied insult Johnson was saved by the common sense of the printer, who struck it out.[71] In 1775, towards the end of his life, bitterness welled up again in his sudden ejaculation, 'Patriotism is the last refuge of a scoundrel'.[72] Thus far had the Patriot of 1738 travelled.

The eclipse of politics is also discernible in Johnson's second great poem, 'The Vanity of Human Wishes', published by Robert Dodsley in 1749. Though also based upon Juvenal (the tenth Satire), it forsakes the political and social satire of 'London' in favour of grand brooding on the transitory nature of human greatness. The political comments and contemporary allusions are marginal rather than central.[73] The choice of Charles XII of Sweden to stand for Hannibal in Juvenal's original was certain to remind Jacobites of their own prince, Charles Edward Stuart, four years after Culloden.[74] After stunning success, each had met with defeat and exile. Charles XII had even given assistance to the Jacobite cause in the 1710s. But the parallel should not be pushed too hard. Charles XII would readily spring to mind in the 1740s as a spectacular instance of military vicissitude. His exploits were well known, Voltaire's *Life* had come out in 1732, and Johnson himself had started work on a play about him in 1742. It is not wise to dwell upon Charles XII's appeal to the English as a Protestant hero without acknowledging that Charles Edward's Catholicism was a major stumbling-block to Stuart restoration.

---

[70] It was scarcely a simple case of desertion. Gower had taken office in 1742 on the fall of Walpole, but resigned in Dec. 1743 because more Tories had not been brought in. Later in 1744 he was negotiating for a total end to Tory proscription and the reproach levelled against him was that he had settled for inadequate terms. Within eighteen months of resuming office, he had been given promotion in the peerage.

[71] This is Johnson's own account to Boswell in 1777. The difference between the note Boswell made of the conversation and the version he printed is a reminder how careful we must be in assessing editorial intervention. By 1744 Gower was regarded as leader of the Tories. Boswell noted the insult to Gower as 'under the word Renegade (alluding to his having deserted the old Jacobite interest *I doubt not*)'. But in the printed version, he gave the remark to Johnson himself: 'Lord Gower forsook the old Jacobite interest.' Boswell's first mistake was not to distinguish Jacobite from Tory, his second to transfer the identification to Johnson. *Life*, i. 296, 544.   [72] Ibid. ii. 348.

[73] Johnson's lines on the electorate seem to foreshadow the rough treatment handed out in *The Patriot* in 1774: 'Our supple tribes repress their patriot throats; | And ask no questions but the price of votes; | With weekly libels and septennial ale, | Their wish is full to riot and to rail.'   [74] Erskine-Hill, 'The Political Character of Johnson', 127–32.

Johnson's later remarks on the Stuarts in the 1750s are characterized by a dispassionate tone. In 1753 he was responsible for the preface to the index of the *Gentleman's Magazine*, in which the rising of '45 was described as

a rebellion which was not less contemptible in its beginning than threatening in its progress and consequences; but which, through the favour of Providence, was crushed at once.[75]

In 1756 he produced for the *Literary Magazine*, of which he was briefly the editor, 'An Introduction to the Political State of Great Britain' which, at the outset of the Seven Years War, traced the development of the maritime struggle between Britain and France. The Stuarts did not come out of it well. James I was dismissed as 'a man of great theoretical knowledge but of no practical wisdom', who neglected the interests of his country; Charles II was accused of allowing the naval power of France to grow, because of his 'fondness of ease and pleasure'; James II 'thought, rightly, that there is no happiness without religion; but he thought very erroneously and absurdly that there is not religion without popery'. His subjects were therefore, under 'the necessity of self-preservation', obliged to drive him from his throne.

The accession of George III in 1760 changed the situation completely. The succession of a king born in this country, glorying in the name of Britain, who had never visited Hanover, removed much English prejudice against the dynasty. Most of the remaining Tories returned to court. But if the Hanoverian dynasty took over a certain amount of the ideological baggage of their rivals in the shape of a desire to stand above party as a national dynasty, it also took over some of their disadvantages. By a curious irony, the fact that the new king's tutor and close friend John, earl of Bute, was a Stuart meant that anti-Scottish feeling could now be re-directed at the court, and paved the way for accusations that George had been brought up on high prerogative and 'Jacobite' notions.[76]

Johnson's position had also changed. The reception of his *Dictionary* in 1755 gave him solid status, if little money, and the pension granted him in

[75] Commented on in E. L. McAdam, Jr., 'Johnson, Walpole and Public Order', in Mary Lascelles *et al.* (eds.), *Johnson, Boswell and Their Circle: Essays Presented to L. F. Powell* (Oxford, 1965), 93–4.

[76] H. Walpole, *Memoirs of the Reign of George III* ed. G. F. R. Barker (London, 1894), ch. 2: 'The Tories . . . abjured their ancient master, but retained their principles; and seemed to have exchanged nothing but their badge, the *White Rose* for the *White Horse*. *Prerogative* became a fashionable word . . .'.

1762 made him financially secure for the first time in his life. A year later he met Boswell. In the relaxed political situation he could speak more freely, especially in private. We have therefore rather more direct evidence and no longer have to be satisfied with hints and inferences. But the new evidence is subject to contamination from two sources: from time, which changes our recollection of what we once felt, and from Boswell himself whose own enthusiasm for Jacobitism, however tempered in practice, was likely to rub off on his portrait of Johnson.

Johnson's acceptance of the pension marked the formal abandonment of whatever reservations he may have had about the house of Hanover. In addition to a good deal of newspaper abuse, the episode also produced two important pieces of evidence bearing on his opinion of Jacobitism.

In 1981, B. H. Davis drew attention to a letter to Lord Bute, dated 15 November 1761, suggesting that a pension be granted to Johnson.[77] It has been attributed to Richard Farmer, a Fellow of Emmanuel College, Cambridge, though it is not, apparently, in his handwriting.[78] Farmer remarked that Johnson's political principles would render him 'incapable of being in any place of trust, by incapacitating him for any such office— but a pension my Lord requires no such performance'. The clear implication was that Johnson was a non-juror who would not be prepared to take the oath of allegiance. Though not all non-jurors were necessarily Jacobites, the argument seems to come close.

There are, however, difficulties in reading too much into Farmer's letter. First, he admitted that he was not personally acquainted with Johnson. It is dangerous to rely upon hearsay when we are dealing with a matter of private conscience. Secondly, the letter is rambling and repetitive. Indeed, the writer wonders whether Bute will think that it comes from 'one whose intellects have been by some accident overturned'. Thirdly, the views attributed to Johnson are at variance with his own account of the subject.

Johnson's own opinion of non-jurors seems not to have been very high. He told Boswell that he 'never knew a non-juror who could reason', that they were hypocrites, and that he had never once been in a non-juring

---

[77] 'The Anonymous Letter Proposing Johnson's Pension', *Transactions of the Johnson Society of Lichfield* (1981), 35–9. A copy of the original letter was sent to Boswell after the publication of the *Life* by the 4th earl of Bute, and was printed in Waingrow (ed.), *Correspondence Relating to the Making of the Life of Johnson* 512–15. The original is in the Bute papers in the British Library, Add. MS 37796, fo. 248. Erskine-Hill discusses the evidence but misdates the letter.

[78] The handwriting has been identified as that of Edward Blakeway of Magdalene College, Cambridge.

meeting-house.[79] Erskine-Hill quotes the evidence of Thomas Cooper the radical that Johnson had no belief in the divine right of kings, but dismisses it with the remark that the anecdote was 'doubtless what Cooper wanted to hear or have heard'.[80] But there is plenty of independent confirmation of Cooper's report. Boswell himself wrote categorically that Johnson did not believe in divine right:

Mr Johnson is not properly a *Jacobite*. He does not hold the *jus divinum* of kings. He said to me once that he did not know but it was become necessary to remove the king at the time of the Revolution.[81]

The second piece of evidence is a conversation which Johnson had with Boswell two months after they had made each other's acquaintance. They had dined well at the Mitre on 14 July 1763, when Boswell, in his inimitable fashion, taxed Johnson with the 'numerous reflections' which had been made upon his acceptance of the pension:

'Why, sir', (said he, with a hearty laugh), 'it is a mighty foolish noise that they make . . . I am the same man in every respect that I have ever been; I retain the same principles. It is true, that I cannot now curse (smiling) the House of Hanover; nor would it be decent for me to drink King James' health in the wine that King George gives me money to pay for. But, Sir, I think that the pleasure of cursing the house of Hanover, and drinking King James' health, are amply overbalanced by three hundred pounds a year.'[82]

The problem is to catch the tone of the conversation and to know how seriously to take the 'confession'. Boswell himself commented that Johnson was admitting the charge of disaffection in order to shrug it off. Erskine-Hill writes that the admission 'brings Johnson to the very brink of treason in any Hanoverian view'.[83] This is hardly doing justice to the playful, almost whimsical nature of the exchange, or to the occasion, which was convivial rather than solemn. What comes across is the cheerfulness with which Johnson would see both kings damned for £300 p.a. The same note of detachment is found later in the conversation when Johnson declared that if, by holding up his right hand, he could have secured victory at Culloden for Prince Charles Edward, 'he was not sure

[79] *Life*, ii. 321; iv. 286–8.

[80] Cooper is quoted in E. A. and G. L. Duyckinck, *Cyclopaedia of American Literature*, (New York, 1855), ii. 333, as reporting that Johnson told him: 'I believe in no such thing as the *jure divino* of kings . . . I believe rather that monarchy is the most conducive to the happiness and safety of the people of every nation, and therefore I am a monarchist but as to its divine right, that is all stuff.' Erskine-Hill's comment is in 'Political Character', 124.

[81] *Tour*, 162–3.   [82] *Life*, i. 429.   [83] 'Political Character', 114.

he would have held it up'. It is hardly the tone of a zealot, scarcely of a
retired zealot.

Another conversation on the same subject took place in April 1773,
when Johnson was alone with Boswell:

> Talking of the family of Stuart, he said, 'It should seem that the family at present
> on the throne has now established as good a right as the former family, by the long
> consent of the people; and that to disturb this right might be considered as
> culpable. At the same time, I own, that it is a very difficult question when
> considered with respect to the house of Stuart. To oblige people to take oaths as
> to the disputed right, is wrong. I know not whether I could take them; but I do not
> blame those who do.'[84]

The opening remark is as clear a repudiation of indefeasible hereditary
right as one could find, in favour either of prescription or of popular
endorsement. Johnson's observations about his personal attitude towards
the oath sound less like a declaration from a lifetime of conscious principle
than a rather casual admission that the question had never arisen. Erskine-
Hill comments that, if Boswell was telling the truth, 'Johnson was a
Jacobite-inclined non-juring Tory, at least until 1773'.[85] I am not sure that
the evidence is strong enough to bear so categorical an interpretation.
Langton had confided to Boswell in July 1763 that Johnson had told him
'nothing has ever offered that has made it worth my while to consider the
question fully'.[86]

An event which might have been expected to demonstrate emphatically
where Johnson's loyalties lay was his visit to the Western Islands in 1773.
It has, of course, been seen as a Jacobite pilgrimage. Johnson slept in the
bed which Prince Charles had occupied and conversed with Flora
Macdonald.

That Boswell was at times deeply moved is not in question. The combination of mountains and mournfulness made a deep impression on him.
Listening to McQueen, the landlord at Glenmoriston and a Culloden
veteran, Boswell 'several times burst into tears':

> There is a certain association of ideas in my mind upon that subject, by which I am
> strongly affected. The very Highland names, or the sound of a bagpipe, will stir
> my blood, and fill me with a mixture of melancholy and respect for courage . . . in
> short, with a crowd of sensations.[87]

Johnson and he, insisted Boswell, shared 'a kind of *liking* for Jacobitism,
something that is not easy to define'. When he did try to define it, he did

---

[84] *Life*, ii. 220.   [85] 'Political Character', 117.   [86] *Life*, i. 430.
[87] *Tour*, 106–7.

not get very far. There was, he felt, 'something pathetic and generous about Jacobitism'. In other words, it had all the charms of a lost cause, and romanticism had taken over. But even Boswell sobered up when it came to practical considerations. 'My calm reasoning stops short at action', he wrote, though what action he had in mind in 1773 is not easy to conjecture. Even talking too much about Jacobitism might 'hurt a man in his rising in life', and he prudently toned down the passage before publishing his *Tour*.[88]

Johnson enjoyed his time on Skye. He talked animatedly with Flora Macdonald about the circumstances of the prince's escape after Culloden, and confided to Boswell that he would 'have given a good deal' rather than not sleep in 'that bed'. But, in writing, he was circumspect. There was no reference to Jacobitism in his published version, which was likely to get into the hands of George III, and his remarks in his letters to Mrs Thrale were guarded. On 24 September he reported:

You may guess at the opinions that prevail in this country, they are however content with fighting for their king, they do not drink for him, we had no foolish healths.[89]

A week later, he passed on the information that the sheets the prince had slept in had been preserved by the mistress of the house and used as her shroud, adding wryly, 'these are not Whigs'.[90]

The last major piece of evidence to be considered is a conversation which Johnson had in 1777 at Ashbourne with his Whig friend Dr Taylor. The exchange became heated. Johnson insisted that the abandonment of hereditary right would, strictly speaking, place in jeopardy the property of every man, and therefore a vast majority of people, fairly polled, would wish to call back the Stuarts:

All those who think a king has a right to his crown, as a man has to his estate, which is the just opinion, would be for restoring the King, who certainly has the hereditary right, could he be trusted with it . . . A right to a throne is like a right to any thing else.[91]

Taylor might have retorted that a powerful motive of those who opposed James II had been to protect property against encroachment by the

---

[88] The original version is printed in *Tour*, 163.

[89] *Letters*, ed. Redford, ii. 83.   [90] Ibid. 91.

[91] *Life*, iii. 156: 'The people, knowing it to be agreed on all hands that this King has not the hereditary right to the crown, and there being no hope that he who has it can be restored, have grown cold and indifferent upon the subject of loyalty, and have no warm attachment to any king. They would not, therefore, risk any thing to restore the exiled family . . . But if a mere vote could do it, there would be twenty to one . . .'.

Crown,[92] but he limited himself, according to Boswell, to dismissing Johnson's argument as a mere 'abstract doctrine', and indeed it does not seem very probable, whatever the logic of the case, that property was in danger in the Britain of Walpole, Henry Pelham, and the duke of Newcastle.

Nevertheless, the argument between Taylor and Johnson was close to the heart of the problems posed by the Glorious Revolution of 1688. The victors on that occasion were, as has been pointed out, 'reluctant revolutionaries',[93] and as soon as James was out of the way they began a process of damage limitation. The immediate aim was to preserve as much of the hereditary principle as possible. The transparent fiction of the warming-pan gave them a pretext for passing over James's infant son. The succession of Mary and Anne in turn, though bumpy, helped to preserve continuity.[94] But the death of Anne's only surviving child, the duke of Gloucester, in 1700 meant yet another breach in the hereditary principle. George I, on his accession to the throne, did his best to reunite religion and hereditary right by assuring Parliament that it had 'pleased Almighty God, of his good providence, to call me to the throne of my ancestors'.[95]

This was by no means a problem for Jacobites and non-jurors alone. Most Tories were extremely uneasy at what had had to be done, and conservative-minded Whigs were also anxious to play down the radical or populist implications of the Revolution. The argument affected not merely property but political stability, since the right of resistance, once granted, might well prove difficult to restrain. Consequently, Edmund Burke began his *Reflections on the Revolution in France* by strongly denying that the throne of Britain had become elective in 1688:

The succession of the crown has always been what it now is, an hereditary succession by law; in the old line it was a succession by the common law; in the new by the statute law, operating on the principles of the common law, not changing the substance, but regulating the mode, and describing the persons.[96]

---

[92] The extent to which James's intervention in the affairs of Magdalen College, Oxford, was seen as an attack upon property rights is indicated by H. Nenner, 'Liberty, Law and Property: The Constitution in Retrospect from 1688', in J. R. Jones (ed.), *Liberty Secured?: Britain Before and After 1688* (Stanford, Calif., 1992), 109–10.

[93] W. A. Speck, *Reluctant Revolutionaries: Englishmen and the Revolution of 1688* (Oxford, 1988).

[94] By 'bumpy' I mean that Mary had to share her claim with that of her husband (and cousin) William, while Anne's succession was postponed to 1702 after Mary's death in 1694.

[95] *Parl. Hist.* vii. 42.   [96] *Reflections*, 19.

Even Burke might have blushed at the speciousness of defining the exclusion of more than fifty Stuart heirs in favour of the house of Hanover as no more than 'describing the persons'.[97] Burke also went as far as possible in asserting that the Glorious Revolution was a unique event, never to be repeated: he would deplore 'the practice of making the extreme medicine of the constitution its daily bread'.[98]

It is scarcely surprising if it has proved hard to establish Johnson's attitude towards the Stuarts. Since the Jacobite cause was treason and the heads of Jacobite lords adorned Temple Bar (where Goldsmith and Johnson had a wry exchange), it was prudent to be guarded.[99] Contemporaries had equal difficulty in assessing the proportions of smoke and fire. Jacobites often pretended to be no more than Tories: Whigs smeared Tories as Jacobites. The ideologies of Tory and Jacobite had much in common. Indefeasible hereditary right was a well-established Tory principle years before the issue of Jacobitism arose, and most men accepted that monarchy had divine origins and divine sanctions. When Samuel Wesley was accused in the *Gentleman's Magazine* of 1785 of having been a Jacobite, John Wesley wrote in some indignation to defend him:

Most of those who gave him this title did not distinguish between a Jacobite and a Tory; whereby I mean 'One that believes God, not the people, to be the origin of all civil power.' In this sense he was a Tory; so was my father; so am I. But I am no more a Jacobite than I am a Turk; neither was my brother.[100]

Some of these difficulties apply to Johnson. We have a number of isolated remarks over a long period, without being absolutely certain what was said.[101] Johnson's ideas, like those of most people, changed over time, as his interests altered and as the Jacobite cause faded. Even a piece of

---

[97] Burke admitted that 'unquestionably there was at the Revolution, in the person of King William, a small and a temporary deviation from the strict order of a regular hereditary succession'. *Reflections*, 15–16.   [98] Ibid. 60.

[99] At Poet's Corner in Westminster Abbey, Johnson murmured to Goldsmith: 'Forsitan et nostrum nomen misebitur istis' (Ovid: 'It may be our names will mingle with those'). When they reached Temple Bar and gazed up at the heads of the Jacobite rebels, Goldsmith repeated the phrase, with emphasis. *Life*, ii. 238.

[100] *Gentleman's Magazine* (1785), i. 246–7, 363–5; ii. 932.

[101] Even granted perfect good faith and acknowledging Boswell's powers of recall, the accuracy of every word can hardly be sustained. The important conversation of 14 July 1763 took place in the Mitre tavern on a rainy night: the meal lasted, according to Boswell, some six hours, during which time they were well fortified with 'thick English port', which Boswell found 'a very heavy and a very inflammatory dose'. For a further discussion of Boswell's accuracy, see P. J. Korshin, 'Johnson's conversation', in G. Clingham (ed.), *New Light on Boswell* (Cambridge, 1991).

evidence which looks at first sight decisive, such as Johnson sleeping in Prince Charles's bed, does not clinch the argument. The geographer Thomas Pennant had visited Skye the year before Johnson, stayed in Flora Macdonald's house, and slept in the bed. Since Pennant was a self-confessed Whig, whose comment on Culloden was that Scotland owed its prosperity to the Duke of Cumberland's victory there, the ritual of sleeping in the Bed begins to look less like a conspicuous gesture of Jacobite loyalty and more like a piece of early Tartan tourism.

Within these limits, Johnson's sympathy for the Stuarts can hardly be doubted. There would have been little need for his repeated disclaimers or for Boswell's editorial explanations had Johnson been a devoted supporter of the Hanoverian dynasty. Sir John Hawkins wrote that in the late 1740s the members of the Ivy Lane club took pains not to provoke Johnson:

The greater number of our company were Whigs, and I was not a Tory, and we all saw the prudence of avoiding to call the then late adventurer in Scotland, or his adherents, by those names which others hesitated not to give them, or to bring to remembrance what had passed, a few years before, on Tower Hill.[102]

Though none of the pieces of evidence is, in isolation, conclusive, the number of hints and references point towards Jacobite sympathies.

How deeply Johnson held these views must be, to some extent, a matter of conjecture. Erskine-Hill writes that the question of Johnson's Jacobite sympathies was one of 'central Johnsonian concern'.[103] That is not quite the same as saying that it was of central concern to Johnson himself. It did not inhibit him from accepting a pension from a Hanoverian monarch nor tempt him, as far as we know, to any rash actions. One may go further and wonder whether politics was ever of central concern to Johnson. There were but two, comparatively brief, periods when he seems to have been politically engaged, and in each of them he was acting under strong personal influence. As soon as Richard Savage left for Wales in 1739, Johnson's political interest appears to have waned. There followed a gap of some thirty years until his political zeal was rekindled by his friendship with the Thrales and his stay at Streatham, where he met politicians of all parties. But the core of his life was scholarship, religion, and the moral order. Indeed, Johnson himself is on record as saying that 'politicks go but a little way with me in comparison of religion'.[104]

---

[102] Hawkins, 106.   [103] 'Political Character', 133.
[104] W. K. Wimsatt and F. A. Pottle (eds.), *Boswell for the Defence 1769–1774* (New Haven, Conn., 1960), 92.

These reservations and uncertainties about Johnson's attitude throw some light on the larger question of the support for and role of Jacobitism in the earlier eighteenth century. Two writers have recently drawn attention to the importance of Johnson in understanding Jacobitism. J. C. D. Clark writes that the experience of Johnson 'provides the key' to comprehending the intellectual changes of the period, and Paul Monod refers to Johnson as the 'archetype' of the tippling and sentimental Jacobite.[105] With both of these observations I am in agreement, though I am less sure to what general conclusion they point. They do not add much weight to the assertion that Jacobitism represented a serious and determined threat to Hanoverian stability.

The last two decades have witnessed a great revival of interest in Jacobitism and a wealth of scholarly investigation. The origins of this historiographical development seem to have been the juxtaposition of two important publications. In 1965 J. H. Plumb's Ford Lectures argued the case for Hanoverian stability and traced the factors which contributed to it.[106] Three years later, in the History of Parliament volume for 1715–54 Romney Sedgwick hazarded the opinion that 'the available evidence leaves no doubt that up to 1745 the Tories were a predominantly Jacobite party, engaged in attempts to restore the Stuarts by a rising with foreign assistance'.[107] This prompted the thought that, if one of the two major parties in the country was treasonable and revolutionary, Hanoverian stability must have been distinctly fragile. Advocates of stability then retorted either that the Jacobite tendencies of the Tories had been much exaggerated or that the risings themselves posed little threat to the Hanoverian regime.

Those who award Jacobitism a key place in the historiography of the period see it in a variety of lights: as a factor making for instability; as a

[105] J. C. D. Clark, *English Society 1688–1832* (Cambridge, 1985), 186–9; P. Monod, *Jacobitism and the English People*, 1688–1788 (Cambridge, 1985), 6. The new introd. to the second edn. of D. J. Greene, *The Politics of Samuel Johnson*, includes a severe and sustained attack upon Dr Clark's accuracy. His remarks on Johnson should certainly be treated with caution. Dr Clark tried to make something mysterious of Johnson's supposed 'absence' during 1745 and observed darkly that Boswell had discovered that Johnson possessed a musket, sword, and belt. He forgot to tell the reader that Boswell added that Johnson had purchased the equipment when required to serve in the London Trained Bands.

[106] *The Growth of Political Stability in England, 1675–1725* (London, 1967).

[107] *House of Commons, 1715–54*, i, p. ix. Sceptical reviews of Sedgwick's thesis were by G. Gibbs, *Welsh History Review*, vii (1974–5), 233–4, and by B. W. Hill, *History*, lvii (1972), 234–40. A recent criticism of Sedgwick's methodology is C. Jones, 'Whigs, Jacobites and Charles Spencer, Third Earl of Sunderland', *English Historical Review*, cix, no. 430 (Feb. 1994), 52–73.

cave of Adullam for the profound discontents of the populace; and as a demonstration and reminder of the continuing importance of religion in Hanoverian England. In each of these propositions there is some truth. It is hardly possible to have a rival dynasty, backed by the most powerful European state, without it posing a considerable threat; there is certainly some evidence of poachers, rioters, and smugglers professing Jacobite loyalties; and the core of Jacobite resistance was based upon Catholics, especially the Catholic Irish, and upon the non-jurors.

But each of these factors may also be substantially qualified. It is often useful for a regime to be able to draw attention to a hated foreign foe and, as Walpole demonstrated, Jacobitism could be employed as a force making for unity and stability. The support it received from Catholic France helped to discredit it, while the fact that so much of its strength came from Scotland and Ireland did little to recommend it to most Englishmen. That historians can find examples of highwaymen and footpads who declared for King James is hardly enough to convince us that they represented a vast general revulsion from Hanoverian rule. Jacobitism was a simple enough ploy, especially on the south coast of England, where a number of sailors turned the honest penny by running agents or Jacobite recruits. It has to be balanced against legions of rogues and ruffians who never bothered their heads with dynastic disputes. If disaffection had been both profound and widespread, it could have hardly asked for a better chance than 1745.[108] Lastly, one wonders if it is strictly necessary to go on reminding people of the continued importance of religion in eighteenth-century Britain. The constitutional settlement after the Glorious Revolution of 1688 was a religious and a political one, and the Hanoverians were summoned to the throne in 1714 specifically because of their Protestantism. The very basis of public life was religious. If, on the other hand, we are concerned with the importance of personal rather than public religion, the dramatic growth of Methodism may be of rather greater significance than the slow decay of non-juring.

Attempts to estimate the size of Jacobite support throughout the country have been bedevilled by methodological difficulties. Interest waxed and waned according to the international situation and in response to the popularity or otherwise of the Hanoverian monarchs. But the prime difficulty has been one of definition: what was a Jacobite? Monod reminds us that we must not make our definition so demanding that none except those in attendance at St Germain would qualify as Jacobites:

[108] See e.g. the comments by F. O'Gorman, 'The Recent Historiography of the Hanoverian Regime', *Historical Journal*, 29/4 (1986), 1005–20.

To be sure, disgruntled Stuart adherents complained at times about 'tippling' Jacobites, who would do no more than toast the Pretender's health, but this was an invidious distinction. If a willingness to die for a cause were the only true indication of resolve then few Englishmen or women in the modern age have been seriously committed to anything.[109]

With respect, this comment is not terribly helpful. The distinction betwen 'tippling' and 'fighting' Jacobites was by no means invidious: it was crucial, and hundreds of Prince Charles's men at Culloden lost their lives because of it. Modern parliamentary government is designed to obviate the need to fight over interests: one can vote for or join a party instead. But it is in the nature of a dynastic dispute that compromise is very difficult. The men who stood with Charles at Derby had every right to ask what expressions of loyalty were worth when the response to his 'now or never' appeal was so pitiful. Lord George Murray, a gallant soldier, put the point bluntly when he reminded the prince that 'if there was any party in England for him, it was very odd that they had never so much as either sent him money or intelligence, or the least advice what to do'.[110]

   If Johnson was, as Monod suggests, no more than a tippling Jacobite, he was not alone, and may indeed be taken as an archetypal or representative figure. The response to Charles's appeal from Derby was a deafening silence. The great Cambridge Jacobite Sir John Hynde Cotton, whose resignation from the government was to be the signal for revolt, decided to remain in office.[111] The great Oxford Jacobite William King did nothing while his prince was 70 miles away but, after Culloden had been safely accomplished, re-emerged in 1749 to make the Sheldonian Theatre ring with his daring eloquence.[112] Of Thomas Rowney, the member of Parliament for Oxford city, who was reputed to have drunk the Pretender's health five hundred times, it was written later that he was 'frightened out of his wits and ordered his chaplain to pray for King George'.[113] Lord Barrymore, a leading Jacobite, was in London, attending the usurper George II's Parliament; his son, at Marbury, on receiving the Pretender's appeal, flung it in the fire and arrested the messenger.[114] Sir Watkin Williams Wynn, whose task was to raise Wales and whose estate was 50 miles from Derby, had had a mere sixteen weeks to make contact

---

[109] *Jacobitism and the English People*, 4–6.
[110] Quoted in W. Speck, *The Butcher* (Oxford, 1981), 91.
[111] *House of Commons, 1715–54*, i. 584–5.   [112] Greenwood, *William King*, 176–7.
[113] Egmont MSS, quoted in *House of Commons, 1715–54*, ii. 394.
[114] Speck, *The Butcher*, 91.

with his prince: nevertheless, his message of devoted support arrived at Derby two days after the retreat had been decided upon.[115]

In a recent article, Ian Christie suggests that nearly half of the Tories returned to Parliament at the general election of 1741 were Jacobites or sympathetic to the Jacobite cause.[116] But of the 56 members identified, *not one* stirred in 1745. 'Sympathy', writes Dr Erskine-Hill, 'stops short of being commitment.'[117] Indeed it does, and perhaps the phrase should have been carved on Prince Charles Edward's tombstone.

[115] Lord Mahon, *History of England* (2nd edn., London, 1839), iii. 415.

[116] 'The Tory Party, Jacobitism and the 'Forty Five: A Note', *Historical Journal*, 30 (1987), 921–31.

[117] 'Political Character', 118. It is sometimes argued in defence of the English Jacobites that they were waiting for a French invasion. But in his specialist study of the French attitude towards the '45, F. J. McLynn concludes that 'the principal obstacle to a successful French landing in England was the poor calibre of the Jacobites themselves . . .'; Chavigny wrote to Louis XV in 1744 that 'there are always malcontents in England but what weight can one put on this . . . [the Jacobites] are good for nothing but ruining themselves and those they draw into their schemes'. *France and the Jacobite Rising of 1745* (Edinburgh, 1981), 3, 25. It looks like on anticipation of Canning's jibe at the Walcheren fiasco: 'Great Chatham with his sabre drawn, | Stood waiting for Sir Richard Strahan. | Sir Richard, longing to be 'at em, | Stood waiting for the Earl of Chatham.'

3

Johnson and Politics

'WE are both *Tories*', Boswell confided to Johnson on their famous tour of
the Western Islands. This evidence is not as useful as one might think,
since Boswell's political career was frenetic and unsuccessful and his
ideology confused and confusing.[1] Boswell's friends were hard put to it to
understand his attitudes. Captain James Francis Erskine thought him 'a
tory with whig principles', while Edmund Burke told him in 1790, perhaps with considerable irony, that he possessed 'the art of reconciling
contradictions beyond any man I know'.[2] Boswell himself claimed that he
and Johnson differed on only two issues, but since these issues were
probably the most important of the day—Wilkes and America—the
agreement is less than might appear. It is true that he and Johnson were at
one on the need for subordination—indeed, Boswell gave particular emphasis to Johnson's concern on the point—but this was an attitude which
they shared with most figures in eighteenth-century public life, few of
whom were egalitarian democrats. Boswell also claimed that they shared a
deep reverence for the monarchical principle. Again, this was scarcely
unusual among Hanoverian gentlemen. But whereas Boswell regarded the
monarchy with something approaching awe—it was, he thought, 'the
image of divine rule'—Johnson's attitude was more secular, dispassionate,
and utilitarian, and certainly did not rule out very sharp comments on
individual monarchs.[3]

We have already seen that Johnson took a keen interest in politics
during his early years in London, adopting a patriot stance: opposition to
the government of the day, suspicion of its motives, concern for the
balance of the constitution, fear of a standing army, and a conviction that
the interests of the nation were neglected, partly by a craven and supine
foreign policy, partly by undue deference to the interests of Hanover. But
Hawkins remarked that Johnson's enthusiasm for politics did not long
survive the fall of Walpole and the collapse of the 'Broad-Bottom' experi-

---

[1] F. Brady, *Boswell's Political Career* (New Haven, Conn., 1965).
[2] Boswell's *Journal*, 9 Apr. 1778, 23 Jan. 1790. Quoted in Brady, *Boswell's Political Career*,
14.   [3] *Letters*, ed. Tinker, i. 68, 81, 213; ii. 273, 319, 320.

ment.[4] Between 1747 and 1755 he was hard at work on the *Dictionary*, and between 1750 and 1752 he was producing copy for *The Rambler* at the rate of two essays a week—leaving little time for sustained political activity.

The publication of the *Dictionary* on 15 April 1755 brought Johnson considerable reputation but little ready cash. He had, in fact, already been overpaid. He therefore needed to eke out his resources by writing the occasional preface, introduction, prologue, or sermon. These may have included political works. In November 1755 a young Scottish member of Parliament, William Gerard Hamilton, delivered a maiden speech of uncommon brilliance. Great things were predicted for him, but the early promise was not fulfilled, and he finished up with the nickname 'Single-Speech Hamilton'.[5] Thomas Birch wrote subsequently to Lord Hardwicke that the speech had been the 'performance of Samuel Johnson, with whom I know he is very intimate'.[6] The suggestion is by no means absurd. Birch was well informed. Johnson's work on the parliamentary debates for the *Gentleman's Magazine* had given him much experience in editing and even writing speeches. A few years later Hamilton employed Edmund Burke as a political assistant and Burke complained bitterly of the work involved.[7] Finally, in 1765 Johnson came to some arrangement to assist Hamilton and, characteristically, composed a prayer in anticipation.[8] It is not clear how long the arrangement lasted, nor how much work was done, but Malone found in Hamilton's papers an essay on corn in Johnson's hand, which he published as one of the fruits of their understanding.[9]

In the spring of 1756 Johnson was appointed editor of the *Literary Magazine*, which was intended to carry a good deal of political and historical comment. It has been suggested that its financial backers were working in the interests of William Pitt.[10] Johnson, as editor and contributor in chief, followed a strange and idiosyncratic line, hardly calculated to win

---

[4] Hawkins, 224–5.

[5] There were, in fact, subsequent speeches and Hamilton spoke often in the Irish Parliament. But the brilliant success was not repeated. See the perceptive entry by John Brooke in *House of Commons, 1754–90*, ii. 572–4.

[6] Add Ms 35400, fo. 268, dated 3 Aug. 1765. *Yale Edition of the Works of Johnson*, i: *Diaries, Prayers and Annals*, ed. E. L. MacAdam, Jr., with D. and M. Hyde (New Haven, Conn. 1958), 98.

[7] T. W. Copeland (ed.), *Correspondence of Edmund Burke*, 10 vols. (Cambridge, 1958–78), i. 182–6.   [8] *Diaries, Prayers and Annals*, 98: 'Engaging in politicks with H—n'.

[9] *Political Writings*, 301–12: 'Considerations on Corn'.

[10] *Political Writings*, 128. Pitt was, at this time, pursuing an opposition patriot line, having been dismissed from his post as Secretary at War in Newcastle's administration in Nov. 1755.

friends. Many of his comments can be seen in a Pittite framework: support for a Militia Bill, which would 'place the sword in the hands of the people'; dislike for Newcastle's subsidy treaties as designed merely to protect Hanover, 'a territory on the continent, of which the natives of this island scarcely knew the name till the present family was called to the throne, and yet know little more than that our king visits it from time to time';[11] and a vigorous defence of the unlucky Admiral Byng, a scapegoat for the real (ministerial) culprits. But in August 1756 Johnson printed his 'Observations on the Present State of Affairs'. It contained a strong attack on the war for Canada, describing the dispute between France and Britain as no more than 'the quarrel of two robbers for the spoils of a passenger . . . Such is the contest that no honest man can heartily wish success to either party'. This was far from a Pittite line. Johnson seems to have given up the editorship and the next issue of the magazine contained a fervent tribute to Pitt and his 'glorious war'.

The accession of George III in 1760 completed the transformation of the political scene by bringing out of the cold the remaining Tories, who had already moved some distance towards reconciliation in the support they had given to Pitt and the war effort. Several leading Tories were appointed to court offices or given honours, though the political promotions were not numerous, partly because many of the Tories did not want the burden of office, and partly because forty years in the wilderness had left them painfully short of political experience.[12] The offer of a pension to Johnson himself in the summer of 1762 may be seen as part of this process of reconciliation, and could hardly fail to facilitate his shift from opposition to support of government. Though he protested violently that he remained his own man, public recognition was bound to take the edge off discontent and make him more receptive to government approaches. Within a year he was in negotiation with Charles Jenkinson, Joint Secretary to the Treasury, for a pamphlet on the peace settlement, and, though the work never appeared, it was an indication of willingness to co-operate with the new management of affairs.[13]

Johnson's pension brought down upon his head a shower of abuse, which he had asked for by trailing his coat so outrageously in the *Dictionary*, where he had defined 'pension' as 'pay given to a state hireling for

---

[11] 'Observations on the Russian and Hessian Treaties', *Literary Magazine* (1756). The commentary offers arguments both for and against the treaties. The shaft against Hanover seems a reminiscence of Johnson's satirical comments in 'London'.

[12] L. Colley, *In Defiance of Oligarchy* (Cambridge, 1982), ch. 10.

[13] N. Jucker (ed.), *The Jenkinson Papers* (London, 1949), no. 203, dated 5 Oct. 1763, is Johnson arranging to collect certain papers on the peace. Nos. 390 and 391 are letters of Oct. 1765 arranging for their return, not having been used.

treason to his country'. John Wilkes and his ally Charles Churchill had a field day. Letter no. 12 of the *North Briton* devoted much heavy sarcasm to the subject:

No man, who has read only one poem of his, *London*, but must congratulate the good sense and discerning spirit of the minister, who bestows such a part of the public treasure on this distinguished friend of the public, of his master's family, and of the constitution of this country.

Nor was the pension the only blandishment proffered by administration. In February 1767 took place the famous audience with George III in the royal library at the Queen's House, which Johnson enjoyed relating. The following year he was asked to advise on the purchasing policy for the royal library and acknowledged with fervour the king's thanks for his services.[14] This is not to suggest that Johnson wrote the later political pamphlets because he had been pensioned, but one may doubt whether he would have written them had he not been.[15]

Boswell met Johnson for the first time in May 1763, just after the close of the Seven Years War. Boswell himself had a keen interest in politics and the search for a seat in the House of Commons was one of the main objectives of his whole life. Two other factors may have helped to increase Johnson's political awareness at this time. The first was the foundation in the winter of 1763–4 of the Club. Among the founder-members were Edmund Burke, returned to Parliament in December 1765 as the member for Wendover, and Anthony Chamier, Secretary at the War Office. They were joined in the course of time by other politicians such as Gibbon, Charles Fox, Sheridan, and John Dunning. For the last twenty years of his life, Johnson was in regular touch with politicians of some consequence. The second factor was his growing involvement with the Thrales, whom he first met in 1764. The following year, Henry Thrale was returned at a by-election as member for Southwark, and when Johnson was given a room to himself at their house at Streatham, he found himself in a family where politics was staple fare.

Though George III undoubtedly intended his crusade against party to usher in a reign of national harmony and reconciliation, he was cruelly disappointed. Peace proved to be more divisive than war. The Pitt–

---

[14] *Letters*, ed. Redford, i. 305–6, 307–14.

[15] Significant is the motto from Claudianus which Johnson placed at the head of the collection of his political writings, published in 1776: 'Fallitur egregio quisquis sub principe credit servitium; nunquam libertas gratior extat quam sub Rege pio.' (He errs who thinks that submission to a noble prince is slavery: never does liberty show more fair than under a good king.) *Stil.* iii. 113.

Newcastle coalition broke up before its task was completed, Pitt resigning in 1761, Newcastle the following year. Both went into strong opposition and succeeded in rousing much public agitation. Lord Bute, the king's chosen minister, dealt his own blows at the intended 'reformation in government', first by resigning after no more than a year, and secondly by his reluctance to fade away, which undermined the position of his successor George Grenville. Pitt, ennobled as Lord Chatham, made his own inimitable contribution to political instability, first by bringing down the Rockingham administration, which had succeeded Grenville, then by abandoning his own ministry between 1766 and 1768.

The situation in which Samuel Johnson's four political pamphlets were written was therefore one of considerable turbulence. Chatham's resignation in October 1768 left his chief collaborator, the duke of Grafton, to carry on the ministry as best he could.[16] He faced two awkward problems: the growing restlessness of the thirteen American colonies, once the threat of France had been removed in 1763, and the fall-out from the decision of the voters of Middlesex in March 1768 to return John Wilkes at the top of the poll.

The success of Wilkes's political career is further testimony to the growing power of the press, which is discussed in Chapter 6. Until the accession of George III, Wilkes was a silent and relatively obscure member of Parliament for Aylesbury, known mainly to a few close friends as an entertaining companion. His ambition was some sinecure or not too demanding post which would bring in a little money, and he hoped to attain it through his connection with Pitt and Temple. Their resignation in the autumn of 1761 dashed his hopes. He therefore resolved to turn patriot journalist and chose for his newspaper the name *North Briton*, the signal for a satirical onslaught against Bute and the Scots.[17] When the terms of the peace negotiation became known, Pitt and Wilkes settled down to attack them. It was not easy to make a treaty whereby Britain acquired Canada and India seem like a national humiliation, but they did their best. It was, suggested Wilkes, like the peace of God, in that it 'passeth human understanding'. Ministers, irritated by the routine insolence of the *North Briton*, frequently contemplated intervention, but it was not until no. 45

[16] Though Grafton had been appointed first Lord of the Treasury in July 1766 when they took office, nobody, least of all Grafton, doubted that Chatham should be the effective first minister. Two years were then spent trying to coax him into acting as such.

[17] The first number came out in June 1762. Bute's paper was the *Briton*, edited by Tobias Smollett. Wilkes and Johnson already had some slight acquaintance, having crossed swords over Johnson's *Dictionary*. But Wilkes had used his influence through Smollett in 1759 to get Frank Barber, Johnson's young black servant, released from the navy.

in April 1763, with its implied censure of the king, that they took out a general warrant for the arrest of all concerned in its production as a seditious libel. Wilkes was arrested and his papers seized. Buoyed up by martyrdom, his career as a friend of liberty took off. Chief Justice Pratt released him the following month on the grounds of privilege of Parliament and subsequently declared general warrants illegal.[18] But before Parliament met, in December 1763, the government, with considerable trouble, obtained a copy of the bawdy *Essay on Woman*, which was thrown into the catalogue of Wilkes's misdeeds to blacken his character. In January 1764 the House of Commons expelled him and declared his seat vacant. The voters of Aylesbury missed their chance to write themselves into history and elected in his place Anthony Bacon, a government contractor. Wilkes fled to France, did not appear to face trial, and was declared an outlaw. His game seemed played out.

In February 1768, having acquired a formidable number of creditors in Paris, Wilkes decided to try his luck again, crossed the Channel and presented himself as a candidate for the city of London. He came bottom of the poll but, unabashed, stood again for the county of Middlesex, which returned him in triumph. He then presented himself for trial and his outlawry was quashed on a technicality. Ten days later he was tried in King's Bench on the two charges of sedition and obscene libel, fined £1,000 and sentenced to twenty-two months in prison. 'He affected ease and indifference by picking his teeth', it was reported to the king.[19]

The House of Commons had now to decide what to do about its troublesome member. Ministers and the king were determined to expel him again: it is, wrote George, 'a measure whereon almost my Crown depends'.[20] But on what grounds? His outlawry had been quashed and he had already been expelled and imprisoned for his two previous offensive publications. Wilkes helped to rescue them from the dilemma. Anxious not to lose momentum, he was more ready than they were to resume hostilities and in December 1768 printed a letter accusing Lord Weymouth, one of the secretaries of state, of masterminding a 'massacre' in St George's Fields during the summer. Summoned to the bar of the House and asked whether he admitted writing the letter, Wilkes replied that he gloried in it.[21] First, the Commons voted the letter a malignant libel; then, in February 1769, it expelled Wilkes once more. Twice the

[18] G. Rudé, *Wilkes and Liberty* (Oxford, 1962), 27, 29–30.
[19] Fortescue, ii. 30.   [20] Ibid. 75.
[21] See *Junius*, 31 n. 1. Wilkes had also petitioned Parliament for redress in order to keep the pot boiling.

voters of Middlesex returned him, and on the third occasion, on 15 April 1769, the House resolved that his opponent, Henry Lawes Luttrell, was duly elected, despite polling 296 votes to Wilkes's 1143.[22]

Meanwhile, a substantial Wilkes lobby had gathered. His remarkable flair for self-publicity had given him exceptional coverage in newspapers throughout the country. His claim, in his earliest court appearance, that he represented 'the middling and inferior class of people' was a deliberate appeal to those who felt themselves excluded from aristocratic and oligarchical politics.[23] Well-wishers on both sides of the Atlantic sent vast numbers of gifts to make his stay in King's Bench prison more comfortable, often in the form of forty-five cheeses, forty-five kippers, or forty-five bottles of wine. In February 1769, a Society of Supporters of the Bill of Rights was formed, with the intention of defending the liberties of the subjects and paying off Wilkes's debts: the first task was perhaps easier. The following month the anonymous writer Junius turned his formidable powers of invective to the defence of Wilkes: 'circumstanced as he is with regard to the public, even his vices plead for him'.[24] The parliamentary opposition succeeded in launching a powerful petitioning movement, which argued that the vote on Luttrell had dealt a blow to the constitution and insisted on a dissolution of Parliament.[25]

Johnson was literally in the midst of these events. Up and down Fleet Street and the Strand swirled the rioters, demanding that householders illuminate in honour of Wilkes on penalty of broken windows. The petition of the loyal merchants on its journey from the city to St James's on 22 March 1769 was ambushed at Temple Bar, some yards from Johnson's house, and few of the petitioners reached the Palace unscathed. At the time of the general election in the spring of 1768 Johnson was in Oxford, where he rejoiced that the University stayed loyal to the old Tory interest,[26] but he wrote Henry Thrale's election address for him and lobbied on his behalf. Thrale's vote with the majority for the expulsion of Wilkes placed him in some jeopardy. The King's Bench prison, in which Wilkes was incarcerated, and St George's Fields, where the 'massacre' had taken place, were in his constituency, and breweries were by no means unattractive targets to the mob. On 10 May 1768 a fellow distiller in

[22] The voting on the motion to return Luttrell was 197–143.

[23] Wilkes's observation, made at his first appearance before Pratt on 6 May 1763, was repeatedly reissued. The best guide to Wilkism's wider appeal is J. Brewer, *Party Ideology and Popular Politics at the Accession of George III* (Cambridge, 1976).

[24] Letter IX, 10 Apr. 1769.

[25] A detailed study of the petitioning movement may be found in Rudé, *Wilkes and Liberty*, ch. 7 and 8.   [26] *Letters*, ed. Redford, i. 299.

Southwark, Edward Russell, had his house and premises broken into by a mob who 'drank spirituous liquor out of their hats'.[27]

The parliamentary and legal proceedings were accompanied by vigorous pamphlet warfare. Opposition—consisting of an uneasy alliance of Rockinghams, Chathamites, and Grenvillites, augmented by some advanced radicals and a few unregenerate Tories—insisted that the issue raised the most profound of constitutional questions: namely, whether ultimate sovereignty resided with the electors or with their parliamentary representatives. The government, whose case in the absence of the first minister in the Lords rested largely upon Lord North, argued that the whole affair was a storm in a teacup, blown up out of all proportion by faction and self-interest; the freeholders who polled for Wilkes threw away their votes.[28] Amid the bewildering welter of argument and abuse, two questions predominated: whether Wilkes's offences were sufficiently heinous to justify expulsion, and whether expulsion, to be effective, must carry with it the incapacity to be returned.[29] The prim answer to the first question, that this must be solely a matter for the House of Commons, which alone was judge of its own privileges, was unlikely to satisfy an increasingly restless, enquiring, and informed electorate. The second was well discussed by Junius in Letter XV, which demanded either a statute confirming incapacity or an indisputable precedent: 'mere assertion will never convince'. There was, he insisted, neither statute nor precedent.[30]

Johnson entered the fray rather late. *The False Alarm* was written in one day and published on 17 January 1770. Johnson preferred it to any of his other political pamphlets, finding in it a 'subtlety of disquisition', which may not be readily apparent to all readers.[31] It was, by this time, hard to introduce new arguments and Johnson's main assumption, that expulsion implied incapacity since it would otherwise be null and void, had been heard many times. He therefore contented himself with a fairly plain statement of the government's position. But his account of rent-a-mob politics was a masterpiece of knockabout humour.

For his main argument, Johnson fell back upon 'the great and pregnant principle of political necessity':

---

[27] Deposition of William Hipgrave, quoted in Rudé, *Wilkes and Liberty*, app. I.

[28] *Parl. Hist.* xvi. 595.

[29] See e.g. *The Case of the Election for the County of Middlesex Considered* (*1769*), probably by Jeremiah Dyson: 'incapacity is the necessary effect of expulsion'.

[30] Blackstone and the court claimed that there were precedents, notably the expulsion of Robert Walpole in 1712. King's Lynn returned him again and the House declared the election void. The precedent did not quite fit. The controversy then degenerated into elaborate exegesis on whatever examples could be discovered.   [31] *Life*, ii. 147.

All government supposes subjects; all authority implies obedience ... Laws which cannot be enforced, can neither prevent nor rectify disorders ... If the Commons have only the power of dismissing for a few days the man whom his constituents can immediately send back, if they can expel but cannot exclude, they have nothing more than nominal authority ...

But it is when he moved to attack the hyperbole of patriotism that Johnson got into his stride and the pamphlet took off:

The progress of a petition is well known. An ejected placeman goes down to his county or his borough, tells his friends of his inability to serve them, and his constituents of the corruption of the government. His friends readily understand that he who can get nothing, will have nothing to give. They agree to proclaim a meeting, meat and drink are plentifully supplied, a crowd is easily brought together, and those who think that they know the reason of their meeting, undertake to tell those who know it not ... A speech is then made by the Cicero of the day, he says much, and suppresses more, and credit is equally given to what he tells and what he conceals. The petition is read and universally approved. Those who are sober enough to write add their names, and the rest would sign it if they could. Every man goes home and tells his neighbour of the glories of the day; how he was consulted and what he advised; how he was invited into the great room, where his lordship called him by his name; how he was caressed by Sir Francis, Sir Joseph or Sir George; how he eat turtle and venison, and drank unanimity to the three brothers ... Of the petition, nothing is remembered by the narrator, but that it spoke much of fears and apprehensions, and something very alarming, and that he is sure it is against the government ...

Johnson professed no surprise that the petitioners demanded a dissolution of Parliament and an immediate general election:

The year of election is a year of jollity; and what is still more delightful, a year of equality. The glutton now eats the delicacies for which he longed when he could not purchase them, and the drunkard has the pleasure of wine without the cost. The drone lives a while without work, and the shopkeeper, in the flow of money, raises his prices. The mechanic that trembled at the presence of Sir Joseph, now bids him come again for an answer; and the poacher, whose gun has been seized, now finds an opportunity to reclaim it.

The tone of banter should not deceive. The underlying note is savage irony which betrays how deep were Johnson's fears that the world might be turned upside down once more, as it had been during the Commonwealth and Protectorate.

Towards the end of the pamphlet, Johnson chided the Tories for their 'frigid neutrality' on the Wilkes issue. This does not quite represent the real position. The Tories were not neutral but divided. Proscription before 1760 had held them together; toleration, after 1760, pulled them apart. Though George III did not succeed in extirpating party, he certainly confused it. While a number of Tories had taken the opportunity to abandon opposition, others, as Johnson pointed out, found it difficult to break the habits of a lifetime: 'being long accustomed to signalise their principles by opposition to the court, do not yet consider that they have at last a king who knows not the name of party.' On general warrants, in February 1764, the Tories split 41 with opposition, 45 with government; on the repeal of the Stamp Act in February 1766, they split 34 in favour and 39 against .[32] On the crucial vote in 1769 on the seating of Henry Lawes Luttrell, those Tories of the 1761 intake who were still in Parliament split 17 for administration, 23 for opposition.[33] The true irony of the situation is well illustrated by Johnson's own University of Oxford. At the general election of 1768, Johnson had rejoiced at the choice of Francis Page: 'the virtue of Oxford has once more prevailed . . . they joined to Sir Roger Newdigate their old representative, . . . an Oxfordshire gentleman of no name, no great interest, not perhaps any other merit, than that of being on the right side.'[34] But this splendid new Tory proceeded to vote for Wilkes, while Newdigate voted on the other side.[35] Oxford Tories were no less confused than the rest.

The *Gentleman's Magazine* gave Johnson's pamphlet a long and friendly review.[36] Admitting that it cited no precedents, referred to no books, and might be read in half an hour, it found 'a strain of masculine eloquence . . . that has seldom been equalled, never exceeded in our language'. Though late in the field, it attracted considerable attention. Junius himself did not reply. He was stalking bigger game, having published the previous month his attack upon the king and assisted in bringing about the resignation of the first minister.[37] But the opposition found other champions. Johnson's authorship was known within days. *The Constitution Defended, and Pensioner Exposed: In Remarks on the 'False Alarm'* was a predictable response.[38] Attributed to Wilkes himself was *A Letter to*

[32] L. B. Namier, 'Country Gentlemen in Parliament', in *Personalities and Powers* (London, 1955), 73–4.

[33] Namier identified 113 Tories returned at the general election of 1761. Of these, 33 were dead by 1769 and another 27 were no longer in Parliament. Of the remaining 53, 10 were absent; the votes of 3 are uncertain; the rest divided 17–23 against government.

[34] *Letters*, ed. Redford, i. 299.

[35] For comment on Newdigate's changing views at this time, see P. D. G. Thomas, 'Sir Roger Newdigate's Essays on Party, *c*.1760', *English Historical Review*, 102 (1987), 394–400.

[36] *Gentleman's Magazine* (1770), 32–6.

[37] Letter to the king pub. 19 Dec. 1769; duke of Grafton resigned 27 Jan.; Junius's next letter, another attack on Grafton, dated 14 Feb. 1770.

[38] It has been attributed to John Scott, the Quaker poet from Amwell, but *DNB* remarks that Scott was and remained a good friend of Johnson.

Samuel Johnson, LL.D., which insisted on the supremacy of the electors over the House of Commons: 'do you conceive the full force of the word CONSTITUENT? It has the same relation to the House of Commons as Creator to creature.'[39] On the other side, Johnson was defended by Percival Stockdale in less than immortal verse:

> Great is thy prose; great thy poetic strain;
> Yet to dull coxcombs, are they great in vain.[40]

Despite desperate attempts by the opposition to keep excitement going with fresh grievances to complain of, the Wilkes pot went off the boil fairly quickly, partly because North's handling of it was relaxed, partly because Wilkes out of gaol in April 1770 was a less appealing figure than the patriot martyr.[41] The first hints of renewed colonial conflict also served to divert attention from the sufferings of the Middlesex electors, and late in 1770 the opposition stumbled upon an issue that was even more promising. An incident in the remote Falkland Islands between a tiny British garrison and a Spanish expeditionary force brought about a protracted threat of war. Many opposition members calculated either that war would bring a demand for the recall of the great Chatham or that the government, in a desperate search for peace, would make a spineless and ignominious settlement. Nor were these hopes fanciful. Walpole's long hold on power began to weaken when in 1739 he was forced into war against the Spaniards, and the twelve-year rule of the duke of Newcastle came to an abrupt end in 1756 when the Seven Years War opened with the capitulation of Minorca and the court martial of Admiral Byng.

Though Chatham and the opposition maintained that the Treaty of Paris in 1763 had been grossly inadequate, and Britain's chief negotiator, the duke of Bedford, was accused of betraying his country,[42] the two

---

[39] Reviewed, with favourable comments towards Johnson, in *Gentleman's Magazine* (1770), 78. Boswell tells us of the reply that Johnson considered making: 'the idea of a Creator must be such that he has a power to unmake or annihilate his creature. Then it cannot be conceived that a creature can make laws for its Creator.' *Life*, iv. 30–1.

[40] A poem entitled 'The Remonstrance'. Stockdale left memoirs with references to Johnson.

[41] Junius had already written sardonically that, if pardoned, Wilkes would soon 'Fall back into his natural station—a silent senator . . . It is only the tempest that lifts him from his place.' *Junius*, Letter XXXV, 19 Dec. 1770. When Wilkes and Junius struck up a correspondence and alliance in Aug. 1771 Junius had to eat his words rather awkwardly.

[42] Junius to the duke of Bedford, 19 Sept. 1769 (*Junius*, Letter XXIII): 'your patrons wanted an ambassador, who would submit to make concessions, without daring to insist upon any honourable condition for his sovereign. Their business required a man, who had as little feeling for his own dignity as for the welfare of his country; and they found him in the first rank of the nobility.'

Bourbon powers smarted under their humiliations. Though Spain was by far the weaker, Charles III was more forward in pursuing a policy of *revanche*, while France, where Louis XV was embroiled in protracted disputes with his *parlements*, maintained a more cautious stance. In 1770 the dispute over the Falkland Islands provided what appeared to be an ideal opportunity for a show-down. Britain had its full share of domestic difficulties, the new first minister was relatively untried, and there was growing antagonism with her American colonies.

The islands in dispute were first discovered in the sixteenth century and named by the British after Viscount Falkland, 1st Lord of the Admiralty, in the 1690s. The French claimed that sailors from St Malo had landed on the islands and called them Malouines, from which the Spaniards gave them the name Islas Malvinas. There were no settlements until after the Seven Years War. In 1765 an expedition under Commodore Byron established a small base and erected a wooden blockhouse, naming the settlement after Lord Egmont, 1st Lord of the Admiralty. The French, at the same time, made over their claims to Spain. In June 1770 a superior Spanish force arrived, immobilized the frigate *Favourite* by removing its rudder, and ordered the British garrison to leave. Receipt of the news in Britain in the autumn of 1770 was made more dramatic by the fact of the French acquisition of Corsica, greatly publicized by Johnson's new friend James Boswell. The two pieces seemed to confirm Bourbon resurgence and support Chatham's worst fears.

North handled the negotiations, his first major test, with considerable skill. He made open and vigorous preparations for war and in December 1770 carried a motion for the Land Tax at four shillings in the pound—the wartime rate. At the same time, his representations to Spain were directed at the governor of Buenos Aires, Bucareli, giving the Spanish government the chance to disavow his actions if it wished, and he offered private assurances that, provided restitution was made, the British would eventually withdraw. But the critical decision was made at Versailles, where Louis XV, beset with problems, dismissed his minister Choiseul and begged Charles III to adopt a pacific stance. When Parliament reassembled in January 1771, North was able to lay before it a compromise settlement, whereby Port Egmont was restored to British possession, but the question of sovereignty left unresolved.

Opposition, which before Christmas had accused North of over-reacting, now attacked him with equal assurance for pusillanimity. Colonel Barré, always excitable, talked wildly of blood and of the vengeance of the nation on guilty ministers; Burke denounced the settlement as 'scandalous, base and dishonourable'; and Chatham, in the Lords, thought it an 'ignominious compromise'. Despite this, North carried approval of the settlement by the comfortable majority of 271 against 157.[43]

For a few weeks, excitement was at fever pitch. Junius was greatly agitated in both his private and public capacities, and did his best to blow the coals. 'Depend upon the assurance I give you', he wrote to his printer, 'that every man in administration looks upon war as inevitable.' When the war did not come, he was beside himself. Letter XLII of 30 January 1771 was a savage attack upon the king: 'it is not probable that he would appear again before his soldiers, even in the pacific ceremony of a review . . . his guards would blush for him.' He followed it up with another letter under the pseudonym of Vindex, which contained such direct accusations of cowardice against the king that Woodfall refused to print it in full.[44]

Though the ministry's majorities were ample, North was sufficiently concerned to approach Johnson for a defence, in itself an indication that the *False Alarm* had won approval in some quarters. But delays on both sides meant that the pamphlet *Thoughts on the Late Transactions Respecting Falkland's Islands* did not come out until 16 March 1771, at the very end of the controversy. Even then it was withdrawn by North for further adjustments.[45] One may guess at his reasons. George Grenville had died in November 1770 and North hoped to inherit his followers.[46] Consequently, Johnson's jibe at Grenville's stolid virtues was deleted, leaving the uncharacteristically lame remark, 'If he was sometimes wrong, he was often right'.[47]

Johnson's pamphlet began with a detailed and satirical sketch of the history of the Falklands and an account of recent developments. He was not at pains to represent the Falklands in any very desirable light:

What have we acquired? . . . a bleak and gloomy solitude, an island thrown aside from human use, stormy in winter, and barren in summer; an island which not the southern savages have dignified with habitation; where a garrison must be kept in a state that contemplates with envy the exiles of Siberia; of which the expense will be perpetual and the use only occasional . . .

---

[43] *Parl. Hist.* xvi. 1335–46, 1358–80.   [44] *Junius*, 224, 487–9.

[45] Johnson to Bennet Langton, 20 Mar. 1771 (*Letters*, ed. Redford, i. 356).

[46] North to the king, 16 Nov. 1770: 'Lord North thinks there is an opening to acquire not only Mr. Wedderburn, but all Mr. Grenville's friends.' Fortescue, ii, no. 835. Wedderburn took office as Solicitor-General in Jan. 1771 and Lord Suffolk became Lord Privy Seal at the same time.

[47] The original passage remarked of the Manila ransom that, if Grenville could have got it, 'he could have counted it'. Johnson was not the only one to think Grenville honest but unimaginative. See *Life*, ii. 135.

The two most remarkable passages were a sharp attack upon Junius, who had taken so prominent a part in the onslaught on North's handling of the dispute, and a sombre reminder of the realities of war:

He has sometimes sported with lucky malice; but to him that knows his company, it is not hard to be sarcastic in a mask. While he walks like Jack the Giant-Killer in a coat of darkness, he may do much mischief with little strength. Novelty captives the superficial and thoughtless; vehemence delights the discontented and turbulent. He that contradicts acknowledged truth will always have an audience; he that vilifies established authority will always find abettors.

Junius, insisted Johnson, was one of the opposition who endeavour to let slip the dogs of war, 'ignorant whither they are going, and careless what may be their prey':

It is wonderful with what coolness and indifference the greater part of mankind see war commenced. Those that hear of it at a distance, or read of it in books, consider it as little more than a splendid game . . . The life of a modern soldier is ill represented by heroick fiction. War has means of destruction more formidable than the cannon and the sword. Of the thousands and ten thousands that perished in our late contests with France and Spain, a very small part ever felt the stroke of an enemy; the rest languished in tents and ships, admist damps and putrefaction; pale, torpid, spiritless and helpless; gasping and groaning, unpitied among men made obdurate by long continuance of hopeless misery; and were at last whelmed in pits, or heaved into the ocean, without notice, and without remembrance.

He concluded with an attack on the motives of the patriot opposition: 'they wish for war, but not for conquest; victory would defeat their purposes equally with peace . . . their hope is malevolence and their good is evil.'

Horace Walpole, who had no reason to be fond of Johnson because of his early attacks upon Sir Robert, though conceding that he had 'a lumber of learning and strong parts', wrote disdainfully of the pamphlet.[48] Johnson himself was dismissed as an 'odious and mean character':

His manners were sordid, supercilious and brutal; his style ridiculously bombastic and vicious; and, in one work, with all the pedantry, he had all the gigantic littleness of a country schoolmaster.

Johnson's charge of factiousness and self-interest against the opposition

---

[48] *Memoirs of George III*, ed. Barker, iv. 196–7. Horace Walpole had dismissed the incident at an early stage of the dispute as one of trifling significance. To Mann he wrote nonchalantly on 4 Oct. 1770: 'England, that lives in the north of Europe, and Spain that dwells in the south, are vehemently angry with one another about a morsel of rock, that lies somewhere at the very bottom of America . . .' (*Correspondence of Walpole*, xxiii. 239–40).

was much resented by some. Two years after Johnson's death, Burke, a fellow member of the Club, was 'intemperately abusive' about Johnson himself:

He ascribed to opposition an endeavour to involve the nation in a war on account of Falkland's Islands, which he knew to be a false charge. He imputed to them the wickedness of his own opposition to Walpole.[49]

It is never easy to bring home a charge of faction. Some of the opposition were political opportunists and there was certainly much dabbling in the funds. But one agitated spectator was sufficiently obliging to make a record of his own motives, which do not sound very lofty. Philip Francis, then a clerk in the War office, wrote later in a private memoir:

Still however we thought a Spanish war inevitable and that Chatham must be employed. Lord Weymouth on that occasion resigned the Secretary of State's office, and I lost five hundred pounds in the stocks. By that loss however I gained knowledge enough of transacting business in the Alley, to deter me into entering into such traffic again. The convention with Spain sunk me and my hopes to a lower state than ever.[50]

If Francis was also Junius,[51] then Johnson had scored a direct hit.

This feverish political activity kindled Johnson's interest in the possibility of obtaining a seat in the House of Commons for himself. Whether he was wise to entertain such projects may be doubted. He would have been starting a new career when above 60. Nor would an eighteenth-century House of Commons have accorded him the respectful attention to which he was accustomed. His fellow club member Gibbon, who entered the House at the general election of 1774, never spoke, and confessed that 'the great speakers fill me with despair, the bad ones with terror'.[52] Edmund Burke, another club member, was more admired by posterity than by contemporaries and complained bitterly and repeatedly of the ribaldry with which he was greeted. But, on 30 March 1771, a fortnight after the *Thoughts* had appeared, the printer William Strahan wrote to one of the Secretaries at the Treasury to sound out the government's response. Johnson, he suggested, possessed 'a great share of manly, nervous and ready eloquence' which could not fail to impress the House, and his reverence for the king would ensure that he would be a reliable

---

[49] G. Scott and F. A. Pottle (eds.), *Private Papers of James Boswell from Malahide Castle* (New York, 1930–4), xv. 234.

[50] J. Parkes and H. Merivale (eds.), *Memoirs of Sir Philip Francis* (London, 1867). The Alley was the Stock Exchange.　　　　[51] The evidence is reviewed in *Junius*, app. 8.

[52] *House of Commons, 1754–90*, ii. 494.

government supporter. North pondered the proposition and took no action, remarking characteristically that Johnson, 'like the elephant in the battle, was quite as likely to trample down his friends as his foes'.[53]

Wilkes's campaign lost impetus after his release from gaol in April 1770. The Rockinghams soon tired of their troublesome radical allies.[54] A very public split in the ranks of the Society of the Supporters of the Bill of Rights in April 1771 was followed by a secession and by an acrimonious newspaper dispute between Wilkes and John Horne Tooke, in which the latter, if he did not get the better of the exchanges, delivered some doughty blows.[55] Wilkes consolidated his personal position in London by election as Alderman (1770), Sheriff (1771), and Lord Mayor (1774). Four radical supporters—Glynn, Bernard, Oliver, and Bull—won parliamentary seats in the metropolitan area at by-elections in the course of the 1768 Parliament and were certain to make a big push to extend their influence at the next general election.[56] Few government supporters were keen to stand and fight. Henry Lawes Luttrell, feeling no doubt that he had done his bit, arranged to retire to the more peaceful borough of Bossiney in Cornwall, which boasted fewer than thirty voters and which he had given up in 1769 in order to contest Middlesex. Lord Percy could perhaps rely upon the duke of Northumberland's extensive property to see him safe for Westminster, with some help from government employees and the Guards. Though Percy was by no means a reliable government supporter, it was probably the best North could hope for. But Henry Thrale, who had voted solidly against Wilkes, was in an extremely exposed position in Southwark, and the financial crisis in 1772, which had brought his brewing business close to bankruptcy, had not enhanced his prospects of re-election.

As far as Middlesex was concerned, the government would have been wise to let in Wilkes unopposed. They had enough trouble with America to keep them busy. Though North's own instincts may well have been that way, the king and the more zealous supporters of the ministry would not hear of so craven a course. The result was that North's efforts to find some

---

[53] Boswell printed Strahan's letter in *Life*, ii. 136. North's remark, which sounds authentic, was passed down by Lord Stowell to Croker, Boswell's later editor, who printed it. The proposal to find Johnson a seat seems to have been revived in the spring of 1775, judging from his ill-informed letter in *Letters*, ed. Redford, ii. 184.

[54] Burke to Richard Shackleton, *c.* 15 Aug. 1770. See *Correspondence of Burke*, ii. 150–1, 174–6.

[55] Burke to Rockingham, 29 Dec. 1770. The exchange was in the *Public Advertiser*.

[56] John Glynn, Wilkes's lawyer, came in for Middlesex in Dec. 1768; Sir Robert Bernard for Westminster in Apr. 1770; Richard Oliver for London in July 1770; and Frederick Bull for London in Dec. 1773.

country gentleman, even remotely sympathetic towards government, to stand against Wilkes degenerated into farce.[57] He was more successful at Westminster, where heavy pleading persuaded the duke of Newcastle to put up Lord Thomas Pelham-Clinton with Percy, and they carried the day against two young aristocratic radicals. But the city of London gave all four seats to radical candidates in 1774, Thomas Harley, the government's chief supporter, abandoning the struggle and standing for Herefordshire instead.[58]

To catch opposition unawares, North had dissolved Parliament well before its seven years were up. Johnson and the Thrales received news of the dissolution while staying with Burke at Beaconsfield on the way back from their tour of North Wales, and hastened to the borough at once to make up lost ground. Though Thrale was a native of Southwark and a major employer, whose father had once held the seat, it was a demanding and unpredictable constituency. The scot and lot electorate numbered about two thousand and an uncontested election, such as Thrale had obtained in 1765, was a considerable rarity. One experienced Southwark voter confided to Mrs Thrale that 'if Jesus Christ and St Paul were to stand candidate next election, our folks would raise an opposition in favour of Barrabas'.[59] Henry Thrale was confronted by two radical candidates: Nathaniel Polhill, a local tobacco merchant, and William Lee, a half-American.[60] Mrs Thrale reported that her husband found his constituents 'run mad with republican frenzy', adding 'the Patriots have the Mob, of course'.[61] Government found Thrale a running mate in Sir Abraham Hume, whose uncle had once represented the constituency, but, as soon as it became known that he had prudently taken out a hedge at Petersfield, his candidature went into headlong decline.[62]

Johnson threw himself into the campaign with gusto, helping to draft Thrale's advertisements and addresses, and haunting the committee rooms.[63] The outcome was a very creditable defensive victory for Thrale,

---

[57] *House of Commons, 1754–90*, i. 334.

[58] The voting was: John Sawbridge, 3,456; George Hayley, 3,390; Richard Oliver, 3,354; Frederick Bull, 3,096; William Baker, 2,802; Brass Crosby, 1,913; John Roberts, 1,398. Hayley was Wilkes's brother-in-law. For the general showing of radicals in 1774, see I. R. Christie, 'The Wilkites and the General Election of 1774', repr. in *Myth and Reality in Late-eighteenth-century Politics* (London, 1970). [59] *Thraliana*, i. 115.

[60] For Polhill, see *House of Commons, 1754–90*, iii. 306. William Lee was a brother of Arthur Lee, whom Johnson met at Dilly's in 1776 at the dinner party with Wilkes. Born in Virginia, he became sheriff of London in 1773 and an alderman in 1775.

[61] *Thraliana*, i. 316; *Letters*, ed. Chapman, i. 413.   [62] Fortescue, iii. 144.

[63] *Thraliana*, i. 201. Johnson's assistance is traced in some detail in J. D. Fleeman, 'Dr. Johnson and Henry Thrale, MP', in Powell (ed.), *Johnson, Boswell and their Circle*, 170–89.

who took the second seat comfortably.[64] We have triumphed, wrote
Johnson, over 'a very violent and formidable opposition'.[65]

In the course of the campaign, Johnson was persuaded to go into print
once more. The character of the opposition at Southwark and the presence of a half-American candidate can hardly fail to explain the choice of
title, *The Patriot*. A combative and vigorous piece, it was written in
Johnson's usual haste, though it does not seem to have appeared in time to
have influenced the Southwark result.[66]

Johnson took as his epigraph a quotation from John Milton, whose
poetry he admired more than his politics: 'License they mean, when they
cry Liberty.'[67] His main theme runs close to the great speech which Sir
Robert Walpole had delivered in February 1741, when he had assured the
House:

The very idea of true patriotism is lost, and the term has been prostituted to the
very worst of purposes. A patriot, Sir! Why patriots spring up like mushrooms! I
could raise fifty of them within the four-and-twenty hours. I have raised many of
them in one night. It is but refusing to gratify an unreasonable or an insolent
demand, and up starts a patriot.[68]

Johnson offered a more elaborate paraphrase:

He that has been refused a reasonable or unreasonable request, who thinks his
merit underrated, and sees his influence declining, begins soon to talk of natural
equality, the absurdity of 'many made for one', the original compact, the foundation of authority, and the majesty of the people. As his political melancholy
increases, he tells, and perhaps dreams of the advances of the prerogative, and the
dangers of arbitrary power; yet his design in all his declamation is not to benefit his
country, but to gratify his malice.[69]

Johnson could not resist an attack upon the rabble. A man may be judged,
he wrote, by the company he keeps:

---

[64] Polhill, 1,195; Thrale, 1,026; Lee, 741; Hume, 457.

[65] Johnson to John Taylor, 20 Oct. 1774 (*Letters*, ed. Redford, ii. 151).

[66] The Southwark poll ended on 13 Oct. and was reported the following day in the *Public
Advertiser*. House of Commons, *1754–90*, i. 387, is in error in giving the date of return as 18
Oct. Johnson commented on the origins of the pamphlet in his letter to Boswell of 26 Nov.
1774 (*Letters*, ed. Redford, i. 155). *The Patriot* appeared on 12 Oct.

[67] From Milton's sonnet 'On the Detraction which Followed upon My Writing Certain
Treatises'.

[68] Walpole was replying to the debate on Sandys's motion asking the king to dismiss him.
This extract is not included in the account by the *London Magazine* nor in that prepared by
Johnson for the *Gentleman's Magazine*. It was first published in 1798 by William Coxe in his
Memoirs of Sir Robert Walpole and was said to be taken from notes in the Houghton MSS.

[69] The quotation is from Pope's *Essay on Man*, iii. 242.

If his first or principal application be to the indigent, who are always inflammable; to the weak, who are naturally suspicious; to the ignorant, who are easily misled; and to the profligate who have no hope, but from mischief and confusion; let his love of the people be no longer boasted.

But though contempt and abuse were plentiful, Johnson packed into the short pamphlet a surprising number of arguments. A true Patriot, who loved his country, would not endeavour to undermine a constitution that had served it so well for so long; would not plunge it into war lightly or capriciously; would not encourage its American colonists in thoughts of resistance. The great Wilkes grievance was at an end, since any constituency was free to return him if it chose. As for the Parliament which had just been dissolved and which had been attacked so fiercely as servile and slavish, it had proffered two concessions to public liberty which ought not to be overlooked: the curtailment by members of their privilege of immunity from certain legal actions,[70] and their confirmation, in the face of government resistance, of Grenville's Election Act, a genuine attempt to ensure that disputed parliamentary elections would be decided fairly and no longer on a purely party basis.[71]

Grenville's Election Act, pushed through by the former first minister in the last months of his life, was a measure of some importance, and the campaign in 1774 to make it perpetual was of considerable political significance. Before 1770, disputed election petitions were heard by the whole House, and were almost invariably decided by the government majority with scant regard to the merits of the case. A wealthy candidate could spin out the proceedings in the hope that the petitioners would lose heart, and it was alleged by many members that the issue was commonly decided by cheerful diners who poured into the House for the division, having heard little or nothing of the evidence. Governor Johnstone, in the debate of 1774, asserted that the procedure was worth at least thirty seats to the government at every general election. A more equitable method commended itself to opponents of party, those suspicious of government influence, and members hoping to curtail election expense. By Grenville's reform, the matter was left to a select committee of fifteen, chosen by a complicated process which allowed each side in turn to strike off opposing

---

[70] 10 George III c. 50. For a remarkable example of a member of Parliament who relied upon privilege to preserve him from his creditors, see Edward Wortley Montagu in *House of Commons, 1754–90*, iii. 661–2.

[71] The original statute was 10 George III c. 16, made perpetual by 14 George III c. 15. The first statute had to be amended by 11 George III c. 42 to allow for cases where there was more than one petitioner against the return.

zealots, in the hope that the remaining members would be as free from bias as humanly possible.[72] It was carried against Lord North in 1770 by 185 votes to 123.[73] Sir William Bagot, a Tory from Johnson's own Staffordshire, explained that the Tories were not, as it might seem, abandoning their support of administration, but were anxious to see the strength of the landed interest restored. Edmund Burke, a strong party man and Whig who liked his demonology simple and found it hard to comprehend reforming Tories, complained that, nowadays, 'a Tory was the best species of Whig'.[74]

The motion to render the Act perpetual (it had originally been for a trial period of seven years) led to an ever sharper rebuff for Lord North in February 1774. His habitual supporters deserted in droves, led astray, according to the king, by 'a false love of popularity'.[75] North went down to defeat by 250 votes to 122. Governor Johnstone, in the course of the debate, remarked upon the 'strange coalition of parties' supporting the measure, radicals like Oliver and Sawbridge rubbing shoulders with Tories like Sir Roger Newdigate and William Drake. But the coalition was not all that strange. Each group mistrusted the executive and the Tories had long advocated various reforms of Parliament. In one sense, the coalition represented the past and the future combined against the present, since the Tories harked back to a golden age in the seventeenth century when the gentlemen had represented their local boroughs, while the radicals had their gaze fixed upon liberalism and democracy.[76]

Though the Grenville Act was scarcely as important as Chatham maintained, it was of consequence.[77] First, it set in train a cautious and

---

[72] The process was known colloquially as 'knocking the brains out of the committee'.

[73] Fortescue, iii, no. 1395, gives the speakers in this debate, but mistakenly dated it 1774.

[74] *Parl. Hist.* xvi. 902–23. Bagot referred to his parliamentary friends as 'country gentlemen of the same connection as himself'. Burke then attacked them as Tories and delivered an exposition of his own Whig creed. Bagot counter-attacked calling Burke a secret Jesuit.

[75] Fortescue, iii, no. 1405. No. 1403 is a memo for the king reporting that 32 placemen deserted to opposition and no fewer than 84 supporters who were generally friends. Henry Thrale was among the government supporters who deserted on this occasion. The transcription is carelessly done and should be used with caution.

[76] On p.77 we analysed 53 Tories who were still in Parliament in 1769. Of these, 9 had died by 1774, 2 had resigned, and 17 did not vote. Two more of Namier's Tories of 1761 had made their way back into Parliament: Herbert Mackworth Pride and Richard Holt. Of these 27, 22 voted for perpetuation and 5 with administration. Ten of the 22 were regarded by the king as members who were normally friends.

[77] In his usual extravagant way, Chatham described the bill as 'the last prop of Parliament; should it be lost in its passage, the legislature will fall into incurable contempt and detestation of the nation.' It would, he added, 'endear for ever the memory of the framer'. W. S. Taylor and J. H. Pringle (eds.), *Correspondence of William Pitt, Earl of Chatham*, 4 vols. (London, 1838–40), iv. 331–2.

pragmatic reform of Parliament. The first case to be heard under the new arrangements was that of the delinquent borough of New Shoreham in Sussex, where the bribery had been so outrageous that an act was passed to reform the borough by extending its representation to the neighbouring hundred.[78] Although subsequent attempts to reform some other corrupt boroughs, such as Hindon, Shaftesbury, Helston, Barnstaple, and Penryn failed, Cricklade was reformed in 1782, Aylesbury in 1804, Grampound in 1821, and East Retford in 1830. For decades this seemed the most practical method of introducing change into the electoral system, and, though in the end it turned out to be something of a blind alley, the idea that the ancient constitution was sacrosanct and to be preserved in every detail had been dealt a blow.

The Grenville Act also marked a shift in the spirit of the age. Parliament was becoming more sensitive to public opinion. Two other important concessions came as a direct result of the Wilkes affair. At the trial in June 1770 of Henry Sampson Woodfall, publisher of the *Public Advertiser* charged with seditious libel for printing Junius's letter to the king, the jury insisted upon its right to declare whether the matter complained of was libel, and refused to confine itself to the mere fact of publication. Few things could be more important in establishing the proper limits of political comment than taking the matter out of the hands of the judges and giving it to jurors. This extension to the scope of public opinion was confirmed by Fox's Libel Act in 1792. Secondly, as a result of a clash between the House of Commons and the city of London, carefully orchestrated by Wilkes, Parliament was forced to abandon its efforts to prevent the publication of its debates. Thus, a cause to which Johnson had contributed as a young man in the 1730s triumphed some forty years later.

There were other indications that the mood of the country was becoming more receptive to innovation and that a different, more positive concept of government was emerging. Though Jeremy Bentham's *Fragment on Government*, published in 1775, did not at first attract much attention, it registered, rather than anticipated, a more utilitarian attitude, reinforced by humanitarian impulses derived from evangelicalism. In 1773 government took on new responsibilities in relation to India, which could no longer be left to an unregulated private company.[79] Lord North, whose

---

[78] 11 George III c. 55 was clearly part of a well-organized opposition campaign to take advantage of the success of the Grenville Act to outmanœuvre the government.

[79] The main feature of North's Regulating Act, 13 George III c. 63, was the appointment by the Crown of a Governor-General, with supervisory powers over the other presidencies. It did not work very well and led, in due course, to the impeachment of the first Governor-General, Warren Hastings.

forte was finance, was responsible for an important Treasury minute of 22 February 1776 that, henceforth, promotions in the department would be based on merit, and he followed this up in 1780 with the establishment of a Commission on the Public Accounts, to provide Parliament with systematic and impartial scrutiny. The 1770s saw the beginning of the movement for economical reform and the abolition of sinecures which, pursued piecemeal by a number of ministers over fifty years, ultimately produced a significant shift in the balance between legislature and executive. Unlike his predecessor at the Treasury Sir Robert Walpole, North did not make a fortune from his long tenure of that office. The old lax attitude towards the balances held by the Paymaster-General, which had made great fortunes for Chandos and Lord Holland, came under sterner inquiry, as Richard Rigby discovered when taken to task in 1782.[80] There were concessions to Protestant and Catholic dissenters, even if the bastion of the Test Act remained untouched.[81] In social matters, the stirring of the public conscience was marked. Granville Sharp's campaign against slavery produced in 1772 Mansfield's famous judgment in the case of James Somerset, which, in effect, ended slavery in Britain.[82] There were moves for inquiries into the operation of the press-gang and into the conditions in private madhouses. In 1775 Thomas Gilbert carried a motion for a committee on the poor laws, telling the Commons that, as a result of population change, the parish system had virtually broken down, and his efforts culminated in the very important Act of 1782.[83] John Howard began the process of drawing to the attention of the public the state of the prisons.[84] In November 1770 Sir William Meredith moved for

[80] Rigby had been Paymaster-General from 1768 to 1782, all through the American War. He was an early victim of the new Commission of Public Accounts, which reported to the Commons in June 1782 that the balances held had been excessive. In the debate of 25 June Rigby had a rough ride, and the House agreed that in future the Paymaster should receive a fixed salary, while the interest on the balances accrued to the public. This was effected by Burke's Acts, 22 George III c. 81, amended by 23 George III c. 50. *Parl. Hist.* xxiii. 115–35.

[81] Catholics were relieved of some of their disabilities by Sir George Savile's Act of 1778, which led to the Gordon riots. In 1779 dissenting ministers were released from their obligation to subscribe to the 39 Articles. See Ch. 1.

[82] Lord Mansfield's judgment was more limited than is sometimes suggested, establishing that a master could not take his slave out of Britain. See J. Walvin, *England, Slaves and Freedom, 1776–1838* (London, 1986), 40–5, 103. The Society for the Abolition of the Slave Trade was set up in 1787. Walvin comments that 'the work of Granville Sharp had the incalculably important effect of transforming issues, which had hitherto been overwhelmingly abstract or theoretical, into substantive political, legal and public matters'.

[83] Described by Webbs, *English Poor Law History* (London, 1963), i. 171, as 'the most carefully devised, the most elaborate and perhaps the most influential . . . of poor law statutes between 1601 and 1834'.

[84] Howard gave evidence to the House of Commons on 4 Mar. 1774 and was thanked for

a committee to investigate the proliferation of capital offences, and, though a bill to incorporate the committee's recommendations to reduce the number foundered in the Lords in 1772, Meredith returned to the attack with a remarkable and passionate speech in May 1777. He pointed to the hanging at Tyburn of Mary Jones, aged 19, whose husband had been taken off by the press-gang and who, to feed her children, had attempted to steal linen from a shop. 'The true hangman', declared Meredith, 'is the member of Parliament . . . he who frames the bloody law'.[85]

Johnson was by no means out of sympathy with this changing mood. To Boswell he wrote in 1776 of the need to keep the laws in repair as society developed.[86] For the religious concessions, it is true, he had little enthusiasm. But many of the other reforms had his strong approval. In particular, he had been a staunch advocate of reform of the criminal law years before it had become a fashionable cause, and it may not be a coincidence that the chairman of the Commons committee of 1770, Sir Charles Bunbury, was a member of the Club, a friend of Johnson, and a pallbearer at his funeral.

In the 1740s there had been much public concern at the lawlessness and debauchery of teeming London. In January 1751 Henry Fielding the novelist, recently appointed to the bench, published an important tract entitled *An Inquiry into the Causes of the Late Increase in Robbers*. His analysis was orthodox and conventional. The laws of England were celebrated for their mildness; a love of luxury had corrupted the poor; and the remedy was stronger policing. In particular, the frequent granting of pardons was an imprudent and self-defeating leniency. That Fielding's was the received wisdom is demonstrated by the fact that the Commons committee, set up on 1 February 1751 to find means of suppressing violent crime, was much influenced by his proposals.[87] Three months later

his humanity and zeal. *CJ*, xxxiv. 535. Two Acts were then passed. 14 George III c. 20 abolished gaoler's fees, non-payment of which kept many acquitted persons in prison, and 14 George III c. 59 sought to improve living conditions in gaols, by charging JPs with responsibility for improving ventilation and sanitation, and appointing a surgeon to carry out regular inspections. Howard's *The State of the Prisons* was pub. in 1777.

[85] *Parl. Hist.* xvi. 1124–7; xvii. 449–53; xix. 235–41; *CJ*, xxxiii. 27, 365, 682, 691, 695, 777. Though the bill dealt with only a few offences, it was the first attempt to reverse the process of adding to capital crimes. See L. Radzinowicz, *A History of the English Criminal Law and Its Administration from 1750* (London, 1948), i. 427–46, 473–6. Meredith published his speech as a short pamphlet. [86] 3 Feb. 1776 (*Letters*, ed. Redford, ii. 286–9).

[87] See Radzinowicz, *A History of the English Criminal Law*, i. 399–424, and M. C. Battestin, *Henry Fielding, a Life* (London, 1989), 519–20. The Commons committee resulted in legislation. 25 George II c. 37 was an Act 'for better preventing the horrid crime of murder'. Its introduction explained the need for 'some further Terror and peculiar marks of infamy'. Its provisions included speedier executions and dissection of the corpse, since these were aspects which the criminal classes were believed to regard with particular horror.

Johnson took up the issue in no. 114 of *The Rambler*. His diagnosis was the very opposite of Fielding's. Johnson deplored the 'periodical havock of our fellow-beings' in the 'legal massacre' of the trip to Tyburn, and he placed the blame on 'vindictive and coercive justice'. He complained particularly of the disproportion between many crimes and punishments and of the relentless multiplication of capital offences. Savage punishments, argued Johnson, have long been tried without success: was it not time to consider a relaxation of the laws? The death penalty should be, not a habitual remedy, but the very last resort: 'to equal robbery with murder is to reduce murder to robbery'. If only murder were punishable by death, very few robbers would stain their hands with blood:

The frequency of capital punishments therefore rarely hinders the commission of a crime, but naturally and commonly prevents its detection, and is, if we proceed only upon prudential principles, chiefly for that reason to be avoided. Whatever may be urged by casuists or politicians, the greater part of mankind, as they can never think that to pick the pocket and to pierce the heart is equally criminal, will scarcely believe that two malefactors so different in guilt can be justly doomed to the same punishment.[88]

At the end of the decade, in *The Idler*, Johnson had turned his attention to the plight of thousands of debtors in gaol:[89] 'We have now imprisoned one generation of debtors after another, but we do not find that their numbers lessen.' Though Johnson's arguments were, in the main, utilitarian—the waste to the community of keeping thousands of able-bodied citizens in hopeless captivity—there is little doubting the intensity of his moral feeling:

Surely, he whose debtor has perished in prison, though he may acquit himself of deliberate murder, must at least have his mind clouded with discontent, when he considers how much another has suffered from him; when he thinks of the wife bewailing her husband, or the children begging the bread which their father would have earned. If there are any made so obdurate by avarice or cruelty, as to revolve these consequences without dread or pity, I must leave them to be awakened by some other power, for I write only to human beings.

In the spring of 1777 Johnson was given the opportunity to reaffirm his principles when he was approached by the Countess of Harrington on behalf of Dr William Dodd, who faced the capital charge of forging a bond

[88] M. R. Zirker, *Fielding's Social Pamphlets* (Berkeley, 1966), 137, comments on the contrast with 'the rich humanity of Johnson's attitude to the poor ... in nearly every instance, one finds Johnson more liberal, humane or understanding'. It is worth pointing out that Johnson was writing 13 years before the publication of Cesare Beccaria's celebrated treatise *Dei delitti e delle pene*. See also *Sermons*, no. 26.

[89] Nos. 22 and 38 (16 Sept. 1758 and 6 Jan. 1759).

in the name of his former pupil, the earl of Chesterfield. Johnson was not in good health, knew Dodd only slightly, and did not care for him, mistrusting his sincerity and finding his preaching florid and shallow. Nevertheless, he flung himself with great vigour into a campaign to save him. The remarkable wave of public sympathy towards Dodd which developed after he had been sentenced to hang owed a good deal to Johnson's efforts. He wrote appeals for clemency, drafted a petition for the city of London and a sermon delivered by Dodd to his fellow prisoners in Newgate.[90] To Charles Jenkinson, with whom Johnson had some acquaintance, he wrote:

The supreme power has, in all ages, paid some attention to the voice of the people; and that voice does not least deserve to be heard, when it calls out for mercy. There is now a very general desire that Dodd's life should be spared. More is not wished; and, perhaps, this is not too much to be granted.[91]

When it became apparent that all attempts had failed, Johnson wrote to Dodd with compassion and understanding:

Be comforted; your crime, morally or religiously considered, has no very deep dye of turpitude. It corrupted no man's principles; it attacked no man's life. It involved only a temporary and reparable injury . . . Let me beg that you make in your devotions one petition for my eternal welfare.

The 14th Parliament of Great Britain, elected in October 1774, was soon plunged into crisis. The lull in American affairs which followed North's abandonment of most of the Townshend duties did not last. In June 1772 Rhode Island patriots seized and burned the revenue cutter *Gaspée*. In December 1773 North's concessions to the East India Company were met by the Boston Tea Party, which was repeated in New York harbour in April 1774. While the British general election was taking place, a congress was in session in Philadelphia to co-ordinate colonial resistance. The king's speech to the new Parliament drew attention to 'violence of a very criminal nature . . . and unlawful combinations'. His private opinion expressed to North was that 'blows must decide whether they are to be subject to this country or independent'.[92]

The case for Congress was contained in a declaration issued on 14 October 1774. It denied that the British Parliament had any right to legislate for America. Since the colonists could not 'from their local and

---

[90] Boswell gives a full list of Johnson's 'extraordinary exertions' on behalf of Dodd. *Life*, iii. 139–48.

[91] *Letters*, ed. Redford, iii. 29, 32–3.   [92] 18 Nov. 1774 (Fortescue, iii, no. 1556).

other circumstances' be properly represented at Westminster, it followed that they could be taxed only by their own provincial legislatures. They did, however, out of regard for the mutual interests of the two countries, 'cheerfully consent' to bona fide trade regulation. Perhaps more ominous than the legal arguments was the ease with which the colonists had slipped into referring to the two countries.[93]

Despite his very satisfactory general election victory, North's position in the spring of 1775 was delicate. In response to the views of the king and his own right wing, North had to appear firm and prepare for war, but in Parliament a vociferous opposition insisted that the ministry had brought disaster upon itself by its own ineptitude and tyranny. In the struggle for public opinion, a reply to Congress's declaration was needed and, through William Strahan and Grey Cooper, the government approached Johnson to prepare one. The result was the best-known of his pamphlets, *Taxation No Tyranny*, which made its appearance on 8 March 1775.[94]

There were two ironies involved in the government's approach to Johnson for help. His previous writings on the subject of colonies suggested that he was doubtful of their value, and the threatened departure of the Americans might not seem to him an unmixed catastrophe.[95] Secondly, he produced a powerful statement of the ministers' case on taxation at just the moment when they were about to abandon it. Consequently, the negotiations with Strahan and Cooper were not without difficulties. 'I am going to write about the Americans', Johnson confided to Boswell on 21 January 1775. When they were shown the draft during February, ministers asked for some passages to be toned down. 'I am sorry to see', wrote Johnson to Strahan on 1 March 1775, 'that all the alterations proposed are evidence of timidity . . . I do not wish to publish what those for whom I write do not like to have published.'[96] But Johnson was not unaware of the difficulties of North's position. He was at Oxford when news of North's unexpected conciliation proposals was received.[97] To Strahan he wrote:

[93] Congress also made arrangements for economic sanctions until the Coercive Acts against New England were withdrawn, and prepared to meet again in 1775 if redress was not forthcoming.

[94] For a more detailed account of Johnson's dealings with the government, see Greene (ed.), *Political Writings*, 401–9.

[95] e.g. 'Every inhabitant gained to the colonies is lost to the mother country' ('On a Letter from a French Refugee', *Literary Magazine*, 15 May 1756); 'it will very little advance the power of the English to plant colonies on the Ohio by dispeopling their native country' (Review of Lewis Evans's Map, *Literary Magazine*, 15 Sept. 1756).

[96] *Letters*, ed. Redford, ii. 170–1, 184–5.

[97] On 20 Feb. 1775 North surprised both friends and opponents by proposing that, if the

They are here much discouraged by the last motion and undoubtedly every man's confidence in government must be diminished, yet if lives can be saved, some deviation from rigid policy may be excused.[98]

Johnson did not intend to confine himself to the American critics of government policy. Most prominent among domestic opponents were Chatham, the setting sun, and Edmund Burke, the rising sun. Chatham was not a man for niceties. 'I will carry it to my grave', he told the Lords on 27 May 1774, 'that this country has no right under heaven to tax America.' Burke's view was different: the argument about right was sterile and unproductive. In his great speech on conciliation on 22 March 1775, a few days after Johnson's pamphlet appeared, Burke explained: 'I am resolved this day to have nothing at all to do with the question of the right of taxation—it is less than nothing in my consideration.' But, though the attitude of both men was majestic and magnanimous, the rest of their remarks revealed the extent to which they were living in the past, and a past, perhaps, that had never truly existed. Chatham's advice was to treat the Americans as children who had erred: 'proceed like a kind and affectionate parent over a child whom he tenderly loves.' Burke was, if anything, even vaguer and more fatuous: the British Parliament should 'restore the former unsuspecting confidence of the colonies in the mother country'. Events had long moved past the point when such well-meaning platitudes could be of assistance. For good measure, Chatham wrapped his discourses in party rhetoric which could hardly fail to provoke Johnson. At precisely the moment that Johnson was thinking about starting work, Chatham declared: 'The cause of America is allied to every true Whig. They will not bear the enslaving America . . . many millions of Whigs, averse to the system, would come together to resist coercion.'[99]

Johnson did not accept the distinction between internal and external taxes, or between taxation and legislation, which had been advanced by a number of politicians and pamphleteers. 'Those who are subject to laws', he wrote, 'are liable to taxes.' He based his argument squarely upon the nature of sovereignty. In every state, of whatever kind, there must exist a supreme authority, to allocate subordinate powers, to adjudicate, enforce and, if necessary, revoke. By definition it must be absolute, since if it is not

colonists would propose some means of sharing the costs of defence, Parliament would suspend its right of taxation. It was an abrupt change of direction, if not a volte-face, and many of his supporters complained that he was truckling to rebels. The resolution was approved on 27 Feb.

[98] *Letters*, ed. Redford, ii. 185–6.

[99] For Chatham, see *Parl. Hist*. xvii. 1356; xviii. 159. For Burke's remarks, ibid. xviii. 506.

absolute, it cannot be said to be supreme. The supreme authority in Britain and its empire is that of Parliament. Colonial legislatures existed merely by a grant of temporary authority, which might, under certain circumstances, be revoked:

> In sovereignty there are no gradations. There may be limited royalty, there may be limited consulship; but there can be no limited government. There must in every society be some power or other from which there is no appeal . . . It is not infallible, for it may do wrong; but it is irresistible, for it can be resisted only by rebellion, by an act which makes it questionable what shall be thenceforward the supreme power.

The colonists claimed that, by crossing the Atlantic, they did not give up their rights as Englishmen, which included the right to be taxed only by their own consent. Johnson objected that many of them had never had votes in the first place and could not claim additional rights; that they had freely chosen to place themselves in a position where they could not cast votes and must abide by the consequences of their own decision; that along with rights went obligations, which could not be shuffled off at will, and among these was the obligation to pay taxes; that the great majority of Englishmen were not represented, either having no vote at all or casting it for the losing candidate.

One of the more effective passages was where Johnson made fun of the ambivalent attitude of Congress towards the French Canadians. They had just denounced North's Quebec Act as a sinister attempt to enlist arbitrary-minded papists by buying them off with concessions to their religion. It would however be extremely convenient if the French Canadians could be persuaded to make common cause with the thirteen colonies. Congress therefore addressed an appeal to them to set aside 'low-minded infirmities', to ignore the fact that Congress was on record as believing that popery held 'sanguinary and impious tenets', and to join the rebellion in 'hearty amity'. Johnson could scarcely miss.

Most of Johnson's contempt was reserved, not for the Americans, but for their British allies and abettors:

> To love their country has been considered as virtue in men, whose love could not be otherwise than blind, because their preference was made without a comparison; but it has never been my fortune to find, either in ancient or modern writers, any honourable mention of those who have with equal blindness hated their country. These anti-patriotic prejudices are the abortions of Folly impregnated by Faction, which being produced against the standing order of nature, have not strength sufficient for long life.

Johnson reserved his most telling thrust against the Americans until the end of his pamphlet:

We are told that the subjection of Americans may tend to the diminution of our own liberties: an event, which none but very perspicacious politicians are able to foresee. If slavery be thus fatally contagious, how is it that we hear the loudest yelps for liberty among the drivers of negroes?

Whether it was wise of Johnson to lean so heavily upon an abstract doctrine of sovereignty may be doubted. There was nothing at all unusual or immoderate about it. We are told that the view that there existed within every state 'a final and absolute authority' was the 'starting point of *Court Whig* thought'.[100] But in the charged atmosphere of 1775 it was bound to be misinterpreted. What Johnson intended as a political commonplace seemed to others a daring and arbitrary proposition. If the existence of an absolute authority is inescapable, and is the most important attribute of all governments, no distinction can be drawn between a despotic and a limited government. Since this was perhaps the most contentious issue in eighteenth-century politics, it was unlikely that Johnson would command total support. Readers who took their views from Hobbes and Hume might approve, but not the admirers of Locke and Rousseau.

Johnson's political pamphlets have not attracted much favourable comment, and *Taxation No Tyranny* least of all. First in the field were the newspapers, with paragraphs on Johnson's pension and reputed Jacobitism; his honorary degree from Oxford, where Lord North was Chancellor, three weeks after the pamphlet appeared, was taken to be his wages. One publisher reprinted *Marmor Norfolciense* to demonstrate how Johnson's views had changed. Next followed a number of pamphlets, *Resistance No Rebellion*, *Taxation Tyranny*, *Tyranny unmasked*, and the like. 'The patriots pelt me with answers', wrote Johnson cheerfully on 8 April.[101] Even the *Gentleman's Magazine*, usually friendly towards its former contributor, abandoned him, commenting on his main tenets:

If these positions are admitted, we have profited little by the boasted Revolution; and the British nation has shifted sovereigns to very little purpose if only to change their names.[102]

---

[100] Reed Browning, *Political and Constitutional Ideas of the Court Whigs* (Baton Rouge, La., 1982), 196.　　　　　　　　　[101] To John Taylor, *Letters*, ed. Redford, ii. 197–8.

[102] It reviewed two replies. *An Answer to a Pamphlet Entitled Taxation No Tyranny* it described as masterful. The second, *Taxation, Tyranny*, quoted Magna Carta and the Bill of Rights among the subject's defence against supreme authority. The journal declared it was not necessary to read any further refutations of Johnson's work. *Gentleman's Magazine* (1775), 135, 189, 238.

James Boswell, when composing the *Life* years later, was also embarrassed by the pamphlet and declined into mournfulness:

The extreme violence which it breathed appeared to me so unsuitable to the mildness of a Christian philosopher, and so directly opposite to the principles of peace which he had so beautifully recommended in his pamphlet respecting Falkland's Islands that I was sorry to see him appear in so unfavourable a light.[103]

Nor have later commentators found much to admire. That Americans should have resented Johnson's tone is understandable.[104] But many English historians of the Whig–Liberal tradition also found it unpalatable. Macaulay dismissed it as 'a pitiable failure'.[105] Leslie Stephen, writing in the *Dictionary of National Biography*, found the pamphlet 'arrogant and offensive . . . illiberal and irritating'. They were, of course, entitled to their opinions, since literary judgement is not yet an exact science, but it would be a mistake to allow the chorus of disapprobation to persuade us that Johnson had taken up a peculiarly extreme or indefensible posture.

Chatham identified the cause of America so closely with Whiggism that there is a natural tendency to presume that his opponents must have been Tories, and violent Tories at that. Johnson was clearly greatly influenced in his pamphlet by Chatham: there are a number of scornful references to the Great Actor of Patriotism, and so on, and a concluding attack which Johnson wisely cancelled before printing.[106] But it was Chatham rather than Johnson who was out of touch and in political isolation. Johnson's view of sovereignty was conventional enough. Though it ran counter to

[103] Boswell was in the rather strange position of being a pro-American Tory. He saw that Johnson's argument was decisive only if the Americans were colonists and no more. 'That I am a Tory, a lover of power in monarchy, and a discourager of much liberty in the people, I avow. But it is not clear to me that our colonies are compleatly our subjects.' *Life*, ii. 312. He told Johnson that the power of the Crown would be greater if in direct contact with all its dominions rather than 'through that dense and troublesome body, a modern British Parliament'. Consequently he did not approve of the Declaratory Act.

[104] J. W. Krutch, *Samuel Johnson* (London, 1948), 394–5, wrote that *Taxation No Tyranny* was 'the most unfortunate of his literary productions, concerning which his admirers, British as well as American, seem generally to assume the less said the better . . . it is hardly worth while to attempt any defence'. J. P. Hardy, Professor of English at the University of England, New South Wales, has written that 'Johnson was, of course, opposing the tide of history'. J. P. Hardy (ed.), *The Political Writings of Dr. Johnson* (London, 1968), p. xix. It must be agreeable to be sure where the tide of history is flowing and it is not necessarily intellectual error to oppose it.

[105] Art. on Johnson for the *Encyclopaedia Britannica*, in Thomas Babington Macaulay, *Selected Writings*, eds. J. Clive and T. Pinney (Chicago, 1972), 156.

[106] See Greene (ed.), *Political Writings*, 455 and illus. The ending was turning into a rant about Whiggism, together with some rather heavy jokes about the Americans asking Chatham to be their king.

Lockean contract theory, many Hanoverians had long been uneasy at the radical implications of Locke's thought.

That Johnson's pamphlet should greatly impress John Wesley, who used it as the basis for his own *A Calm Address to our American Colonies*, may not seem particularly significant: Wesley's pedigree was High Tory.[107] But the argument that Johnson put forward was very similar to that of Josiah Tucker, dean of Gloucester, an ardent and active Whig politician.[108] The war against the American colonies had the support of the vast majority of the British people, and, when it went wrong, it was its wisdom rather than its justice that was in doubt. Peter Thomas, in a work of detailed scholarship on American policy in the 1760s, concludes that, despite appearances, there was a 'great consensus' of opinion in Parliament.[109] The Declaratory Act, which reaffirmed British sovereignty and which greatly offended American patriots, was, after all, the work of the Rockingham Whigs.[110] This consensus lasted through most of the 1770s and North's ministry was supported by handsome majorities. Chatham's motion in January 1775 to withdraw troops from America was defeated in the House of Lords by 68 votes to 18; Burke's conciliation resolutions went down in the Commons by 270 votes to 78.[111] Lord North strongly denied Charles Fox's charge that he was pursuing a Tory policy and was

---

[107] Wesley, in the introd. to a later edn. of *A Calm Address*, claimed a sale of 100,000 copies and admitted that he had been convinced by Johnson's pamphlet. Though he was accused of gross plagiarism by Revd Augustus Toplady in *An Old Fox Tarred and Feathered*, Johnson seems not to have resented Wesley's extensive borrowing, and wrote amiably, 6 Feb. 1776, that 'to have gained such a mind as yours, may justly confirm me in my own opinion'. By comparison with Wesley, Johnson seems restrained. Of the argument that taxation without representation was slavery, Wesley wrote: 'I answer, I have no representative in Parliament, but I am taxed; yet I am no slave . . . Who, then is a slave? Look into America and you may easily see. See that Negro, fainting under the load, bleeding under the lash? He is a slave.' It was not a very calm address.

[108] Tucker got his reply to Congress into print before Johnson's. *The Respective Pleas and Arguments of the Mother Country and of the Colonies Distinctly Set Forth* was pub. at Gloucester, 20 Jan. 1775. Johnson certainly read it, because he referred to Tucker's proposal to let the colonists go. Tucker also opened with a discussion of sovereignty: 'In all societies there must be a dernier resort, and a *Ne Plus ultra* of ruling power. To suppose a series of Ruling Powers one above another, ad infinitum, is to suppose as great an absurdity as can be conceived.' For commentary on Tucker's writings, including his repudiation of Locke, see G. W. Shelton, *Dean Tucker and Eighteenth-century Economic and Political Thought* (London, 1981).

[109] *British Politics and the Stamp Act Crisis: The First Phase of the American Revolution, 1763–1767* (Oxford, 1975), 364–71.

[110] 6 George III c. 12 declared that the said colonies 'have been, are, and of Right ought to be subordinate unto, and dependent upon, the Imperial Crown and Parliament of Great Britain . . . in all cases whatsoever'.   [111] *Parl. Hist.* xviii. 168, 540.

an enemy to freedom: on the contrary, he was contending for the rights of Parliament.[112]

With considerable justice, John Courtenay, the member for Tamworth, turned in 1781 upon those who believed that the war had been a despotic and Tory one:

The asserting an unlimited sovereignty over America was a Whig principle, maintained by Whig statesmen, and confirmed by repeated acts of a Whig parliament.[113]

After 1775 Johnson's interest in politics waned, though he published the four political pamphlets in a collected edition in 1776. From 1777 onwards he was engaged on the *Lives of the Poets* and in his later years was preoccupied with his health. Once fighting had broken out in the colonies, there was little to be done save wait upon the fortunes of war, which swayed backwards and forwards. The entry of France and Spain into the conflict in 1778 and 1779 made the war more popular, by draping it in patriotic colours, even if it worsened the strategic situation. Johnson was by no means singular in supporting the war while doubting the capacity of the ministers: his doubts were shared, among others, by the prime minister himself, who begged repeatedly to be allowed to resign.[114]

As long as Henry Thrale retained his seat, Johnson had a direct line to and concern with politics. Thrale's business affairs recovered from the shake of 1772–3 and he continued to give general support to North's government.[115] But in June 1779 he suffered a severe stroke, caused, in his wife's opinion, by gross overeating. Though incapacitated for the rest of his life, Thrale clung to his parliamentary seat. But the odds were against him in such a borough as Southwark: a candidate who might not live to requite favours was not an attractive proposition. A new and formidable antagonist made his appearance in the shape of Sir Richard Hotham, another native of the borough, once a hatter, and a supporter of opposition. During the early summer of 1780 there were persistent rumours

[112] Parl. Hist. xviii. 771, debate of 26 Oct. 1775: 'If he understood the meaning of the words Whig and Tory . . . it was the characteristic of Whiggism to gain as much for the people as possible, while the aim of Toryism was to increase the prerogative. That in the present case, the administration contended for the right of Parliament, while the Americans talked of their belonging to the Crown. Their language was therefore that of Toryism.'

[113] Ibid. xxi. 1281.

[114] 'Lord North', in H. van Thal (ed.), *The Prime Ministers* (London, 1974), i. 176–9.

[115] In his biography of Thrale, Namier discussed whether he held a government contract. *House of Commons, 1754–90*, iii. 528–9.

that North would try another snap election. On 25 April Johnson vetted an address by Thrale to his constituents, trying for damage limitation.[116] On 3 May Mrs Thrale reported that 'Sir Richard Hotham is busy in the Borough, it seems, and spends money very liberally, but it will not do, I think', and the following day:

The Borough people want my Master among them, but he must not come: Southwark is a scene of riot and bustle and it would soon petrify him even to see and hear the confusion, if he took no active part in it . . . he is not safe from another apoplexy, he is not indeed . . . and his appearance among his constituents would *do him no good*.[117]

Johnson replied urging her to come instead, as John Perkins, Thrale's business partner, insisted: 'Money, Mr P. says, must be spent.' Next day Johnson reinforced his advice in a letter which gives a nice insight into the arts of managing an open borough:

My opinion is that you should come for a week, and show yourself, and talk in high terms, for it will certainly be propagated with great diligence that you despair and desist, and to those that declare the contrary, it will be answered why then do they not appear? To this no reply can be made that will keep your Friends in countenance. A little bustle, and a little ostentation will put a stop to clamours, and whispers, and suspicions of your friends, and calumnies of your opponents. Be brisk, and be splendid and be publick . . .

It is always necessary to show some good opinion of those whose good opinion we solicit. Your friends solicit you to come, if you do not come, you make them less your friends by disregarding their advice. Nobody will persist long in helping those that will do nothing for themselves.

The voters of the borough are too proud and too little dependent to be solicited by deputies, they expect the gratification of seeing the Candidate bowing or courtesying before them. If you are proud, they can be sullen.[118]

On the 9th Johnson repeated his advice, adding: 'Mr Polhill, as I suppose you know, has refused to join with Hotham, and is thought to be in more danger than Mr Thrale.[119]

Mrs Thrale left her sick husband at Bath and spent a week canvassing the borough. Johnson reported to Queenie Thrale that her mother 'has

---

[116] To Mrs Thrale, then in Bath, Johnson wrote: 'you had mentioned his sickness in terms which gave his adversaries advantage, by confirming the report which they had already spread with great industry, of his infirmity and inability. You speak . . . with too little confidence in your own interest. By fearing, you teach others to fear.' *Letters*, ed. Redford, iii. 244–6.

[117] *Letters*, ed. Chapman, ii. 352–3.

[118] *Letters*, ed. Redford, iii. 252–3.   [119] Ibid. 253–5.

been very busy, and has run about the Borough like a Tigress seizing upon every thing that she found in her way. I hope the Election is out of danger.' Johnson continued to keep an eye on Southwark, though in June the Gordon riots drove electoral matters out of sight for several weeks.[120]

In July 1780 John Robinson, Secretary to the Treasury, made one of his assessments of the possible result of a general election. He thought that the government's working majority of just over fifty might be more than doubled, and he noted Thrale as a supporter and Polhill as an opponent. Under Southwark he wrote:

Sir Abraham Hume has sometimes been talked of to stand here, but he is no better for government than Mr. Polhill and has not yet come forward to declare—Mr Thrale it is hoped is secure.

30th. July. Altho' it is now said they mean to push at him.[121]

In September government resolved to call an election in order to cash in on the change wrought in public opinion by the riots. Mrs Thrale commented:

The late riots have done for the ministry what the rebellion did for the house of Hanover; established their authority and made their government popular; any thing say we now but a mob to rule over us: in short, any government that will protect our property is the present cry, and if the Tories would but take advantage of the spirit *de ce moment*, they might fasten what rulers and what rules they would on us.[122]

Even in a relatively open borough like Southwark the engines of influence could be put to work. Lord Westcote, a close friend who had been with Thrale on the Grand Tour and was now a Lord of the Treasury, engaged the interest of Peter Champion, a prominent merchant; Bamber Gascoyne, a Lord of the Admiralty, 'spoke to the officers' in his department and assured Mrs Thrale that the interest he had among the wharfingers would be at Thrale's disposal. Once polling had started, even the prime minister was not safe from Mrs Thrale's importunities. North dutifully consulted a colleague on a doubtful legal point, adding that he

[120] Ibid. 256.
[121] Robinson's lists may conveniently be found in the Camden Miscellany xxx, Camden 4th ser., 39 (1990), 442–97, edited by Ian Christie. Robinson was too optimistic. For the eventual outcome, see I. R. Christie, *The End of North's Ministry, 1780–1782* (London, 1958), 157–63. North carried the first divisions in the new House by 203–134 and 212–130. But in Feb. 1781, in a gloomy moment, Robinson put the government majority at no more than six.
[122] *Thraliana*, i. 450.

had 'heard a good account of the conduct of all the Customs House officers today'.[123]

Mrs Thrale had looked forward to the election campaign with trepidation. In the event, the disaster could scarcely have been more spectacular. Johnson wrote a number of addresses on behalf of Thrale, admitting that his recovery 'from a very serious distemper is not yet perfect', but begging the voters to understand. Polhill and Hotham remained in the field. But the day before voting began, the Thrales visited church to demonstrate that he was still fit for active service. Mrs Thrale wrote:

I had the mortification to see him seized with such illness as made him look a perfect corpse in the full view of an immense congregation.[124]

Though Thrale was got into action once more, he was hopelessly behind and forced to decline.[125]

Amazingly, Thrale did not even then give up his search for a seat. On the day he declined, Johnson wrote to Strahan asking his good offices in finding Thrale a seat 'less uncertain', and added, vaguely, 'there are, I suppose, men who transact these affairs, but we do not know them'. A little later he drafted a letter to Lord North on Thrale's behalf asking for government help in finding some snug borough, of the sort that Edward Eliot had in Cornwall: 'I do not mean to stand a contest, but to receive a nomination,' Thrale added.[126] The letter suggests how little Thrale and Johnson knew about the situation. There were no vacancies at any of Eliot's six Cornish seats and Eliot himself was totally devoted to opposition, having refused to re-elect Edward Gibbon at Liskeard. There were plenty of government refugees, Gibbon among them, looking for shelter and with better prospects of tenure than Thrale.[127] In October Johnson tried to find Thrale a seat for Steyning in Sussex, where there was a vacancy on Filmer Honywood, the sitting member, deciding to take his

[123] John Rylands Library, Manchester, Piozzi MS 891. The first two letters are dated 9 and 31 May. North's letter is undated but must have been written early in Sept. 1780.

[124] *Life*, iii. 440; *Thraliana*, i. 453. To a friend Mrs Thrale wrote: 'he was again taken very ill the day before the poll, at a church crowded with voters, who came to see the rival candidates; in whose presence likewise this fatal accident happened. His friends now considered him as dying, his enemies as dead. I was to call physicians, to provide a substitute for him upon the hustings, to consult counsel concerning the polling business, and to prove my husband's existence by showing myself in the streets, while my duty called me to his bedside.' Quoted in J. L. Clifford, *Hester Lynch Piozzi* (Oxford, 1941), 190.

[125] The numbers were Hotham, 1300; Polhill, 1138; Thrale, 855. Government therefore lost a seat to opposition.

[126] *Letters*, ed. Redford, iii. 314; *Letters*, ed. Chapman, ii. 403–4.

[127] J. E. Norton (ed.), *Letters of Edward Gibbon* (London, 1956), ii, nos. 472, 481, 483, 485, 487.

seat for Kent instead. But Honywood was a close friend of Charles Fox and a dedicated oppositionist, and brought in John Bullock, another supporter of Fox. Henry Thrale's parliamentary aspirations finished on 4 April 1781, when he suffered his final stroke.[128]

The political scene during the rest of Johnson's life was dominated by the fall-out from the American disaster. The general election of 1780 gave Lord North's uneasy ministry a further lease of life, but in November 1781 he received news of Cornwallis's surrender at Yorktown, which spelled the end. Even then it required from North a sharp reminder of political realities before the king himself could be persuaded to political surrender: 'the torrent is too strong to be resisted. Your Majesty is well apprised that, in this country, the Prince on the Throne cannot, with prudence, oppose the deliberate resolution of the House of Commons.'[129] The Rockinghams and the remnants of the old Chathamites, led by Lord Shelburne, took office after more than fifteen years in opposition. Johnson watched these developments with lack-lustre eyes: 'the Men are got in, whom I have endeavoured to keep out', he wrote on 30 March 1782, 'but I hope they will do better than their predecessors; it will not be easy to do worse.'[130]

The new ministry made a brisk start on its two main objectives: winding up the American war and introducing a programme of economical reform. But the death of Lord Rockingham in less than three months brought the tensions between his supporters and those of Lord Shelburne into the open and, during the early days of July 1782, the administration broke up. Portland, Fox, Burke, and the Cavendishes went out leaving Shelburne as first minister. 'All is yet uncertainty and confusion,' wrote Johnson to Taylor on 8 July: 'I did not think Rockingham of such importance as that his death should have had such extensive consequences. . . . These are not pleasant times.'[131] A fortnight later he remarked: 'Mr. Burke's family is computed to have lost by this revolution twelve thousand a year. What a rise, and what a fall. Shelburne speaks of him in private with great malignity.'[132] But, at this juncture, Johnson seemed

---

[128] *Letters*, ed. Redford, iii. 316–17. The editor does not seem to have realized that Steyning was a parliamentary borough and that there was a vacancy there.

[129] Fortescue, v, no. 3566.   [130] *Letters*, ed. Redford, iv. 29.   [131] Ibid. 59–60.

[132] Ibid. 62. The rumours of Burke's losses were not as extragavant as they might seem. His own place as Paymaster had a salary of £4,000 p.a.; his brother Richard was Secretary to the Treasury at £3,000 p.a.; his son was Deputy-Paymaster at £500 p.a.; and his cousin William had been appointed Deputy-Paymaster in India at £2,000 p.a. In addition, Burke was busy trying to land the Clerkship of the Pells, worth £4,000 p.a., for his son for life. Burke did not intend economical reform to get out of hand. *House of Commons, 1754–90*, ii. 151–2; *Correspondence of Burke*, v. 10–14.

more concerned with the effect of the government changes on his friend Sir Robert Chambers, in India as a judge of the Supreme Court, and under close scrutiny. 'Shelburne seems to be his enemy,' commented Johnson on 22 July 1782, but, in the event, Chambers survived. When his superior Sir Elijah Impey was recalled, Chambers succeeded to the office of Chief Justice.[133]

There was little in the events of the remaining two years of Johnson's life to give him much pleasure. Not only had the Americans established their independence, with the Irish in hot pursuit, but at times it seemed that the much-vaunted British constitution had broken down. Lord Shelburne's ministry lasted a mere eight months and his defeat in February 1783 was followed by a six-week crisis during which the king contemplated abdication rather than surrender to the Fox–North coalition. 'Almost all news is bad,' Johnson wrote in August 1782; 'perhaps no nation not absolutely conquered has declined so much in so short a time. We seem to be sinking.'[134] In January 1783 he wrote to his old friend Taylor, 'I am afraid of a civil war'.[135] At the beginning of April the coalition took office, and Johnson reported at some length to Chambers in India:

The state of the Publick, and the operations of government have little influence upon the private happiness of private men, nor can I pretend that much of the national calamities is felt by me; yet I cannot but suffer some pain when I compare the state of this kingdom, with that in which we triumphed twenty years ago. I have at least endeavoured to preserve order and support Monarchy.[136]

On 13 June 1783 Johnson wrote to Mrs Thrale that his 'powers and attention have for a long time, been almost wholly employed upon my Health'.[137] Four days later he suffered a stroke, which did not make it any easier to keep at bay 'the black dog'.[138] In November 1783 Charles Fox introduced the India Bill. Johnson, through his friends Fowke, Chambers, and Jones, had a good second-hand knowledge of Indian matters: 'I doubt whether the government, in its present state of diminished credit, will do more than give another evidence of its own imbecility.'[139] The sombre mood remained. In December Fox and North were turned out to make way for William Pitt. 'To any man who extends his thoughts to national considerations,' Johnson wrote to Mrs Thrale, 'the times are dismal and gloomy. But to a sick man, what is the publick?'[140]

---

[133] *Letters*, ed. Redford, iv. 58, 62–3.   [134] Ibid. 64.
[135] Ibid. 109. This is a full discussion of Johnson's views on a reform of Parliament and is looked at in some detail in Ch. 4.
[136] Ibid. 124–9.   [137] Ibid. 148.   [138] Ibid. 160.
[139] Ibid. 248.   [140] Ibid. 267.

With the new year in 1784 came the great battle in the House of Commons to see whether Pitt could wear away the coalition's majority. Johnson seemed no longer to care much either way:

The tumult in government is, I believe, excessive, and the efforts of each party outrageously violent, with very little thought on any national interest, at a time when we have all the world for our enemies, when the King and Parliament have lost even the titular dominion of America, and the real power of government every where else. Thus Empires are broken down when the profits of administration are so great, that ambition is satisfied with obtaining them . . .[141]

A last visit to Oxford with Boswell in the summer of 1784 gave Johnson a chance to fight old battles and parade his true-blue feelings once more. They dined with Thomas Nowell, Regius Professor of Modern History and Principal of St Mary's Hall, where he had succeeded the Jacobite William King. In 1772 Nowell had been involved in a bizarre episode which showed how easily old passions could be rekindled. Invited to deliver the annual Fast sermon to the House of Commons (or more truthfully to the Speaker and four members who attended at St Margaret's) on the anniversary of the execution of Charles I, Nowell had praised Charles as a spotless prince, condemned the Puritans as men who 'spurned at all order, disdained subordination, despised government' (words that Johnson might well have used), and condemned those who had 'artfully revived' these old disputes. Though the sermon does not seem very extreme, after it had been published Tommy Townshend moved that it be burned by the common hangman, only for North to point out that the House had already recorded its thanks. Newdigate, Dolben, and the old Tories seem to have been bounced by the opposition and the vote of thanks was rescinded. Gibbon, in a splendidly cynical comment, thought that Nowell's publisher would bless the zeal of Townshend and that Nowell himself would be speedily promoted. He was not, but the position he already enjoyed was enough to provide Johnson with a convivial evening in 1784, drinking 'Church and King' toasts after dinner 'with true Tory cordiality'. A fortnight later, back in London, Boswell took his leave of Johnson, after they had dined alone with Reynolds. Boswell dropped Johnson at Bolt Court from his coach and declined Johnson's characteristic request to stay just a little longer: 'when he had got down upon the foot-pavement, he called out "Fare you well", and without looking back, sprung away with a kind of pathetic briskness.'[142]

---

[141] *Letters* ed. Redford, iv. 277.
[142] *Life*, ii. 152; iv. 295–6, 339; *Parl. Hist.* xvii. 245, 312–17, 319; J. E. Norton (ed.), *Letters of Edward Gibbon* (London, 1956), i. 309–10. There is a copy of Nowell's *Sermon Preached*

No doubt ill health explains much of Johnson's dejection at this time, though he was by no means the only one who presumed that the sun of Britain's greatness had set. But Burke himself found a way to cheer the dying man and sent a copy of his speech on Indian matters, which ran to more than one hundred pages of close text. 'I will look into it,' replied Johnson.[143]

We are now left with the task of explaining what was meant by the term 'Tory' in the middle years of the eighteenth century and to what extent Johnson fitted into that category. Neither question is straightforward.

Many of the problems of party historiography arise from the nature of the evidence. Since there was no mass party membership, it follows that there are no lists of members. People could call themselves anything or nothing. There is a number of lists of members of Parliament, drawn up by party organizers and managers, but they are notoriously difficult to use. Not infrequently the same man would be claimed by rival parties and there were many members whose behaviour or absence baffled the commentator.[144]

Before the Honourable House of Commons at St. Margaret's, Westminster on Thursday XXX January 1772 in Durham University Library.
    The sequel to the rescinding of thanks provides yet another example of Johnson's comparative coolness on these questions. Following up their victory, the opposition moved on 2 Mar. that the Fast Day on 30 Jan. be abolished, but were defeated by 125–97. Johnson's reply to Boswell, when asked whether he would have deplored the abolition, was very measured: 'Why, Sir, I could have wished that it had been a temporary act, perhaps, to have expired with the century. I am against abolishing it, because that would be declaring it was wrong to establish it; but I should have no objection to make an act, continuing it for another century, and then letting it expire.' *Life*, ii. 151–2. The national Fast, which Stephen Fox remarked was widely disregarded, was eventually abolished in 1859.

[143] *Letters*, ed. Redford, iv. 277.
[144] John Robinson's *State* for 1780 contains many examples. Robinson was writing at a time when party names, as we have seen, were causing difficulty, but the problem of pinning down behaviour would have been found at other periods. Of William Drake, member for Amersham and an old Tory, he wrote: 'Mr. Drake, senr. is offner with Govt. than against: in Ministerial Questions he may be against, but in great constitutional points he will always be with, if the questions are to affect the Govt. or constitution'; his monumental inscription described Drake as 'attached to no party'. Of Lord Ongley, member for Bedfordshire, who at the outset of his political career had been called 'a determined Tory', Robinson wrote: 'I put Lord Ongley down for, because he generally is so, except in some of the questions on economy and reform, and I think he may be mostly depended upon, if attended to and humoured a little, for I have generally on trial found him practicable'; of Samuel Whitbread, the brewer and member for Bedford, 'a very doubtful uncertain man for either side'; of Lord Newhaven, member for Canterbury, 'is sometimes with, at others against, but he professes great friendship'. Resistance to party and determination to preserve independence of action remained strong with many members.

It is no easier to ascertain the party views of ordinary voters. There are, of course, a large number of poll books in existence and they provide valuable information. But throughout the period 1701–1832 about two-thirds of the elections for counties and boroughs were uncontested, and therefore no poll books were called for.[145] Even when poll books exist, their interpretation is difficult. Frequently the voters were not given a choice on a party basis.[146] Where there was a clear choice, with one Tory standing against two Whigs, one cannot be certain whether a voter gave his support because the candidate was a Tory or despite it, since other considerations such as local loyalties, personal friendships, or money changing hands cannot be ruled out.[147]

The historian, in his hunt for party, is therefore forced back onto ideology, whether in the form of speeches, pamphlets, public statements, or private letters. Here again there are difficulties. There were no formal party manifestos or resolutions for party conferences. Parliamentary speeches are often ill reported or not reported at all. Statements of principle are somewhat rare and often distressingly vague. On the hustings candidates often took refuge in fervent tributes to the constitution, without much attempt to explain what they took the constitution to be: one candidate is even on record as eschewing political discussion on the grounds that it frequently led to dissension.[148] With, in effect, only two parties to accommodate the nation, each had to be a broad church. It is not unknown today for fellow members of the Conservative or Labour parties to hold sharply different views: similarly, in the Hanoverian period, we

[145] These figures are for England only and exclude the two University constituencies and by-elections. The evidence suggests that the 40 counties were contested on 308 occasions out of a possible 1,160, giving an average of 27%. The 203 boroughs were contested on 2,068 occasions out of a possible 5,887, giving an average of 35%. The overall position gives an average of 33% contested. At the general election of 1761, the 177,000 freeholders had scarcely any party choice, even if they were zealots. In 36 of the 40 counties, accounting for 167,000 voters, there was no contest. About 10,000 freeholders voted in the other elections.

[146] Even in the four contests in 1761, party allegiance was not always clear. Jacob Houblon, a Tory, gained a seat in a three-cornered contest in Hertfordshire. In Co. Durham, a candidate said to be of Tory antecedents was supported by the duke of Newcastle, the Whig first minister. Rutland was fought out between aristocratic interests. It was not at all clear what the two successful candidates were. Thomas Cecil was abroad all through the Parliament of 1761–8; Thomas Noel was a Tory who adhered to Newcastle. Westmorland was a contest to prevent the county falling totally into the hands of Sir James Lowther.

[147] Much helpful discussion of voting behaviour is in F. O'Gorman, *Voters, Patrons and Parties: The Unreformed Electorate of Hanoverian England, 1734–1832* (Oxford, 1989). The limitations of the evidence seem to me to have dogged the discussion of 'deference' among the voters.

[148] Daniel Parker Coke refused to answer questions at Nottingham in 1784. It did him no harm. He was returned unopposed. *House of Commons, 1754–90*, ii. 233.

find radical Whigs and conservative Whigs, old Whigs and new Whigs, Court Whigs and Country Whigs, Hanoverian Tories and High-Flyers. Tories often preferred to call themselves the Church party or the country party.

Since there is no copyright on names, anyone could provide his own definition. The original names of Whig and Tory were terms of abuse, and many eighteenth-century definitions come from political opponents and tend to caricature. Though the historian knows that he must allow something off for partisanship, he does not know to what extent. Each of the two parties experienced great vicissitudes in this period, from heady triumph to stark disaster. This often has a remarkably bracing effect upon attitudes and ideology. We have seen the extent to which, in the 1980s, the prospect of permanent opposition concentrated the mind of the Labour party and produced important changes of policy. It would be surprising if in Hanoverian England, with no party conference to face, no bloc vote to organize, no national executive to persuade, the adjustment of ideology to assist party fortunes should have been less apparent.

Toryism in the early eighteenth century sometimes went by the name of the landed interest, the old interest, or the Church interest. It was above all the creed of the squire, the parson, and the cathedral clergy. Its pillars had been the monarchy and the Church of England, and the reason why James II's conduct dealt such a blow to the Tories is that he managed to bring the two into conflict. Most Tories, faced with the choice, stood by their Church and supported the Glorious Revolution, though the concessions they were obliged to make in the process weakened the Church's exclusive position. Once the immediate crisis was over, many of them began to regret the religious concessions, looked askance at Protestant refugees from abroad, and complained of the pernicious practices of some of the dissenters. They identified early on the great financial and commercial changes of the period and were haunted by the spectre of the moneyed interest prevailing over the landed interest.

With these major principles went certain attitudes, sometimes unacknowledged. Though they professed great respect for the monarchy, they had a deep mistrust of government and of the court. Their area of interest was usually the shire, or even their own section of the shire. They were unlikely to be offered places at court, which went to the greater aristocracy, and their addiction to country pleasures made them unwilling to spend the time in London that government office demanded. It was often with some reluctance that they left their counties in November for the session of Parliament, and party managers were well aware that they could not be relied upon for much heavy action after Easter. Their ideal was a low-spending government which could keep the land tax down to two shillings in the pound and stay clear of foreign entanglements, which often involved subsidies. Their dislike of bankers and brewers in the earlier period gave way later to an equal detestation of Indian nabobs, West Indian planters, and government contractors. Since parson and squire were a formidable combination in the villages of Hanoverian England, their opinions were echoed by perhaps a majority of the nation.

The last four years of Anne's reign, when Johnson was a small boy, saw the Tory high-water mark. In 1710, thanks to growing weariness with the war and Whig mismanagement of the Sacheverell impeachment, the Tories swept back with a majority of about 150, to be repeated at the general election of 1713 with 360 members against 190 Whigs. Suspicion of government did not desert the Tories even when the government was, in theory, their own, and in February 1711 the backwoodsmen formed the October Club to watch for treachery and keep the ministers to proper Tory principles.

The staggering defeat of 1714–15 was certain to have its effect upon Tory thinking. A number of them refused to accept the Hanoverian succession and threw in their lot with the Stuarts, with greater or lesser commitment. Though the majority adhered to the new regime and their tradition was to support the monarchy, it was difficult to feel quite the same enthusiasm for that principle when the main use that the monarch made of his power was to banish the Tories. The result was not so much a change of principle as a reversion to views that had always been held, but less prominently exhibited. The new Hanoverian connection encouraged a Little England attitude towards foreign affairs. The sight of government patronage and influence in the hands of their rivals reminded the Tories how much they had always distrusted overweening government. Above all, their devotion to the constitution waned a little when it seemed to work so much to their disadvantage and they became more receptive to suggestions for reform—the elimination of placemen, shorter parliaments, and curbs on electoral bribery. Toryism acquired a radical tinge. Even if the depth of their conversion was suspect, propaganda often converts those who proffer it more than those who are the recipients. David Hume noted in 1742 that 'the Tories have been so long obliged to talk in the republican style that they seem to have made converts of themselves by their hypocrisy'.[149]

---

[149] Essay IX, 'Of the Parties of Great Britain', in *Essays, moral, political and literary* (1752).

Whig ideology was also much modified by time and circumstances. By origin, the Whigs were a parliamentary group towards the end of Charles II's reign, insisting upon the legitimacy of resistance to an arbitrary or tyrannical ruler. Their ideological guru was John Locke and their political martyrs were Lord Russell and Algernon Sidney, who perished on the scaffold as a result of the Rye House plot of 1683.[150] The events of 1688 strengthened the understanding between the Whigs and the Protestant dissenters, who were rewarded by the Toleration Act and whose considerable electoral influence was usually placed at Whig disposal. The identification of the Whigs with the commercial and moneyed interest increased Tory dislike. Johnson was not the only one to accuse them of hardness of heart and the worship of Mammon.

The transformation of the Whigs from a party of resistance and opposition to a party of government began soon after the Glorious Revolution. For a time they remained anxious to limit the powers of the Crown, but the emphasis on the legitimacy of resistance became feebler as it became clear that it was a doctrine more likely to benefit Jacobites than Whigs. This tendency to forget the republican traditions of Whiggism was all the more marked after 1714, when they enjoyed the full and undivided confidence of the new Hanoverian monarchs. By 1722, John Trenchard and Thomas Gordon could complain that English parties were as variable as the English weather: 'a *Tory* under oppression and out of place is a *Whig*: a *Whig* with power to oppress is a *Tory* . . . We change sides every day, yet keep the same names for ever.'[151] The process of adaptation was well described by John, Lord Hervey, in his Memoirs written in the 1730s:

The original principles on which both these parties were said to act, altered so insensibly in the persons who bore the names, by the long prosperity of the one, and the adversity of the other, that those who called themselves Whigs arbitrarily gave the title of Tory to every one who opposed the measures of the administration, or whom they had a mind to make disagreeable at court; whilst the Tories (with more justice) reproached the Whigs with acting on those very principles and pushing those very points which, to ingratiate themselves with the people and to assume a popular character, they had at first set themselves up to explode and abuse.[152]

The end of the Tories' long proscription was brought about by two

---

[150] Sidney had served against the king in the civil wars, being wounded at Marston Moor. Russell was too young to have served, but his father, the earl of Bedford, had fought for Parliament at Edgehill. Russell was friendly towards Nonconformity and his wife's mother had been a Huguenot. Sidney had close friends among the Quakers, including Penn himself.

[151] *Cato's Letters* (1722).   [152] Croker (ed.), *Memoirs of John Lord Hervey*, i. 4–6.

events: the collapse of the Jacobite cause after Culloden and the accession of George III in 1760. There had, of course, been many previous indications that the ice was melting. Hervey records how George II in 1734 irritated his Whig ministers by telling them how much better organized the Tories were. A few Tories had taken office after the fall of Walpole, though the experiment was not a vast success.[153] There was a considerable increase in the number of Tories appointed to the bench after 1742.[154] The shattering defeat at Culloden in 1745 cut off a possible Tory strategy and persuaded all but the most obdurate that the Hanoverians were here to stay, but it also made the old reproaches of Jacobitism seem stale and implausible. Had Frederick, Prince of Wales, lived to inherit, his succession would have been the signal for reconciliation.[155] As it was, George III's famous speech to Parliament in November 1760 was taken not only as a snub to Hanover, but as an assurance that he would be king, not just of the Whigs, but of the whole people. 'A nation of *Whigs* we may now justly be called', wrote John Douglas soon after the accession.[156]

The first two decades of George III's reign saw yet another adjustment in the position of the two parties and a corresponding shift in their political ideologies. Many of the old Tories accepted the invitation held out to them, made their appearance at court, and drifted towards general support of administration, losing interest in place bills, annual parliaments, and the nostrums of the 1740s. Newcastle and his Whig friends, to their considerable indignation, found themselves in opposition in the autumn of 1762, and, though the formation of the Rockingham ministry in July 1765 held out hopes that this was merely a temporary setback and that normal service would be resumed, the ministry was out a year later. As the years of opposition began to lengthen, the Whigs too began to recall their radical past, looked around for popular causes, picked up some of the reform proposals dropped by the Tories, and developed a more critical attitude towards the court and the government. No longer satisfied with a

---

[153] Partly as a result of the feud between the Pelhams and Carteret, three Tories—Cotton, Philipps, and John Pitt—took office in Dec. 1744. Cotton, appointed Treasurer of the Chamber, had been a Lord of Trade in the last Tory ministry in 1714; he continued to flirt with Jacobitism and was dismissed in May 1746. Philipps voted with opposition during the winter and was dismissed after three months. John Pitt settled down as a lifelong holder of minor office.

[154] N. Landau, *The Justices of the Peace, 1679–1760* (Berkeley, Calif., 1984), 160–9.

[155] For the Tories' negotiations with the prince, see Colley, *In Defiance of Oligarchy*, ch. 9.

[156] *Seasonable Hints from an Honest Man*, quoted by Mary Peters, '"Names and Cant": Party Labels in English Political Propaganda, *c*.1755–1765', *Parliamentary History*, 3 (1984), 103–27.

monarch who appeared to mistrust them, they joined forces in 1769 and 1770 with genuine radicals. Chatham, the Whig of Whigs, declared himself in 1771 a convert to reform of Parliament, and, though that medicine was too strong for most of the Rockingham Whigs, they embraced economical reform as a means of curtailing the influence of the Crown and adjusting once more the constitutional balance.

Bearing in mind the vicissitudes of both parties and the malleability which the names Whig and Tory had to demonstrate if they were to adapt to the changes of the century, it is not surprising that many people are hard to classify. In particular, there seems to be, at times, a distinct shortage of Tories, despite the popularity of Tory attitudes in the country at large. In the earlier period, Swift, Pope, and Hume have often been described as Tories.[157] But Pope wrote to Swift in 1730, without irony, 'you are a Whig, as I am'.[158] David Hume in 1748 described himself as a Whig, 'but a very sceptical one'.[159] Forty years later Edward Gibbon was still wrestling with the same problem, denouncing 'those foolish, obsolete, odious words, Whig and Tory'.[160]

At least there is no doubt that Johnson thought of himself as a Tory. Indeed, Mrs Thrale wrote that he gloried in it. But it might be more true to say that he was, in essence, an anti-Whig. The mere mention of the word 'Whig' was enough to start him snorting and pawing the ground. 'The first Whig was the devil', he told Boswell; Whiggism was 'a negation of all principle'.[161] Of his close friend Richard Bathurst, dead in the West Indies, Johnson recalled fondly, 'Dear Bathurst was a man to my very heart's content; he hated a fool, and he hated a rogue, and he hated a *Whig*. He was a very good *hater*.'[162]

Since hatred is often more vivid than admiration, it follows that Johnson, like many other people, had a reasonable image of his own side, but held to an absurd caricature of his opponents. To him, the word

[157] L. I. Bredvold, 'The Gloom of the Tory Satirists', in J. L. Clifford and L. A. Landa (eds.), *Pope and His Contemporaries: Essays Presented to George Sherburn* (Oxford, 1949), 1–19; E. C. Mossner 'Was Hume a Tory Historian?', *Journal of History of Ideas*, 2 (1941), 225–6. There is a valuable discussion of this point in J. A. Downie, 'Walpole, "The Poet's Foe"', in J. Black (ed), *Britain in the Age of Walpole* (London, 1984), 183–4.

[158] 4 Mar. 1730 (*Correspondence of Pope*, ed. Sherburn, iii. 95). For comment, see H. T. Dickinson, 'The Politics of Pope', in C. Nicholson (ed.), *Alexander Pope: Essays for the Tercentenary* (Aberdeen, 1988). For Swift on his 'old Whig principles', see letter to Lady Elizabeth Germain, 8 Jan. 1733 (*Correspondence of Jonathan Swift*, ed. H. H. Williams (Oxford, 1963–5), iv. 100).

[159] J. Y. T. Greig (ed.), *Letters of David Hume* (Oxford, 1932), i. 111.

[160] Gibbon to Lord Sheffield, 7 Aug. 1790 (*Letters of Gibbon*, ed. Norton, iii. 195).

[161] *Life*, i. 431; iii. 326.   [162] *Miscellanies*, i. 204.

'Whig' conjured up images of death and destruction: he saw rebels, king-killers, surly malcontents, men who would brook no authority. Though he acknowledged that the Tory position had changed over time (indeed, he reproached the Tories for not recognizing the fact), his archetypai Whig remained a roundhead, a commonwealthman, a plotter—types which had disappeared before he was born: hence his dictionary definition of Tory as 'one who adheres to the ancient constitution of the state and the apostolic hierarchy of the Church of England', while Whig was dismissed as 'the name of a faction'.[163]

On a rational level, Johnson was aware that this stereotype of Whig did not apply to Sir Robert Walpole, still less to Lord Rockingham and the duke of Portland. But we are dealing with the grip that the past has upon people. Johnson's past was the city of Lichfield, whose lovely cathedral had suffered so much during the civil wars. Staffordshire Tories had a lot to remember, and it is not surprising that Boswell did not believe that Staffordshire Whigs existed.[164] It did not take much to bring that past alive again for Johnson.[165] On his visit to St Andrews in 1773 he surveyed the ruins of the cathedral with rapt contemplation, before bursting out with 'Knox had set on a mob without knowing where it would end'.[166]

If this were all, Johnson would be no more than an extreme example, a quaint relic, a case-study of a man trapped in the past. He would deserve Leslie Stephen's dismissal as 'the embodiment of sturdy prejudice, or staunch beliefs which had survived their logical justification . . . the last of the Tories.'[167] But, first of all, if Johnson felt strongly, he was not alone. The language of eighteenth-century polemic was robust and the Tories were plastered in their turn as servile supporters of power.[168] Nor were his feelings unusual. The memory of the civil wars had a deep effect upon many of his contemporaries. It explains their deep distrust of standing armies, which could be used to overawe the people, as Cromwell and

---

[163] We have however been warned not to try to derive too much of Johnson's personal position from his dictionary definitions, nor to exaggerate the starkness of his antitheses. It was common to define by opposites and Johnson's definition of Whig is more restrained than that of some of his predecessors. See James Sledd and G. Kolb, 'Johnson's definitions of *Whig* and *Tory*', *Publications of the Modern Language Association of America* (1952), 882–5, and *Notes and Queries*, 198 (1953), 161.

[164] *Life*, iii. 326. Johnson's reply was: 'Sir, there are rascals in all countries.'

[165] See e.g. *Sermons*, no. 23, commented on in Ch. 1.   [166] *Life*, v. 61–3.

[167] *English Thought in the Eighteenth-century* (London, 1902), ii. 206.

[168] Among the abuse Johnson collected as a consequence of *Taxation No Tyranny* was 'mercenary reptile', 'bookworm', 'tool of traitors', 'scribbling prostitute', 'apostate pedant', 'old surly pensioner'. See H. L. McGuffie, 'Dr. Johnson and the Little Dogs: The Reaction of the London Press to Taxation No Tyranny', in D. H. Bond and W. R. McLeod (eds.), *Newsletters to Newspapers: Eighteenth Century Journalism* (West Virginia, 1977), 191–206.

James II had tried to do; it explains the profound dislike of religious enthusiasm, which could slip its leash at any moment and degenerate into fanaticism; it explains the widespread admiration for the constitution which had rescued the country from these perils and the anxious monitoring of its health; it explains the dislike of party, even among many who practised it, as a mechanism which could divide the nation and set up warring factions.

Deep in Johnson was a desire to shock and provoke and we must distinguish Johnson sounding off from Johnson reflecting and writing with deliberation. He acknowledged that much of his original Tory fervour came from his youthful encounters with Gilbert Walmsley, mentor and Whig. Party zeal, he told Boswell on their tour of the Hebrides, 'is much increased by opposition. There was a violent Whig with whom I used to contend with great eagerness. After his death, I felt my Toryism much abated'.[169] Johnson was often more moderate than his language. The stream of jokes at the expense of the Scots did not prevent him from being on terms of friendship with a large number of them, including Boswell, Strahan, MacBean, Beattie, Frank Stewart, and Robertson. Dr Maxwell wrote of him that he was by no means a party man: 'in politicks he was deemed a Tory, but certainly was not so in the obnoxious or party sense of the term; for while he asserted the legal and salutary prerogatives of the crown, he no less respected the constitutional liberties of the people.'[170] He was critical of the behaviour of the Tories in Parliament and his respect for authority in general did not lead to slavish admiration for ministers. Of Lord Bute, who had, after all, given Johnson his pension, he wrote dispassionately that, though a very honourable man and a man who meant well, he 'had his blood full of prerogative, was a theoretical statesman, a book-minister, and thought this country could be governed by the influence of the Crown alone.'[171] One of his best-known essays is an attack upon the credulity of 'political zealots'.[172] He was far too independent to surrender his judgement to party and was deeply shocked by Edmund Burke's defence of party loyalty:

I remember being present when he [Burke] shewed himself to be so corrupted, or at least something so different from what I think right, as to maintain, that a member of Parliament should go along with his party right or wrong . . . It is maintaining that you may lie to the publick.[173]

[169] *Life*, v. 386.   [170] Ibid. ii. 117.   [171] Ibid. 353.
[172] *Idler*, no. 10 (17 June 1758).   [173] *Life*, ii. 223. See also v. 36.

In January 1784, when the parliamentary struggle was still undecided, he wrote glumly to Taylor that all was party, 'the *outs* and the *ins* . . . with very little thought on any national interest'.[174]

In his quieter moments Johnson was ready to acknowledge the wide consensus that had developed in Hanoverian England, despite the appearance of often acute party strife. In May 1781 he made a very deliberate statement in answer to Boswell, when they were alone. Boswell added that 'I begged of him to repeat what he had said and I wrote down as follows':

A wise Tory and a wise Whig, I believe, will agree. Their principles are the same, though their modes of thinking are different. A high Tory makes government unintelligible: it is lost in the clouds. A violent Whig makes it impracticable: he is for allowing so much liberty to every man, that there is not power enough to govern any man. The prejudice of the Tory is for establishment: the prejudice of the Whig is for innovation. A Tory does not wish to give more real power to government; but that government should have more reverence. Then they differ as to the Church. The Tory is not for giving more legal power to the clergy, but wishes they should have a considerable influence, founded on the opinion of mankind: the Whig is for limiting them and watching them with a narrow jealousy.[175]

One could hardly have a more dispassionate statement. Halifax had conquered and all were Trimmers. It was, as Hume insisted, a question of balance. Sometimes the wind blew towards authority, sometimes towards liberty. The crew would move from one side of the ship of state to the other to keep it steady. In Johnson's opinion there had been, during his lifetime, a vast expansion in the scope of public opinion and comment: it was now time to try to strengthen the Crown. The conclusion of most modern historians is that he was right, and that, despite appearances, the Crown was growing weaker.[176]

Far from being a man living in the past, an obdurate defender of the status quo, Johnson welcomed many of the changes taking place and found much in Hanoverian society that distressed him. In the battle of the

---

[174] *Letters*, ed. Redford, iv. 277.

[175] *Life*, iv. 117–8. During the last year of his life, Johnson repeated this view, denying that there existed 'great enmity' between Whig and Tory. 'Why, not so much I think, unless when they come into competition with each other. There is none when they are only common acquaintance, none when they are of different sexes. A Tory will marry into a Whig family, and a Whig into a Tory family, without any reluctance,' Ibid. 291.

[176] See particularly I. R. Christie, 'Economical Reform and "The Influence of the Crown", 1780', repr. in *Myth and Reality in Late-eighteenth-century British Politics* (London, 1970), 296–310.

books, he sided with the moderns against the ancients. He took delight in the spread of newspapers and periodicals. He was wholly in favour of the education of the poor, whom, according to Mrs Thrale, he loved as no man ever did.[177] He was far from deploring the commercial progress of the age and was keenly interested in the new science. He did not call for more savage punishments or more capital offences, but argued for mildness and leniency. While Boswell, from a younger generation, defended slavery, Johnson detested it.[178] Even in the political pamphlets, which have so often been used as evidence against him, his language is fierce but not outrageous by contemporary standards, and his basic position is moderate. At home and abroad, though he defended authority, it was the authority of Parliament, challenged by the Americans and by the Wilkites. In each case he was probably speaking for the great majority of his fellow countrymen.

It is not easy to focus the nature of Toryism, since a word which has survived as a political term for more than three hundred years is bound to have undergone many changes of meaning and emphasis. Johnson himself was acutely aware that he was living in a time of change. Twentieth-century historians tend to regard Hanoverian Tories as obstructive, resisting the growth of stability and the established order. But such a formulation begs the question, whose order? A traditional society based upon land and its relationships was giving way to one based upon trade and finance. In that setting, Whigs could appear as disrupters and innovators, and so Johnson saw them. He was suspicious of what Coleridge, at a later date, called the 'magic wealth-machine'.[179] But he also saw that there were merits as well as dangers in the new order, and he was not content, like many of his friends, merely to mourn the passing of a way of life. He was never querulous, wrote Boswell, 'never prone to inveigh against the present times . . . on the contrary, he was willing to speak favourably of his own age; and indeed maintained its superiority in every respect, except in its reverence for government'.[180]

By the end of the nineteenth century, the landed interest had shrunk so much that it could no longer sustain a national party and the Tories moved over to become the champions of business and industry. With the move came changing values, and the cross-over makes it hard to understand Johnson's brand of Toryism. While modern Tories are suspicious of

---

[177] *Miscellanies*, i. 204.   [178] *Life*, iii. 203–5.
[179] 'On the Constitution of Church and State', in J. Colmer (ed.), *Collected Works of Samuel Taylor Coleridge* (Princeton, NJ, 1976), ii. 63.
[180] *Life*, iii. 3.

welfare as a solvent of individual initiative and responsibility, Johnson placed a high order on charity as a Christian duty. While he had a clear vision of society as a network of obligations and duties, they are apt to regard it as a mere rhetorical device of the Left, the excuse for incessant demands.

To describe Johnson as a Tory, let alone an arch-Tory, is not wrong, but it is inadequate. It begs too many questions in a changing party situation, provides too few answers and, above all, fails to do justice to the complexities of a singularly complex man. It is asking too much of one word to expect it to do such heavy duty.

4

Johnson and the Constitution

JOHNSON was a seven-week-old baby when Dr Henry Sacheverell, Fellow of Magdalen College, Oxford, delivered from the pulpit of St Paul's his famous sermon *The Perils of False Brethren*. Rarely can a sermon have caused a greater stir. It was hastily printed and a large number of copies sent out to Lichfield and other cathedral cities. The most immediate result was to bring about a grand debate on the settlement of 1689 and the principles of the constitution, since the Whig government decided to prosecute Sacheverell for sedition by impeaching him before the House of Lords.

The terms of the Articles of Impeachment, drawn up by the Commons, set out the Whig case. It rehearsed how in 1688 the country had been rescued from the perils of popery and arbitrary power by the 'glorious enterprise' undertaken by William of Orange. As a consequence, the laws and liberties of the kingdom had been preserved, true religion established, toleration granted to dissenters, and 'the prospect of happiness for future ages' held out by the union of England and Scotland. In his sermon, the prosecution maintained, Sacheverell had suggested that the means by which the revolution had been brought about were 'odious and unjustifiable', that the toleration granted was 'unreasonable and unwarrantable', that the Church of England was in danger, and that the ministers had been guilty of general maladministration. Sacheverell, 'a public incendiary', had kept up a 'distinction of factions and parties', instilled groundless jealousies, fomented destructive divisions, and excited subjects to arms and violence. To add insult to injury, the sermon had been preached on 5 November, anniversary of the very day William had landed at Brixham, and at a service intended as a thanksgiving for that happy deliverance.

Sacheverell's defence was that he was merely expounding the true and accepted doctrines of the Church of England, which he had a duty as well as a right to do. Those doctrines went out of their way to emphasize that passive obedience and non-resistance were obligations on the subject at all times: indeed, the clergy were directed, if they did not preach on 5 November, to read one of the homilies against rebellion. Was it not strange that his zeal in trying to preserve the Church of England and to draw attention to the perils that surrounded it should be turned to his disadvantage?

Thus, those strains and anxieties that had afflicted many Tories and some Whigs in 1688 came to the surface twenty-two years later. They were rendered more intense by religious developments in the meantime. The toleration granted had not, as many had hoped, led to the dissenters being comprehended within a broader Church of England, but to their taking root outside it. In the eyes of many Anglicans, they had not merely taken root but had flourished exceedingly, making many wonder whether toleration had not become an engine which would, in due course, undermine the Church and the revolutionary settlement. There were, in addition, a number of factors which made the impeachment far from an abstract or theoretical discussion. Sacheverell's remarks came in the middle of a bitter and gruelling war, in which national unity was all the more necessary. The Whig partnership of Marlborough and Godolphin was in difficulties and, with the queen known to be devoted to the Church of England, it was possible that the impeachment might be used as a lever to turn out the administration and replace it with a Tory one. Moreover, the impeachment proceedings were punctuated by nights of violent rioting in London, with dissenting chapels burned and destroyed and passers-by forced to testify their admiration for the Doctor. This extra dimension of terror underlined the question that puzzled politicians and philosophers alike: how to claim rights for themselves and deny them to others, how to defend the right of resistance in an emergency without inviting any disgruntled group to throw off allegiance whenever it chose?

John Locke, whose *Two Treatises on Government* were much used as a defence of the Glorious Revolution, had certainly argued a contract theory, insisting that if the monarch broke the contract his subjects had a right to take action. Locke's subsequent reputation has been strange. At one time he was regarded as an arch-conservative, since he believed that the preservation of property was the chief aim of government; more recently, the radical and popular implications of his writings have been stressed, and it has been suggested that he fell into disfavour with the Hanoverian establishment.[1] In the last chapter of his work, Locke addressed himself directly to the question of whether he was not giving an invitation to malcontents and rebels:

---

[1] H. T. Dickinson, *Liberty and Property: Political Ideology in eighteenth-century Britain* (London, 1977), 125–32.

It will be said that the people being ignorant and always discontented, to lay the foundation of government in the unsteady opinion and uncertain humour of the people, is to expose it to certain ruin; and no government will be able long to subsist if the people may set up a new legislative whenever they take offence at the old one. To this I answer, Quite the contrary. People are not so easily got out of their old forms as some are apt to suggest . . . Great mistakes in the ruling part, many wrong and inconvenient laws, and all the slips of human frailty will be borne by the people without mutiny or murmur.

Though at the impeachment of Sacheverell Tories were ranged against Whigs, at the revolution of 1688 they had made common cause, and at the trial tactical considerations urged them not to adopt an extreme posture. Sir Simon Harcourt, speaking on behalf of Sacheverell, offered a double defence: first that there had been no occasion to resist supreme authority in 1688 since Lords and Commons had taken the lead; secondly, that the Doctor had, in one passage of his sermon, specifically admitted that there must be exceptions to every rule, and that 1688 was the exception to non-resistance. Otherwise, Harcourt conceded, it would be a slavish doctrine. Indeed, Humphrey Henchman later pointed out that Sacheverell had drawn attention to a maxim necessary for the safety of all governments: namely, 'that no innovation whatsoever should be allowed in the fundamental constitution of any state, without a very pressing, nay unavoidable necessity for it'. By definition, there could be such necessities.[2]

The managers on the Whig side were not completely agreed how strongly to urge contract theory. Nicholas Lechmere adopted a bold line, asserting an original contract between ruler and subjects and contending that it was the duty of the people to resist if it were broken. The success of the resistance to James II showed that Heaven itself had approved that cause. James Stanhope agreed with him in postulating a compact. Sir Constantine Phipps, for the defence, was sarcastic: 'when the Original Contract was made, that learned gentleman did not think fit to inform us . . . I never met with it in any of our law-books, in my little experience.' The prosecution retorted by quoting from Richard Hooker, the great defender of the Anglican Church, who had admitted that there must have been some 'Original Conveyance' of power and authority from the whole body politic to kings.

Harcourt's first proposition—that the Revolution had been effected by legal authority—stood on shaky ground. The participants in the Glorious

---

[2] G. S. Holmes, *The Trial of Doctor Sacheverell* (London, 1973).

Revolution had been at pains to demonstrate that there had not been any breakdown or hiatus in power, and they had drawn on the precedents from 1660. Even so, the means whereby continuity was preserved were something of an Indian rope trick. The parallel with 1660 was awkward. Then there had been a king to be brought in, by general agreement, and it was easy to accept that he had been king since the moment of his father's execution in 1649. In 1689 there was a king to be kept out, ultimately by the pretence that he had abdicated, which he strenuously denied. Even had he abdicated, the normal descent would have brought to the throne the infant Prince of Wales, who could be kept out only by another pretence that he was a supposititious child. James had made life even more difficult for his opponents by dropping the Great Seal into the Thames and burning the writs still to be sent out for the Parliament he had summoned for January 1689. His kingdom was thereby reduced to as near a state of nature as could be, with the contract, if contract there had ever been, by implication repudiated.

The proceedings taken to restore some kind of authority were strange. An informal meeting of some thirty lords and bishops at the Guildhall on 11 December adjourned without taking action. James then returned from his first effort to escape. On 21 December the Lords met and three days later asked William to summon a Parliament. On the 26th a very odd group, unique in composition, assembled. It included surviving members from Charles II's Parliaments (but not from James's), thus ensuring a Whig majority, augmented by the Lord Mayor, Aldermen, and Common Council of the city of London. Not surprisingly they were at first at something of a loss to know how to proceed. On the 28th and 29th, circular letters were issued in William's name, 'in this extraordinary juncture' summoning a Parliament under the existing electoral arrangements to meet in January 1689. This body, the Convention, offered the throne to William and Mary. It next passed what purported to be a statute, 1 William and Mary c. 1, which received the royal assent on 22 February, declaring itself to be a Parliament, 'notwithstanding any other defect or default whatsoever'. For good measure, and on the belt and braces principle, the next Parliament in 1690 passed legislation confirming the validity of its predecessors' statutes. All this repeated the formula used in 1660. It was probably the best that could be done in the curious circumstances, but Jacobites had a fairly easy task in arguing that the whole settlement was erected on a foundation that was palpably unlawful. Sacheverell's reopening of the issue was not therefore very welcome to the majority of post-revolutionary politicians.

The results of the impeachment were inconclusive. The immediate advantage went to the Tories. Though Sacheverell was found guilty by the votes of 69 peers against 52, his punishment—suspension of preaching for three years—was so light as to be a virtual commendation. When the Whigs tried to stiffen it by carrying a resolution that he should not be eligible for preferment during the period of his suspension, they failed by 60 votes to 59. Sacheverell, assisted by Tory patrons and welcomed by Tory corporations, went on to triumph and affluence. The Whigs' hold on power had been fatally weakened and the queen alienated; in August 1710 Godolphin was dismissed and Robert Harley took office. The subsequent elections of 1710 and 1713 gave the Tories a massive majority in the House of Commons.

But the long-term advantage may possibly have fallen to the Whigs. Harley found his High Tory allies difficult to handle and it proved costly to stoke the fires of religious animosity just before the Hanoverians came over to claim the throne under the terms of the Act of Settlement. Putting to one side the question whether many of the Tories were crypto-Jacobites, the Lutheran George I was bound to have more in common with moderate latitudinarian Anglicans than with High-Flying, passive-obedience, non-resistance clerics of the Sacheverell ilk. The revival of Tory concern about the limits of religious toleration also helped to cement the alliance between the Whigs and the Protestant dissenters.

With the unopposed succession of George I, the bottom fell out of the theoretical argument that had dominated the impeachment of Sacheverell. There was not much point in continuing the debate on the validity of the 1688 settlement when a fresh settlement had been superimposed and showed every indication of sticking. High-Flyers who had preached non-resistance in the hope that it might bring back the Stuarts fell silent when a repeat of the argument could only work to the advantage of the Hanoverians. Though the new dynasty did not abandon its claim to divine sanctions, George I dropped the practice of touching for the King's Evil and it was not even revived by George IV, that connoisseur of instant tradition.[3] Those few Tories who clung to the belief that 1688 had been illegitimate took the logical step of throwing in their lot with the Pretender. The rest looked to the future. The new king might tire of one-party rule; the Whigs might split; the electorate might prove resistant to government influence; the Prince of Wales might set up in

---

[3] Touching for the Evil, which English monarchs had borrowed from the French, was resumed by Charles X of France in 1824. He lasted only another six years.

opposition to his father and call in the Tories. Few members of that party can have realized in 1714 that they were on the long march to oblivion and that the wheel of fortune, which had turned so merrily between 1688 and 1714, was now jammed.

Theological controversy was slowest to die down. In 1717 the Bangorian controversy over the Low Church opinions of Bishop Benjamin Hoadly provoked a storm of pamphleteering, but the Whigs moved fast and the prorogation and then the discontinuation of Convocation took away the High-Flyers' platform.[4] Many Tories began to remember with pride that the Glorious Revolution had been as much a Tory as a Whig achievement. There was no reason why, as a party, they could not lay claim to some of its benefits. The principles of 1688 ceased to be a party issue and became a national heritage, which all true Englishmen could defend.

An early indication of a changing situation was the publication in 1717 of an acute analysis by Paul de Rapin-Thoyras, a Huguenot refugee.[5] Though Rapin-Thoyras' sympathies were with the Whigs, largely for religious reasons, his analysis was remarkably detached. The English were congratulated that alone among the peoples of Europe they had preserved their liberties against the advance of princely despotism. The Glorious Revolution had been effected 'to the inexpressible joy of the people'. Rapin-Thoyras began with a warning against placing too much faith in party names which were 'obscure and equivocal terms':

The names Torys and Whigs convey to the mind certain confused idea, which few are capable of rightly distinguishing . . . the same person may be either Whig or Tory, according to the subject in hand . . . When the Church only is concerned, the episcopal party are to be considered only as Torys. But how many even of these are Whigs with respect to the government . . . Every man uses this confusion of ideas, occasioned by the name of Whig and Tory, to accuse his adversaries of what is most odious in both parties.

Party warfare induced each party to caricature its opponents. Tories would persuade the public that all Whigs were commonwealthmen, longing to re-establish a republic; Whigs retorted that all Tories were High-Flyers, in whose hands toleration was not safe. 'But this is only an artifice to render one another mutually odious.'

There was much greater agreement on constitutional matters than was often supposed, Rapin-Thoyras suggested:

---

[4] The Bangorian controversy originated with an attack by Hoadly upon the non-jurors.
[5] *Dissertation sur les Whigs et Torys.* (Amsterdam, 1717); tr. John Ozell (1717).

It is not true that all Church-men are Torys, or all Presbyterians Whigs, in point of government, as is commonly imagined . . . Many Church-men, even bishops themselves, are Whigs, very good Whigs, as to the government.

On purely secular matters, there was consensus: 'the moderate State-Whigs and Torys', he wrote, 'are almost of the same sentiments . . . the moderate Whig and Tory form almost the same party, under the common appellation of Whig.' Though the impeachment of Sacheverell had roused great excitement, at the end of the day there was not a lot dividing the two sides, since hardly anyone denied that resistance might on certain occasions be justified, while even fewer wished to make it more than an extraordinary and unusual occurrence.

In these changing circumstances, the aims of most public men were to preserve the constitution and the revolutionary settlement. They were reinforced in their views by the stream of admiration directed at the mixed or balanced constitution from continental commentators. Rapin-Thoyras' *Dissertation* was followed by an *Histoire d'Angleterre*, translated by Nicholas Tindal and published in 1725. It achieved enormous success. Rapin-Thoyras' respectful message was driven home by a bullish preface dedicated to the Prince of Wales. The English constitution, the prince was reminded, 'in which the Prerogative of the Crown and the Privileges of the Subject are so happily proportioned', was a precious survival from Saxon times.

In 1733 Voltaire, much influenced by Bolingbroke, published his *Letters Concerning the English Nation*.[6] The preface declared how much the English abhorred flattery, presumably on the principle that Decius Brutus employed with Caesar, and Voltaire continued:

The English are the only people upon earth who have been able to prescribe limits to the power of Kings by resisting them; and who, by a series of struggles, have at last established that wise government, where the Prince is all powerful to do good, and at the same time is restrained from committing evil; where the Nobles are great without insolence; and where the People share in the Government without confusion.

Montesquieu, in *De l'esprit des lois*, written in 1748 and translated two years later, was hardly less respectful to the constitution of England, 'this beautiful system invented first in the woods . . . they know better than any

---

[6] The English edn. came out first. The French edn., under the name *Lettres philosophiques*, came out in 1734. If Voltaire's intention in choosing a vague title was to diffuse attention, it failed: his book was burned by order of the Paris *parlement*.

other people upon earth how to value, at the same time, these three great advantages—religion, commerce and liberty'.[7]

It did not much matter if foreigners were more fervent than accurate. Voltaire greatly exaggerated the extent of British liberties, perhaps to point the contrast, and Montesquieu found the secret of the constitution in a separation of powers that did not exist. Englishmen were not likely to be too critical towards analyses which showed them in so agreeable a light.

As a consequence, political discussion moved away from fundamentals. Bolingbroke and the opposition to Sir Robert Walpole did not attack the constitution; on the contrary, they claimed to be defending it against influence and bribery: 'it is our duty to preserve it, as far as we are able, in its full strength and vigour.' That could be done only by constantly monitoring its operation.[8]

But it was hardly to be expected that commentaries would remain scrupulously abstract and disinterested. Oppositions tended to the mournful conclusion that the liberties of the subject were in danger; governments, that they had never been in safer hands. In the course of the long ascendancy of Sir Robert Walpole, a 'country' opposition programme was formulated, on which the Tories and dissident Whigs might agree. It deplored reliance upon foreign mercenaries rather than the native militia; peered suspiciously at excise and a standing army; called for shorter parliaments; denounced the spread of government influence and corruption; lamented the loss of independence of the county freeholders, the yeomen of England; and hinted darkly that Parliament itself was sinking into subservience under a torrent of gold, supplied by stock-jobbers and city bankers. The fact that these accusations were regularly voted down by the House of Commons merely showed the depths to which the majority had sunk. Lord Hervey, Sir Robert's most useful ally, picked off nicely the monotony of the *Craftsman*'s jeremiads in his poem 'Journalists Displayed':

> To frighten the Mob, all Inventions they try,
> Ribbledum, Scribbledum, Fribbledum, Flash,
> But Money's their aim, tho' their Country's the Cry,
> Satyrum, Traytorum, Treasondum, Trash.
> Popery, Slavery, Bribery, Knavery,
> Irruptions, Corruptions, and *Somebody's Fall*,
> Pensions and Places,

---

[7] BK. XI, ch. 6.   [8] *Craftsman*, nos. 124, 371, 375, 394, 413.

Removes and Disgraces,
And something and nothing, the Devil and all.[9]

Old party labels became increasingly unhelpful. 'To determine the nature of these parties', wrote David Hume in 1741, 'is perhaps one of the most difficult problems that can be met with.'[10] His experience a few years later when he published the *History of England* bore out the point. Hume claimed to be impartial. But 'Lord Elibank says, that I am a moderate Whig, and Mr Wallace that I am a candid Tory'.[11] For good measure, Warburton thought Hume to be that rare monster 'an atheistical Jacobite'.[12] Who were the true Whigs, who the true Patriots? Where did the greater danger to the constitution lie, in the growth of executive power or the emergence of factions? If, as Polybius and the classical writers maintained, the constitution must, in the end, fall out of equilibrium, which way would it topple? Towards monarchy and despotism, or towards democracy and confusion? Hume believed that, in its final euthanasia, the constitution would expire into the arms of absolute monarchy: 'the tide has run long, and with some rapidity, to the side of popular government, and is just beginning to turn towards monarchy.'[13] If the choice was between that or a decline into republicanism, Hume preferred the former as 'the easier death'. Horace Walpole, a theoretical republican and advanced Whig, was in agreement that the balance would tip towards monarchy, though he deplored the fact and spent much of his life waiting for a royal *coup*.[14]

A third possibility was that the aristocracy would steal influence from Crown and Commons alike and achieve, not a balancing, but a preponderant influence in the constitution. This was the situation that existed in Poland, had developed in Sweden after the death of Charles XII, and was attempted in Russia in 1730 and again in 1740. Though there

---

[9] *London Journal* (6 Feb. 1731), in M. O. Percival (ed.), *Political Ballads Illustrating the Administration of Sir Robert Walpole* (Oxford, 1916), 48–9. The attribution to Hervey is probable.   [10] 'Of the Parties of Great Britain', in *Essays*, ix.

[11] Greig (ed.), *Letters of Hume*, i. 185.

[12] Quoted in E. C. Mossner, *The Life of David Hume* (Edinburgh, 1954), 309.

[13] 'Whether the British Government Inclines More to Absolute Monarchy or to a Republic', in *Essays*, vii.

[14] 'The legislature consists of the three branches of King, Lords and Commons. Together they form our invaluable constitution, and each is a check on the other two. But it must be remembered at the same time that while any two are checking, the third is naturally aiming at extending and aggrandizing its power. The House of Commons had not seldom made this attempt like the rest. The Lords, as a permanent and as a proud body, more constantly aim at it; the Crown always.' D. Le Marchant (ed.), *Memoirs of George III*, i. 322; see also A. F. Steuart (ed.), *Last Journals* (London, 1910), ii. 413.

was much mistrust of great lords among the Tory gentry, it was not until the development of Wilkite radicalism in the 1770s that this critique found coherent and sustained expression.

Whether party had a legitimate place in the constitution was a problem that exercised many minds. In the early Hanoverian period there were few advocates of party as such and considerable sympathy for Bolingbroke's vision of a non-party state under a patriot king—even if many found it ironical that Bolingbroke of all men should be the messenger. One of the strongest attacks upon party as a conspiracy against the rest of the nation came from David Hume:

> As much as legislators and founders of states ought to be honoured and respected among men, as much ought the founders of sects and factions to be detested and hated: because the influence of faction is directly contrary to that of laws. Factions subvert government, render laws impotent, and beget the fiercest animosities among men of the same nation, who ought to give mutual assistance and protection to each other. And what should render the founders of parties more odious is, the difficulty of extirpating these weeds, when once they have taken root in any state.[15]

So strongly did Hume feel that, in his plan for a perfect commonwealth, published in 1752, he proposed that any of the hundred senators found forming parties or groups should be at once expelled from the legislature.[16] Not until Burke's *Thoughts on the Cause of the Present Discontents*, published in 1770, did party begin to find principled and resolute defenders.[17]

Another issue which attracted attention was the effect that the growth of executive influence was having upon the balance of the constitution. That there had been a substantial expansion of the army, navy and administration could hardly be denied. The debate went back at least as far as the Act of Settlement in 1701, when the Tories had carried a clause forbidding all persons holding pensions or places of profit under the Crown from sitting in the House of Commons. Though the clause was considered impracticable and was soon modified, suspicion remained. Opposition newspapers frequently printed division lists, drawing atten-

---

[15] *Essays*, i. 127–8. [16] 'Idea of a Perfect Commonwealth', in *Political discourses*, xvi.

[17] 'Party is a body of men united, for promoting by their joint endeavours the national interest, upon some particular principle in which they are all agreed . . . Men thinking freely, will, in particular instances, think differently. But still, as the greater part of the measures which arise in the course of public business are related to, or dependent on, some great *leading general principles in government*, a man must be peculiarly unfortunate . . . if he does not agree with them nine times in ten.'

tion to the number of placemen in the government majority. Defenders of administration argued that some influence was necessary if government was to work at all: otherwise legislature and executive might clash without possibility of adjustment.

Part of the difficulty lay in deciding whether the influence was that of the Crown or of the ministers. If they were in agreement, it did not much matter, but at times of contention the question was critical. If the influence belonged to ministers, Commons and Crown were equally in danger of being suborned. Ministers and their friends were understandably touchy on the subject. In February 1734 Sir William Milner, a former Tory who had deserted to Walpole, complained to the House that he had been falsely accused of accepting a pension of £500 p.a. to vote for the government.[18] 'The reflecting upon members of this House', he expostulated, 'has been a common practice of late years, by the enemies of our constitution, to render His Majesty's government odious, to inflame the nation, and to lessen the dignity and authority of this House.' The Commons upheld his complaint and sent the offender into custody to learn prudence. But place bills and pension probes continued to be part of the stock-in-trade of eighteenth-century oppositions, since they demonstrated devotion to the constitution, while embarrassing and weakening the government.

In these issues, Johnson took a keen interest. Sir John Hawkins wrote of his profound reverence for and knowledge of the constitution.[19] In the 1740s he was in detailed discussion with Edward Cave about 'our historical design', which may have been a history of Parliament.[20] At a later period, among his many projects was a history of the Constitution.[21] Dr Wetherell, the Master of University College, Oxford, said that he would have given 100 guineas had Johnson written a constitutional commentary by way of a preface to the collected edition of the political pamphlets.[22] But, since none of these proposals saw the light of day, we are reduced to piecing together Johnson's views from a variety of sources.

It is true that on one occasion, in conversation with Sir Adam Fergusson, Johnson declared that he would not give half a guinea to live under one form of government rather than another. Macaulay berated Johnson for this and, indeed, it does seem the comfortable view of a man living in a decent society. But in his anxiety to score points, Macaulay

---

[18] *Parl. Hist.* ix. 392–3.   [19] Hawkins, 224.
[20] *Life*, i. 155. It is discussed by Kaminski, *Early Career of Johnson*, 184–7.
[21] Hawkins, 286.   [22] *Life*, ii. 441.

omitted to mention the rest of the conversation, which made it clear that Johnson was not in the least indifferent to, still less sympathetic towards, despotism. As though perceiving that he had not expressed himself very clearly, Johnson added:

When I say that all governments are alike, I consider that in no government, power can be abused long. Mankind will not bear it. If a sovereign oppresses his people to a great degree, they will rise and cut off his head. There is a remedy in human nature against tyranny, that will keep us safe under every form of government.[23]

Johnson's remark verges on complacency, though we should remember that the terrors of totalitarian rule were in the future. But it was certainly not the observation of a man disposed to tolerate despotism.[24]

The episode reminds us of three things: first, that Johnson had no interest at all in the old Tory doctrine of non-resistance—indeed, he is the last man one would expect to lie down under oppression. Secondly, there is the characteristic distaste for elaborate theory. The appeal to nature might suggest that Johnson was a believer in natural law, and there has been a learned controversy on the subject.[25] But Johnson's remark seems to me to signify a lack of confidence on his part in the ability of men to lay down precise rules and principles when resistance becomes permissible. His approach is consequently robust pragmatism. Thirdly, in the course of the conversation Johnson exclaimed to Sir Adam, 'Sir, I perceive you are a vile Whig'. This has often been regarded as an intemperate outburst. The circumstances make that rather unlikely. He had just met Fergusson, a well-connected Scottish baronet, in a public place. The tone is more likely to be one of jocular extravagance.

This dislike of theory is evident in Johnson's approach to the question of the origins of civil society. He rejected the doctrines of Right and Left in favour of a rather matter-of-fact pragmatism. We have seen his opinion that the divine right of kings was 'all stuff',[26] and he showed no interest in

---

[23] Ibid. 170. Pope put much the same point in the famous couplet in the *Essay on Man*: 'For forms of government let fools contest, Whatever's best administered is best.' Pope was also denounced for not declaring a preference for liberty. He was forced to explain that he had followed Aristotle in believing that what really mattered was results, and that no form of government, *in itself*, could succeed, unless characterized by virtue.

[24] In *Sermons*, no. 24, Johnson observed that, since all government was by the few over the many, 'it is apparent that nations cannot be governed but by their own consent'. He was here following what Hume had said in *Of the First Principles of Government*.

[25] D. J. Greene, 'Samuel Johnson and "Natural law"', *Journal of British Studies*, ii/I(May 1963) 59–75; riposte by P. J. Stanlis and further comment by Greene, ibid. 76–87; F. Oakley, 'Greene and Stanlis on Dr. Johnson and the Natural Law: A Medieval Postscript', *ibid.* iv/I (Nov. 1964), 1–5.   [26] See ch. 2, n. 80.

tracing authority either to religion or to the family. On the other hand, he repudiated the Whig doctrine of a formal social contract. Consequently, his explanation was one of almost pure historical description: the first authority must have constituted itself.[27] Men joined together in civil society for utilitarian ends, to promote peace and justice, and to co-operate in social advancement. 'I think that every people have the right to establish such government as they may think conducive to their interest and happiness,' he told Cooper.[28]

Johnson's well-known concern for order and stability and his evident worry about civil war has led some writers to equate his views with those of Hobbes, whose argument was that men formed governments in order to escape from the terrors of the state of nature.[29] But Johnson was by no means as fearful as Hobbes, nor as gloomy about the nature of men. His concept of government was not purely defensive but contained positive and ameliorative elements. The sources of this attitude were, no doubt, many and complex, but Hooker and Grotius took a similar view, and it was not dissimilar to the attitude of Richard Cumberland, known as the founder of utilitarianism, whose work Johnson knew and commended. Whether Johnson's practice of compassion towards unfortunates derived from his theory, or his theory from his practice, is a nice question, but he placed great emphasis on sociability, in both public and private life. In *Sermons*, no. 24, he declared that government was necessary 'to the safety of particular men and the happiness of society', and in *Rambler*, no. 99, he remarked that man had 'a general tendency to congenial nature' and that he tried to 'improve the condition of his existence, by superadding friendship to humanity, and the love of individuals to that of the species'.[30]

It followed that, if there was no contract to be broken on either side, nor any divine authority to dictate obedience, the problem of when subjects had a right to resist was empirical. Johnson treated it as such. The remarks to Sir Adam Fergusson were no isolated outburst. They repeat very closely a discussion on the same subject which Johnson had

---

[27] 'The first laws had no laws to enforce them: the first authority was constituted by itself.' *Works* (1787 edn.), x. 8, quoted in Greene, *The Politics of Samuel Johnson*, 206.

[28] See Ch. 2, n. 80. Hawkins, 223, suggested that Johnson derived his views from Richard Hooker, as expounded by Hoadly, the hero of the Bangorian controversy. If this was so, it was a distinctly Whiggish pedigree.

[29] Greene, *The Politics of Samuel Johnson*, 246, commented on by P. J. Stanlis in *Journal of British Studies*, ii/2 (May 1963), 79–83.

[30] For comment on Johnson's utilitarianism, see R. Voitle, *Samuel Johnson the Moralist* (Cambridge, Mass., 1961), ch. 4; P. K. Alkon, *Samuel Johnson and Moral Discipline* (Evanston Ill., 1967).

with Goldsmith ten years earlier. 'If the abuse be enormous,' Johnson remarked, 'Nature will rise up, and claiming her original rights, overturn a corrupt political system.'[31]

Johnson seems less concerned that he might have opened a gate to permanent revolution than one might have expected from his zeal for subordination. He seems to follow Locke's argument in repudiating the accusation that no stable government could be erected on so loose a footing:

Lawful and settled authority is very seldom resisted when it is well employed . . . Men are easily kept obedient to those who have temporal dominion in their hands, till their veneration is dissipated by such wickedness and folly as can neither be defended nor concealed.[32]

This rather low-keyed secular approach meant that Johnson did not get very excited about the revolution of 1688. He certainly did not regard it as either treason or sacrilege, as a Jacobite or a non-juror would have done, but noted merely that 'the necessity of self-preservation impelled the subjects of James II to drive him from the throne'.[33] On a subsequent occasion he remarked that, though necessary, the Revolution 'broke our constitution'.[34] He may merely have meant that it destroyed the balance of the constitution by weakening the Crown unduly, though 'broke' is a powerful word, or he may have meant that lawful authority disappeared in 1688 and a new self-validating regime had to be established—in which case, he was once more close to a historical paraphrase of what had actually happened in 1688 and 1689.

Johnson was no more anxious than Locke or any other gentleman of education or property to see 1688 taken as a signal by the lower orders that resistance was permissible, and he insisted that the obligation to obey the law was not removed if governments made mistakes or judges fell into error. The fallibility of human beings meant that even the best government would sometimes make errors. He followed the view of Cumberland that perfect security could never be obtained under any human government.[35] Imlac presumably represented Johnson's own opinions when he commented in *The History of Rasselas*:

No form of government has been yet discovered by which cruelty can be wholly prevented. Subordination supposes power on one part and subjection on the

---

[31] *Life*, i. 424.   [32] *Rambler*, no. 50.
[33] *An Introduction of the Political State of Great Britain*; *Life*, ii. 341.
[34] *Life*, iv. 170
[35] *A Philosophical Enquiry into the Laws of Nature* (Dublin, 1750), 83.

other; and if power be in the hands of men, it will sometimes be abused. The vigilance of the supreme magistrate may do much, but much will still remain undone.[36]

Injustice may sometimes have to be borne and the innocent suffer. In the summer of 1775 Boswell sought Johnson's advice on a legal case turning on corrupt practices by certain of the burgesses of the corporation of Stirling. Johnson's reply ran wider than the burgh:

The objection, in which is urged the injustice of making the innocent suffer with the guilty, is an objection not only against society, but against the possibility of society. All societies, great and small, subsist upon this condition; that as the individuals derive advantages from union, they may likewise suffer inconveniences.[37]

At this point, one may feel some impatience with Johnson. But there is no rule to tell us when oppression has become intolerable nor will any two individuals necessarily agree. Johnson developed the point in his review of Soame Jenyns's *Free Inquiry*. Though there was much in that volume to which he took exception, Johnson agreed with Jenyns that evils could never be totally eliminated. Wise men would do their best to minimize them, 'but the question, upon which all dissension arises, is when that excess begins, at what point men shall cease to bear, and attempt to remedy'. Though in his later writings he placed stress on authority, nowhere did Johnson show any disposition to applaud arbitrary government.[38]

A remarkable example of Johnson's belief in limited government comes from his early play *Irene*, set in the Ottoman empire. It may be that the exigencies of the plot demanded some explicit denunciation of arbitrary rule, but Johnson's treatment seems somewhat intrusive. In the first draft of the play, on which he was working in the later 1730s, the Sultan's Grand Vizier, Cali, steps forward and confides to the audience that he is an admirer of constitutional government. The stage directions read:

He launches into the misery of absolute governments . . . then breaks out into the praises of that country, (after having blamed the Eastern tyranny), which he has heard of in the North.

---

[36] *The History of Rasselas, Prince of Abissinia*, ed. R. W. Chapman (Oxford, 1972), ch. 8.
[37] *Life*, ii. 373–4.
[38] Ibid. 118. Dr Maxwell wrote that to charge Johnson with arbitrary principles was a gross calumny and misrepresentation. See also *Sermons*, no. 24, in which Johnson declared that 'established property and inviolable freedom are the greatest of political felicities'.

> Where King and People own one common law,
> One common interest, mutual duties
> And feel one happiness and one misfortune.[39]

The finished text read:

> Such are the Woes when arbitrary Pow'r,
> And lawless Passion, hold the Sword of Justice.
> If there be any Land, as Fame reports,
> Where common Laws restrain the Prince and Subject
> A happy land, where circulating Pow'r
> Flows through each Member of th'embodied State
> Sure, not unconscious of the mighty Blessing,
> Her grateful Sons shine bright with ev'ry Virtue . . .

Cali's strange speech has been variously interpreted, as a statement of the Tory vision of society or as an underhand attack upon Sir Robert Walpole as an arbitrary minister.[40] It seems to me to be no more than a generalized statement of the advantages of the rule of law, such as might occur to any Hanoverian gentleman, though perhaps surprisingly progressive for a fifteenth-century Turk. By the time it was performed at Drury Lane in 1749 *Irene* had lost any topical allusion it ever possessed and the epilogue was provided by Sir William Yonge, who had been one of Walpole's most loyal followers.[41]

Even in his later years, when he had drifted into a more authoritarian position, Johnson showed no sympathy for absolutist government. In a conversation of April 1775 he showed his usual preciseness in identifying one of the ineradicable defects of autocratic rule. To a gentleman who offered the opinion that, had Charles II become absolute, 'it would have done no harm', Johnson offered the mild rebuke:

Absolute princes seldom do any harm. But they who are governed by them are governed by chance. There is no security for good government.[42]

Johnson's acceptance of the revolutionary settlement in principle did not prevent him from having reservations in detail. Time had not stood still.

---

[39] D. Nichol Smith and E. L. MacAdam, Jr. (eds.), *The Poems of Samuel Johnson*, 2nd edn. (Oxford, 1974), 382.

[40] Smith and MacAdam (eds.), *Poems* 290; B. H. Bronson, 'Johnson's Irene', in *Johnson Agonistes and Other Essays* (Cambridge, 1946), 141.

[41] In its review, the *Gentleman's Magazine* (1749), 79, quoted the passage beginning 'If there be any land . . .'.

[42] *Life*, ii. 370.

When Johnson went up to Oxford, that settlement was forty years in the past. Johnson came to the conclusion that the powers of the Crown had been substantially curtailed in 1689 and had declined further subsequently.

First there were the limitations placed upon the Crown by the financial and constitutional settlement itself. The acceptance of the Declaration of Rights, subsequently given statute form, together with the changes in the coronation oath came close to making the choice of monarch a formal contract, based upon a written constitution. The revised coronation oath (1 William and Mary c. 6) sought to remove 'doubtful words and expressions' and impose 'one uniform oath'. Monarchs were to swear in future to rule 'according to the statutes in Parliament agreed on'· and to preserve 'the protestant reformed religion established by law'. When George III and George IV protested that their coronation oath did not permit them to accept Catholic emancipation, they were not merely making use of a debating ploy. A further limitation on the freedom of action of the monarch was a financial settlement in 1689 which was deliberately ungenerous.[43]

A number of historians have argued that the restrictions placed upon the Crown in 1689 were marginal,[44] and it is true that, in the choice of ministers, the granting of honours, the power of dissolution, and the right of veto, the Crown retained important weapons. But in a continental context, the limitations do not look insubstantial. The Augsburg confession of 1555 had given rulers the power to dictate the religion of their subjects; in the Bill of Rights, subjects dictated to their rulers. The Habsburgs would not have regarded the change as of little consequence. Nor would the clause forbidding the existence of a standing army in peacetime without the consent of Parliament have seemed trifling to the Hohenzollerns, who used their army to suppress parliamentary and aristocratic opposition. One wonders why William III soon contemplated abdication if the limitations on his power were so slight.

Further restrictions were imposed by the Triennial Act of 1694, which William had tried to veto, and by the Act of Settlement of 1701.[45] The

---

[43] J. Cannon and R. Griffiths, *Oxford Illustrated History of the British Monarchy* (Oxford, 1988), 431–3.

[44] For a convenient summary of recent historiography, see L. G. Schwoerer (ed.), *The Revolution of 1688–1689: Changing Perspectives* (Cambridge, 1992), 'Introduction'.

[45] The restrictions imposed by the Act of Settlement were largely Tory devices to hamper the Hanoverians. Many of them were removed by the Whigs before they came into effect. They included provisions that the monarch should not leave the realm without parliamentary consent; that advice given in the Privy Council should be signed; that no person born

need to deal with an annual Parliament imposed its own limitations on the monarch's choice of ministers: they must be able to command a parliamentary majority and to put on some kind of parliamentary performance.[46] Perhaps most of all, the Crown and its ministers had to come to terms with the growth of an informed public opinion, to which Johnson paid frequent tribute.

The increase in royal power which Johnson advocated was a reassertion within the confines of a balanced constitution. There is little evidence of a 'servile attitude towards monarchy and the established order' or of Johnson placing his faith in an 'absolute monarch'.[47] But his mistrust of party and his concern lest freedom of speech and protest should get out of control induced him to lean towards royal authority. This tendency was reinforced as he grew older by the Wilkite and American agitations, in the course of which public criticism of the monarch reached unprecedented heights,[48] and no doubt by his own pension and by the gratifying audience he had with George III in February 1767. 'I find it does a man good to be talked to by his sovereign,' Johnson told his friends.[49]

Though he is frequently described as an ardent royalist, Johnson's statements on the subject are neither as frequent nor as fervent as that term might imply. We have already seen that he was not a believer in divine right and possessed little religious awe towards the Crown. Until 1760 he may have been restrained by Tory reserve towards George II. It is true that, in his encounter at the Pantheon with Sir Adam Fergusson on 31 March 1772, he spoke emphatically in support of the monarchy: 'why all this childish jealousy of the power of the crown? The crown has not power enough.'[50] But the context of the conversation makes it clear that it was concerned with preserving the balance of the constitution.

outside the Kingdom could serve in Parliament or the Privy Council; that no person holding a place of profit under the Crown could serve in Parliament; that judges should hold office *quamdium se bene gesserint*; that royal pardons could not be granted against impeachment proceedings.

[46] Court favour was no longer enough. In seventeenth-century conditions, there seems no reason why Spencer Compton, the favourite of George II, or Lord Bute, the favourite of George III, could not have been enduring ministers.

[47] The phrases are used by J. L. Clifford, 'A Survey of Johnsonian Studies, 1887–1950', in D. J. Greene (ed.), *Samuel Johnson: A Collection of Critical Essays* (New Jersey, 1965).

[48] Horace Walpole described Junius's letter to the king, pub. Dec. 1769, as 'the most daring insult ever offered to a prince but in times of open rebellion'. Tom Paine in *Commonsense* (1776) referred to George III as 'the royal brute' and included a sharp attack upon 'crowned ruffians'.

[49] *Life*, ii. 42.

[50] Ibid. 170. Johnson seems to have been provoked by Fergusson in this meeting and Boswell commented that Sir Adam was 'unlucky in his topics'. But Johnson repeated the

Johnson acknowledged that this balance might be threatened from any side. In his life of Addison, written in 1779, he offered a neat example of all three parts committing aggression in turn. He disapproved of the use made of the royal prerogative in 1712 to create twelve peers and override the House of Lords, an act of 'violent authority'; he condemned the Commons for the Septennial Act, whereby a House 'chosen by the people for three years, chose themselves for seven'; and he thought the Peerage Bill of 1719 an attempt to create a 'despotic and irresistible aristocracy'. Noting that in the pamphlet warfare on the Peerage Bill, which grew acrimonious, Addison and Steele took opposite sides, Johnson sounded, for almost the last time, one of the great chords from 'The Vanity of Human Wishes': 'Among the uncertainties of the human state, we are doomed to number the instability of friendship.'

For much of the time, Johnson's attitude to the constitution seems to have been relaxed, if not positively laconic. In *Rambler*, no. 50, far from defending the old order, he remarked benignly that all elderly people feel that respect is on the slide and authority in danger:

Every old man complains of the growing depravity of the world, of the petulance and insolence of the rising generation. He recounts the decency and regularity of former times, and celebrates the discipline and sobriety of the age in which his youth was passed; a happy age, which is now no more to be expected, since confusion has broken in upon the world, and thrown down all the boundaries of civility and reverence.

On another occasion, he observed philosophically that people say what suits them:

the power of the crown is always thought too great by those who suffer by its influence, and too little by those in whose favour it is exerted; and a standing army is generally accounted necessary by those who command it, and dangerous and oppressive by those who support it.[51]

Towards the end of his life Boswell asked him whether he had not been extremely indignant when the Commons in April 1780 had voted that the influence of the Crown had increased, was increasing, and ought to be diminished. Not a bit, Johnson replied: 'Sir, I have never slept an hour

opinion while on tour in the Hebrides, telling Boswell that 'our great fear is from want to power in government. Such a storm of vulgar force has broke in . . . '. *Tour*, 37.

[51] Quoted in Krutch, *Samuel Johnson*, 77.

less, nor eat an ounce less meat. I would have knocked the factious dogs on the head, to be sure; but I was not vexed.'[52]

Reverence, even for authority, did not come easily to Johnson and in his writings he peppered kingship and individual monarchs with unflattering and disparaging remarks. In his early work *Marmor Norfolciense* Johnson implies that kings rarely approach their subjects save to demand money from them. In 1740, in the *Life of Barretier*, he remarks that kings are the last to perceive merit. In his review of *Memoirs of Frederick the Great* in 1756 he explains that kings normally 'see the world in a mist'. They have, like the rest of us, to take their chance as to whether they are intelligent: 'princes draw with meaner mortals the lot of understanding'. They find it unusually difficult to practise moderation in prosperity: 'forbearance of revenge when it is within reach is scarcely ever to be found among princes.' Kings, he told his readers the following year, rarely know what is happening: 'it is a misfortune of a king that he seldom, but in cases of public calamity, knows the sentiments of his people.' Individual monarchs are tossed just as boldly. Of James I he remarked that, since 'the ready way to gain king James' favour was to flatter his speculations', aspiring courtiers found vast merit in his writings. Charles II, 'by his affability and politeness, made himself the idol of the nation, which he betrayed and sold'; William III was 'one of the most worthless scoundrels that ever existed'; George I 'knew nothing and desired to know nothing'; George II he treated 'with prodigious violence'. Of the young George III Johnson wrote patronizingly to Baretti in June 1761: 'the young man is hitherto blameless; but it would be unreasonable to expect much from the immaturity of juvenile years, and the ignorance of princely education.' Johnson's views may be perverse, brutal, or ill-informed; they are scarcely servile.[53]

A sustained and coherent statement of the pro-royal case in the 1760s comes from Oliver Goldsmith, and, though it would be wrong to try to infer Johnson's views from somebody else's writings, it is clear that the two men were much closer than Boswell's *Life of Johnson* suggests. To Boswell, Goldsmith was largely a figure of fun—a buffoon and a butt. To Johnson, he was 'a very great man'. *The Traveller* was 'a very fine performance' and Johnson read it with tears in his eyes. *The Deserted*

---

[52] *Life*, iv. 220–1. 'Factious dogs' was perhaps a picturesque embellishment by Boswell: in his notebook he wrote, merely, 'knock 'em on the head'.

[53] *An Introduction to the Political State of Great Britain; An Essay on An Account of the Conduct of the Duchess of Marlborough; Life*, ii. 342; *Letters*, ed. Redford, i. 196–201. These sentiments, particularly towards William III, seem at variance with opinions expressed by Johnson elsewhere.

Village was 'first-class'. Johnson contributed a number of lines to each poem. He was responsible for the publication of *The Vicar of Wakefield*, finding Goldsmith destitute with a half-finished manuscript. Johnson wrote the prologue for the play *The Good Natured Man*, and Goldsmith dedicated *She Stoops to Conquer* to him. Goldsmith was a founder member of the Club and Johnson wrote the Latin epitaph for his tomb in Westminster Abbey.

Goldsmith's *The Traveller* came out in 1764, though he had been working on it, off and on, for ten years. In the preface, addressed to his brother Henry, Goldsmith went out of his way to launch an attack upon party, which 'entirely distorts the judgement, and destroys the taste'. When the Traveller returns from his European tour, he finds his native land in the grip of a struggle between an arrogant aristocracy and their only effective adversary, the Crown:

> But when contending chiefs blockade the throne,
> Contracting regal power to stretch their own,
> When I behold a factious band agree
> To call it freedom, when themselves are free;
> Each wanton judge new penal statutes draw,
> Law grinds the poor, and rich men rule the law . . .
> Fear, pity, justice, indignation start,
> Tear off reserve, and bare my swelling heart;
> Till half a patriot, half a coward grown,
> I fly from petty tyrants to the throne.

Goldsmith continued his criticism of the aristocracy in his article 'The Revolution in Low Life', which appeared in *Lloyd's Evening Post*, 14–16 June 1762. It relates a visit to a village in which there is a society divided between the 'immensely rich and miserably poor'. This was also the theme of Goldsmith's best-known poem *The Deserted Village*, which came out in 1770.

The most elaborate exposition is in chapter 19 of Goldsmith's *Vicar of Wakefield*, and is scarcely demanded by the exigencies of the story.[54] The Vicar is invited to a country house by a 'well-dressed gentleman', who turns out to be the butler, playing up while his master is away. Before the butler is unmasked, a political dialogue takes place, or rather a political diatribe, since the butler hardly gets a word in sideways. The butler soon

---

[54] It may have been required more by the exigencies of the author, since Johnson seems to have found the novel finished up to ch. 17. If it had to be padded out, all was grist to Goldsmith's mill. See J. Ginger, *The Notable Man: The Life and Times of Oliver Goldsmith* (London, 1977), app.

identifies himself as a liberty man.[55] The Vicar's retort takes a mere thousand words:

The generality of mankind are of my way of thinking, and have unanimously created one king, whose election at once diminishes the number of tyrants, and puts tyranny at the greatest distance from the greatest number of people . . . I am then for, and would die for, monarchy, sacred monarchy . . . and every diminution of his power in war, or in peace, is an infringement upon the real liberties of the subject.

It is an argument which, I think, Johnson would have endorsed.

We are not required to share Johnson's views, but merely to note two things: first, that they were by no means extreme or unusual at that period, and secondly that historical scholarship has tended to confirm that he was correct in his assessment of what was happening to the Hanoverian constitution. The proposition that there was a remarkable reassertion of royal power in the 1760s has long been abandoned, and explained largely as the invention of Horace Walpole and Edmund Burke. Dunning's motion that the influence of the Crown was increasing was as inaccurate as it was elegant. The growing complexity of public business, the rise of party, the shrinking of royal finances, and the rise of an educated public all helped to undermine the Crown's position. Of the three component parts which contemporaries identified as maintaining the balance of the constitution, the first to collapse was the Crown, in the early nineteenth century. The aristocratic part, by a series of concessions and manœuvres, maintained its influence, though a diminishing one, into the early twentieth century. The popular element triumphed, in the end, in the form of parliamentary democracy. Euthanasia did not deliver up the constitution to the Crown but to the people. David Hume was wrong and Samuel Johnson right.

The most considered commentary by Johnson on the law and the constitution is subject to severe methodological difficulties. In 1766 he was asked by his younger friend, Robert Chambers, for help in preparing the Vinerian lectures at Oxford, which were to follow Blackstone's initial and extremely distinguished lecture course. Chambers was, not unnaturally, diffident, and, in addition, was liable to be fined by the University for non-delivery. There is no doubt that Johnson's collaboration was

---

[55] ' "Can it be possible," cried our entertainer, "that there should be any found at present advocates for slavery? Any who are for meanly giving up the privileges of Britons? Can any, Sir, be so abject?" '

substantial, and Mrs Thrale even included the Vinerian lectures among Johnson's works.[56] Johnson paid at least six visits to Oxford between 1766 and 1769 to assist Chambers and it is clear from his letters that they worked side by side: 'come up to town', wrote Johnson in 1766, 'and lock yourself up from all but me, and I doubt not but lectures will be produced. You must not miss another term.'[57]

E. L. MacAdam, who first drew attention to the collaboration, maintains that one can distinguish Johnson's contribution on the basis of style.[58] This is always a precarious undertaking and Thomas Curley has shown that Chambers's prose can sound, in its more florid moments, much like Johnson's.[59] One cannot with certitude say what Johnson's contribution was. But it seems reasonable enough to presume that Chambers would not have asked Johnson for help had they not seen eye to eye on most legal and constitutional questions. The lectures cannot however be used to infer Johnson's opinions, unless they are strongly supported by evidence from elsewhere.

But, while clearing up one difficulty, Curley may have introduced another. He suggests that the tone of Chambers's Vinerian lectures was significantly more authoritarian than that of his predecessor Blackstone, and that this may perhaps be traced to Johnson's influence.[60] In Chambers, Curley argues, we see 'the sweeping disavowal of a Whig interpretation'. However, Curley offers little evidence that Blackstone's interpretation was Whiggish and, indeed, the suggestion would greatly have surprised Blackstone himself. His pedigree was thoroughly Tory. He was turned down by Newcastle for the Regius Chair at Oxford in 1752 because he was not prepared to give assurances about his political conduct.[61] He then resolved to give his own course of lectures at Oxford and began in 1753 the programme on which the *Commentaries* were based.

---

[56] *Thraliana* i. 204. The collaboration is not as strange as it may sound. Boswell consulted Johnson on a number of legal cases in which he was involved, and Johnson often dictated or sent lengthy and informed answers.

[57] *Letters*, ed. Redford, i. 276–7.

[58] *Dr. Johnson and the English Law* (Syracuse, NY, 1951).

[59] Thomas M. Curley, 'Johnson's Secret Collaboration', in J. J. Burke, Jr., and Donald Kay (eds.) *The Unknown Samuel Johnson* (Madison Wis., 1983). See also T. M. Curley, 'Johnson, Chambers and the Law', in Korshin (ed.), *Johnson After Two Hundred Years*. For the complete Chambers lectures, see *A Course of Lectures*.

[60] Curley refers to the 'pronounced conservatism' of the lectures, emphasizing 'law and order rather than liberty'. In the introduction to *A Course of Lectures*, i. 31, he adds that 'Blackstone had undoubtedly espoused a Whig reading of the national constitution'.

[61] J. Holliday, *Life of Mansfield*, 88–9, quoted in W. R. Ward, *Georgian Oxford* (Oxford, 1958), 197.

He was regarded as a bastion of Oxford Toryism, worked as an organizer for the Tory interest in the famous Oxfordshire election of 1754, and represented the Tory candidates before the House of Commons when they petitioned. Returned to the House of Commons in 1761, he was marked 'Tory' on Newcastle's list, and during his nine years in Parliament he made his mark by his defence of authority in both the Wilkes and the American questions. It is true that in the *Commentaries* he advocated a reform of Parliament, but that, as we have seen, was a very standard part of the Tory programme.[62]

Far from standing forth as an advocate of change, Blackstone was regarded as an almost unredeemed supporter of the status quo. 'Everything-as-it-should-be Blackstone' was the jibe of the young Jeremy Bentham, who had been a member of his audience.[63] Holdsworth, while defending Blackstone, admitted that there was truth in the charge that he was 'an indiscriminating apologist for all things established' and the *Dictionary of National Biography* described him as 'conservative almost to rigidity'.[64] He was certainly proud of the English constitution and the praise which it had attracted, but that had long ceased to be a specifically Whig attitude. His observation that the laws of England were so gentle and moderate 'that no man of sense or probity would wish to see them slackened' may be contrasted with Johnson's opinion on the same subject.[65]

Nor can the suggestion that Chambers's lectures were Tory in character be wholly accepted. Indeed, Curley's own description of the tenor of the lecture course makes it sound distinctly Whiggish in flavour: 'according to the *Lectures*, history is fundamentally a story of human progress generated by the pursuit of individual happiness in the course of mankind's pilgrimage to attain spiritual fulfilment.'[66]

In sections of Lecture 5, which MacAdam believes can safely be attributed to Johnson, there were warnings against elaborate intellectual systems and against attempting to trace the principles of the constitution too far back into the past. They undoubtedly sound Johnsonian in the vivacity of exposition and the bluntness of the approach:

---

[62] *House of Commons, 1754–90*, ii. 76.

[63] *The Book of Fallacies*, in J. Bowring (ed.), *The Works of Jeremy Bentham* (New York, 1962), ii. 443.

[64] W. Holdsworth, *A History of English Law*, (7th. edn., London, 1923–72) xii. 727; G. P. Moriarty, in *DNB*.

[65] *Commentaries on the Laws of England*, bk. I, ch. 1, sect. 144.

[66] *A Course of Lectures*, i. 35.

Our political historians too often forget the state of the age they are endeavouring to describe—an age of tyranny, darkness and violence, in which perhaps few of the barons, to whom the contrivance of this wonderful system of government is ascribed, were able to sign their names to their own treaties, and in which there-fore there could be little foresight of the future because there was little knowledge of the past. When they thought themselves oppressed by the regal power, they endeavoured to set themselves free as a horse unbroken shakes off his rider; but when they had obtained a present relief, they went back to their castles and their tenants and contrived little for themselves and nothing for posterity.[67]

Curley points out that Chambers placed little emphasis on Magna Carta by comparison with Blackstone. First, we should note that Blackstone was editing Magna Carta for Clarendon Press while preparing his lectures, so it is hardly surprising if it was in the forefront of his mind. But Hawkins confirmed that Johnson gave little weight to Magna Carta, looking upon later concessions such as the Petition of Right, Habeas Corpus Act, and the Bill of Rights as of greater importance.[68] The lack of emphasis on Magna Carta was neither inadvertence nor authoritarianism, but an indication of the greater historical sense which commentators have praised in the Chambers lectures.[69]

In Curley's view, the two outstanding features of Chambers's lectures were, first, an insistence on the need for some governing authority and on the view that the first law must base itself on its own authority; and, secondly, the requirement that parliamentary sovereignty must be absolute, since any power which could limit it must itself be the supreme power. Each proposition is close to Johnson's position, particularly as expounded in *Taxation No Tyranny*, when Johnson may have been working from reminiscences or even notes of Chambers's lectures. As we saw in Chapter 3 this was not, in the context of the period, an authori-tarian attitude, since the emphasis on parliamentary supremacy enabled supporters of the American war to maintain that their position was essentially a Whiggish one.

In other respects, Chambers and Johnson seem independently to agree. In his first lecture, Chambers dealt with the objectives of civil government:

---

[67] *A Course of Lectures*; 133–4. The argument that resistance was scarcely principled but an empirical matter sounds similar to the argument expressed on p. 130. The phrase 'this wonderful system of government' is more like the irony of an established writer in his late fifties than a nervous and inexperienced lawyer of 29.

[68] Hawkins, 224.

[69] Rupert Cross, 'The First Two Vinerian Professors: Blackstone and Chambers', *William and Mary Law Review*, 20 (1979).

But by whatever means political bodies were first *framed*, they are clearly *supported* by these two foundations: 1. a desire of social life, to which both reason and instinct (if I may be allowed the expression), incline men; and 2. a certain rule of obedience established in every state, to which every member of it chooses rather silently to submit, than to exchange the protection and pleasures of society, for the solitude and horrors of a desert.[70]

This was very much a reminiscence of Hooker, one of Johnson's favourite authors.[71]

In his third lecture, 'The King and the Coronation Oath', Chambers dismissed the religious origins of kingship so dispassionately as to suggest scepticism:

While men are gross and ignorant, unskilled in the arts of reasoning, and enjoying few opportunities of information and instruction, they are much influenced by unusual and splendid ceremonies . . . Nations as well as individuals have their childhood, and the mind, unformed by reflection and unoccupied by knowledge, must receive its whole intelligence immediately from the senses. When coronations were first contrived they were probably of great use. As they procured veneration to the person of the king, they at least *confirmed* his authority though they did not *give* it . . . In that age of prejudice and ignorance, . . . it was necessary to invest the king with something of a sacred character, that might secure obedience by reverence, and more effectively preserve his person from danger of violation. For this reason it was necessary to interpose the clerical authority, that the crown being imposed by a holy hand might communicate some sanctity to him that wore it.[72]

MacAdam is convinced that the passage was 'almost wholly' by Johnson. It may be so, though it seems remarkably secular, even for him. But we should remember that Johnson had joined in a piece on the coronation of 1761 and it would seem probable that this was one of Chambers's themes to which he felt able to contribute.[73]

A passage which may strike readers as characteristically Johnsonian is on 'Civil Rank, Order and Precedence', delivered as Lecture 12. It was probably given in early April 1767, and we know that Johnson was staying with Chambers at New Inn Hall from March until 9 April, when he wrote in his diary 'returned from helping Chambers at Oxford'. It was a subject

[70] *A Course of Lectures*, i. 88.
[71] *Of the Laws of Ecclesiastical Polity*, bk. I, ch. 10: 'Two foundations there are which bear up public societies: the one, a natural inclination, whereby all men desire sociable life and fellowship; the other, an order expressly or secretly agreed upon touching the manner of their union in living together.' [72] *A Course of Lectures*, i. 153–4.
[73] 'Thoughts on the Coronation of George III', in Greene (ed.), *Political Writings* 290–300.

dear to Johnson's heart, and well suited to his assistance, since it did not necessitate specialist legal knowledge. In places, it reads not unlike a *Rambler* essay:

Political society is that state of man in which some govern and others are governed; it therefore necessarily implies subordination, and ranks those of which it is composed in different degrees . . . As experience immediately shows that but a very small number of any society are qualified to regulate manners or supervise the interest of the rest, and that these qualifications must be the effect of study and inquiry not easily made consistent with manual labour or the constant solicitudes of husbandry or trade, almost every civilised nation has distributed its inhabitants into different orders and, by conferring established precedence and hereditary honours, has in some sense designated from the birth a certain number to public cares and liberal employments.[74]

The lecturer presumed that the obligation to govern must be hereditary since there would otherwise be a constant struggle for supremacy, and he was in no way abashed by the assumption that this must, in the end, mean entrusting the state to wealth:

Riches long continued in a family constitute a kind of nobility without any positive designation, and where the rank of nobles is established by an edict of the sovereign authority, riches have always been considered as a motive to preference. Of all kinds of superiority that of riches is most notorious and least disputable . . . Wealth is the only superiority than can be successively transmitted. The son of a rich man will be rich, but the son of a wise man will not always be wise. Wealth is therefore perhaps the only ground of hereditary greatness.[75]

In the last twenty years of Johnson's life there arose an agitation for reform of Parliament which, in both extent and intention, went a good deal further than anything previously seen. The object of most earlier reform proposals had been to adjust the balance of the constitution, bringing it back to some real or imagined norm. Pressure from the Tories for the exclusion of placemen had been designed to strengthen the legislature against the growth of executive influence, while their dislike of rotten boroughs, admiration for the county representation, and concern for more effective laws against bribery were all intended to support the landed against the moneyed interest.

That strand of reform continued, especially in the shape of economical reform, taken up by the Rockingham Whigs in the 1770s. But arising from the Wilkite and American agitations came suggestions of a far more

---

[74] *A course of Lectures*, i. 249.   [75] Ibid.

fundamental character, many of which challenged the very concept of a balanced constitution.

The limits of Tory reform can be gauged from the little flurry of success which it had in the closing years of George II's reign. In exchange for their support for his war measures, Pitt allowed the Tories a few concessions. They were sore that the great Oxfordshire election had been decided against them on the grounds that copyholders were eligible to vote in shire contests. In the spring of 1758 they were permitted to reverse that decision and, by the terms of the Freeholders Act, copyholders were disqualified.[76] This meant a considerable reduction in the electorate in some counties. A second success followed in early 1760, when a measure to tighten up the property qualification for members of Parliament went through.[77] The committee appointed in January 1760 to prepare the bill reads like a roll-call of the Tory party.[78] The duke of Newcastle, guardian of the Whig conscience, was said to have been 'very averse but forced to swallow it . . . , as Pitt insisted that something must be done to gratify the Tories'.[79] But on a third measure the Tories overplayed their hand. In February 1758 Sir John Glynne moved to repeal the Septennial Act and bring in shorter Parliaments. This was more serious stuff and he was defeated by 74 votes to 190. Lord Chesterfield dismissed it as 'a little popular squib'.[80]

Not many country gentlemen, of whatever persuasion, would relish the more radical proposals coming up in the 1760s and 1770s. John

---

[76] 31 George II c. 14.

[77] The original Act had of course been one of the high-water Tory successes after their election victory in 1710 and was intended to retain the House of Commons as a preserve for country gentlemen. By 33 George II c. 20 a signed schedule and an oath were required.

[78] Sir John Philipps (Petersfield), William Beckford (London), Thomas Staunton (Ipswich), William Cartwright (Northants), Sir Thomas Palmer (Leicestershire), Sir John Morgan (Herefordshire), Sir Richard Glyn (London), Robert Vyner (Lincolnshire), Sir Robert Long (Wiltshire), Richard Lowndes (Bucks.), Edward Kynaston (Montgomeryshire), Richard Lyster (Salop), William Craven (Warwickshire), Henry Pye (Berkshire), Thomas Foley (Droitwich), Rowland Holt (Suffolk), Charles Barrow (Gloucester), William Grove (Coventry), William Drake (Amersham), Isaac Whittington (Amersham), Edward Smith (Leicestershire), Sir John Hynde Cotton (Marlborough), Sir Robert Burdett (Tamworth), Sir Thomas Stapleton (Oxford), William Northey (Calne), Jarrit Smith (Bristol), Sir Charles Mordaunt (Warwickshire), Nathaniel Curzon (Derbyshire), and James Wigley (Leicester). Tellers for the third reading were George Grenville (Buckingham) and Sir Walter Blackett (Newcastle). The Tories had held on well in the shires and the larger towns.

[79] H. Walpole, *Memoirs of The Reign of George II*, ed. J. Brooke (New Haven, Conn., 1985), iii. 107. In the Commons, it was carried by 121–76 and 95–46. In the Lords, despite opposition from Richmond, Gower, and Hillsborough, it passed by 50–16.

[80] B. Dobrée (ed.), *Letters of Lord Chesterfield* (London, 1932), v. 2288.

Almon, bookseller and publisher, through his *Honest Elector's Proposal* in 1767 resurrected the case for secret ballot, hardly mentioned since the seventeenth century.[81] It was a suggestion that would strike at the influence which gentlemen felt property should have. In 1771 the Society of the Supporters of the Bill of Rights mapped out a programme of radical reform, including annual Parliaments, place bills, anti-bribery legislation, and a more equal representation.[82] Wilkes himself, in March 1776, having been allowed to take his seat for Middlesex, moved in the House of Commons for manhood suffrage, though his proposal was voted down *nem. con.* and without debate.[83] In 1780 the Westminster committee, strange allies of the moderate movement for economical reform, produced a programme which anticipated, in every detail, that of the People's Charter, more than fifty years later.[84] Even more distressing was the comment that property was 'the grand enchantress of the world' which could only lead to a 'lust of despotic power': to most gentlemen it was the very basis of civilized life. Though one must not exaggerate the appeal of these new policies outside London and a few large cities, there is no doubt that the political agenda was being rewritten.

Johnson, nearly 60 when Wilkes's election for Middlesex took place, found little to admire in the new programme. The importance he attached to the need for leisure, experience, and education in government meant that, like most of his circle, he could not comprehend how tapsters and bargemen, tailors and farriers, could use political power with judgement and moderation. It was not that he despised the poor and humble—the whole of his life testifies against that—but that he feared their ignorance, hastiness, and impressionability. Classical wisdom, in which he was soaked, insisted that the poor were the natural prey of demagogues and mountebanks. Nor did the example of those few constituencies where the franchise permitted some of the lower orders to vote do much to assuage such misgivings. Preston, Coventry, and Westminster were notorious for riotousness; Honiton, where nearly half the borough's adult males could vote, was a sink of bribery.[85]

---

[81] It was repeated by 'Regulus' in Almon's *Political Register* for March 1768 to coincide with the election campaign. Secret ballot had been advocated by Harrington in *Oceana* and by David Hume in his *Plan for a Perfect Commonwealth*.

[82] A convenient account of the eleven points is in *Junius*, 404.

[83] *Parl. Hist.* xviii. 1286–98.

[84] More accurately, the programme was produced by the second sub-committee of the Westminster committee, under the chairmanship of Thomas Brand Hollis, the veteran radical. Wyvill, i. 235: 27 May 1780.

[85] Honiton's unlucky patron, Sir George Yonge, was reported to have said that his father left him £80,000, his wife brought him another £80,000, and government added a further

Before we deplore Johnson's bigotry, we should note two things. First, compulsory elementary education was not introduced in Britain until 1870—nearly one hundred years after his death. It was then brought in partly as a response to the second Reform Act, which had for the first time extended the vote to large numbers of the working classes: 'we must educate our masters', was Robert Lowe's brilliant sneer. Secondly, more than fifty years after Johnson's death, Macaulay, an advanced Whig and an ardent defender of the first Reform Act, explained why the Chartist case for manhood suffrage must be resisted at all costs:

Universal suffrage is utterly incompatible with the very existence of civilization. I conceive that civilization rests on the security of property . . . We never can, without absolute danger, entrust the supreme government of the country to any class which would, to a moral certainty, be induced to commit great and systematic inroads against the security of property . . . How is it possible that, if you give them this power, it would not be used to its fullest extent.[86]

Democracy, in short, was a raging tiger that must never be let loose.

Much as he disliked these new proposals, Johnson could hardly prevent them from lapping round his door. There was a strong radical group in Thrale's constituency of Southwark and it needed careful handling. Sir Joseph Mawbey, Thrale's fellow member in the 1760s, was an ardent Wilkite and a busy politician. On 1 March 1769 a public meeting was held in the borough to issue 'instructions' to its two members—a well-established technique of agitation dating back to the seventeenth century. Mawbey defended the right of his constituents to instruct their members; Thrale prudently 'acquiesced'.[87] A twelve-point programme was then

£80,000, but Honiton had swallowed the lot. Though the figures are a little too pat, Sir George fell into financial difficulties and finished up as Governor of the Virgin Islands. *Notes and Queries*, 11th ser. (1842), i. 191.

[86] *Hansard's Parliamentary Debates*, 3rd ser. (1910), lxiii. 43–52. In 1848 *The Economist* added its voice to the argument: 'Granting to them [the lower orders] the best intentions and the most unselfish views, their haste, their impressibility, their openness to deception and their inevitable ignorance, must ever make, and has ever made the government of the lower classes fatal beyond all others to freedom, to prosperity, to peace . . .'. Quoted in K. B. Smellie, 'Victorian Democracy: Good Luck or Good management?', in *Ideas and Beliefs of the Victorians* (London, 1949), 293.

[87] The *Gentleman's Magazine* (1769), 161–2, carried a lengthy report of the meeting. Mawbey was in some trouble for having signed a requisition to bring troops from the Tower to defend the King's Bench prison against the mob. His lame excuse was that Thrale had signed first, which was denied. Croker suggested that Johnson might have written the report. It does not seem unlikely that he had a hand in it, and the final reproach to Mawbey sounds distinctly Johnsonian: 'when he shrinks from vulgar resentment, let him not employ falsehood to cover his retreat.'

adopted. Many of the items were uncontroversial: the preservation of the liberties guaranteed by 'our excellent constitution', the protection of trial by jury, habeas corpus, and so on. But the last point demanded a return to shorter Parliaments.

The grievances of the Middlesex electors were kept before the public by a number of initiatives. Mawbey and his supporters held another meeting in the borough in October 1769 and adopted a petition which, when presented, bore the signatures of 1200 of the Southwark electors. We may safely presume that the Southwark resolutions and Thrale's tactics were discussed in the Streatham household. The day before Mawbey's October meeting, Johnson burst out in conversation:

This petitioning is a new mode of distressing government, and a mighty easy one. I will undertake to get petitions either against quarter-guineas or half-guineas, with the help of a little hot wine. There must be no yielding to encourage this.[88]

It is not clear what Johnson's opinion at this time was on the issue of shorter Parliaments. It had, of course, once formed part of the Tory programme of reform. His general attitude towards radical proposals was that they were empty rhetoric and that the dangers anticipated were figments of inflamed imaginations. He refused, for example, to believe that the question of general warrants, raised by the Wilkes case, was of much consequence: all governments needed discretionary powers of that kind and, if one were to offer subjects exemption from the threat of general warrants at a halfpenny a time, 'very few would purchase it'.[89] This, added Boswell severely, was a typical example of his lax way of talking.

Unfortunately, Boswell's account of Johnson's views on shorter Parliaments is brief and confused.[90] Johnson was reported to have said:

The duration of Parliament, whether for seven years or for the life of the King, appears to me so immaterial, that I would not give half a crown to turn the scale the one way or the other. The *habeas corpus* is the single advantage which our government has over that of other countries.

[88] *Life*, ii. 90. He was sufficiently irritated to refuse to allow Boswell to read the petitions from the *London Chronicle* to him; F. Brady and F. A. Pottle (eds.), *Boswell in Search of a Wife, 1766–1769*, (New Haven, Conn., 1957) 351.

[89] *Life*, ii. 72–3.

[90] Ibid. 73. Boswell admitted that he was not, at this time, keeping notes as carefully as he would have wished. Johnson's comments on shorter Parliaments do not seem to be reported in Boswell's private journals. In the *Life* they are attached to the discussion of general warrants and are printed for Sept. 1769. But, in the private journal, the reference to general warrants is given for Mar. 1768, before Wilkes's election for Middlesex had taken place.

Croker seemed puzzled by Johnson's reference to habeas corpus and could only suggest that it must have been intended as paradox. But a more probable explanation is that the conversation referred to the Irish Parliament, that Boswell had noted it on a separate piece of paper, that he moved it eighteen months later, and that he presumed that it had arisen from the Wilkes issue. Until the accession of George III, the Irish Parliament remained in being throughout the lifetime of the king, and the one dissolved by George II's death in 1760 had been in existence for thirty-three years. From 1760 onwards there was vigorous agitation in Ireland for a Septennial Act which, though a badge of oligarchy in England, would be a radical measure for Ireland. This agitation came to a head in the spring of 1768, and an Octennial Act was finally conceded in February 1768. The reference to habeas corpus, odd if not unintelligible in an *English* context, makes perfect sense if the discussion had been about Ireland, where there was no habeas corpus and a demand for it had formed part of the agitation. The English Privy Council, which retained the right of veto over Irish legislation, refused a habeas corpus bill in April 1768, on the grounds that disaffection was still too widespread.

Though it is unwise to try to read too much from a garbled and misplaced account, it looks as if Johnson was expressing, as he often did, sympathy for Irish national aspirations. It would not however be surprising had he lost whatever enthusiasm he may once have felt for shorter Parliaments in general. It would demonstrate the extent to which events had modified old Tory attitudes. Political life had lurched so much towards the radical left in the 1760s that most of the Tories had done an about-turn on the issue. Until the accession of George III, they were still concerned with their struggle against the oligarchical Whigs and were pressing for the repeal of the Septennial Act as late as 1758. But once, with Wilkes and Liberty, democratical ideas began to circulate, it became a matter of defending the landed interest and property against rampant egalitarianism. The Septennial Act no longer seemed an insupportable grievance. When Boswell asked Mrs Thrale in 1775 whether Johnson had not laid himself open to the charge of trimming by accepting his pension, she replied: 'he had not changed but the court had changed. While the court was Whig, he opposed it: was then a patriot. Now it has become Tory, he is a friend to it.'[91] But more than the court had changed after 1760. The political scene outside Westminster was changing and the defences against radicalism needed to be manned.

[91] *Boswell: The Ominous Years 1774–1776*, (New Haven, Conn., 1963), ed. Ryskamp and Pottle, 123. Boswell did not use this material in the *Life*.

Johnson was as much committed to preserving property as Locke had been. In *Sermons*, no. 24, he described 'established property and inviolable freedom' as the greatest of 'political felicities'. His strongest argument for 'female chastity' was that infidelity placed in jeopardy the rightful descent of property. He was an unabashed supporter of the view that property must and should exert political influence: it was the ballast in the ship of state. Were he a country gentleman, he told Bennet Langton, 'he would turn out all his tenants who did not vote for the candidate whom he supported'. Old family interests, 'the permanent property of the country', must be maintained.[92] In a discussion with Boswell on the way to St Andrews, he defended the influence which many members of the peerage had over seats in the House of Commons: 'influence must ever be in proportion to property and it is right it should.'[93] Of course, Johnson added the rider that influence should not be fraudulent or improper and that wealth would only be respected if it was used responsibly. But of the correctness of the relationship between property and power he had no doubt.

Since he did not for one moment agree with the critics, domestic or American, that the House of Commons had shown itself corrupt, Johnson had no wish to see reforms.[94] He was not in the least embarrassed by the oddities of the representative system—that great towns like Birmingham, Manchester, and Sheffield remained unrepresented, while tiny hamlets like Aldborough, Great Bedwyn, Heytesbury, and Grampound had two members of Parliament each. Johnson's views, it has been suggested, may be inferred from Lecture 15 of Chambers's Vinerian course.[95] The Americans' claim of no taxation without representation led the lecturer to comment on the representative system of Britain:

If we attempt to subdivide this representation and consider what proportion the representing powers bear to the numbers represented, we shall find nothing but deficiency, vacuity and confusion—small villages with two representatives, the greatest city in the world with only four, and many large and opulent towns to

---

[92] *Life*, ii. 167, 340. But see also *Life*, v. 304, where Johnson argued that landlords ought to grant their tenants long leases and not keep them as 'perpetual wretched dependents' upon their will.

[93] *Tour*, 18 Aug. 1773. A more subtle defence of the influence of the peers in the Commons was that it prevented the working mechanism of the constitution from becoming uncoordinated and jarring components.   [94] *Life*, iii. 206.

[95] MacAdam, *Dr. Johnson and the English Law*, 106–7, attributes this passage to Johnson. It seems probable, since it is of a general rather than specialist character and deals with Ireland and America, on which Johnson held strong views. The argument is similar to that of *Taxation No Tyranny*.

which, having risen since the original regulation, no representatives have been ever granted.

Our House of Commons, therefore . . . can now be considered only as a body of men summoned to consult the general interest of the community with very little or no reference of particular men to particular places. The value of pecuniary property is now known by the weight of taxes to bear no small proportion to the weight of our land; but 130 millions, now circulating in our funds, have no representative assigned them, nor confer the right of a single vote. Surely it cannot be charged as injustice that we do not do for our colonies what we do not do for ourselves . . . If we are content that the owners of land should tax those whose possessions are in money, if we do not permit our trading companies to delegate to the Great Council any particular guardians of their interests, if we allow equal authority to the voice of him who represents half the inhabitants of a village almost uninhabited as to him who is deputed by a fourth part of the inhabitants of London, it may surely be allowed us to include our colonies in this extensive legislation and commit them to the care of the Parliament on the same terms as we commit ourselves.

Chambers/Johnson next dealt with the argument that the British Parliament might be ignorant of the views of the colonists or indifferent to their interests:

If it be argued that on these principles the colonies may be taxed without due attention or full knowledge of their abilities, the same argument might be used by the trading companies. If it shall be said that they may be taxed wantonly, because the legislators pay no part of the tax imposed upon them, it must be considered that if they are useful and beneficial to their mother country it can never be our interest to diminish their usefulness or obstruct the benefits that we receive ourselves. We have the same interest in their preservation and their happiness as a representative of Cornwall can have in the trade or prosperity of Leeds or Manchester. We shall be restrained from oppression by that great principle which holds all Empires together, 'that the happiness of the whole is the happiness of its parts.'

Many Americans would have regarded this description as specious, interested, and sentimental. Johnson's reply was to wonder how the American colonists had acquired the strength to contemplate independence or the wealth to defy the mother country.[96]

[96] 'We are ready to conclude that those restrictions are not very oppressive which have been found consistent with this speedy growth of prosperity, and begin to think it reasonable that they, who thus flourish under the protection of our government, should contribute something towards its expence' (*Taxation No Tyranny*). The reference in the lecture to Cornwall's interest in the well-being of Leeds and Manchester is reflected in the pamphlet's burlesque account of Cornish declaration of independence, issued from Truro.

The political pamphlets of the 1770s, in which the question of authority, sovereignty, and the constitution is repeatedly raised, have been discussed earlier (Ch. 3). The agitation for reform faded in the early years of the American conflict but revived in the later 1770s in the shape of the Association movement for economical reform. This, in turn, led to parliamentary reform being once more canvassed. In May 1782 Chatham's son William Pitt moved for a select committee to discuss the issue. He was studiously moderate, praising the ancient constitution, seeking only to restore its vitality, and offering no specific proposals. He went down to defeat by 161 votes to 141, a division which greatly exaggerated the prospects for reform. Wyvill and his fellow Associators resolved to devote the autumn and winter of 1782–3 to a fresh attempt to awaken the country in anticipation of a further motion in the session of 1783.

Wyvill's campaign opened up a Pandora's box of reform, moderates vying with radicals, local interests with national ones. Shorter Parliaments, place bills, secret ballot, payment of members, franchise extension, redistribution of seats were all canvassed once more. There were demands that copyholders should have the vote restored to them, on the grounds that they might well be men of substance. Wyvill faced great difficulty in holding his troops together. With the end of the American war in sight and a prospect of lower taxation, fair-weather friends fell away. Others objected to particular policies. From Bedford, William Belchamp wrote angrily to protest against abolishing fifty rotten boroughs and giving their hundred members to the counties: it would, he declared, 'convert the constitution into an aristocracy'.[97] Sir George Onesiphorus Paul reported from Gloucestershire how much damage the radical proposals of the Westminster Committee, Granville Sharp, and Major Cartwright were doing to the cause.[98]

Johnson's clerical friend Dr Taylor, with whom he stayed often at Ashbourne, was a strong Whig and in the thick of a campaign to rouse Derbyshire. On 16 January 1783 Samuel Shore of Norton Hall told Wyvill that a county meeting had been summoned and an advertisement placed in the London newspapers: the intention was to produce a moderate petition, avoiding all issues but representation, and addressing in general terms. Wyvill replied encouragingly that Derbyshire would be 'a most important addition to our strength'; the prudence shown would help

[97] Wyvill, iv: 25 Nov. 1782.   [98] Ibid. 241–7: 6 Dec. 1782.

to conciliate the powerful Cavendish family.[99] Accordingly, when the Derbyshire petition was brought forward, it was respectful in tone, praising the constitution, and begging only for some consideration of the inadequate state of the representation.[100]

It is not clear whether Johnson learned of these developments by letter from Taylor or from reports in the London papers. But on 21 January 1783 he wrote a long letter to Taylor on the subject:

I am glad that your friends are not among the promoters of equal representation, which I consider as specious in theory but dangerous in experiment, as equitable in itself, but above human wisdom to be equitably adjusted, and which is now proposed only to distress the government.

An equal representation can never form a constitution, because it can have no stability, for whether you regulate the representation by numbers or by property, that which is equal today, will be unequal in a week.[101]

The difficulty which Johnson saw as insuperable was met in 1949 by the establishment of boundary commissioners, charged with monitoring the size of constituencies and proposing periodic adjustments. But Johnson's second point had more substance and identified the problem of 'Finality', heatedly discussed in the debates on the Great Reform Act of 1832:

To change the constituent parts of government must be always dangerous, for who can tell where changes will stop. A new representation will want the reverence of antiquity, and the firmness of establishment. The new Senate will be considered as Mushrooms, which springing in a day may be blasted in a night.

What will a Parliament chosen in any new manner, whether more or less numerous, do which is not done by such Parliaments as we have? Will it be less tumultuous if we have more, or less mercenary if we have fewer?

Johnson ended sombrely with the risk of civil war: 'the business of every wise man seems to be now to keep his ground.'

Johnson's course was nearly run. Tired and dispirited, he observed in April 1783 that, at least, he had done his best to preserve order and support monarchy.[102] Two months later he suffered a stroke. One senses that Johnson knew that the writing was on the wall, for himself and for the

---

[99] Wyvill, iv: 275–6, 276–8: 16, 24 Jan. 1783.

[100] *CJ*, xxxix. 230, recd. 17 Feb. 1783. Some of the inhabitants of Derby also took the opportunity to petition. Of 12,000 inhabitants, some 2,000 were householders, but the franchise was confined to some 430 burgesses. The corporation retained control by creating honorary burgesses, 'the greatest part of whom never come near it . . . except to vote at elections' (*CJ*, xxxix. 239).

[101] *Letters*, ed. Redford, iv. 109.   [102] Ibid. 124–9.

old order. One of Wyvill's correspondents, the mayor of Petersfield, a snug parliamentary borough in Hampshire, had replied with indignation to the request for support: 'You and your Association will do much injury to Old England.'[103] Johnson would have cried, 'Amen!'

Johnson's views on the constitution were not forgotten. Five years after his death, the grand debate on the French Revolution began. Edmund Burke begged his readers to shun the French example and contrasted the crazy structure of the new French regime with the solid evolution of the English constitution:

Thanks to our sullen resistance to innovation, thanks to the cold sluggishness of our national character, we still bear the stamp of our forefathers . . . We are not the converts of Rousseau; we are not the disciples of Voltaire; Helvetius has made no progress amongst us. Atheists are not our preachers; madmen are not our lawgivers.[104]

He was answered by Tom Paine in *The Rights of Man*. England, declared Paine, did not have a constitution:

Can Mr Burke produce the English constitution? If he cannot, we may fairly conclude, that though it has been so much talked about, no such thing as a constitution exists . . . Much is to be learned from the French constitution.[105]

Johnson, Paine continued, had been correct in maintaining that in any civil society there should be a superior and ultimate controlling power, but wrong in placing that power in the government rather than in the constitution itself. It was a fair point, though Johnson could hardly have placed it in the constitution if Paine was right that none existed. But it showed that Johnson remained a name to be conjured with and an authority to be overthrown.

---

[103] Wyvill, ii. 97–8.   [104] *Reflections*, 83.
[105] 8th edn. (London, 1791), 57, 63 50–1.

5

Johnson and Aristocracy

'SUBORDINATION' was one of Johnson's favourite words. To him it meant, not humiliation or degradation, but order, harmony, stability, and security. On respect for authority rested all those advances towards civilization that mankind had so painfully made. Johnson was a volunteer in the cause. 'I have great merit in being zealous for subordination and the honour of birth,' he told Boswell, 'for I can hardly tell who my grandfather was.'[1]

Why did Johnson feel so strongly? First, because of his early life in Lichfield, which we discussed in Chapter 1: disrespect bred rebellion, and rebellion bred ruin: 'civil wars are the greatest evils that can happen to a people'.[2] Secondly, because during Johnson's lifetime were felt tremors of that earthquake which was to bring down the old order, sweeping aside the rule of kings and noblemen alike.

In his political essays, written in the early 1740s, David Hume had drawn attention to the vital role played by opinion in the support of government. The approbation of mass opinion, whether enthusiastic or merely acquiescent, enabled, in all states, the few to govern the many. Above all, if the feeling prevailed that the existing arrangements were sensible, natural, and fair, it provided a massive buttress to rulers. Johnson was in full agreement with Hume: 'what is it but opinion, by which we have a respect for authority, that prevents us, who are the rabble, from rising up and pulling down you, who are gentlemen from your places, and saying, "We will be gentlemen in our turn".'[3]

Hume did not however discuss a more interesting question, which causes historians considerable difficulty: why and how opinion changes,

---

[1] *Life*, ii. 261. This was pardonable hyperbole, for Johnson knew perfectly well who his grandfathers were. His father's father had died some forty years before Johnson was born, but his maternal grandfather, Cornelius Ford, was well-connected. Johnson's great-uncle was a barrister, his uncle a physician, and his first cousin a Fellow of Peterhouse, Cambridge.

[2] *A course of lectures*, i. 175.

[3] *Life*, ii. 153. This is a further example of Johnson's gift for pointing up his argument by picturesque exaggeration. He did not really think of himself as part of the rabble, but he was teasing Boswell.

often over a comparatively short period. In a few decades at the beginning of the eighteenth century, belief in witchcraft ceased to be a nearly universal opinion and became the badge of rural eccentricity. In an equally brief period, votes for women moved from being a captious and daring proposition to a mere commonplace. In the course of the eighteenth century, the predominance of the aristocracy ceased to be unquestioned. Chief among the ideological concepts challenging aristocracy was the doctrine of equality, perhaps the most potent slogan of the modern world.[4]

When tracing such broad concepts, the historian has to be content with distressingly approximate explanations. The term 'equality' is itself so abstract that it means little save in specific situations and related to specific questions. We are not necessarily looking for mass conversions or mass changes of heart. Most ideas and concepts are in existence at any given moment, even if in crude or unarticulated form. 'Jack's as good as his master' is not a particularly sophisticated idea and must have existed from early times. Often what takes place is less a shift in intellectual persuasion than a change in the balance of economic or political power, whereby minority opinion, which has been submerged or disregarded, is more freely expressed or even becomes the dominant view. One does not have to be an unreconstructed Marxist to believe that what we often take to be a universal opinion is no more than the prevailing orthodoxy of a powerful group. The effective challenge to aristocratic domination came, not from peasants, but from middle-class professional and commercial men in the more advanced countries of France, Holland, and Britain. Henry Thrale, a wealthy brewer whose grandfather had been a poor Hertfordshire labourer and whose mother is unknown, is a case in point, even if kitted out with an Oxford education and a fine country house. It was harder to argue that a man who gave employment to hundreds did not deserve political influence than to hold at bay the aspirations of a Cumberland shepherd or a Dorset ditcher.

Nor should we expect a purely cerebral explanation. Ideas and concepts exist in a changing world, and it would be hard to decide whether gunpowder, printing, education, or the steam engine was the great leveller. We must not be too sentimental or expect people to be disinterested. Few eighteenth-century liberals were also democrats. What people demand for

---

[4] Its rivals are either national self-determination or 'the career open to talent', a slogan of great appeal since few people believe they are without some talent. This also did damage to aristocratic ascendancy but may in some ways be regarded as a subsection of the doctrine of equality, i.e. equality in action.

themselves, as Johnson pointed out, they often deny to others. Religious sects frequently claimed freedom of worship in order that they should more effectively supplant or suppress their rivals. The Dutch burghers who shrugged off monarchical and aristocratic rule were not noticeably egalitarian when their own turn came.

Though it is possible to trace the concept of equality in classical thought, it remained a minority opinion. Plato and Aristotle may have implied equality within the ruling élite, but the main assumptions behind their ideas of government were hierarchical and aristocratic. Not until the Stoics and Cicero was the basic equality of mankind urged, partly in justification of a republican rather than a monarchical regime. Early Christian thought had strong egalitarian tendencies, and the early Christians were themselves regarded as subversives, but with their advent to power their priorities began to change. Romans overcame Galatians.[5] The concept of equality lived on, particularly in monastic institutions such as the Benedictine order, which held everything in common, but in most countries it became a submerged tradition.

Since the context of political and constitutional discourse was essentially religious, it is natural that challenges to orthodoxy took a religious form. The later medieval heretics, such as the Lollards and the Hussites, held egalitarian views and the authorities did not take kindly to them. John Ball, who preached to a mass audience at Blackheath in 1381 on the text 'When Adam delved and Eve span, who was then the gentleman?', was hanged, drawn, and quartered at St Albans; the body of John Wycliffe, his spiritual mentor, was exhumed in 1428, burned, and the ashes tipped into the river Swift. With the splintering of Christendom at the Reformation, the concept of equality emerged more strongly. In Calvinism the doctrine was confined to the elect and balanced by the large number of the ungodly. But the egalitarian attitude of Anabaptists, leading some of them to community of goods and of women, earned for them a reputation as destroyers of society. Some of their doctrines re-emerged in seventeenth-century England among Baptists, Quakers, and Socinians. The refusal of the Quakers to recognize titles or to remove their hats and their use of the term, 'thou' were deeply alarming to a society in which the king was

---

[5] Gal. 3 declared: 'there is no such thing as Jew and Greek, slave and freeman, male and female; for you are all one person in Christ Jesus'; the message of Rom. 13 was: 'Every person must submit to the supreme authorities. There is no authority but by act of God, and the existing authorities are instituted by him: anyone rebelling against authority is resisting a divine institution.'

served his dishes on bended knee and children stood bareheaded in the presence of their parents.[6] Their principles, Charles II was warned, were 'inconsistent with any kind of government',[7] and it has been suggested that fear of the Quakers was a factor in bringing about the restoration of the monarchy.[8]

The Restoration saw a powerful reassertion of traditional values. Though the abolition of the monarchy and the House of Lords in 1649 had been tactical rather than ideological, it seemed to many a dramatic example of the consequences of egalitarianism. In revulsion, the doctrines of the divine right of kings and of non-resistance were promulgated in their most extreme forms. The emergence of the full-bottomed wig, which was borrowed from France and retained its popularity for more than a hundred years, was another reminder of the importance of rank, since its aim was to distinguish gentlemen from plebeians, and it rested on the assumption that fishmongers and ploughmen would look silly wearing one. Though the doctrine of equality in the sight of God was not abandoned, neither was it pressed to disagreeable lengths by the gentry and peerage: services did not begin until they made their appearance; they had private pews at the front of the church; and, even in death, they were buried nearer to the altar than ordinary people.[9] The spectre of equality was however never quite defeated. The Quakers abandoned their initial fierceness, advocated pacificism, and became an inward-looking sect, while the Baptists lost much of their original fervour. But the spread of Methodism in the later 1730s began the controversy all over again with many members of the élite finding much to trouble them in the mass meetings and the emphasis on the sinfulness of all men. Catherine, duchess of Buckingham, spoke valiantly for her order when she wrote to reprove Selina, countess of Huntingdon, for fraternizing with the enemy: 'their doctrines are most repulsive, and strongly tinctured with impertinence, and disrespect towards their superiors. It is monstrous to be told that you have a heart as sinful as the common wretches that crawl the earth. I cannot but wonder that your ladyship should

---

[6] One surviving bastion of the hat as a symbol of authority seems to be degree ceremonies in British universities, where elaborate doffing is still much in vogue.

[7] *Records of the Governor of Massachusetts Bay* (Boston, 1853), iv. 165–6.

[8] B. Reay, *The Quakers and the English Revolution* (London, 1985). The *Calendar of State Papers Domestic* contains many alarmist reports of Quaker meetings from 1660 onwards. In Nov. 1660 more than a thousand of these 'monsters' were reported meeting in Bristol; in Jan. 1661 they were said to be running naked through the streets in Yorkshire shouting strange doctrines against the government.

[9] A good example is Shrivenham church, where the memorial tablets of the Barrington family, though only Irish peers, cluster round the altar.

relish any sentiments so much at variance with high rank and good breeding.'[10]

Aristocracy and hierarchy were defended in a variety of ways: by biblical authority, by appeals to the theory of noble blood, by parallels with the family, and by a number of political and legal arguments. One of the more abstract justifications, which had a long life, was that of the Great Chain of Being. It has been expounded in a book of remarkable scholarship.[11] It was in origin an inductive argument from divine attributes, among which was included plenitude. From the theory that it is better to exist than not to exist, and that God must necessarily prefer the better, it was inferred that there was a continuous chain of creation, running from God through the archangels and angels to man, and from man through brute creation to the smallest living organism. The gradations were infinitely small and every possibility was taken up—hence the theory that this was the best of all possible worlds.[12]

Though the concept of the Great Chain of Being had been in existence in classical times, it achieved its greatest popularity in the post-Renaissance world. Shakespeare offered a version of it as the basis for Ulysses' speech in *Troilus and Cressida*,[13] and Pope and Young were still exploiting its poetical possibilities in Johnson's time.[14] Clearly such a concept derived its appeal less from its intrinsic merits than from an intense desire to believe that the universe was one of purpose and design. There was no necessary reason why the theory should have had political implications, since there might well have been equality *within* the component parts,

---

[10] *The Life and Times of Selina, Countess of Huntingdon, by a Member of the Houses of Shirley and Hastings* (London, 1839–40), i. 27. The duchess was an illegitimate daughter of James II by Catherine Sedley, so perhaps she was laying it on thick. Her husband built Buckingham House, later purchased by George III and developed into Buckingham Palace.

[11] A. O. Lovejoy, *The Great Chain of Being* (Cambridge, Mass., 1936).

[12] It is a theory much associated with Leibniz and was the target of Voltaire's attack in *Candide*. It is often seen as fatuously optimistic, but it really stems from the simple proposition, which is hard to deny, that God, being good, would have created a better world if he could have done.

[13] Act I. iii. 75–137.

[14] In bk. I of the *Essay on Man*, Pope obligingly prints a summary of the concept: 'That throughout the whole visible world, an universal order and gradation in the sensual and mental faculties is observed, which causes a subordination of creature to creature, and of all creatures to man . . . How much farther this order and subordination of living creatures may extend, above and below us; were any part of which broken, not that part only, but the whole connected creation must be destroyed' (Arguments VII–VIII). This led to the lines (i. 245–6): 'From Nature's chain whatever link you strike | Tenth or ten thousandth, breaks the chain alike', and to his triumphant conclusion that 'One truth is clear, "Whatever IS, is RIGHT"'.

whether of men or of crocodiles. But the idea of a chain of creation was
easily taken as a model for human government by those with a natural
interest in or disposition towards hierarchy, and as an indication that,
from the beginning of time, it had been a world of rank and degree. Soame
Jenyns in his small volume of 1757, *A Free Inquiry into the Nature
and Origin of Evil*, spelled out the political message: 'thus the universe
resembles a large and well-regulated family, in which all the officers and
servants, and even the domestic animals, are subservient to each other in
a proper subordination.'[15] The dramatic consequences of breaking the
chain could then be demonstrated—confusion, disorder, anarchy and
chaos—even if, strictly speaking, it is not clear either how the chain could
be broken, save possibly by extirpating one of the lesser species, or
why the extinction of earthworms or dodos should necessarily bring
irreparable discord among men. The powerful imagery of ropes breaking,
chains snapping, and foundations collapsing meant that the logic of the
concept was not closely scrutinized.

How seriously this hypothesis was taken must be in some doubt.[16] But
in a period before a theory of evolution, when a single act of creation was
taken for granted, it was difficult to deny a purposeful, rational, and
benevolent plan. Lovejoy remarked that Voltaire and Johnson were the
most cogent critics of the concept and he seemed surprised that Johnson's
were the more telling objections.[17] Johnson's criticisms were contained
in the review of Soame Jenyns's book which he wrote for the *Literary
Magazine*. He had several reasons for writing a lengthy counterblast
rather than a review. He disliked Jenyns's tone, finding it nonchalant and
unbecoming, doubted Jenyns's capacity to deal with such a solemn subject
as the origins of evil, and deeply mistrusted abstract theorizing. Johnson
objected that there was not continuity but a great gulf between the lowest

[15] 4th edn. (London, 1761), 70–1.
[16] Lovejoy's lectures, first given in 1933, were reinforced by E. W. Tillyard's *The
Elizabethan World View* (London, 1943), which leaned heavily on the concept. More recently
there has been scepticism as to its widespread acceptance and influence. A. D. Nuttall, *Pope's
Essay on Man* (London, 1984), 209, has remarked that Johnson did not seem to have come
across it much and attributed it to 'the Arabian metaphysicians'. He can only suggest that
Johnson 'blanked out' and became 'blundering and myopic'. But Johnson was not ill-read,
and it is at least possible that his remark should be taken as a warning against giving the
concept too much prominence. For a valuable discussion of the use of the 'Great Chain of
Being' concept in Hanoverian social analysis, see P. J. Corfield, 'Class by Name and Number
in Eighteenth-century Britain', *History*, 72/234 (Feb. 1987), 38–61.
[17] This seems to me to be a residue of the disdainful attitude that Johnson was a man of
'strong prejudices' and to ignore the fact that he was an acute and precise thinker.

infinite being and the highest finite creature; at the other end of the chain, there must be a gulf between the lowest finite creature and nothing. Within the existing gradations could be inserted an infinite number of further gradations. It was easy enough to imagine more and more specimens of every creature. 'This scale of being', Johnson concluded, 'I have demonstrated to be raised by presumptuous imagination, to rest on nothing at the bottom, to lean on nothing at the top, and to have vacuities from step to step, through which any order of being may sink into nihility without any inconvenience, so far as we can judge, to the next rank above or below it.' The idea that imperfection implied evil Johnson denied. The concept of higher and lower organisms was one which human beings imposed on the universe from outside: 'the weed as a weed is no less perfect than the oak as an oak.'

Johnson returned to the theme towards the end of his life. He presumed that Jenyns had lifted his theory from Pope, and the *Life of Pope*, completed in the spring of 1781, gave him a second chance. Johnson admired Pope's poetry more than his philosophy, but, as he remarked, 'philosophy and poetry have not often the same readers'. His comments on the *Essay on Man* were a sustained and contemptuous onslaught:

The poet was not sufficiently master of his subject; metaphysical morality was to him a new study; he was proud of his acquisitions, and supposing himself master of great secrets, was in haste to teach what he had not learned . . . Having exalted himself into the chair of wisdom, he tells us much that every man knows, and much that he does not know himself: that we see but little, and that the order of the universe is beyond our comprehension (an opinion not very uncommon), and that there is a chain of subordinate beings 'from infinite to nothing', of which himself and his readers are equally ignorant. But he gives us one comfort which, without his help, he supposes unattainable, in the position 'that though we are fools, yet God is wise.'

'Never', concluded Johnson, 'was penury of knowledge and vulgarity of sentiment so happily disguised. The reader feels his mind full, though he learns nothing.'

But while the review of Jenyns, followed two years later by *Rasselas*, was sufficient to demonstrate Johnson's dislike of egregious optimism, his own position was not free from difficulty. If God is the great architect of the universe and indubitably good, it is hard to avoid belief in a benevolent creation. Johnson faced this problem when, in the 'Vanity of Human Wishes', he rehearsed the harsh vicissitudes of fate and fortune, and asked:

> Must helpless Man, in ignorance sedate
> Roll darkling down the torrent of his Fate?

The answer was not very dissimilar from Pope's. Humans, in this unpredictable and volatile world, should turn to God:

> Implore his aid, in his decisions rest,
> Secure whate'er he gives, he gives the best.

In *Rambler*, no. 184, Johnson had written:

Nothing can afford any rational tranquillity but the conviction that . . . nothing in reality is governed by chance, but that the universe is under the perpetual super-intendence of him who created it; that our being is in the hands of omnipotent goodness, by whom what appears casual to us is directed for ends ultimately kind and merciful.

In *Sermons*, no. 16 he wrote:

Heaven and earth, and the whole system of things, were created by an infinite and perfect being, who still continues to superintend and govern them. He knows that this Great Being is infinitely wise and infinitely good; so that the end which he proposes must necessarily be the final happiness of those beings that depend upon him, and the means, by which he promotes that end, must undoubtedly be the wisest and the best.

It is not clear that, philosophically, this differs very much from Pope's position.

Though he repudiated the concept of the Great Chain of Being, Johnson remained wedded to a belief in subordination. The grounds for his belief were secular and utilitarian rather than theological or speculative and mark a shift towards a more modern world. His argument was simply that the task of government was to create the greatest happiness possible in society and that this was best achieved by due subordination.[18] 'I would no more deprive a nobleman of his respect than of his money,' he told Boswell:

I consider myself as acting a part in the great system of society, and I do to others as I would have them to do to me. I would behave to a nobleman as I should expect he would behave to me, were I a nobleman and he Sam Johnson . . . There would be a perpetual struggle for precedence were there no fixed invariable rules for the distinction of rank.[19]

Johnson's 'perpetual struggle for precedence' is no bad description of what used to be known as the 'rat race', and among redundant chief

---

[18] *Life*, i. 408.   [19] Ibid. 447.

executives there may be some sympathy for Johnson's concept of a less frenetic and competitive society. Johnson did not deny that life was hard for the poor and unfortunate, and he did his best to relieve their wants, but, since suffering was an inescapable part of human existence, submission was the more prudent course: 'it is better that some should be unhappy than that none should be happy, which would be the case in a general state of equality.'[20]

Aristocratic supremacy raised the question of property, its rights and obligations, since one of the most obvious manifestations of that supremacy in Hanoverian England was the vast disparity in income and life-style between rich and poor. We have seen in Chapter 4 Johnson/ Chambers suggesting that wealth was the only true ground of hereditary greatness. Certainly it was the foundation.

There were other reasons why the question of property rights began to play a more prominent part in public debate in the eighteenth century. In the Tudor period, when comparatively wealthy burghers left a bed and some stools, there was little to discuss. But the seventeenth century saw a significant increase in and dispersal of wealth, some of it from early capitalist enterprises,[21] some the fruits of the new colonial empires. The growth of state power and the ceaseless search for more revenue which accompanied it led to extended debates on sovereignty, resistance, and the rights of subjects. These issues were fought out less in constitutional treatises than in fierce disputes about forced loans, benevolences, immunities, ship money, *capitation*, excise, income tax, and the like.

The exceptional circumstances of the breakdown of government in England in the 1640s allowed a brief airing for advanced views on

---

[20] Life, iii. 26.

[21] One example in point, which impinged on Johnson's life, was the growth of large-scale brewing. The notable increase in the size of towns permitted large-scale ventures, which could overcome the crippling transport costs. Commercial production of beers and ales began to compete with home production. Southwark was established as a brewing centre for London as early as the sixteenth century. The first brewer to become a member of Parliament was probably Sir John Parsons, owner of the Red Lion brewery at Aldgate, returned for Reigate in 1685. Southwark elected two brewers, J. Cholmeley and C. Cox in the 1690s. See P. Mathias, *The Brewing Industry in England, 1700–1830* (Cambridge, 1959). As a warning against stereotypes, it may be worth noting that Parsons was a Jacobite/Tory.

The Anchor brewery was established at Southwark in 1616 by James Monger. It passed via his son to James Child, thence to Edmund Halsey, who married Child's daughter, and thence to Halsey's nephew, Ralph Thrale. After her husband's death, Mrs Thrale sold it to their chief clerk, John Perkins. Barclay–Perkins merged with Courage in 1956, were in turn taken over by Imperial Tobacco, and now form part of the Elder empire of Australia. The headquarters is still called Anchor House.

property. A tiny minority repudiated it altogether. Gerrard Winstanley and the Diggers saw covetousness as the supreme evil, setting man against man: 'so long as such are rulers as calls the land theirs, upholding this particular propriety of Mine and Thine, the common people shall never have their liberty, nor the land ever be freed from troubles, oppressions and complainings.'[22] In Winstanley's brave new world, any attempt to reinstate private property would be punishable by death. A larger number of people went with the Levellers in accepting private property as an institution, but wishing to place on it restrictions in the interests of smaller men. By the second Leveller agreement of 1648, interest rates were not to be allowed above six per cent, excise was forbidden, and estates of less than £30 p.a. were not to be subject to national taxation.[23] But Leveller influence waned after the surrender at Burford in 1649.

The Glorious Revolution, unlike the civil wars, did not let loose a torrent of radical speculation, and its organizers were anxious that it should not do so. Though it has been demonstrated that Locke's two *Treatises on Government* were written during the Exclusion crisis, they were brought out, given a topical preface, and passed off as a contribution to the 1689 debate.[24] Since Locke did not accept Hobbes's contention that the life of man in a state of nature was intolerable, he could not argue that the primary purpose of civil government was merely survival. Its first objective was the preservation to every man of his property.[25] This, though important, was a more limited aim than Hobbes's. Consequently there was no obligation to postulate that individuals had to surrender to government all their rights: the agreement was a contract, and a right of resistance remained if the contract were broken.

There were not many people in England after 1688 who denied the validity of property rights. The debate therefore tended to move in a

---

[22] *The New Law of Righteousness* (London, 1649), 159.

[23] D. M. Wolfe (ed.), *Leveller Manifestoes of the Puritan Revolution* (New York, 1967), 291–303. The Levellers also advocated an end to imprisonment for debt and the abolition of the death penalty, save for murder and trying to destroy the Agreement. Among other improvements, they urged Parliament to rid the kingdom of 'those vermin and caterpillars, the lawyers, the chief bane of this poor nation'.

[24] The preface announced that its intention was 'to justify to the world, the people of England, whose love of their just and natural rights, with their resolution to preserve them, saved the nation when it was on the very brink of slavery and ruin'.

[25] Ch. 9, 'Of the Ends of Political Society and Government': '. . . the enjoyment of the property he has in this state is very unsafe, very unsecure. That makes him willing to quit a condition, which, however free, is full of fears and continual dangers . . . to join in society with others . . . for the mutual preservation of their lives, liberties and estates, which I call by the general name, Property. The great and chief end, therefore, of Men's uniting into Commonwealths and putting themselves under government, is the preservation of their property'.

different direction. It was argued that some forms of property were more stable and acceptable than others, and that landed property, which could not be transferred out of the kingdom, should be the basis of political power. The high-water mark of this belief was the Tory success in 1711 in carrying the property qualification for members of Parliament, whereby borough members were obliged to possess landed estates worth £300 p.a.; and county members, landed estates worth £600 p.a. It is significant that this Tory measure was not repealed by the triumphant Whigs after 1714: indeed, it was strengthened and extended into local government in 1732 by an act requiring Justices of the Peace to hold landed property to the value of £100 p.a.[26] Secondly, as prosperity trickled downwards fears began to be expressed that too great a diffusion of wealth would enervate and corrupt the people. The example of Rome was brought forward as evidence of a great empire undermined by the spread of luxury.

A publication arguing the contrary opinion, which succeeded in setting the cat among the pigeons, was Bernard Mandeville's verse homily *The Fable of the Bees*. This started life in 1705 as a doggerel broadsheet, was revised and added to, and had a *succès de scandale*.[27] It produced a hail of replies and in 1723 was presented, rather belatedly, by the Grand Jury of Middlesex as a public nuisance. Mandeville was Dutch by origin. His technique was to take an aspect of truth and present it in provoking and piquant form. His thesis was that private vices were of public benefit, since luxury, extravagance, and high living made for employment, trade, and the rapid circulation of money. Johnson himself commented later in life how stimulating he had found Mandeville when he first read him.[28] Mandeville did not, however, persuade everyone that luxury was good.

[26] The first Act was 9 Anne c. 5, the second 5 George II c. 18.

[27] The 1705 poem was entitled 'The Grumbling Hive'. In 1714 it was reissued with a prose commentary. Another edition in 1723 included an essay on charity schools which attracted much attention.

[28] 'I read Mandeville forty, or, I believe, fifty years ago,' he told Boswell in 1778; 'he did not puzzle me: he opened my views into real life very much.' Johnson's comments show that, although he accepted Mandeville's argument that luxury had good effects, he rejected the fragile paradoxes. Once more, the utilitarian argument is brought to bear: 'The fallacy of that book is, that Mandeville defines neither vices nor benefits. He reckons among vices everything that gives pleasure. He takes the narrowest system of morality, monastick morality, which holds pleasure itself to be a vice . . . and he reckons wealth as a publick benefit, which is by no means always true. Pleasure of itself is not a vice. Having a garden, which we all know to be perfectly innocent, is a great pleasure . . . Mandeville puts the case of a man who gets drunk in an alehouse; and says it is a public benefit, because so much money is got by it to the publick. But it must be considered, that all the good gained by this, through the gradation of ale-house keeper, brewer, maltster, and farmer is overbalanced by the evil caused to the man and his family by his getting drunk. This is the way to try what is vicious, by ascertaining whether more evil than good is produced by it upon the whole.' *Life*, iii. 292.

Denunciations of its pernicious effects became part of the stock-in-trade of the opposition to Sir Robert Walpole, accused of undermining the independence of Parliament by places, pensions, and patronage. Pope made it a central theme of his political poems in the 1730s, and Johnson added his own voice when he published 'London' in 1738:

> But lost in thoughtless ease, and empty show
> Behold the warrior dwindled to a beau;
> Sense, freedom, piety, refin'd away,
> Of France the mimick, and of Spain the prey.

Prophets of doom can usually obtain a hearing, and as late as 1757 John Brown achieved great, if fleeting, success with a repetition of the argument that luxury would destroy the country, insisting that Britain stood on the very brink of disaster. His *Estimate of the Manners and Principles of the Times* went up, according to William Cowper, 'like a paper kite'.[29] Brown saw his country as characterized by a 'vain, luxurious and selfish effeminacy'. There could be but one outcome of the struggle against the French: 'by a gradual and unperceived decline, we seem gliding down to ruin: we laugh, we sing, we feast, we play.'[30] From these melancholy prospects Britain was saved, and Brown plunged into an optimism he could hardly bear, by Plassey, Quebec, and Quiberon Bay.[31]

It was now France's turn to suffer introspective national gloom and a new lease of life was given to the rather tired controversy about property by the writings of Jean-Jacques Rousseau, drawing on Hobbes, Locke, Mandeville, and others. Rousseau was three years younger than Johnson and had spent a trying year in 1740 as tutor to the children of a nobleman, de Mably, whose brothers the Abbé de Mably and Condillac became distinguished savants.[32] Rousseau's breakthrough came in 1749 when the

---

[29] *Table Talk* (London, 1782), 20–1.

[30] *Estimate of the Manners and Principles of the Times* (London, 1757), i. 29, 144.

[31] Unabashed, Brown turned the tape over and began again. 'Victory hath at length restored peace to our bleeding country,' he wrote in 1765, 'but in vain the sword of war is sheathed, if in time of peace, the poignard of licentiousness and faction is drawn.' *Thoughts on Civil Liberty* (London, 1765), 9–10. Brown had attacked Mandeville in his *Essays on the Characteristicks of the Earl of Shaftesbury* (London, 1751). After the Seven Years War, he corresponded with Catherine the Great and began advising her on the development of education in Russia. He committed suicide in 1766.

[32] Mably was three years older than Rousseau and also attacked property, developing the concept of a communistic society: 'equality must produce all the benefits because it unites men, elevates their souls, and prepares them for mutual sentiments of well-being and friendship . . . Inequality produces all the evils because it degrades men, humiliates them, and sows among them division and hate.' *Of Legislation, or the Principles of Laws* (Lausanne, 1776). Condillac, three years younger than Rousseau, became a celebrated authority on

Dijon Academy invited essays on the question of whether the progress of the sciences and the arts had contributed to purify or to corrupt morals. Rousseau's prize-winning answer was that in many respects the march of civilization had failed to promote human happiness and had weakened many generous impulses natural to man. Real virtue was to be found, not among sophisticated men, but in primitive societies, free from hypocrisy, aggression, and guile. In awarding him the first prize, the Dijon Academy let a genie out of the bottle in the form of the Noble Savage.[33]

Four years later Rousseau entered another Dijon competition on the subject on inequality. Turning Locke on his head, Rousseau argued that property, far from being a natural right, was a usurpation and a fraud: 'the first man who, having enclosed a piece of land, thought of saying "This is Mine", and found people simple enough to believe him, was the true founder of civil society.' How much better would it have been for the human race had someone denounced this impostor immediately. The main characteristic of natural man was spontaneous compassion. The inequality which exists among civilized people—the fact 'that a child should govern an old man, that an imbecile should lead a wise man, and that a handful of people should gorge themselves with superfluities while the hungry multitude goes in want of necessities'—is contrary to the law of nature.[34]

The counter-attack was not long in coming—indeed, it began before the book was published. Voltaire wrote gravely to acknowledge the complementary copy which Rousseau had sent him: 'I have received, Monsieur, your new book against the human race.' He peppered his volume with scathing marginal notes: 'behold, the philosophy of a beggar, who would like the rich to be robbed by the poor'; 'all this is abominable'; and so on.[35] Fréron, who did not much like any of the *philosophes*, thought Rousseau 'the enemy of mankind', and the Président de Brosses found the *Discourse* 'smashing everything and . . . still frightening . . . even though

educational psychology, another subject close to Rousseau's heart. It may not be unfair to suggest that the tutor learned more than the two pupils, whom Rousseau confesses he would at times have cheerfully murdered.

[33] An English translation of Rousseau's prize essay appeared in 1752.

[34] *Discours sur l'inégalité* (Amsterdam, 1755). Curiously enough, though Johnson disagreed totally with Rousseau's conclusion, his contribution to Chambers's Vinerian lectures contained an almost exact paraphrase: 'it were natural to expect that no man would be left long in possession of superfluous enjoyments, while such numbers are destitute of real necessaries.' *A course of lectures*, i. 305–6.

[35] R. A. Leigh (ed.), *Correspondance complète de Jean-Jacques Rousseau* (Geneva, 1966), iii. 156–8. Voltaire's comments are printed in the notes to *A discourse on Inequality*, ed. M. Cranston (London, 1984).

toned down by friends'. The Academy of Dijon decided that it had done enough for Rousseau and did not award him the prize a second time.[36]

It took some years for Rousseau's reputation to reach England and it was not until the publication of *Nouvelle Héloïse* (1761), *Émile* (1762), and *Du contrat social* (1762) that he became well known. The later books were better received. Indeed, in *Du contrat social* Rousseau attempted to show how the defects of civil society, to which he had drawn attention earlier, might be overcome. It was also presumed that the artificiality of society, which Rousseau found so irksome, was French rather than English. Consequently, Rousseau found some admirers. Among the more surprising was David Hume, at least until he met Rousseau. James Boswell, who collected celebrities, managed by his usual importunity to gain several audiences with the great man, assuring him in advance, 'your books have melted my heart, have elevated my soul, have fired my imagination'.[37]

They did not melt Johnson's heart. Although Boswell was convinced that his two distinguished friends would have got on famously, one may venture to doubt it. Apart from the fact that both were failed schoolmasters, rarely in short supply, one can hardly imagine two men with less in common.[38] Johnson tried painfully to bring reason to bear upon problems and to clear his mind of cant; Rousseau wallowed in feeling. Johnson was a man of strict sexual probity; Rousseau luxuriated in amorous intrigue, some of it enjoyable. Johnson had a deep, perhaps exaggerated, sense of his own defects and shortcomings; Rousseau was an egotistical monster. Johnson loved society and shunned solitude; Rousseau was ill at ease with his fellow men.[39] Johnson attached the deepest importance to civilization; Rousseau thought it had corrupted man.

Johnson's dismissal of Rousseau as a scoundrel and his treatise on inequality as a childish desire for novelty was no mere emotional spasm, but the product of profound intellectual disagreement. Johnson, 'the Tory', believed in the Whiggish idea of progress; Rousseau, 'the progressive', believed that history showed decay and decline. Johnson was

---

[36] L. G. Crocker, *Jean-Jacques Rousseau: The Quest 1712-58* (New York, 1968), i. 271-2.

[37] *Letters*, ed. Tinker, ii. 60.

[38] Mrs Piozzi also claimed to see much common ground between them. M. Temmer, *Samuel Johnson and Three Infidels* (Athens, Ga., 1988), argues a similar case. It is more ingenious than convincing.

[39] Rousseau's remark to Malesherbes (Leigh (ed.), *Correspondance complète de Rousseau*, letter no. 1622) was: 'je suis né avec un amour pour la solitude'. Johnson, in *The Adventurer*, no. 67, wrote that 'Man may indeed preserve his existence in solitude, but can enjoy it only in society'.

convinced that Rousseau's thinking was flawed from the outset. Natural man was not good. 'Pity', he told Boswell, 'is not natural to man. Children are always cruel. Savages are always cruel. Pity is acquired and approved by the cultivation of reason.'[40] Had he been born a Red Indian, Johnson remarked on one occasion, 'I must have starved, or they would have knocked me on the head, when they saw I could do nothing'.[41]

As for the tranquillity which Rousseau claimed for primitive men, Johnson could not credit it: 'as to care or mental uneasiness, they are not above it, but below it, like bears.'[42] Equality was not therefore the answer; it was a mere will-o'-the-wisp, an ignis fatuus:

'Sir, Your levellers wish to level *down* as far as themselves. . . . They would all have some people under them; why not then have some people above them?' I mentioned a certain author who disgusted me by his forwardness, and by shewing no deference to noblemen into whose company he was admitted.

JOHNSON: 'Suppose a shoemaker should claim an equality with him, as he does with a Lord. How he would stare. "Why, Sir, do you stare?", says the shoemaker. "I do great service to society. 'Tis true, I am paid for doing it; but so are you, sir, and I am sorry to say it, paid better than I am, for doing something not so necessary. For mankind could do better without your books, than without my shoes." '[43]

The 'certain author' Boswell referred to may well have been Samuel Foote, playwright, mimic, and one-man entertainer, for Sir Joshua Reynolds recalled Johnson's indignation at Foote's pertness towards men of quality, calling them by their surnames:

The foolish fellow fancied that lowering them was raising himself to their level: this affectation of familiarity with the great, this childish ambition of momentary exaltation obtained by the neglect of those ceremonies which custom has established as the barriers between one order of society and another, only showed his folly and meanness.[44]

Johnson's insistence on the need to treat the nobility with respect may be contrasted with the attitude of Rousseau, who wrote to Malesherbes: 'I hate the great. I hate their rank, their harshness, their prejudices, their pettiness, and all their vices.'[45] Johnson had found a hater who out-hated him with ease.

---

[40] *Life*, i. 437.   [41] Ibid. iv. 210.   [42] Ibid. ii. 73.   [43] Ibid. i. 448.
[44] 'Two Dialogues by Sir Joshua Reynolds in Imitation of Johnson's Style of Conversation' [1816], *Miscellanies*, ii. 243. Croker's note confirms that 'the substance of the dialogues did really occur' and they certainly appear to reflect Johnson's sentiments and style.
[45] Letter no. 1654, 28 Jan. 1762 (Leigh (ed.), *Correspondance complète de Rousseau*, x. 66). The passage begins: 'je hais les grands . . .'.

Since the nobility had so prominent a role in Johnson's moral and social order, it was important not only that they should be respected but that they should deserve respect. Johnson welcomed the increased use of entails so that noblemen would not find themselves deprived of their estates and bring their order into disrepute.[46] Gross and shameful deviations of rank and *mésalliances* should be punished, not indeed by formal penalties, but by ostracism and contempt.[47] Johnson would not hear the common suggestion that the nobility lived frivolous and debauched lives: it was merely that the sins of duchesses found their way into newspapers when the sins of shopgirls did not:

> Few lords will cheat; and, if they do, they'll be ashamed of it: farmers cheat and are not ashamed of it: they have all the sensual vices too of the nobility, with cheating into the bargain . . . the licentiousness of one woman of quality makes more noise than that of a number of women in lower stations . . . So far as I have observed, the higher in rank, the richer ladies are, they are the better instructed and the more virtuous.[48]

One of the primary purposes of inequality was to provide a few people with leisure: without leisure for some, there would be no cultivation of the arts, no learning.[49]

Though Johnson was an enthusiastic supporter of rank and hierarchy, we should note a number of reservations that go some way to modifying his position. First, he believed that hierarchy promoted human happiness: though by temperament gloomy, his view of government was positive. Like many elderly men, he deplored the growing disrespect of his age, but he acknowledged that there was another side to the coin. One of the most remarkable of his essays was 'The Bravery of the English Common Soldiers', written during the Seven Years War.[50] The rank and file, recruited from the lower orders, were frequently pert and irreverent. 'From this neglect of subordination,' Johnson conceded, 'I do not deny that some inconveniences may from time to time proceed.' But it should be remembered that the impertinence often displayed in private life was

---

[46] *Life*, v. 101.

[47] Even then, Johnson added that a daughter who married beneath her should be helped by her father, but only to support her in the condition she had herself chosen. *Life*, ii. 328–9.

[48] Ibid. iii. 353.

[49] Ibid. ii. 219: 'all intellectual improvement arises from leisure: all leisure arises from one working for another.'

[50] *British Magazine* (Jan. 1760).

transformed on the battlefield into self-respect and initiative: 'Insolence in peace is bravery in war.'

Secondly, Johnson was at pains to point out that rank and wealth were great privileges, which carried with them great responsibilities. In *Sermons*, no. 24, written for Dr Taylor, he reminded the upper classes that their 'superiority is not to be considered as a sanction for laziness, or a privilege for vice ... they are to look upon their power, and their greatness, as instruments placed in their hands, to be employed for the publick advantage'. Johnson placed such weight on public and civic responsibility, both for the governors and the governed, that at times he sounds like an anticipation of Maximilien de Robespierre: 'the only uniform and perpetual cause of publick happiness is publick virtue. The effects of all other things which are considered as advantages will be found casual and transitory. Without virtue, nothing can be securely possessed or properly enjoyed.'

Thirdly, although Johnson defended the superiority of the landed interest, he was not hostile to the commercial and industrial changes that were transforming his country, and he did not believe in a rigid economic and social structure. We have seen that he had little patience with the fashionable view that 'luxury' was undermining the nation. He had considerable interest in and understanding of trade and manufacture. The aristocratic ideal was essentially rural and land remained for decades the basis of noble wealth and influence. But the clash between landed and commercial wealth, which threatened briefly during the War of the Spanish Succession, did not materialize:[51] bankers, merchants, brewers, and industrialists bought seats in Parliament and were incorporated into the system; noblemen invested heavily in mining, in the great chartered companies, and in urban development. Johnson thought it of consequence that the mixing process should be encouraged: there should always be some landed estates on the market so that new blood could buy in.[52] He was proud of England's commercial vitality. *The Adventurer*, no. 67, is a paean of delight at the extraordinary ingenuity of vendors and tradesmen:

[51] See, for example, Swift's pamphlet *The Conduct of the Allies, and of the Late Ministry, in Beginning and Carrying on the Present War*, which had a great sale in 1711. 'What have we been fighting for all this while?', Swift asked. 'The answer is ready; we have been fighting for the ruin of the publick interest, and the advancement of a private. We have been fighting to raise the wealth and grandeur of a particular family [the Marlboroughs]; to enrich usurers and stock-jobbers; and to cultivate the pernicious designs of a faction, by destroying the landed interest.'

[52] *Life*, ii. 428.

'there is, indeed, no employment, however despicable, from which a man may not promise himself more than competence, when he sees thousands and myriads raised to dignity, by no other merits than that of contributing to supply their neighbours with the means of sucking smoke through a tube of clay.' One of the reasons why he did not agree with Soame Jenyns that the poor had better remain ignorant was that it was against the national interest:

To entail irreversible poverty upon generation after generation only because the ancestor happened to be poor is in itself cruel, if not unjust, and is wholly contrary to the maxims of a commercial nation, which always suppose and promote a rotation of property, and offer every individual a chance of mending his condition by his diligence.[53]

Johnson's vision was hierarchical, but it was neither rigid nor immobile.

Johnson's interest in trade and manufacture was not confined to theory. He took a keen interest in the details of the manufacturing process. During the late summer of 1774 he went on a tour of the West of England and North Wales with the Thrales. During that time he visited Lombe's silk-mill at Derby; brass, copper, and iron works at Holywell, where he noted that the sheers and hammers were all worked by water; and, on the way back, the china factory at Worcester, a papier-mâché factory at Birmingham, and Matthew Boulton's great Soho factory, producing buttons, watch chains, and the like.[54] He went out of his way to praise inventors and entrepreneurs, contrasting them with the great conquerors who burned cities: 'I would wish Caesar and Catiline, Xerxes and Alexander, Charles and Peter, huddled together in obscurity or detestation', he wrote in *The Adventurer*, no. 99. Of projectors, who were so frequently jeered at when their plans went awry, he remarked:

That the attempts of such men will often miscarry, we may reasonably expect; yet from such men, and such only, are we to hope for the cultivation of those parts of nature which lie yet waste, and the invention of those arts which are yet wanting to the felicity of life. If they are, therefore, universally discouraged, art and discovery can make no advances.

[53] 'Review of Soame Jenyns, *A Free Inquiry into the Nature and Origin of Evil*' [1757], in D. J. Greene (ed.), *Samuel Johnson* (Oxford, 1984), 522–43. Johnson made the same point in conversation with Boswell when he explained that trade 'gives men an opportunity of improving their situation. If there were no trade, many who were poor would always remain poor.' *Life*, ii. 98.
[54] Johnson's own diary of the North Wales tour is printed in *Life*, v. 427–61. For a good discussion on his interest in these matters, see J. H. Middendorf, 'Johnson on Wealth and Commerce', in Powell (ed.), *Johnson, Boswell and their Circle*, 47–64.

His respect for rank did not mean that Johnson despised the poor and humble. Soame Jenyns was only one of many writers who insisted, with what degree of sincerity one knows not, that the poor had a great deal to be thankful for. Johnson doubted that. He corrected sharply Jenyns's amiable definition of poverty as 'want of riches': it was 'want of *necessaries*'.[55] If people of rank really believed that the poor were happier, the remedy was in their own hands:

Sir, all the arguments which are brought to represent poverty as no evil, shew it to be evidently a great evil. You never find people labouring to convince you that you may live very happily upon a plentiful fortune.[56]

He warned repeatedly against the demoralizing effect of poverty and preached the importance of frugality in avoiding it: 'Poverty will enforce dependence, and invite corruption: it will almost always produce a passive compliance with the wickedness of others.'[57] He urged Boswell to every effort to keep his affairs in order and stop the slide into insolvency:

Poverty, my dear friend, is so great an evil, and pregnant with so much temptation, and so much misery, that I cannot but earnestly enjoin you to avoid it.[58]

To those who insisted that there would always be poor, Johnson replied with an argument that seems to anticipate the concept of a welfare state:

Riches cannot be within the reach of great numbers, because to be rich is to possess more than is commonly placed in a single hand; and, if many could obtain the sum which now makes a man wealthy, the name of wealth must then be transferred to still greater accumulations. But I am not certain that it is equally impossible to exempt the lower classes of mankind from poverty; because, though whatever be the wealth of the community, some always will have least, and he that has less than any other is comparatively poor; yet I do not see any coactive necessity that many should be without the indispensable conveniences of life; but am sometimes inclined to imagine, that, casual calamities excepted, there might, by universal prudence, be procured an universal exemption from want; and that he who should happen to have least, might notwithstanding have enough.[59]

Johnson's profound concern to avoid at all costs the perils of dependence leads us to a discussion of his views on literary patronage, and again suggests that his attitude towards the nobility was not one of unalloyed approbation.

---

[55] Review of Jenyns, *Free Inquiry*.   [56] *Life*, i. 441.   [57] *Rambler*, no. 57.
[58] Letter of 28 Mar. 1782 (*Letters*, ed. Chapman, ii. 474–5). See also 7 Sept., 7 Dec. 1782; ?4 Feb. 1783 (ibid. 504–5, 517–19; iii. 6–7).
[59] *Rambler*, No. 57.

Johnson was born into a world in which patronage was all-important
to anyone who wished to rise. Artistic patronage was but one subdivision
of that great network of dependence that ran all through society. Colonels,
postmasters, doorkeepers, chaplains, necessary women, regius professors,
messengers, housekeepers, customs officers, physicians, deans, paper-
hanging makers, matrons, constables, storekeepers all had their patrons
and friends. Candidates who were abashed to ask on their own behalf
explained that it was a duty they owed to their family. Publications like the
Court and City Register or the *Royal Kalendar* listed the jobs available and
the salaries attached. Aspiring dentists could note that the position of
Operator to the Royal Teeth was in the gift of the Lord Chamberlain;
starving curates that the chaplaincy to the Governor of Gibraltar brought
in £121. 13s. 4d. a year. The *Kalendar* was conveniently pocket-sized.

In artistic and literary matters, royal and ecclesiastical patronage was in
decline. Wolsey was perhaps the last magnificent clerical patron; Charles
I, with his keen interest in painting and in masques, the last great royal
patron of the arts. After the Restoration, royal patronage went mainly to
architects and builders: Charles II undertook vast building projects at
Greenwich, Chelsea, and Windsor, while William III and his successors
extended and embellished Hampton Court and Kensington Palace. But
royal favour still counted for a good deal. Handel profited much from the
support of George II and was accordingly opposed by the Prince of
Wales's set, who established a rival opera: 'the affair grew as serious as that
of the *Greens* and the *Blues* under Justinian,' wrote Lord Hervey. On a
more modest footing, Queen Caroline extended patronage to Stephen
Duck, the thresher-poet from Wiltshire, and found him a job as a Yeoman
of the Guard before he became ordained. But decades of war and
parliamentary control of finances meant that the scale of royal patronage
was much reduced.

As court patronage waned, aristocratic patronage grew in importance.
One of the most lavish of patrons was James Brydges, 1st duke of
Chandos, who made a vast fortune as Paymaster-General during the War
of the Spanish Succession. At Cannons, his house in Middlesex, he
maintained a whole orchestra and choir. Handel spent nearly two years
there writing anthems. Chandos subscribed for fifty copies of Gay's
collected poems in 1720, and is said to have given Pope £500 for his *Epistle
to Lord Burlington*.[60] Burlington himself was another great patron,

---

[60] C. H. C. Baker and M. I. Baker, *The Life and Circumstances of James Brydges, 1st Duke
of Chandos* (Oxford, 1949). Chandos's patronage was highly successful, in that Handel's
compositions in his service are known as the Chandos Anthems, and have helped to preserve
his name for posterity.

employing Colen Campbell the architect, and patronizing Handel, Pope, Gay, and William Kent, the landscape artist and painter. John Gay went through a number of patrons, including the dowager duchess of Monmouth, Clarendon, Chandos, Burlington, and Harcourt, before finishing up under the protection of the duke and duchess of Queensberry. A good deal of the energies of Richard Savage, Johnson's strange friend, was spent in a fruitless hunt for patronage, particularly after he had quarrelled in 1734 with Lord Tyrconnel. One of the luckier artists was the sculptor Roubiliac, who was an unknown Frenchman when in the 1730s he picked up at Vauxhall Gardens a pocket-book belonging to Sir Edward Walpole, son of the prime minister. Through Walpole's good offices, Roubiliac was employed to provide a bust of Handel at Vauxhall, the basis for his very successful career.

Though it is customary to dwell upon the frustrations experienced by artists and poets, one may spare a thought for the patrons themselves. The drain on resources was not inconsiderable: both Chandos and Burlington ran into financial difficulties.[61] Literary men often displayed a remarkable capacity for biting the hand that was feeding them, and as soon as a quarrel took place, decencies were cast to one side: 'the Right Honourable Brute and Booby' was Savage's description of his former patron Tyrconnel. There was remorseless importuning from writers and wits, 'an undistinguish'd race, Who first his Judgement ask'd, and then a Place'.[62] Few things were harder than to agree on what was an appropriate and adequate reward. Philip, duke of Wharton, gave the poet Edward Young an annuity of £100 in 1719 'for the encouragement of learning and the polite arts'. On the strength of this, Young claimed to have turned down other preferments and the ultimate outcome was a protracted legal action. In 1726 Young received a pension from the king worth £200 p.a., and two years later was appointed chaplain to George II. In 1730 he obtained the lucrative living of Welwyn, worth £300 p.a. He remained unsatisfied. His next line of advance was to pay court to the Prince of Wales, but in 1742 complained in his 'Fourth Night': 'I've been so long remembered, I'm forgot'.[63]

[61] It is only fair to say that Burlington's problems were brought about largely by his building enterprises. Chandos spent lavishly on Cannons and was also the softest of touches for projectors and swindlers of all kinds.

[62] Pope, *An Epistle to Dr Arbuthnot*, ll. 237–8. He is describing *Bufo*, usually taken to be Dodington.

[63] Young caught something of the misery of the hanger-on in his lines: 'When in his courtier's ear I pour my plaint, | They drink it as the nectar of the great, | And squeeze my hand and beg me come tomorrow.' Young's reputation as a poet of unusual profundity was destroyed by an acid review from George Eliot entitled 'Worldliness and Other-Worldliness: The Poet Young', *Westminster Review* (1857). She remarked of Young that 'he has a fervid

If patronage could be so irksome for patrons, why did they do it? The great majority of noblemen, of course, did not. We tend to remember the comparatively few distinguished patrons, which is presumably what they wished. The others contented themselves with buying the occasional portrait or bust, hired plasterers or musicians as required, subscribed to a few books of particular interest to themselves, but did not attempt regular or systematic artistic patronage. More of their disposable income went to charities like the Magdalen Hospital or the Foundling Hospital, or to providing their neighbourhood with a town hall, a school, alms-houses, or assembly rooms, where the return on the investment was more secure.

The motives of the minority of artistic patrons were extremely mixed. They were heirs to the great tradition of aristocratic magnificence, whereby humble folk were dazzled by the spectacle of a lavish life-style. In earlier days, noble pre-eminence was reinforced by the number of liveried retainers. By Johnson's day, the iron barons had been replaced by the silken barons, and education, taste, and good breeding were of more importance than physical prowess. The care lavished on the approaches to the great house—the lodge, the curving drive, the pediment and pilasters, the reception room, and the chandeliers—showed how aware the aristocracy was of impressions. Of course, it could be overdone. General Wade's house in Cork Street, designed by Lord Burlington in 1723, sacrificed all internal convenience to a superb front, leaving Lord Chesterfield to remark that one could not live in it, but it would be worth buying the house opposite to look at it.[64] Some patrons had a genuine love of music and painting. Others wished to shine before relatives and friends. Of the 5th earl of Orrery, Bishop Berkeley remarked unkindly that he 'would have been a man of genius had he known how to set about it'. Johnson, while conceding that Orrery was feeble-minded, commented more charitably that he 'would have been a very liberal patron' of the arts, had he been rich.[65]

Some patrons enjoyed the flattery they received, though one suspects that birthday odes were as tedious to read as to write. For others, artistic patronage was part of social climbing. George Bubb, born an apothecary's son but in transit via an inheritance and the change of name to a peerage,

attachment to patrons in general, but on the whole prefers the Almighty'. An attempt to re-establish Young is H. Forster, *Poet of the Night Thoughts: Edward Young 1683–1765* (Alburgh, Norfolk, 1986).

[64] Walpole to Montagu, 18 May 1748 (*Correspondence of Walpole*, ix. 56).
[65] *Life*, v. 238.

was patron to a host of writers.[66] Young, of course, was there, dedicating to George Bubb Dodington his *3rd Satire* in 1726, with a pleasing forecast:

> Whom my presaging thoughts already view,
> By Walpole's conduct fir'd, and friendship grac'd,
> Still higher in your prince's favour plac'd.

Henry Fielding the novelist was so moved at the contemplation of Dodington in 1741 that he wrote a poem 'On True Greatness', discovering in his patron qualities strangely at variance with his posthumous reputation: 'prone not to change'.[67] In 1750, when *The Rambler* appeared, Dodington sent to invite the author to his house to 'enlarge his acquaintance'. Johnson declined.[68]

If patronage was not always roses for the patron, for the artist it was often frustrating and humiliating. Finding a patron was hard enough, keeping him even harder. There were always rivals in the field. Promises were easily obtained, payment was more difficult. Even to obtain several patrons did not guarantee security. 'They wonder at each other', complained Gay to Swift in 1722, 'for not providing for me, and I wonder at them all.'[69] Writing or composing to order could be tiresome. It is just possible that Richard Savage was deeply affected in 1734 by the departure of the newly-married Prince and Princess of Orange for Holland, but 'The Genius of Liberty: A Poem' scarcely proves it.[70] Colley Cibber, poet

[66] They included Paul Whitehead, James Thomson (who dedicated to Dodington 'Summer' of *The Seasons*), Richard Glover (author of *Leonidas*), and Richard Bentley (poet son of the classical scholar). Savage dedicated to Dodington a poem in honour of the memory of George I, but seems to have been out of luck.

[67] Dodington was unfortunate. He obtained his barony as Lord Melcombe Regis at the accession of George III, but died a year later. Eastbury, his great house in Dorset, went to the Temple family, who pulled it down. The rest of his property, including his papers, went to a cousin, Thomas Wyndham, with the stipulation that only those writings should be published which 'do honour to his memory'. Wyndham's nephew, Henry Penruddocke Wyndham, printed the diary in 1784, with the comment that it showed Dodington's political conduct to have been 'wholly directed by the base motives of avarice, vanity and selfishness'. Much however may be forgiven Dodington for his charming poem 'Shorten Sail', which included the stanza: 'Void of strong desire and fear | Life's wide ocean trust no more, | Strive thy little bark to steer | With the tide, but near the shore.'

[68] J. Nichols, *Literary Anecdotes* (London, 1812–15), v. 38.

[69] C. F. Burgess (ed.), *Letters of John Gay* (Oxford, 1966), 41.

[70] *Gentleman's Magazine* (1738), 315. 'Great Nassau' and 'the beauteous Anna, Britain's eldest pride' are more prosaically described in *DNB*, under George II: 'She was fat, ill-shaped, disfigured by the small-pox, and short, while the Prince was deformed. The princess had leave to refuse him, but replied that she would marry him if he were a baboon. "Well, then," said the king, "there is baboon enough for you".' Johnson, in his *Lives of the Poets*, reports that Savage told him that he only wrote it 'because it was expected from him'.

laureate from 1730, faced with his fourteenth birthday ode to George II, sensibly formed a consortium with four other poets:

> Again on Caesar's natal day,
> In humble strains,
> His grateful swains,
> Their joyous songs shall pay.[71]

Worst of all was the need to be constantly on one's guard, lest one be caught out of step with the patron. John Gay seems to have resented toadying more than most, writing to Mrs Howard:

You must be entirely governed by his friendships and resentments, not your own . . . the method to please these wonderful and mighty men, is never to declare in the morning what you believe 'till your friend has declared what he believes, for one mistake this way is utter destruction.[72]

From this disagreeable situation he was rescued by the enormous success of the *Beggar's Opera*, put on at Lincoln's Inn Fields by John Rich in 1728 and pardonably said to have 'made Rich gay, and Gay rich'.

This system of artistic patronage broke down almost completely during Johnson's lifetime, particularly in literature. It was easier for some artists and craftsmen to emancipate themselves than for others. Architects could hardly be expected to build great country houses on spec. Composers needed the resources of choirs and orchestras and were therefore heavily dependent upon court and clerical patronage. Patronage is not quite the term to describe the relationship of painters with their noble customers, even if they were sometimes given shelter and protection, as Turner was at Petworth: even the wealthiest patron, with several country houses, would scarcely want the complete output of a painter. At a time when portrait painting was still dominant, it was hard for painters to break away from aristocratic service: one could hardly place an unwanted portrait of the 3rd duchess on the market. Hogarth, however, led a move away from aristocratic patronage, using engravings to reach a wider public and choosing popular themes like *Marriage à la Mode* and *The Rake's Progress*. But the vast increase in books and periodicals meant that writers were increasingly able to appeal to the general reader, and they were helped

---

[71] Curiously, Richard Savage is credited with one of the verses, though when the poem appeared in the *Gentleman's Magazine* in Nov. 1744 he had been dead for more than a year. It is not impossible that Cibber had built up a stock of birthday odes, since Johnson told Boswell: 'his friends gave out that he *intended* his Birthday Odes should be bad; but that was not the case, Sir, for he kept them many months by him.' *Life*, i. 402.

[72] Burgess (ed.), *Letters of Gay*, 45–6 (Aug. 1723).

by the spread of circulating libraries. Johnson himself summed up the process, linking it with the diffusion of learning: 'an author leaves the great and applies to the multitude.'[73] One of the first to do so with success was Alexander Pope, who, though on good terms with a number of noblemen, was intensely proud of the fact that he supported himself by his own writings.

Johnson's letter to Lord Chesterfield, probably the best-known of all his writings, coupled with the alteration he made to the 'Vanity of Human Wishes' and his dictionary definition of the word 'patron', has given him a peculiar prominence in the revulsion against patronage. 'Is not a Patron, my Lord,' he asked Chesterfield, 'one who looks with unconcern on a man struggling for life in the water, and, when he has reached ground, encumbers him with help?' But we must not overestimate Johnson's influence nor make his letter too dramatic a turning-point. It was, after all, not intended for publication, and did not appear until 1790.[74] By that time the battle was won. Johnson as a young man was not unwilling to seek patronage and had accepted ten pounds from Chesterfield.

Johnson was far from being the only man to feel and express ambivalence towards the nobility. Edmund Burke quarrelled violently with his first patron, William Gerard Hamilton, for whom Johnson subsequently worked, and, at the end of his life, all his resentment overflowed in his *Letter to a Noble Lord*, in which he demanded to know what the young duke of Bedford had done to justify 'the ponderous mass of his nobility, wealth and titles'.[75] Samuel Foote used the theme in his play *The Patron*, produced at the Little Theatre, Haymarket, in 1764, and Charles Churchill, Wilkes's friend, attacked patronage in his poems 'The Author' and 'Independence', which came out in December 1763 and October 1764. But perhaps the most determined opponent of patronage during Johnson's life was Oliver Goldsmith, whom Sir John Hawkins thought quite quixotic in refusing offers of assistance when he could hardly keep out of debtor's prison. But Goldsmith was in earnest and insisted, in

---

[73] *Life*, v. 59.

[74] In the 1755 edn. of 'Vanity', Johnson substituted 'patron' for 'garret' in ll. 159–60: 'There mark what ills the Scholar's life assail, | Toil, Envy, Want, the Garret and the Jail.' His dictionary definition was: 'Patron—commonly a wretch who supports with insolence, and is paid with flattery.' Boswell obtained a copy of the letter and published it separately in advance of the *Life*.

[75] For Burke's feelings, see I. Kramnick, *The Rage of Edmund Burke: Portrait of an Ambivalent Conservative* (New York, 1977); J. A. Cannon, *Aristocratic Century* (Cambridge, 1984), 167–8.

his *Chinese letter LXXXIV* published in 1760, that patronage was no longer necessary:

At present, the few poets of England no longer depend upon the great for subsistence, they have now no other patrons but the public, and the public, collectively considered, is a good and a generous master . . . A writer of real merit now may easily be rich if his heart be set only on fortune . . . He may now refuse an invitation to dinner, without fearing to incur his patron's displeasure, or to starve by remaining at home . . . he can bravely assert the dignity of independence.

With these sentiments, Johnson was, of course, in complete agreement. Like Pope, he was particularly proud of his professional integrity: 'no man who ever lived by literature', he claimed, 'has lived more independently than I have done.'[76] He warned repeatedly of the corrupting effects of flattery, on both sides, and of the extent to which it rendered impossible honest opinion:

Now learning itself is a trade. A man goes to a bookseller, and gets what he can. We have done with patronage . . . With patronage, what flattery! what falsehood! When a man is in equilibrio, he throws truth among the multitude, and lets them take it as they please; in patronage, he must say what pleases his patron, and it is an equal chance whether that be truth or falsehood.[77]

In *Rambler*, no. 163, he made the point in an entertaining letter in which a poor author complains that, after dancing attendance on the great Aurantius some eight years, he has been offered a small place provided that he marries a young lady with whom the patron has finished. In no. 136 he deplored 'indecent and promiscuous dedication'. Yet Johnson conceded that 'you may be prudently attached to great men and yet independent'[78] and, in his most considered writing on the subject, he turned aside to spare a thought for the patron himself. Of course it was wrong of people to surrender to vanity or to bribe a flatterer, but one should make allowance for the difficulty in dealing with the harassing importunity employed by desperate authors:

If at last, after long enquiry and innumerable disappointments, he find a lord willing to hear of his own eloquence and taste, a statesman desirous of knowing how a friendly historian will represent his conduct, or a lady delighted to leave to the world some memorial of her wit and beauty, such weakness cannot be censured as an instance of enormous depravity. The wisest man may by a diligent solicitor be surprised in the hour of weakness, and be persuaded to solace vexation, or invigorate hope with the musick of flattery.[79]

[76] *Life*, i. 443.   [77] Ibid. v. 59.   [78] Ibid. ii. 10.
[79] *Rambler*, no. 136. For other comments on patronage, see ibid. nos. 21, 104.

The decay of artistic patronage was a two-sided affair. It is easy enough to understand that the artist was glad to be free to express his own thoughts or to pursue his own interests, even if that threw him back on the publishers and the public. But many patrons must also have felt a sense of relief. Dedications had become so extravagant that they were a source of embarrassment rather than pleasure. Clients were often difficult and demanding, and not all of them were talented. Johnson dwelt at considerable length on how tiresome a guest Pope had been and how the life of any household which he graced with his presence had to revolve around him.[80] But Johnson himself could be moody and difficult. Above all, the tastes and values of the nobility itself were beginning to change. The vast increase in peerage numbers towards the end of the eighteenth century weakened its social cohesion: peers did not necessarily know one another and were less taken up with competition. Houses were becoming smaller and more private; there were fewer servants and they were less in evidence. Domestic virtues were challenging the grand aristocratic lifestyle, and the nineteenth century concept of the home as a sanctuary and place of refuge from the world was emerging. In this new vision of family tranquillity there was hardly a place for the tame poet or the artist in residence.

So the world of the artist and the world of the nobleman drifted apart. Though Johnson awarded the aristocracy a vital place in his scheme of things, it is remarkable how little they impinged upon his own life, which was spent among scholars, booksellers, clergymen, and printers. When Boswell remarked how few of the great sought his society, Johnson expressed little surprise: 'great lords and great ladies don't love to have their mouths stopped.'[81] A few noblemen belonged to the Club but they did not take a prominent part. We must not exaggerate the significance of the decline of aristocratic patronage. It was a symptom of retreat rather than a cause. It is doubtful whether there ever was a time when noble society and literary society were fully integrated, and many of the later tributes to the generous and benevolent age of patronage smack of the sentimental. It was only one prop of the aristocratic order that was creaking: others, and stronger ones, continued. Noble economic, social, and political power remained intact. There were many other roles for noblemen to play, as leaders of society, statesmen, patrons of sport, and as presidents, chancellors, and chairmen. Yet the collapse of patronage was a warning sign. The attack upon patronage could easily slide into a more

---

[80] *Lives of the Poets.*   [81] *Life*, iv. 116–17.

general disdain for titles and rank, as it did with Churchill. It raised doubts about Johnson's whole social and intellectual order. Without rank and inequality, he had maintained, there could be no wealth and no leisure, and therefore no civilization and no learning. His own life demonstrated that this was no longer true.

One occasion when Johnson had squarely to face what subordination meant was in 1773 on his journey with Boswell to the Western Islands. His interest had been aroused by Martin Martin's account of the islands, published in Anne's reign and given to Johnson by his father. Johnson set out with the intention of investigating a primitive and isolated society but, as he himself explained, it was to no avail. Under the impact of post-Culloden security measures and the first onset of money and commerce, the clan system was fast breaking down. 'We came thither too late', he wrote, 'to see what we expected, a people of peculiar appearance and a system of antiquated life. The clans retain little now of their original character.'[82]

Johnson had no doubt of the extent of the changes taking place and recognized that much of value was being lost. The payment of rent in kind had almost disappeared, and Johnson commented: 'money confounds subordination, by overpowering the distinctions of rank and birth, and weakens authority by supplying power of resistance, or expedients for escape.'[83] The 'vindictive' measures of government after the '45, coupled with the rapacity of many lairds, had produced an 'epidemical fury of emigration'. Of those Scots who had left for the New World Johnson wrote: 'it may be thought that they are happier by the change; but they are not happy as a nation, for they are a nation no longer.'[84] On government policy towards the Highlands, he was severe:

To hinder insurrection, by driving away the people, and to govern peaceably, by having no subjects, is an expedient that argues no great profundity of politicks. To soften the obdurate, to convince the mistaken, to mollify the resentful, are worthy of a statesman; but it affords a legislator little self-applause to consider, that where there was formerly an insurrection, there is now a wilderness.[85]

Yet Johnson's account of his journey is far from being a threnody, and his general attitude is brisk and detached rather than mournful. He relates a number of bloody and savage atrocities in the previous feuding between clans, and adds: 'if they are no longer martial, they are no longer

---

[82] *Journey to the Western Islands*, 57–8.   [83] Ibid. 113.
[84] Ibid. 59, 89, 131.   [85] Ibid. 97.

quarrelsome.' Disarmament rendered them open, in theory, to foreign invasion or piratical incursions, yet 'the visit of an invader is necessarily rare, but domestic animosities allow no cessation'.[86] An armed warrior, who settles all questions of honour by the sword, 'is a very troublesome and pernicious animal in time of peace'. Johnson found little to admire in the old order. The almost complete absence of books meant that there could be little learning. Limited opportunities and limited horizons meant that most Highlanders were sluggish, unenterprising, and credulous:

> Such is the system of insular subordination, which, having little variety, cannot afford much delight in the view, nor long detain the mind in contemplation. The inhabitants were for a long time perhaps not unhappy; but their content was a muddy mixture of pride and ignorance, an indifference for pleasures which they did not know, a blind veneration for their chiefs, and strong conviction of their own importance.[87]

Even in the 1770s, after the lairds had been deprived of their judicial authority, their influence remained very great, and at an earlier period it had been almost irresistible: 'Kings can, for the most part, only exalt or degrade. The laird, at pleasure, can feed or starve, can give bread, or withhold it.'[88] On the island of Col, which was well looked after, Johnson noted the respect with which the young laird was greeted:

> Wherever we rowed, we were pleased to see the reverence with which his subjects regarded him. He did not endeavour to dazzle them by any magnificence of dress; his only distinction was a feather in his bonnet; but as soon as he appeared, they forsook their work and clustered about him; he took them by the hand, and they seemed mutually delighted.[89]

Boswell was, of course, enchanted with rank and lairdship. Indeed, in his own account of the tour he complained that Young Col's manner was not sufficiently dignified.[90] But when Boswell invited Johnson to endorse a society based almost solely upon tradition and hierarchy, he refused to do so:

> I said I believed mankind were happier in the ancient feudal state of subordination than when in the modern state of independency. Mr. Johnson said, 'To be sure, the *Chief* was. But we must think of the number of individuals. That *they* were less happy seems plain; for that state from which all escape as soon as they can, and to

---

[86] *Journey to the Western Islands*, 92.   [87] Ibid. 89.   [88] Ibid. 85–6.
[89] Ibid. 128.   [90] *Tour*, 258.

which none return after they have left it, must be less happy; and this is the case with a state of dependence on a chief or great man.[91]

One's first reaction may be to believe that Johnson was ambivalent towards the society in transition which he found in the Western Islands. It may even seem perverse that he should find so much to dislike in the past and so much to fear in the future. One commentator has remarked that on these questions 'Johnson's mind was utterly divided, totally uncertain.'[92] But that hardly does justice to Johnson's clarity of purpose or to the complexities of the issues involved. Just as he saw in his 'Bravery of the English Common Soldiers' that intrepidity and insolence were coins from the same mint, so he made a remarkable attempt to strike a fair balance between the old order and the new, and to identify the advantages and disadvantages of each. He disliked the static quality of the old order: 'where there is no commerce nor manufacture, he that is born poor can scarcely become rich.'[93] He went out of his way to defend the unpopular tacksman, who acted as a middleman between laird and tenant, comparing him to industrial and commercial entrepreneurs: 'if the tacksmen be taken away, the Hebrides must in their present state be given up to grossness and ignorance.'[94] The introduction of regular justice had been wholly beneficial. Previously the lairds, who had the dispensation of justice, had themselves been lawless: 'as government advances towards perfection, provincial judicature is perhaps in every empire abolished.' The result was that thieving and cattle-raiding were much reduced: 'thirty years ago no herd had ever been conducted through the mountains, without paying tribute in the night, to some of the clans; but cattle are now driven, and passengers travel without danger, fear or molestation.'[95] Of the impact of commerce on the Highlanders he wrote that 'the possibility of gain will by degrees make them industrious' and alleviate their pitiful poverty.[96] He concluded his journey on a note of hope, reporting his visit to the Deaf-and-Dumb school in Edinburgh, where the students made impressive progress:

[91] *Tour*, 77. This conversation was at Slains Castle and therefore before Johnson had seen the Western Islands at first hand. But there is no evidence that he changed his opinion. For another occasion when Johnson remarked that we should not provide for the happiness of one at the expense of many, see *Life*, ii. 178.

[92] Patrick Cuttwell, '"These Are Not Whigs": Eighteenth-century Attitudes to the Scottish Highlanders', *Essays in Criticism*, 15 (1965), 394–413.

[93] *Journey to the Western Islands*, 85.   [94] Ibid. 86–9.

[95] Ibid. 44–7.   [96] Ibid. 58.

It was pleasing to see one of the most desperate of human calamities capable of so much help: whatever enlarges hope, will exalt courage; after having seen the deaf taught arithmetick, who would be afraid to cultivate the Hebrides?[97]

Johnson's comments on what he found in the Western Islands had a wider application. Throughout the whole of Britain, commercial values and relationships were replacing old paternalistic and hierarchical ones. Part of Johnson's distaste for Whiggism came from the fact that he associated it with the moneyed interest, which he saw as undermining the traditional relationships of responsibility and obligation. In 1778, in a conversation with Boswell, he expanded his remarks:

Subordination is sadly broken down in this age. No man, now, has the same authority which his father had—except a gaoler. No master has it over his servants; it is diminished in our colleges; nay, in our grammar schools . . . there are many causes, the chief of which is, I think, the great increase of money . . . I have explained in my Journey to the Hebrides, how gold and silver destroy feudal subordination. But, besides, there is a general relaxation of reverence.[98]

The trend had, of course, been developing of decades before Johnson was born, though at different rates in different areas of the country and in particular occupations. Contemporaries associated it with the growth of towns, where the bustling newcomers were free from observation and control, the parson and squire had little influence, and relationships were commercial and transitory. Johnson, like Defoe, lived most of his life in London, which may have led him to exaggerate the speed of the decay of the old order. But in all parts of the kingdom the process could be perceived. 'The Laird of Auchinleck now', he reminded Boswell, 'is not near so great a man as the Laird of Auchinleck was a hundred years ago.'[99]

It is significant that Johnson should have led with the problem of servants. It is hard to envisage support for rank and aristocracy without servants, and indeed the virtual disappearance of the servant class is one of the most striking differences between modern Britain and its past. But servants intrude upon privacy , however much they are warned to use the back stairs, and can hardly avoid being aware of embarrassing secrets and foibles of their employers. Throughout the ages, the difficulty of obtaining reliable, discreet, and trustworthy servants has been one of the abiding preoccupations of the upper classes.

---

[97] *Journey to the Western Islands*, 164.   [98] *Life*, iii. 262.   [99] Ibid. 177.

The word 'servant' was in process of change in the course of the eighteenth century.[100] Previously, it had included dependent labourers and retainers, but by the Victorian period it had come to mean only domestic servants. In the early Hanoverian period, the chorus of anxiety seems to have reached something of a crescendo. Servants and their failings were in the forefront of the argument, since it was in relation to them that gentlemen were most likely to encounter the irritation and indignity caused by lack of respect for rank, and through the servant problem they glimpsed a shattered, atomized, and unruly society.

What had been for most gentlemen no more than a worry turned into a nightmare during the French Revolution, when Burke demanded to know what was to prevent the poor cutting the throats of the rich and redistributing their property.[101] Who was better placed to cut the throat of his master than the personal valet? A *frisson* ran through polite society in 1810 when the duke of Cumberland was found in bed, weltering in his own blood, having been apparently attacked while asleep by his manservant.[102]

Throughout the Hanoverian period, servants were subjected to a hail of advice, little of which they could have read, urging them to be pious, discreet, industrious, and honest. Daniel Defoe took a heavily didactic line in 1724 with a volume running to a mere 302 pages, entitled *The Great Law of Subordination Considered; Or, the Insolence and Unsufferable Behaviour of Servants in England Duly Enquired Into*. A collapse in the reliability of domestic servants would be the signal of a complete breakdown of civilized society: 'the poor will be rulers over the rich and the servants governors of their masters . . . order is inverted, subordination ceases, and the world seems to stand with the bottom upwards.' Swift tried irony and sarcasm in his *Directions to Servants*, offering friendly advice on how they could best cheat and rob their masters: 'When you have done a fault, be always pert and insolent, and behave yourself as if you were the injured person.'[103] Chamber pots should not be emptied

---

[100] A. Kussmaul, *Servants in Husbandry in Early Modern England* (Cambridge, 1981).

[101] *Thoughts and Details on Scarcity in the Month of November, 1795* (London, 1800): 'the labouring people are only poor because they are numerous. Numbers in their nature imply poverty. In a fair distribution among a vast multitude, none can have much. That class of dependent pensioners, called the rich, is so extremely small, that if all their throats were cut, and a distribution made of all they consume in a year, it would not give a bit of bread and cheese for one night's supper to those who labour, and who in reality feed both the pensioners and themselves . . .'.

[102] Cumberland recovered but his valet, Sellis, committed suicide.

[103] Pub. 1745 but written in stages earlier. H. Daris (ed.), *Directions to Servants and Miscellaneous Pieces, 1733–1742* (Oxford, 1959), 7, 61.

until they were full, since that made it easier to spill the contents. It could not be expected that the servant problem would escape the attention of Jonas Hanway, who was once described as 'one of the most splendid and indefatigable bores of English history' and who clashed with Johnson on the drinking of tea.[104] 'Perhaps no eighteenth-century writer provided so much advice to servants as did Hanway,' remarked his biographer.[105] *Instructions, Religious and Prudential, to Apprentices and Servants in General* came out in 1763. As late as 1807 Robert Southey, in the guise of a Spanish visitor, was observing the 'general depravity' of servants in England, who were not what they had once been.[106]

The concept of the Great Chain of Being was not, therefore, always employed as a lofty defence of cosmic order, but could be brought into use as an appeal of servants to tend dutifully to creature comforts while remembering their station. In the early Hanoverian period, the argument became involved with the debate about luxury. The word itself was, as Johnson pointed out, somewhat misleading, since there was little real luxury, save at the very top of society.[107] But the improvement in wages was sufficient to offer many people increased consumption and some limited choice in spending, and this was in itself a solvent of the old order. The craftsmen, artisans, mechanics, and shopkeepers of the new towns had more money to handle than the peasants who made up the vast majority in the rest of Europe, and could take their custom where they pleased.

Johnson's views on the need for subordination were not, therefore, unusual, though they were expressed with characteristic vigour. Yet in the treatment he afforded his own servant, Frank Barber, Johnson could

---

[104] Hanway's *Essay on Tea* was attached to his *Journal of Eight Days' Journey from Portsmouth to Kingston upon Thames* (London, 1757). Of the *Journal*, Goldsmith observed demurely that the author lacked 'that novelty of thought and elegance of expression' necessary to treat 'trite materials in new and striking lights'. A. Friedman (ed.), *Collected Works of Oliver Goldsmith* (Oxford, 1966), i. 76. Hanway thought that the lower orders drank too much tea and praised one lady for forbidding her servants from drinking it; Johnson dissented. The opprobrious comment on Hanway is by Charles Wilson, 'The Other Face of Mercantilism', *Transactions of the Royal Historical Society*, 5th ser., 9 (1959), 92.

[105] J. S. Taylor, *Jonas Hanway, Founder of the Marine Society* (London, 1985), 135.

[106] *Letters from England*, ed. J. Simmons (London, 1951), 369.

[107] For comments on the confused usage, see David Hume, 'Of Refinement in the Arts', in *Essays* (1752): 'Luxury is a word of uncertain signification, and may be taken in a good as well as in a bad sense.' For Johnson's comments on Mandeville and luxury, see above, pp. 165–6. There was an echo of the controversy in the 1960s with much earnest discussion of 'materialistic values', but it transpired that one man's materialism was another man's bathroom, and that those who condemned materialism most strongly were usually those who were best off.

hardly have been more considerate, paying for him to be educated and leaving him all his property. In *Rambler*, no. 68, he paid tribute to the perspicacity of servants. 'To be happy at home', Johnson insisted, was the object of all ambition, and it was in his own home that a just estimate of the character of a man could best be made:

The highest panegyric, therefore, that private virtue can receive, is the praise of servants. For, however vanity or insolence may look down with contempt on the suffrage of men, undignified by wealth, and unenlightened by education, it very seldom happens that they censure or blame without justice . . . the servant must commonly know the secrets of a master who has any secrets to entrust . . . the testimony of a menial domestick can seldom be considered as defective for want of knowledge.

Johnson and his contemporaries were right to see that wealth, financial and commercial, posed a threat to the traditional way of life. It was not, as it happens, a world that Johnson much knew or cared for: he is often to be found remarking upon the vacuity of country life and, on his visits to Taylor at Ashbourne, was soon bored by talk of bulls and market prices. But as a vision it retained its appeal. 'A man of family and estate', he remarked, 'ought to consider himself as having the charge of a district, over which he is to diffuse civility and happiness.'[108] Significantly, one of the great literary defences of the ideal came in 1711, during the commercial revolution. Addison and Steele's Sir Roger de Coverley in the *Spectator* owed his enormous success in part to the fact that he stood for virtues and a way of life that were already vanishing. Sir Roger, a baronet of ancient lineage, lived in Worcestershire, on his own estate, with 'the ruins of an old abbey' in the grounds, and the rooks and crows cawing in the aged elms. He was beloved by tenants and servants alike. Visitors noted that Sir Roger's domestic servants, instead of disappearing when needed, clustered around him, eager to do his bidding. He took seriously his duties as a JP, and his death occurred when, wretchedly ill, he insisted on going to see justice done 'to a poor widow and her fatherless children that had been wronged by a neighbouring gentleman'.[109]

Sir Roger was a fiction. That not all squires were kind and generous may be inferred from the anxiety of many young men and women to leave their villages and try their luck in Manchester, Birmingham, London, and

---

[108] *Life*, iii. 249.

[109] *Spectator*, 3 July 1711, 23 Oct. 1712. For a discussion of literary stereotypes, see Speck, *Society and Literature in England, 1700–60*. There were, of course, less flattering representations of booby squires. The old country dance called 'Sir Roger de Coverley' was said to be the invention of Sir Roger's great-grandfather.

Sheffield. But the vision of pastoral felicity outside the park gates lived on and found its expression in the poetry of nostalgia.[110] Goldsmith's *The Deserted Village*, to which Johnson contributed the concluding lines, was published in May 1770. In the dedication to Sir Joshua Reynolds, Goldsmith insisted that he had taken pains to confirm the truth of 'those miseries, which I here attempt to display', and that he sincerely believed what he had written. What remained of 'sweet Auburn', once a thriving village, was forlorn and desolate, one aged crone gathering watercress in the muddy stream, while a gloomy tyrant of new wealth held sway at the hall. Goldsmith admitted that opinion might well be against him in deploring the effects of luxury. In his view, 'wanton wealth' had driven out 'rural virtues' and destroyed a proud and bold peasantry:

> Ill fares the land, to hastening ills a prey,
> Where wealth accumulates, and men decay.

Johnson's view was more balanced than Goldsmith's. He did not deplore the spread of luxury because he did not think there was much of it about. He welcomed improvements in the lot of the poor, admired the ingenuity of tradesmen and entrepreneurs, and applauded the increased independence which the developing commercial society offered. But he saw a darker side to the 'moneyed interest': in a world based on cash relationships, what would happen to those without cash? 'Severity towards the poor', he insisted, was 'an undoubted and constant attendant and consequence of Whiggism'.[111] He feared that the brave new world would prove callous and harsh, and in his *Life of Addison* he drew attention to the *Spectator*'s creation of Sir Andrew Freeport, the city counterpart to Sir Roger de Coverley. Sir Andrew, 'a new man, a wealthy merchant, zealous for the moneyed interest, and a Whig', behaved towards the poor, in Johnson's words, 'in the true spirit of unfeeling commerce'.

This debate is not yet played out. It is a mere freak of nomenclature that Thatcherism should have passed as a form of Toryism when, as has often been remarked, it had far more in common with Manchester school liberalism, even if its theoretical aloofness was mitigated in practice by the personal itch to intervene and direct. Johnson represented an older and deeper Toryism—moderate, balanced, organic, and compassionate. Far from believing that society was a figment of the imagination, he saw it as the context and comfort of human existence. His concern for waifs and

---

[110] See I. Kramnick, *Bolingbroke and his Circle: The Politics of Nostalgia in the Age of Walpole* (Cambridge, Mass., 1968), esp. ch. 8.
[111] *Miscellanies*, i. 204.

strays, and his charity towards beggars whom, according to Mrs Thrale, he wished not merely to relieve but to indulge, were no mere personal whims, but reflected his Christian view of a responsible society. 'Life', he observed, 'was a pill which none of us can bear to swallow without gilding', tolerable only if the rich and fortunate behaved with kindness and understanding. Though, in the late twentieth century, regulated and controlled economies have mostly been abandoned, as tending only to keep people poor and ignorant, few regimes have wholly embraced unrestricted market forces. To balance the freedom of individuals against the needs of society calls for constant reappraisal and delicate judgements. Of the difficulties that lay ahead Johnson was not unaware.

6

Johnson and Enlightenment

AT first sight, Johnson does not look like a member of the fraternity of enlightened thinkers. He has often been exhibited as an archetypal anti-enlightenment figure, England's John Bull, a man of sturdy prejudices who hated infidels, mistrusted metaphysicians, and had no high opinion of *philosophes*, continental or domestic. His constant message was not belief in progress, but fortitude and resignation in the face of those afflictions which the human condition necessarily imposes. Most schemes of improvement, he told Boswell, were very laughable things.[1] To Goldsmith's poem *The Traveller*, Johnson contributed two sombre lines:

> How small, of all that human hearts endure
> That part which laws or kings can cause or cure.

His deep love for the Church and his respect for the clergy seem to set him apart from the strident anti-clericalism of continental circles.

Yet a closer scrutiny prompts doubt. No one has, after all, suggested that Voltaire should not be included in the Enlightenment. But Voltaire's *Candide* and Johnson's *Rasselas* came out in the same year and the parallels are remarkable. If Voltaire's intention was to mock mechanical and heartless optimism and to suggest that we should soldier on, Johnson's was to unmask folly and pretentiousness and to preach endurance of what cannot be avoided. At the end of *Candide*, the remaining members of Pangloss's little party resolve to cultivate their gardens,[2] while at the end of *Rasselas* Imlac and his friends return to Abyssinia, sadder and wiser.[3]

The problem arises in the main from a narrow and somewhat outdated interpretation of the Enlightenment as an essentially French phenomenon, from a concentration on too limited a chronological span, and from a distortion even of the French part of that definition. One can understand

---

[1] *Life*, ii. 102.

[2] The subtitle of *Candide* is *Ou l'optimisme*. See also Voltaire's *Poème sur le désastre de Lisbonne ou examen de cet axiome: Tout est bien.*

[3] Each of them had schemes of improvement but 'they knew none could be accomplished'. For a comparison of Voltaire and Johnson, see D. J. Greene in A. J. Bingham and V. W. Topagio (eds.), *Enlightened Studies in Honour of L. G. Crocker* (Oxford, 1979), 111–32.

how such an interpretation arose in the first place. France was, in the middle of the eighteenth century, a country of great intellectual vitality and distinction. Montesquieu, Voltaire, and Rousseau are a formidable trio, and with a supporting cast of Fontenelle, Mably, de La Mettrie, Diderot, Helvétius, d'Alembert, Mercier, Turgot, Quesnay, Morellet, Chastellux, and Condorcet one is inclined to surrender to mere numbers. But it would be scarcely possible, in seventeenth-century thought, to exaggerate the importance of Bacon, Newton, and Locke, or later to overlook Pope, Bolingbroke, Hume, Gibbon, Bentham, or Paine. Contemporaries certainly did not have a narrow view of the Enlightenment. They referred frequently to its European dimension and to the English contribution. On his famous visit in the later 1720s, Voltaire found the English 'a nation of Philosophers'; Diderot wrote that it was clear 'to all who have eyes, that without the English, reason and philosophy would still be in a state of contemptible infancy in France'; Jean Louis de Lolme, a native of Geneva, visited England in 1769 and rejoiced that, by a fortunate conjunction of circumstances, 'liberty has at last been able to erect herself a temple'; and Jacob Sievers, a Baltic German in Russian service, wrote in 1780 that England was, without doubt, the most enlightened country in Europe.[4]

The traditional interpretation saw the French Enlightenment as radical, egalitarian, progressive, sceptical, and hostile to religion. Support for this view came from furious denunciations of the *philosophes* after the French Revolution by Burke, Barruel, de Maistre, and others, who painted them as negative and destructive wild-eyed fanatics. Burke placed the blame for the Revolution on a 'literary cabal' who had formed a 'regular plan' for the overthrow of Christianity and who cared not what havoc was necessary to reach their goal:

Nothing can be conceived more hard than the heart of a thoroughbred metaphysician . . . It is like that of the principle of evil himself, incorporeal, pure, unmixed, dephlegmated, defecated evil. It is no easy operation to eradicate humanity from the human breast . . . they never see any way to their projected good but by the road of some evil . . . These philosophers consider men in their experiments no more than they do mice in an air-pump . . .[5]

Two years later, Burke was joined by the Abbé Barruel in the conspiracy thesis: in his *Mémoires pour servir à l'histoire du jacobinisme*, Barruel traced

⁴ T. Besterman (ed.), *Voltaire's Correspondence* (Geneva, 1953), ii. 37; Diderot, *Œuvres complètes*, ed. J. Assezat (Paris, 1875), iii. 416; de Lolme, *Constitution d'Angleterre*; Sievers is quoted in R. E. Jones, *The Emancipation of the Russian Nobility* (Princeton, 1973), 268 n.
⁵ *Reflections*, 107–8; *A Letter to a Noble Lord* (London, 1796).

the misfortunes that had overtaken his country to a sinister alliance of *philosophes* and Freemasons. It was then the turn of Britain once more to denounce the 'detestable doctrines' of the Illuminati, with an even stranger volume by the scientist John Robison, the title of which reveals the basic plot: *Proofs of a Conspiracy Against All the Religions and Governments of Europe Carried On in the Secret Meetings of Free Masons, Illuminati and Reading Societies, Collected from Good Authorities.*[6]

But the connection between the French Enlightenment and the French Revolution was never as direct as conservatives suggested, nor were the *illuminés* as radical as subsequent generations believed. Far from wishing to stir up mob violence, most of the *philosophes* were uncommonly anxious that their writings should not fall into the hands of the lower orders and bring down the roof. 'We have never pretended to enlighten shoemakers and servants', wrote Voltaire loftily to d'Alembert.[7] Holbach, though one of the more radical thinkers, explained that his books were intended 'only for that part of a nation which its circumstances, its education and its feelings raise above crime'.[8] Diderot was of like mind, explaining to his publisher that there were some readers whom he would never wish to have: 'I write only for those with whom I should enjoy conversing. I address my works to the philosophers.'[9]

Nor can the assumption that the *philosophes* shared a blithe confidence in the future go unchallenged. We have already noted Voltaire attacking any such attitude in *Candide* in 1759, and Norman Hampson has argued that by the 1760s the bloom had gone off the Enlightenment, as many of the *philosophes* came to realize that they had argued themselves into a deterministic trap.[10] This coincided with much heart-searching about the benevolence of nature, prompted by the Lisbon earthquake of 1755, and despair at the cruelty and cost of the Seven Years War. Vyverberg has gone so far as to argue that a deep strain of pessimism ran through the Enlightenment, and, though his suggestion seems in places a little strained, it serves as a reminder against easy generalization.[11]

---

[6] Readers may be surprised to learn that the secret conspiracy continues. Robison's book was republished in America in 1967 with a foreword explaining that the villains were still at their work and were particularly to be found in universities and seats of learning: 'one tends to think of professors, philosophers and writers as sitting in their ivory towers, perfectly harmless to the world. Robison and history prove otherwise.' *Proofs of a Conspiracy* (Boston, Western Islands, 1967).

[7] *Voltaire's Correspondence*, 70, no. 14239 (2 Sept. 1768).

[8] *Le Christianisme dévoilé* (Londres, 1756).

[9] Quoted in N. Hampson, *The Enlightenment* (London, 1968), 161.   [10] Ibid. 186.

[11] H. Vyverberg, *Historical Pessimism in the French Enlightenment* (Cambridge, Mass., 1958).

Perhaps the most common misunderstanding about the French Enlightenment is that it was opposed to religion. The charge was made
repeatedly, during and after the Revolution, especially in the light of the
short-lived campaign of de-Christianization in France. It is not easy to
establish precisely what were the religious views of the French *philosophes*,
since it was a matter both personal and complex. Their views were subject
to change over time, and, faced by a powerful and suspicious Church
which kept a wary eye open for religious deviation, many writers thought
it prudent to dissemble. Though towards the end of his life Diderot made
little attempt to hide his agnosticism, at an earlier period he had included
in his *Pensées philosophiques* a formal declaration of faith.[12] Most of the
writers seem to have been deists or latitudinarian Catholics. There were
few avowed atheists, though those who were attracted much attention and
the spread of free-thinking was one of the obsessions of the age. Holbach,
an aristocrat and a wealthy man, could afford to risk his atheism, but a
detailed study of the celebrated Holbach circle suggests that, despite its
reputation as a nest of atheists, few of its members were.[13] Jean-Jacques
Rousseau, who came in for much censure after the Revolution, insisted
upon the importance of religion, and his acolyte Maximilien de
Robespierre led the procession in June 1794 for the Feast of the Supreme
Being.[14]

Although the French Enlightenment was far from being anti-religious,
it was certainly anti-clerical, for reasons which are not hard to discern.
The Gallican Church and the *parlements*, especially the *parlement de Paris*,
kept up a running warfare against the *philosophes*. A number of them were
gaoled at various times and almost all of them suffered persecution and
censorship. Voltaire's spell in the Bastille in 1726 helped to persuade him
to make his highly formative visit to England and convinced him that
habeas corpus had much to commend it. The *Lettres philosophiques*, which
were the outcome of the visit, were burned as soon as they appeared in
1734. In 1766 when the young Chevalier de La Barre was tortured and
executed, a copy of Voltaire's *Dictionnaire philosophique* was hung around
his neck. Diderot's *Pensées philosophiques* were burned in 1746, despite the
author's testimony to Catholicism, and in 1749 he spent three months in
prison in Vincennes for the publication of *Lettres sur les aveugles*. The
great *Encyclopédie*, of which Diderot was the editor, was suppressed in

[12] Pensée LVIII. *Œuvres Complètes*, i. 153.
[13] A. C. Kors, *D'Holbach's Coterie: An Enlightenment in Paris* (Princeton, NJ, 1976),
suggests that only d'Holbach himself, Diderot, and Naigeon were atheists.
[14] Robespierre denounced atheism as 'aristocratic'.

1752, putting Diderot to desperate shifts to complete it. Marmontel spent a few days in the Bastille in 1759; Helvetius's *De l'esprit* was burned the same year; and Morellet was sent to the Bastille in 1760. Rousseau's *Émile* was banned in 1762. In 1768, a grocer's apprentice was branded and sentenced to nine years in the galleys for selling a copy of Holbach's *Le Christianisme dévoilé*. Raynal, the author of *Histoire philosophique et politique des deux Indes*, was sent into exile in 1781 and his property confiscated.

It is sometimes argued that the sentences were not usually severe, nor the conditions of imprisonment arduous. Had they been, they might have been more effective deterrents. Control was fussy and irritating, enough to provoke and inflame, hardly sufficient to intimidate or subdue. Diderot was one of many French writers to make rueful comparisons with the situation in England:

In England, philosophers are honoured, respected; they rise to public offices, are buried with the kings. Do we see that England is any the worse for it? In France, warrants are issued against them, they are persecuted, pelted with pastoral letters, with satires and libels.[15]

The contrast is painted in extreme terms and the grass is always greener on the other side. But there is enough in it to account for the sharp difference in attitude between writers in England and in France. The latter drifted, or were pushed, into a critical and oppositionist stance. The reception offered to *Rasselas* and *Candide* makes the point. The first was widely acclaimed and within three years Johnson was given a government pension; the second was burned by order of the Paris *parlement*.

Some indication of the damage which their own heavy-handedness may have inflicted upon the French authorities may perhaps be gained by considering one of the few cases in England where the government moved to suppress criticism. In 1763 John Wilkes's no. 45 of the *North Briton*, attacking the Peace of Paris, was indicted as a seditious libel, and his *Essay on Woman* as an obscene libel. The result was not to intimidate Wilkes but to launch him on an extremely successful career as an opposition martyr, and to give to the reform movement an impetus which it could never have acquired on its own. Lord North and the more intelligent members of the government soon realized that Wilkes was infinitely more of a nuisance outside the House of Commons than inside and that persecution was the

---

[15] *Œuvres complètes*, ed. J. Assezat, ii. 80 n. 1.

oxygen he needed. Deprived of his grievance after 1774, he settled down quietly and became, in time, a reliable supporter of government.[16]

When pondering Johnson's relationship with the French *philosophes*, one must remember the very different social and political contexts in which they lived. Many of the rights for which French authors contended had been long granted in England. It was no longer necessary to make the case for religious toleration, trial by jury, or habeas corpus. It is true that Johnson had to exercise guile and caution in reporting paliamentary debates, but at least there was a Parliament and it had debates. In France, the States-General had not been summoned since 1614.[17] In England, the use of torture had long been forbidden. In France it was still in use, as were hideous punishments: Calas, on whose behalf Voltaire wrote, was broken on the wheel; Damiens, who had tried to assassinate Louis XV, was dismembered by cart-horses; de La Barre, an eighteen-year-old youth, had his tongue ripped out before he was decapitated. It is unlikely that a man as compassionate as Johnson, who wrote angrily on behalf of Admiral Byng and tried to save the unfortunate Dr Dodd, would have been a supporter of the status quo had he lived in France.[18]

If the gap between Johnson and the French *philosophes*, particularly those of his own generation, does not look unbridgeable, an extension of the comparison to include writers from other countries suggests that he may not have been far from the mainstream of enlightened thinking. We have already noted the admiration widely expressed for England's authors, especially her scientists and political philosophers. Other countries also had their admirers. The vigour and extent of the Scottish Enlightenment attracted much attention. The Dutch and the Venetians were frequently applauded as exceptionally tolerant and enlightened. Johann Georg Forster, the German man-of-letters, was surprised in 1784 to find in Prague scholars 'much disposed towards the enlightenment'.[19] In Spain, the leading representative of the Enlightenment was a Benedictine monk, Benito Feijoo, whose work Johnson reviewed. A young and impressionable Jeremy Bentham declared that Beccaria's work on crime

---

[16] Wilkes had strong links with France, particularly with the d'Holbach circle, and lived there in exile between 1763 and 1768. Barré told the government to kill Wilkes by neglect and, when in 1776 Wilkes moved for reform, Lord North treated the matter jocularly.

[17] The Paris *Parlement* was not a Parliament in the English sense, but a law court, with powers of remonstrance and registration.

[18] Robert Shackleton points out that, as one would expect, Johnson was more sympathetic to the earlier and less radical phase of the Enlightenment. 'Johnson and the Enlightenment', in Powell (ed.), *Johnson, Boswell and their Circle*, 76–92.

[19] H. Hettner (ed.), *Georg Forster's Briefwechsel mit S. Th. Sömmerring* (Brunswick, 1877), 102.

and punishment had carried Italy's contribution beyond that of England or France.[20]

In most of these countries, the *philosophes* were Christian, moderate in tone, and much less likely to be found in opposition to their governments. In Scotland, relations between the philosophers and the Church were close. William Robertson, the historian and leader of the Moderate party, was a minister, as were the philosopher Adam Ferguson, the mathematician and geologist John Playfair, the Gaelic scholar William Shaw, Alexander Carlyle (the advocate of a Scottish militia), and the poet Robert Blair. Another cleric was Hugh Blair, whose sermons Johnson persuaded Strahan to print, with enormous success. Thomas Reid, Francis Hutcheson, John Millar, and John Home were sons of clerics.[21] In Germany, Switzerland, and Holland, the leading thinkers were traditional in attitude and enlightened circles included a number of clerics. Boerhaave, the Dutch physician, and Linnaeus, the Swedish botanist, were both sons of the clergy: of Boerhaave Johnson wrote that 'the excellency of the Christian religion was the frequent subject of his conversation'.[22] 's Gravesande, the Dutch popularizer of Newton's work, declared himself proud to be a Christian, and in Germany Christian Wolff, the exponent of Leibniz, employed scepticism as a weapon against deism and atheism. In Austria, Catholic writers collaborated in the reforms of Maria Theresa and Joseph II. Beccaria, an Italian and an aristocrat by birth, was much consulted about practical questions by the government of Lombardy, and was appointed a state councillor in Austria. Only in France were the *philosophes* forced into the role of critics.[23]

In this wider European context, Johnson looks much more comfortable. His deep personal religion no longer marks him off as an antiquated thinker in an era of secular progress, any more than Newton's means that he cannot be regarded as part of the Enlightenment. His admiration for the English constitution does not brand him as an ultra-conservative, since we have seen that such an attitude was a commonplace both at home and abroad, even among liberal thinkers. What placed him in the middle of the Enlightenment was his rationality, a determination, despite his own

[20] E. Halevy, *The Growth of Philosophical Radicalism*, tr. M. Morris (London, 1972), 21, quoting from the Bentham MSS in University College London.

[21] R. B. Sher, *Church and University in the Scottish Enlightenment* (Edinburgh, 1990).

[22] *Gentleman's Magazine* (1739), 175.

[23] Even in France a number of the *philosophes* were in holy orders and, at the beginning of Louis XVI's reign, Turgot, a contributor to the *Encyclopédie*, was appointed Comptroller-General.

strong prejudices and feelings, to think out his position on moral and political issues. His famous remark 'Pray, clear your mind of cant' was not a playful aphorism, but a clue to his mental approach. It was this which Boswell, at the end of the *Life*, identified as Johnson's chief characteristic:

> His superiority over other learned men consisted chiefly in what may be called the art of thinking, the art of using his mind; a certain continual power of seizing the useful substance of all that he knew, and exhibiting it in a clear and forcible manner; so that knowledge, which we often see to be no better than lumber in men of dull understanding, was, in him, true, evident, and actual wisdom.[24]

Norman Hampson has observed that the conviction that social utility took precedence over dogma runs like a leitmotiv throughout the eighteenth century.[25] Such a description fits Johnson, with his interest in useful knowledge. His justification of the church establishment was, as we have seen, in terms of social utility. He argued repeatedly that doctrinal differences were of comparatively little importance. He disapproved somewhat of convents on the ground that 'it is our first duty to serve society; and, after we have done that, we may attend wholly to the salvation of our own souls.'[26] He was interested in the reform of debtors' prisons and he concerned himself with the plight of French prisoners of war in the 1760s. He insisted that the test of a country's civilization was the way it treated its poor, and he took into his own household misfits and unfortunates, the casualties of society. Lasting fame, he wrote in *Rambler*, no. 106, is not within the grasp of most men: 'it may however satisfy an honest and benevolent mind to have been useful'.

If the Enlightenment in France was largely literary and philosophical, in England it retained a more scientific character. The tradition of the powerful founding trio of Bacon, Newton, and Locke was carried on by Boyle, Hooke, Halley, Sloane, the chemist Henry Cavendish, the astronomer Neville Maskelyne, David Hartley, Joseph Priestley, and the botanist Sir Joseph Banks, who was a close friend of Johnson and a pallbearer at his funeral. It would be idle to suggest that Johnson was a great scientist or that science was one of his major interests. But he was in close touch with a considerable number of medical and scientific friends, and was an active member of the Royal Society of Arts, one of the aims of which was the practical implementation of scientific and technological developments. Johnson attended meetings in the late 1750s and early 1760s, and

---

[24] *Life*, iv. 427–8. The stunning brilliance of Boswell's analysis and the beauty of his prose should not go unacknowledged.

[25] *The Enlightenment*, 105.   [26] *Life*, ii. 10.

served on a number of committees, including those concerned with the expansion of the Society's premises, proposals for improvements to a sawmill, and a scheme for a purer water supply.[27] According to Revd Andrew Kippis, Johnson spoke well at the Society on the subject of mechanics, and in January 1762 he proposed his great friend Richard Bathurst, the surgeon, for membership.[28]

Johnson maintained a lifelong interest in chemistry. In one of his earliest writings, in 1739, he referred to it as an 'enchanting subject',[29] and when the playwright Arthur Murphy first called upon him in the summer of 1754 he found Johnson 'all covered with soot like a chimney-sweep, in a little room, with an intolerable heat and strange smell . . . making *aether*'.[30] When Boswell visited him in July 1763 at his lodgings in the Temple, he 'observed an apparatus for chymical experiment, of which Johnson was all his life very fond'; and when Johnson made the acquaintance of the Thrales, they fitted up a kind of garden shed at Streatham where he could continue his experiments.[31] He retained all his life a particular interest in exact calculations and problems of measurement, and took pleasure in visiting factories, foundries, and museums.[32] He also published on the margins of science: the life of Boerhaave, an account for Anna Williams's father of the latter's claim to have discovered a method of ascertaining longitude at sea by magnetism,[33] and several entries, including a revised life of Boerhaave, for the large *Medical Dictionary* of his friend Dr Robert James.[34]

It has also been suggested that Johnson was uncommonly well informed on psychological matters. There is little doubt that the concern he felt for his own mental health prompted him to take a deep interest in the subject and, though without formal training, sharpened his perceptions. His

[27] J. L. Abbott, 'Dr Johnson and the Society', *Journal of the Royal Society of Arts*, 115 (Apr. and May 1967), 395–400, 486–91.

[28] C. H. Hinnant, *Samuel Johnson: An Analysis* (Basingstoke, 1988), shows Johnson's debt to Newton, whose views influenced his moral and theological standpoint as well as his understanding of science.

[29] A passing reference in his life of Boerhaave, printed in the *Gentleman's Magazine* (1739), 37, 72, 114, 172.

[30] *Miscellanies*, i. 306.   [31] *Life*, i. 436; *Miscellanies*, i. 307–8.

[32] R. B. Schwartz, *Samuel Johnson and the New Science* (Madison, Wis., 1971). For measurement of finger nails, see *Miscellanies*, i, no. 75; for his vine, ibid. i, no. 161; for the Lichfield tree, ibid. ii. p. 423.

[33] Zachariah Williams was another of Johnson's medical friends. He failed to persuade most of his acquaintances of the validity of his proposal, and Johnson brought out the treatise, with an Italian translation by Baretti, in the last year of Williams's life.

[34] For the range of Johnson's scientific metaphors, see W. K. Wimsatt, Jr., 'Scientific Imagery in *The Rambler*', in Greene (ed.), *Samuel Johnson*, 138–48.

portrait of the astrologer in *Rasselas*, who became convinced that he could control the weather, is a classic description of schizophrenia;[35] and that the condition of paranoia was well recognized is clear from Johnson's account in *The Idler*, no. 92, of Ned Smuggle, who 'believes himself watched by observation and malignity on every side, and rejoices in the dexterity by which he has escaped snares that never were laid'. Kathleen Grange has suggested that Johnson made 'outstanding contributions' to the understanding which twentieth-century psychologists have inherited from the past.[36]

So far we have been working on the traditional assumption that the Enlightenment is best traced in the writings of individuals or in their common approach to particular issues. That definition runs into considerable difficulties of demarcation, of chronology, and of intellectual coherence. A different way of looking at the question, which has distinct advantages, is to widen the focus from a comparatively small group of authors in order to acknowledge the vast accumulation and dissemination of knowledge, the great increase in literacy, and the improvements in media communications which took place in Europe, not over one or two decades, but throughout the seventeenth and eighteenth centuries. Such an approach would find room for popular as well as classical literature, for popularizers and hack-writers as well as writers of outstanding talent, and for a great variety of publications, many of them humble and instructional, as well as the severely literary and philosophical. It changes the cast on stage, bringing on the printers, teachers, editors, and booksellers to augment the performances of the *philosophes*. It raises the 'harmless drudges', for whom Johnson had a soft spot, and gives them an important role in the transmission of culture. It drops the definite article, and draws attention to the *process* of enlightenment. It looks for the political influence of the Enlightenment, not in a handful of autocratic rulers whose dedication to enlightened principles frequently disappoints when placed under scrutiny, but in the growing ranks of the middling people of Europe, and it points, not towards enlightened despotism, which was a dead end, but towards liberalism and democracy.

One consequence of the change of focus is that England appears, not as

[35] K. M. Grange, 'Dr Samuel Johnson's Account of a Schizophrenic Illness in *Rasselas*', *Medical History*, 6 (1962), 162–8.

[36] 'Samuel Johnson's Account of Certain Psychoanalytic Concepts', in Greene (ed.), *Samuel Johnson*, 149–57. An excellent discussion of Johnson's very considerable medical knowledge is in J. Wiltshire, *Samuel Johnson in the Medical World* (Cambridge, 1991).

a sloop following in the wake of the French, but as the flagship of the enterprise, and Johnson himself is promoted from deck-hand to Admiral of the Fleet; for he was both a shrewd observer of these new developments and a supreme example of them.

Perhaps the most striking illustration of this intellectual revolution was the establishment of a popular press and its emergence as a powerful political force. The decade into which Johnson was born has been described as the most critical in the history of the newspaper, since it followed the decision of Parliament not to renew the Licensing Act in 1695.[37] With pardonable exaggeration, Macaulay called this event one 'which has done more for liberty and for civilisation than the Great Charter or the Bill of Rights'.[38] Until then, newspapers, broadsheets, and news-sheets had had a hard struggle against adversity. They made their first appearance in the 1620s as imitations of German or Dutch *corontos*, occasional and haphazard in publication and prudently eschewing English news and comment. They were confined to London and to a circulation of between 200 and 300. Suppressed between 1632 and 1638, they came into their own during the great crisis of the 1640s. From 1643 to 1645 there were vigorous exchanges between the royalist *Mercurius Aulicus* at Oxford and its parliamentary counterparts in London. The vitality and scurrility of the press caused first the Rump Parliament and then Cromwell to move against it, and restraining measures were continued by Charles II after the Restoration. But the public demand for news continued unabated and was not assuaged by the *London Gazette*, established in 1665 as the vehicle for official information. The upheavals of the 1670s and 1680s—the Popish plot and the Exclusion crisis, Monmouth's rebellion and the Glorious Revolution—provided plenty of fuel for public excitement, which a motley collection of news-sheets and ephemeral papers endeavoured to meet. Many of them were remarkable more for their lewdness than for their learning, but there were significant indications of the new commercial and financial developments in papers that concentrated on shipping news, agricultural items, and other matters of specialized interest.[39]

The decade after the lapse of the Licensing Act saw two important developments in newspaper history. In April 1702, correctly anticipating

---

[37] M. Harris, 'The Structure, Ownership and Control of the Press, 1620–1780', in G. Boyce, J. Curran, and P. Wingate (eds.), *Newspaper History from the Seventeenth Century to the Present Day* (London, 1978), 82–97.

[38] *History of England* (1889 edn.), ii. 503.

[39] G. Cranfield, *The Press and Society* (London, 1978), 32–3.

the effect that the War of the Spanish Succession would have upon the demand for news, a bookseller named Edward Mallet produced the first daily newspaper, the *Daily Courant*.[40] Its circulation for 1704 has been estimated at a modest 800,[41] but it survived until 1735 when it was incorporated into *The Gazetteer*.[42] The second development was the growth of a weekly provincial press. Francis Burges' *Norwich Post* (1701) was followed in quick succession by Bonny's *Bristol Post Boy* (1702), Farley's *Exeter Post-Man* (1704), and the *Worcester Post-Man* (1709).[43] The Norwich and Exeter papers soon had local rivals.[44] By the end of the decade, thirteen papers had been established in nine provincial towns, and only one had failed to survive.[45]

Successive governments, Tory and Whig, watched these developments without enthusiasm. In 1712 Bolingbroke clapped the first duty on the newspaper press.[46] After some immediate casualties, it recovered. Walpole then closed the loophole in 1725,[47] but the development of a strong opposition to his government prompted much journalistic activity, and, in the end, he spent a good deal of money subsidizing a ministerial press.[48] In 1757, at the beginning of the Seven Years War, the duty was doubled. Despite these obstacles, the press, metropolitan and provincial, continued to flourish. Circulation fluctuated according to war and peace, and the fortunes of particular newspapers rose and fell, but the general trend was unmistakably upward.

By 1760 there were four London dailies, six by 1772, and no fewer than fourteen by 1790. Their circulation had risen from hundreds in Anne's reign to thousands: the *Public Advertiser* in the early 1770s was printing

[40] He quickly sold it to Samuel Buckley, printer of the *London Gazette* and publisher of Pope.

[41] Cranfield, *Press and Society*, 32. Triennial evening papers in London catered for the provincial market and achieved larger circulations: the *Post-Man* may have had 3,800 and the *Post-Boy* 3,000.

[42] R. L. Haig, *The Gazetteer, 1735–1797* (Carbondale, Ill., 1960), 3, 10–11.

[43] For the considerable problems in dating early provincial newspapers, see G. A. Cranfield, *The Development of the Provincial Newspaper, 1700–1760* (Oxford, 1962), 13–15.

[44] The *Norwich Gazette* (1706), *Norwich Post-Man* (1706), and *Exeter Post Boy* (1709).

[45] The casualty was a Shrewsbury paper, *A Collection of the Most Material Newes*, which may not have been helped by its unarresting title. The newcomers in 1710 were the *Liverpool Courant*, *Newcastle Gazette*, *Stamford Post*, *Nottingham Post*, and *Nottingham Courant*.

[46] Pamphlets were to pay two shillings per specimen sheet, newspapers $\frac{1}{2}d$. a copy on a half-sheet and 1*d*. on a full sheet. A duty of one shilling was imposed on advertisements. Newspapers evaded the worst effects by turning themselves into small pamphlets.

[47] The Act of 1725 insisted that every sheet should bear a stamp.

[48] The committee established after Walpole's fall in 1742 to investigate his conduct reported that William Arnall, his chief journalist, had received £11,000 from secret service funds in four years.

more than 3,000 copies, and the *Gazetteer* claimed 5,000.[49] The increase in the provincial press was even more marked. By 1760 there were some 35 provincial papers in existence, 50 by 1780, and 150 by 1821. They supplied not only their immediate towns but large adjacent areas: the *York Courant* in 1743 claimed agents in 43 towns and villages throughout the North, and *Felix Farley's Bristol Journal* in 1752 claimed 37, ranging from Penzance to Liverpool. Circulation is more difficult to establish because of the fluctuating success of particular papers, but some indication can be gained from the number of stamps issued. The stamp duty brought in a mere £911 in its first year in 1713, but by 1781 was bringing in more than £40,000 p.a. and making a substantial contribution to revenue. Seven million stamps were issued in 1750, ten million by 1756, twelve million by 1775, fourteen million by 1780, and thirty-nine million by the accession of Victoria.

The remarkable expansion of newspapers was augmented and supported by the simultaneous growth of periodical literature. Among the earliest in the field was Defoe's *Review*, started in 1704 and surviving until 1713. Intended as political comment in the Harley interest, it came out thrice weekly and sold between 500 and 1,000 copies each edition.[50] Richard Steele's *Tatler*, founded in 1709, was concerned with social comment.[51] In 1711, he joined forces with Joseph Addison to launch the *Spectator*, which, ambitiously, came out daily, and was soon selling more than 3,000 copies a time.[52] The literary success of Steele and Addison was not repeated and a gradual diversification of the periodical press followed. The *Craftsman* began in 1726 in opposition to the Walpole regime and at one stage was selling 10,000 copies. Most spectacular of all successes was that of Edward Cave's *Gentleman's Magazine*, started in 1731 and prompting a number of imitations, of which the *London Magazine* was the most enduring. By mid-century, the output of publications was sufficient to float regular reviews: the *Monthly Review* began in 1749, Smollett's *Critical Review* in 1756, and the *Literary Magazine*, which Johnson edited for a time, in the same year. The young Edmund Burke was employed as editor for Dodsley's *Annual Register*, launched in 1758 during the Seven

---

[49] The *Public Advertiser*'s sales books are in Add. MS 38169; Haig, *The Gazetteer*, 79.

[50] J. A. Downie, *Robert Harley and the Press: Propaganda and Public Opinion in the Age of Swift and Defoe* (Cambridge, 1979), 8–9.

[51] R. P. Bond in his edn. of the *Tatler* (Oxford, 1987) puts its circulation at 3,000–4,000.

[52] D. F. Bond (ed.), *The Spectator* (Oxford, 1965) i, pp. xxv–xxix. Certain numbers sold many more. Two printing houses had to be used to meet the demand. It sold at 1*d.* a copy until the Stamp Act of 1712, which imposed a duty of $\frac{1}{2}d.$, when the price was raised to 2*d.*

Years War. Tapping another new group of readers were journals aimed specifically at women: John Dunton produced the *Ladies Mercury* as early as 1693; the *Ladies Diary* ran from 1704 to 1841; and there was a *Female Tatler* written by Eliza Haywood from 1744 to 1746, and a *Ladies Magazine*.[53] John Newbery, one of the busiest of publishers, identified the growing market for children's books with his 'Juvenile Library', specially bound in attractive Dutch covers, though his attempt at a children's magazine, *The Lilliputian*, failed in 1751.[54] Newbery was also responsible for one of the first religious journals, the *Christian Magazine*, which ran from 1760 under the editorship of the unfortunate Dr Dodd, whom Johnson tried to save from the gallows.[55]

Within this steady progress, there were spectacular publishing *coups*, particularly in pamphlet literature. As early as 1693, Richard Sault, an eccentric mathematician, is reported to have sold 30,000 copies of his pamphlet, the *Second Spira*, in six weeks. This was a sensational piece describing the despair of a dying atheist and is, in itself, a warning against exaggerating the appeal of free-thinking and scepticism.[56] The political excitement of Anne's reign produced a crop of hard-hitting pamphlets. Daniel Defoe's *True-born Englishman*, a defence of William III, which came out in 1701, was said to have sold 80,000 copies; Henry Sacheverell's St Paul's sermon, *The Perils of False Brethren*, was said to have sold 40,000.[57] Swift was delighted with the success of his *Conduct of the Allies* in 1711, and claimed that 11,000 copies had been sold within two months.

A more surprising best-seller was Bishop Sherlock's pastoral letter of 1750 warning that the earthquakes that had afflicted London in that year were testimonies to the wrath of God for lewdness and infidelity: it was said to have sold 105,000 copies.[58] Books and plays could also bring great

---

[53] C. L. White, *Women's Magazines, 1693–1968* (London, 1970).

[54] Johnson satirized Newbery as Jack Whirler in *Idler*, no. 19: 'when he enters a house, his first declaration is that he cannot sit down, and so short are his visits that he seldom appears to have come for any reason but to say he must go.'

[55] Earlier examples were *The Christian's Amusement* (1740) and *Glasgow Weekly History* (1741), supported by George Whitefield. See S. Durden, 'A Study of the First Evangelical Magazines, 1740–1748', *Journal of Ecclesiastical History*, 76 (1976), 255–75.

[56] The 'first' Spira was an Italian advocate who died in the 1540s. Sault's publisher was John Dunton, who seems to have developed doubts about the pamphlet's authenticity, commenting later that it was one of the few books he regretted publishing.

[57] This is Burnet's figure, but Holmes, *The Trial of Dr Sacheverell*, 75, puts the real figure at nearer 100,000.

[58] Sherlock's success is a good example of the ambivalence of much evidence. The numbers sold testify to the growth of the reading public, and one of the bishop's complaints was about the swarm of indecent books being published. But his insistence that the earthquakes represented divine displeasure suggests that Bayle's rational works of the 1680s had

profit to the lucky publisher. *Gulliver's Travels* in 1726 was reported to have sold 10,000 copies in three weeks and the printer, Benjamin Motte, could not keep up with the demand. In 1729 William Bowyer printed 10,500 copies of John Gay's sequel to the *Beggar's Opera*, entitled *Polly*, and this did not prevent the publication of pirate editions. John Cleland's pornographic novel *Fanny Hill, or the Memoirs of a Woman of Pleasure* is reported to have made £10,000 for the publisher, Ralph Griffiths, in 1750; the author had to be content with 20 guineas, though he was subsequently given a pension by the Privy Council to desist from such corrupting enterprises.

There was also a good market for more scholarly works. Cadell and Millar made £6,000 out of Robertson's *History of Scotland* in 1759, and his *History of Charles V* in 1769 brought him in £4,500. Gibbon's *Decline and Fall*, a book of 586 pages, sold 1,000 copies in the first six weeks of publication in the spring of 1776. Burke's *Reflections on the Revolution in France*, a substantial volume, sold 19,000 copies in the six months from November 1790 to May 1791.[59] This, in turn, was dwarfed by the sales of Tom Paine's reply, *The Rights of Man*, estimated to have sold 200,000 copies by 1793.[60]

Though most of the publishing triumphs were metropolitan, there was also a remarkable expansion in the provincial book trade. Liverpool had 11 booksellers in 1766, 34 by the 1790s, and 98 by 1800. Newcastle upon Tyne had 2 booksellers in 1700, 25 in 1776, and 38 by 1787.[61] Ireland remained a source of irritation to English authors and publishers, since the English laws of copyright did not apply there. Dublin is said to have had 13 booksellers in 1690, 27 in 1710, and 46 by 1760.[62]

The substantial growth in the reading public is reflected in the increasingly important position held by publishers in Hanoverian England. Jacob Tonson, in Anne's reign, was secretary to the Kit-Kat Club; his nephew who took over the publishing firm died worth £10,000; and his great-nephew Richard became a member of Parliament. Thomas Osborne, for whom Johnson wrote the preface to the catalogue of the earl of Oxford's

---

still converts to make. The letter ran to 15 pages, sold at 3*d.* a copy, and many were distributed free of charge to the poor of London. Whether they were also read is another matter.

[59] *Correspondence of Burke*, vi. 177 n. 6.

[60] Paine's editions were of course much cheaper. M. D. Conway, *Life of Paine* (New York, 1892), i. 346; P. S. Foner, *The Complete Writings of Thomas Paine* (New York, 1961), ii. 190.

[61] J. Feather, *The Provincial Book Trade in Eighteenth Century England* (Cambridge, 1985), 29.

[62] R. Munter, *History of Irish Newspapers, 1685–1780* (Cambridge, 1967), 18.

library, claimed to be worth £40,000. Charles Dilly was famous for his dinner parties at the Poultry, at one of which Johnson had his meeting with John Wilkes, and he was said to have left a fortune of £60,000. William Strahan, one of the many Scots who after the Act of Union took the high road to England with success, published Adam Smith, Mackenzie, Gibbon, Robertson, and Blackstone, and became a member of Parliament in 1774. Johnson, who never had his own coach, called Strahan's coach 'a credit to literature', and at one of Strahan's dinner parties the guests included David Hume, Benjamin Franklin, the physician Sir John Pringle, and Mrs Thrale. Robert Dodsley, whom Johnson called his 'patron' since he had published 'London', started life as a footman; his successes included *The Preceptor*, for which Johnson wrote the preface in 1748 and which Boswell described as 'one of the most valuable books for the improvement of young minds that has appeared'.[63] Another remarkable career was that of James Lackington, in early life a West-country pie-man, who built up an enormous emporium in Finsbury Square. Lackington went for the emerging mass-market on the principle that 'small profits do great things', refused credit even to aristocratic customers so that he could sell cheap, and by 1791 claimed to be selling 100,000 volumes a year, at a profit of £4,000.[64]

To what extent were these English developments replicated throughout the rest of Europe? The situation varied greatly from country to country, since the vigour and vitality of the press was much affected by the attitudes of different rulers. In Germany, the position of the author was retarded by political disunity, since there was no copyright for the whole country until the nineteenth century.

The production of books in sixteenth-century Europe was stimulated by the Reformation, which placed great emphasis on regular Bible reading. But the application of the new technique to the distribution of news

---

[63] *Life*, i. 192. Johnson corrected his preface for the second edn. and wrote a contribution entitled 'The Vision of Theodore, the Hermit of Teneriffe'. The preface may be found in A. T. Hazen (ed.), *Samuel Johnson's Prefaces and Dedications* (New Haven, Conn., 1937). It is a long and earnest piece, explaining the intended use of the book and its various sections. 'The Vision', intended as the key to the book, was printed in *Gentleman's Magazine* (Apr. 1748). It is an elaborate homily on climbing the Mountain of Existence, resisting Appetite, Desire, Lust, Vanity, Intemperance, Indolence, and other snares. The defence is to cling fast to Reason and, above all, Religion. As a school-book and for readers inexperienced in the sciences, it had considerable success and was reprinted in 1754, 1758, 1763, 1769, 1775, 1783, 1793.

[64] James Lackington, *Memoirs of the First Forty-five Years of the Life of James Lackington, Bookseller* (1791): 'Reflecting on the means by which I have been enabled to support a carriage adds not a little to the pleasure of riding in it.' For a general account, see J. Feather, *A History of British Publishing* (London, 1988).

was much slower. Early presses could not print quickly and paper was expensive. Communications were so poor that both the gathering and the dissemination of news was difficult. For many decades, events reached the reader weeks or even months after they had taken place.

In the world of newspapers, the most crucial decades were in the early seventeenth century, a period of war and turmoil. Antwerp is reported to have had the *Nieuwe Tydigen* by 1605, and it was followed by papers published on a regular basis at Augsburg (1609), Basle (1610), Cologne (1610), Frankfurt (1615), Berlin (1617), Hamburg (1618), Vienna (1622), and Copenhagen (1634). By the early 1620s papers were being printed in Amsterdam for the English market. The first daily newspaper is believed to have been the *Einkommende Zeitung*, published in Leipzig from 1650.

The later development of newspapers and magazines was held back in a number of countries by censorship and official disapprobation, particularly in Spain and Austria. But the eighteenth century saw the establishment in most European countries of a vigorous press. In Ireland, the *Dublin Intelligence* appeared in 1690 to report William's campaigns; it did not survive his reign, but its place was taken by the *Flying Post* (1699), *Pue's Occurrences* (1703), and *Whalley's News Letter* (1714).[65] Scotland produced an *Edinburgh Gazette* in 1699, the *Edinburgh Flying Post* (1707), the *Glasgow Courant* (1715), and the *Caledonian Mercury* (1720).[66] In France, the official *Gazette* was established as a weekly by Richelieu in 1631, more than thirty years before its London counterpart. The *Mercure galant*, a monthly literary magazine, followed in 1672: according to Hampson, it was available in 26 French towns by 1748 and in 55 by 1774.[67] The development of the French provincial press was inhibited by the domination of Paris, but it gathered pace in the second half of the eighteenth century. The *Affiches de Province* began as a Parisian journal in 1752, but it had been preceded by the *Affiches de Lyon* (1750) and was followed by the *Affiches de Nantes* (1757), the *Affiches de Normandie* (1762), the *Affiches de Bordeaux* (1758), *Affiches de l'Orléanais* (1764), the *Affiches de Picardie* (1770), and the *Affiches de Dijon* (1771). Circulations remained small for some years, however. In 1776 the *Affiches de Reims*, established four years earlier, had fewer than 250 subscribers.[68] But progress, if unspectacular, was steady. An estimate of French literacy

---

[65] R. R. Madden, *The History of Irish Periodical Literature* (London, 1867).

[66] M. E. Craig, *The Scottish Periodical Press, 1750–1789* (Edinburgh, 1931).

[67] Hampson, *The Enlightenment*, 143.

[68] *Histoire générale de la presse française* (Paris, 1969–76), 323–7; J. Sgard, *Dictionnaire des Journaux, 1600–1789* (Paris, 1991).

suggests that it rose among men between 1686 and 1786 from 29 per cent to 47 per cent, and among women from 14 per cent to 27 per cent.[69]

In Germany, though political divisions held back a national mass readership, they encouraged local magazines and newspapers. Most important towns had their own newspapers by the end of the seventeenth century and by 1784 it was estimated that there were 217 newspapers published in Germany. The *Hamburg Patriot*, set up in 1724, had 5,000 subscribers. Book production made slower progress, but Becker's *Noth-und-Hülfsbuch*, an encyclopaedia of knowledge, printed 30,000 copies in 1787 and had sold eleven more authorized editions by 1791.[70] In Russia, Peter the Great made an attempt to encourage literacy and publication, but it was not until the reign of Catherine that the process picked up speed. Sumarokov's magazine *Busy Bee* made its appearance in 1759, and the first Russian weekly journal, an imitation of the *Spectator*, was *All Sorts of Things* (1769). During the whole of the seventeenth century Russian presses had produced no more than 500 books, most of them of a devotional nature; in the single year 1788 more than that number were published.[71] In Scandinavia, Stockholm had its *Ordinari post tijdende* by 1645 and Copenhagen its *Post Tidende* in 1749.

Though for reasons of conciseness we have concentrated on newspapers, books, and periodicals, the spread of enlightened ideas, the diffusion of knowledge, and the growth of a more sophisticated society can be observed in many other ways. The early eighteenth century witnessed a remarkable proliferation of clubs, societies, and associations, many of them based on coffee-houses and taverns. Johnson placed great emphasis on the civilizing effects of public conviviality, defined a club as 'an assembly of good fellows meeting under certain conditions', and noted that almost everyone he knew belonged to some club. William Maitland, commenting in 1739 on the spread of clubs in London, agreed that 'though these societies consist of the meanest and rudest of the citizens, yet by their admirable regulations and constitutions (of their own making) they are kept in the best order and decorum'.[72] The spread of masonry after the establishment of the Grand Lodge in 1717 was confined to the more

[69] Quoted in I. Woloch, *Eighteenth-century Europe* (London, 1982), 225.

[70] W. H. Bruford, *Germany in the Eighteenth Century* (Cambridge, 1965).

[71] G. Marker, *Publishing, Printing and the Origins of Intellectual Life in Russia, 1700–1800* (Princeton, NJ, 1985), 19, 105; I. de Madariaga, *Russia in the Age of Catherine the Great* (London, 1981); P. L. Alston, *Education and the State in Tsarist Russia* (Stanford, Calif., 1969).

[72] *The History and Survey of London from its Foundation . . . to the Present Time*, quoted by

prosperous classes, but there were other clubs for all manner of men: booksellers, goldsmiths, tradesmen, artists, farmers, and beggars.[73] The pleasure gardens of Vauxhall and Ranelagh flourished as never before. In provincial centres like York, Stamford, Shrewsbury, and Lincoln, assembly rooms and reading rooms were opened and subscription concerts, theatres, and libraries established. The Three Choirs Festival at Gloucester, Worcester, and Hereford dates from 1713; at Manchester, subscription concerts were held from 1744 onwards. Robert Thomlinson, a cleric, established the first public library in Newcastle upon Tyne in 1741.

Reactions to these developments were mixed. Many were glad to hail an improvement in the tone of social life and a decline in coarse and boisterous manners. Others were concerned that luxury would ruin the nation. Part of the interest in Gibbon's volumes in the 1770s and 1780s stemmed from the country's preoccupation with unwonted comfort and elegance, and a desire to discover to what extent luxury had contributed to the decline of Rome. Each social group began to condemn the effrontery of the group immediately below it. Circulating libraries were blamed for turning the heads of young ladies. Cobbett, at the end of the century, deplored the fact that farmers' daughters demanded pianos and learned French; he preferred the days when they would have been out milking cows.

Some perceived political dangers in these developments, arguing that they must, in the course of time, undermine respect for monarchical and aristocratic supremacy. As early as 1676 there was a somewhat half-hearted attempt by the government to suppress the new coffee-houses on the grounds that they were 'places where the disaffected met and spread scandalous reports concerning the conduct of His Majesty and his ministers'.[74] Bernard Mandeville, in 1713, thought that the country was in danger of producing too many literate persons: 'a certain proportion of ignorance in a well-ordered society' was necessary.[75] In 1721 an anonymous correspondent wrote to the government in some agitation from Birmingham that 'in every alehouse, people have the *London Journal* in their hands, shewing to each other with a kind of joy the most audacious

John Brewer in *The Birth of a Consumer Society*, ed. N. McKendrick, J. Brewer, and J. H. Plumb (London, 1982), 203.

[73] Extensive lists of London clubs are given in *Notes and Queries*, 9th ser., vols. iv, vi, viii, ix, x, xi.

[74] Bryant Lillywhite, *London Coffee Houses* (London, 1963), 18.

[75] Quoted in H. Monro, *The Ambivalence of Bernard Mandeville* (Oxford, 1975), 97.

reflections therein contained'.[76] The ministers took this information sufficiently seriously to buy up the newspaper a year later. Clubs founded for
primarily social or charitable purposes could easily acquire political objectives. A society among 'the lower kind of burgesses' at Shrewsbury in
1767 had a fund to support aged and infirm members, but also declared
that they would be unanimous in voting on all occasions.[77]

Of course, one must not overstate the speed and extent of change,
particularly in the more remote parts of Europe. It is, after all, novelty that
catches the eye of commentators and invites attention. It may be doubted
whether the majority of eighteenth-century Europeans ever had a book or
a newspaper in their hands or were aware that they were living in an age
of enlightenment. Russian and Polish serfs, Spanish and Irish peasants,
lived very much as their forefathers had.

Even in countries where the state showed considerable initiative in
education, the objectives were limited and the results often meagre.
Frederick the Great wrote that his 'country people' should receive instruction 'designed to keep them in villages and not influence them to
leave', while all the efforts of Catherine the Great served only to produce
the situation that, between 1786 and 1803, of 1,432 children in Archangel
schools, only 52 earned a leaving certificate.[78] Nevertheless, society was
changing and at an increasing speed.

The political influence of the press is hard to gauge. It has been pointed
out that early newspapers contained little comment and, partly to avoid
brushes with the authorities, concentrated largely upon foreign news,
filling up the rest with advertisements. Many of the attitudes expressed
were traditional, if not complacent, with much emphasis on the blessings
of the system of government.[79]

But that is not the whole story. It did not take British printers long to
realize that sustained panegyrics on the government of the day did not sell
many newspapers and within a few years they were vying with each other
in audacity. 'The expectation of readers runs so high', warned a correspondent of the *Freeholder's Journal* in 1722, 'that unless you journalists
now and then cut a bold stroke, they give you over; cry, you are grown

---

[76] Quoted in J. R. Sutherland, 'The Circulation of Newspapers and Literary Periodicals,
1700–30', *The Library*, 4th ser., 15 (1934), 110–24.

[77] *House of Commons, 1754–90*, i. 364.

[78] Alston, *Education and the State in Tsarist Russia*, 19.

[79] See J. Black, *The English Press in the Eighteenth Century* (London, 1987), esp. ch. 8; and
J. Black, 'Calculated upon a very Extensive and Useful Plan: The English Provincial Press
in the Eighteenth Century', in P. Isaac (ed.), *Six Centuries of the Provincial Book Trade in
Britain* (Winchester, 1990), 61–72.

insipid, or, what is worse, turn'd *Pensioners*.'[80] The contents of news-papers changed considerably in the course of the century. They became much larger, found more room for domestic news, and introduced features such as readers' letters, which were an attraction of Henry Sampson Woodfall's *Public Advertiser* in the 1760s. Some of the London papers adopted an overtly political stance from an early period. Mist's *Weekly Journal* was a thorn in the side of Walpole during the 1730s and the editor was frequently prosecuted; the *Middlesex Journal* followed an ardent radical line in the 1770s; and Cobbett's *Political Register*, which ran from 1802 until 1835, pursued a crusade for reform of Parliament and sold in unprecedented numbers.

It can hardly be stressed too strongly how limited were the sources of ideas and knowledge open to ordinary people before the invention and development of printing. Though the full potential of the press took time to be realized, there was little doubt of the direction in which events were moving, or of its role in challenging the exclusive and hierarchical charac-ter of political life.

Of these developments during his lifetime Johnson was well aware and, for the most part, he welcomed them. The country had become 'a nation of readers', he wrote in the 1781 preface to the *Lives of the Poets*, and in *The Adventurer*, no. 115, he offered a comic if barbed account of what he described as 'an epidemical conspiracy for the destruction of paper':

The present age . . . may be styled, with great propriety, the Age of Authors; for, perhaps, there never was a time in which men of all degrees of ability, of every kind of education, of every profession and employment, were posting with ardour so general to the press. The province of writing was formerly left to those who, by study, or appearance of study, were supposed to have gained knowledge unattain-able by the busy part of mankind; but in these enlightened days, every man is qualified to instruct every other man.

In the old controversy of the Ancients versus Moderns, Johnson, despite his deep love for the classics, had no hesitation in taking the side of the Moderns:

I am always angry when I hear ancient times praised at the expence of modern times. There is now a great deal more learning in the world than there was formerly, for it is universally diffused.[81]

He denied that Greece or Rome were more advanced civilizations:

[80] Quoted in Sutherland, 'The Circulation of Newspapers', 118–19.
[81] *Life*, iv. 217.

Sir, the mass of both of them were barbarians. The mass of every people must be barbarous where there is no printing, and consequently knowledge is not generally diffused. Knowledge is diffused among our people by the newspapers.[82]

In Essay no. 7 of *The Idler*, he dealt more fully with the role of the press:

All foreigners remark, that the knowledge of the common people of England is greater than that of any other vulgar. This superiority we undoubtedly owe to the rivulets of intelligence, which are continually trickling among us, which every one may catch, and of which every one partakes.

Johnson followed Bernard Mandeville in defending luxury. He had little patience with the Scottish baronet Sir Adam Fergusson, whom he and Boswell met in the newly-opened Pantheon in Oxford Street. All this, declared Sir Adam, would encourage luxury. 'Sir,' replied Johnson, 'I am a great friend to public amusements, for they keep people from vice'; were Boswell not with them, he added, he would no doubt be with a whore.[83] But he differed sharply from Mandeville on the imprudence of educating the lower orders.

Much of the attention which Mandeville had attracted derived from his attack upon charity schools, as institutions which would educate the poor above their stations in life. Soame Jenyns, in his *Free Inquiry*, had followed Mandeville, suggesting that ignorance was an opiate necessary to render the drudgery of life endurable to the poor: 'it is a cordial administered by the gracious hand of Providence, of which they ought never to be deprived by an ill-judged and improper education. It is the basis of all subordination.'[84] Johnson's concern to preserve rank and due submission might have led him to agree with Jenyns, but he seems to have been greatly provoked by Jenyns's condescension. After making the point that the interests of a great commercial nation demanded that the mass of the people should have an opportunity to improve their lot, Johnson continued:

---

[82] *Life*, ii. 170.

[83] Ibid. 169–71. See also his exchange with Goldsmith in 1773, who was worried that the English people were physically degenerated by luxury. Johnson: 'Sir, in the first place, I doubt the fact. I believe there are as many tall men in England now, as ever there were. But, secondly, supposing the stature of our people to be diminished, that is not owing to luxury; for, Sir, consider to how very small a proportion of our people luxury can reach. Our soldiery, surely, are not luxurious, who live on six-pence a day; and the same remark will apply to almost all the other classes.' Ibid. 217–18.

[84] It is only fair to Jenyns to note that it was an ill-judged or inappropriate education which he deplored. Such an attitude was commonplace and continued to be so for decades. Hannah More defended her Mendip schools with the assurance that she only fitted the poor for their role as servants.

I am always afraid of determining on the side of envy or cruelty. The privileges of education may sometimes be improperly bestowed, but I shall always fear to withhold them, lest I should be yielding to the suggestions of pride, while I persuade myself that I am following the maxims of policy; and, under the appearance of salutary restraints, should be indulging the lust of dominion and that malevolence which delights in seeing others depressed.[85]

We can, however, go further than suggesting that Johnson welcomed the expansion of education and of printing that was taking place. He personified it. The whole of his life, from beginning to end, serves as a commentary on the theme we have been tracing. He was born the son of a bookseller and died in the house of a printer.[86] Having failed as a teacher, he stayed in Birmingham in the house of Thomas Warren, publisher of the *Birmingham Journal*, one of the many provincial newspapers struggling for existence. To its pages Johnson contributed his first essays, and it was for Warren that he translated Father Lobo's *Voyage to Abyssinia* from a French version. On his visit to London in the spring of 1737 he made straight for the house of John Wilcox, a bookseller in the Strand, who is reported to have advised him to seek his fortune as a porter rather than as a poet.[87] His first steady employment in London was as parliamentary reporter for Cave's *Gentleman's Magazine*, which had been in existence a mere seven years. The first work to push him into national prominence was the *Dictionary*, testimony to the demands of the growing reading public.[88] All his life he was surrounded by printers and editors; the booksellers were, he said, 'his best friends' and 'generous liberal-minded men'. Unlike Pope in his villa at Twickenham, he did not cultivate an aristocratic life-style, nor did he spend much time in the houses of the great. Johnson's habitat was the library, the bookshop, the tavern, the printing office. Pope distrusted the great expansion of printing as an invitation to a deluge of mediocrity, a vast tide that would engulf all that

[85] Greene (ed.), *Samuel Johnson*, 529.

[86] Edward Allen, printer at Bolt Court, was Johnson's 'dear friend' and a member of the Essex Street Club. When he died in July 1780, Thomas Bensley took over the printing works. Donald Greene has hailed Johnson as 'the first journalist', though Defoe would run him close. 'Samuel Johnson, Journalist', in Bond and McLeod (eds.), *Newsletters to Newspapers*, 87–101.

[87] Nichols, *Literary Anecdotes*, viii. 416.

[88] The proliferation of dictionaries and encyclopaedias was one of the characteristics of the age. Ephraim Chambers's *Cyclopaedia or Universal Dictionary of Arts and Sciences* came out in 1728 and went through many editions. A proposal to translate it into French eventually led to the production of the great French *Encyclopédie*. Johnson said that he had based his style on Chambers's proposals for his second edition and in his later sixties was prepared to consider editing it, since he 'liked that *muddling* work'. *Life*, ii. 203 n. 3. The *Encyclopaedia Britannica* made its appearance in 1768.

was noble and exalted, and end in the triumph of the dunces.[89] Johnson thought Pope narrow-minded, censorious, and self-important.[90] He rejoiced in his own ability to turn his hand to anything literary, a pen for hire, and he submitted willingly to the judgement of the common reader.[91] He had great sympathy for hack-writers and struggling authors, devoting no. 145 of *The Rambler* to abridgers, compilers, and translators, mere 'drudges of the pen':

A race of beings equally obscure and equally indigent, who because their usefulness is less obvious to vulgar apprehensions, live unrewarded and die unpitied, and who have been long exposed to insult without a defender, and to censure without an apologist . . . Surely though they cannot aspire to honour, they may be exempted from ignominy, and adopted into that order of men which deserves our kindness though not our reverence.

Nor was his sympathy abstract and literary only. Arthur Murphy, actor and dramatist and a member of the Essex Head club, wrote of him after his death:

Authors, long since forgotten, waited on him as their oracle, and he gave responses in the chair of criticism. He listened to the complaints, the schemes, and the hopes and fears of a crowd of inferior writers, 'who', he said, in the words of Roger Ascham, 'lived men knew not how, and died obscure, men marked not when.' He believed, that he could give a better history of Grub-Street than any man living.[92]

Can we be sure that the real meaning of the Enlightenment is not to be found among the 'harmless drudges' of Grub Street rather than in the salons of Paris?

---

[89] See, particularly, Pope's commentary on *The Dunciad* as Martinus Scriblerus: 'He lived in those days, when (after providence had permitted the invention of printing as a scourge for the sins of the learned) paper also became so cheap, and printers so numerous, that a deluge of authors covered the land . . . till in conclusion all shall return to their original chaos.'

[90] In his *Lives of the Poets*, Johnson wrote: 'In the letters both of Swift and Pope there appears such narrowness of mind as makes them insensible of any excellence that has not some affinity with their own, and confines their esteem and approbation to so small a number, that whoever should form his opinion of the age from their representation would suppose them to have lived amidst ignorance and barbarity, unable to find among their contemporaries either virtue or intelligence, and persecuted by those that could not understand them.'

[91] See A. Kernan, *Printing Technology, Letters and Samuel Johnson*, (Princeton, NJ, 1987), 226–40, subsequently pub. as *Samuel Johnson and the Impact of Print* (Princeton, NJ, 1989).

[92] 'An Essay on the Life and Genius of Samuel Johnson', in *Miscellanies*, i. 414.

7

Johnson and Nationalism

At the Club, on 7 April 1775, with Boswell, Gibbon, Langton, Reynolds, and Beauclerk in attendance, Johnson came up with perhaps his best-remembered observation: 'Patriotism is the last refuge of a scoundrel.' Unfortunately, it is one of the least understood. The word 'patriotism' had acquired in Hanoverian England a scornful meaning as the mask for factious opposition. Johnson's remark was, in fact, the opposite of what it is commonly taken to mean.[1]

The source of the confusion is twofold. First, Johnson's own position changed considerably between the 1730s, when he was a staunch member of the opposition to Walpole, and the 1770s, when he had become, however unreliably, a supporter of government. Secondly, the word 'patriotism' had changed its meaning as successive oppositions had hijacked it. Hence, Johnson was using it to mean the noisy and insincere rhetoric of a man who made a trade out of his concern for his country.[2]

The evolution of both points may be traced in Johnson's own writings. In his first poem, 'London', his stance was patriot opposition. Henry V and Elizabeth duly made their appearance to remind readers of Britannia's departed glories. As for the corrupt present:

> Here let those reign, whom pensions can incite
> To vote a Patriot black, a courtier white.

'Patriot' had not then, for Johnson, acquired its pejorative meaning. In his *Dictionary* of 1755, the word was still neutral, defined as 'one whose ruling passion is the love of his country'. But by 1773, after a decade of Wilkite agitation, Johnson added: 'ironically for a factious disturber of the government'. In his short pamphlet *The Patriot*, written a year later, he explained how false patriots could be distinguished from genuine ones,

---

[1] *Life*, ii. 348. Boswell explained Johnson's remark with some care: 'he did not mean a real and generous love of our country, but that pretended patriotism which so many, in all ages and countries, have made a cloak for self-interest.'

[2] It acquired the label 'patriotism' because it became part of the rhetoric of opposition to lament that the nation's interests were being neglected by a supine and incompetent government and to appeal to a glorious national past in contrast to a shameful present.

and deplored that opposition had been able 'to arrogate to themselves the name of patriot'. Thence, it was a short throw to his muttered remark in the London tavern.

Contemporary usage can be illustrated from among Johnson's fellow members of the Club. Young Charles Fox made a brilliant début in the House of Commons in 1768, adopted a fiercely anti-Wilkite line, talked contemptuously of the rabble, and was rewarded with a place at the Board of Admiralty. In February 1772, disliking the Royal Marriages Bill, he resigned. Edward Gibbon, not yet a member of Parliament, wrote sardonically: 'Charles Fox is commenced Patriot, and is already attempting to pronounce the words *Country*, *Liberty*, *Corruption*, etc., with what success time will discover.' If Fox's resignation was opportunistic rather than principled, it was a classic case. In less than a year he was brought back into the government as a Lord of the Treasury.[3]

The concept of nationalism has been almost as troublesome to historians as the practice of it has been to rulers. The word itself is comparatively recent. It did not feature in Johnson's *Dictionary*, and its first recorded use is believed to have been in Barruel's *Mémoires*, published in 1798–9. At its simplest, it is a sense of loyalty, a sense of belonging, and it is distinguished from religious, family, or regional loyalty by the desire to use the nation as the basis for the governmental unit. But it bristles with problems. How should it be distinguished from patriotism? Is it a natural feeling or can it be artificially fostered? How does it relate to other loyalties, and particularly to religion and class? Is it a neutral and dispassionate concept, or does it carry with it an inescapable baggage of aggression and assertiveness?

If nationalism is basically a feeling, or state of mind, it follows that it will be fitful, and that the development of national consciousness can hardly be a regular process. Time and place intervene. The people of Dorset in the fourteenth century were less likely to have anti-Scottish feelings than the people of Northumberland, who bore the full brunt of Scottish border raids and incursions. Warfare, started for whatever purpose, is likely to stimulate national feeling, which may or may not fall back to its previous level at the peace. We should expect national

---

[3] Gibbon to Holroyd, 21 Feb. 1772 (*Letters*, ed. Norton, i. 309). Fox defended Johnson in the House of Commons in 1774 from a sharp attack by Tommy Townshend, who insinuated that he had had his pension doubled for writing on behalf of administration. Fox, though complaining of scandalous reporting, would never persecute 'men of great literary abilities'. *Parl. Hist.* xvii. 1058.

consciousness to move in fits and starts. It would be surprising were there not to be signs of advance in English nationalism during the Hundred Years War against France, the struggle against Spain, the Seven Years War, the Napoleonic Wars, the Great War, and the Battle of Britain. National consciousness will mix with other feelings. There was clearly a powerful Protestant element in English national feeling during the seventeenth century, just as Catholicism fused with nationalism in Ireland and in Poland. It can also pick up strong racial tones, as it did in Wilhelmine and Nazi Germany.

The overwhelming consensus of opinion has been that nationalism is a recent development and may be traced largely to the French Revolution. Hans Kohn, one of the most influential of scholars and writing in 1943 under the shadow of war, insisted that 'nationalism, as we understand it, is not older than the second half of the eighteenth century. Its first great manifestation was the French Revolution.'[4] A succession of scholars then provided variations upon the main theme. Boyd Shafer adopted a rather peremptory tone: 'any use of the word nationalism to describe historical happenings before the eighteenth century is probably anachronistic . . . Nationalism has been falsely seen long before it came into being.'[5] To Kedourie, writing in 1960, nationalism was 'a doctrine invented in Europe at the beginning of the nineteenth century'.[6] Kenneth Minogue, in 1967, drew a sharp distinction between patriotism and nationalism: 'until late in the eighteenth century, this modern modification, indeed transformation of patriotic feelings was quite unpredictable.'[7] Repetition began to harden into orthodoxy. 'Writers about nationalism', wrote John Plamenatz in 1976, 'mostly agree that there was little or none of it in the world until the end of the eighteenth century.'[8] As late as 1989, it could be written that 'received opinion holds that nationalism in the modern sense does not date back further than the revolutionary political turmoil that troubled the second half of the eighteenth century. It was born in France.'[9]

Such unanimity is intimidating, but a closer inspection reveals that many of the authors harboured considerable doubts or reservations. Kohn went on to explain that nationalism, though modern, 'had its roots deep in the past . . . some feeling of nationality, it may be said, existed before

---

[4] *The Idea of Nationalism: A Study in its Origins and Background* (New York, 1944), 3.

[5] B. C. Shafer, *Nationalism, Myth and Reality* (London, 1955), 5.

[6] E. Kedourie, *Nationalism* (London, 1960), 1.

[7] K. R. Minogue, *Nationalism* (London, 1967), 24.

[8] 'Two Types of Nationalism', in E. Kamenka (ed.), *Nationalism, the Nature and Evolution of an Idea* (London, 1976), 23.

[9] Peter Alter, *Nationalism* (London, 1989), 56.

the birth of modern nationalism, but it was largely unconscious and inarticulate'.[10] This itself raises the question of whether a feeling that is unconscious can be a feeling. When we are told later that 'nationalism is first and foremost a state of mind, an act of consciousness', the difficulty is compounded. If nationalism is an act of consciousness, what can unconscious nationalism possibly be? Even Shafer sounded the retreat later in his book, admitting that 'sentiments akin to nationalism are possibly as old as man and society'.[11] Not only does this seem to be flying from one extreme to the other, but it leaves the poor reader to distinguish between nationalism and 'sentiments akin to nationalism'.

It may seem impertinent to suggest that those writers who cannot detect nationalism before the French Revolution may not have looked very hard. Indeed, since the declaration that nationalism is a post-1789 phenomenon often comes in the opening paragraph, further enquiry might have been supererogation. But there have always been a number of historians standing out against the creeping orthodoxy of political science, and the thrust of more recent scholarship has been to push the roots of nationalism deeper into the past. The fact that a particular word was not in existence in the medieval world is no evidence that the feeling was not there: Huizinga has remarked briskly that on that showing there were no cosmic rays in the middle ages.[12]

That the French Revolution and the wars that followed gave encouragement to emergent nationalism by breaking the patterns of the past and by stimulating the resentment of millions of Germans, Italians, Spaniards, and Russians, who did not take kindly to the blessings thrust upon them by 'la Grande Nation', will not be disputed. But the French Revolution was far from being the only, or even the most important, dynamic of nineteenth-century European nationalism, and the more enthusiastic advocates of its unique contribution seem to have fallen into one of the more common historical errors, that of mistaking trends for origins.

The evidence to the contrary is too voluminous to be treated fully in this work. Nevertheless, since the subject remains controversial and it is important to try to see Johnson in his correct setting, some account must be attempted.

No study of the larger European countries could fail to discern the existence of recognized national identities centuries before the French

---

[10] *The Idea of Nationalism*, 3, 6, 10.   [11] *Nationalism, Myth and Reality*, 60.
[12] 'Patriotism and Nationalism in European History', in J. Huizinga, *Men and Ideas: History, the Middle Ages, the Renaissance* (London, 1960), 99.

Revolution. Halvdan Koht argued that, in the course of the twelfth century, 'a truly national consciousness, though limited in its scope, burst forth almost simultaneously in many of the European countries'.[13] Other scholars have drawn attention to a renewed outburst of national feeling at the end of the fifteenth and the beginning of the sixteenth centuries.[14] In *The Praise of Folly*, written in 1509, Erasmus preached common humanity and tolerant Christianity, and deplored the animosities that were splitting Europe apart:

Nowadays, the Englishman generally hates the Frenchman, for no better reason than that he is French. The Scot, simply because he is a Scot, hates the Englishman, the Italian hates the German, the Swabian the Swiss, and so on.

Perhaps, like the middle classes, national feeling has always been rising.

The limitations Koht mentioned were, of course, considerable, and the obstacles to national unity formidable. On the one hand there were local and provincial loyalties, manifested in local dialects, local institutions, and local customs. On the other there were international or supranational loyalties—to the Papacy, to the Empire, or to the broader concept of Christendom—which pulled in the opposite direction. But within the larger states, and particularly in the face of a foreign foe, a sense of common purpose and identity was growing.

It is often argued that supreme loyalty, in the medieval or early modern period, was to the monarch, in a personal capacity. But too sharp an antithesis between dynastic and national loyalty is misleading, since monarchs were seen as the leaders of their nations. There was no necessary clash of loyalty. Aquinas, in the mid-thirteenth century, wrote that kings were 'sometimes called the fathers of their people, and they rule them for the common good'.[15] A modern historian has suggested that a kingdom 'was never thought of merely as the territory to be ruled by a king. It comprised and corresponded to a "people".'[16] Monarchs represented the nation, were often called by its name, and appealed to it for support. The relationship was symbiotic: monarchs helped to create nations by imposing common laws, common coinage, and common institutions, while nations supported their monarchs as symbols of unity

---

[13] H. Koht, 'The Dawn of Nationalism in Europe,' *American Historical Review*, 52 (1947), 266.

[14] R. Aubenas, 'The Papacy and the Catholic Church', in G. R. Potter (ed.), *New Cambridge Modern History, 1493–1520* (Cambridge, 1971), 88, 94.

[15] *De Regimine Principum*, bk. I, ch. 1.

[16] Susan Reynolds, *Kingdoms and Communities in Western Europe, 900–1300* (Oxford, 1984), 250.

and for security. National identity and royal power grew together. Later, the concept of the nation was turned against monarchs, as a rival source of authority. Charles I, in Westminster Hall in 1649, was indicted for the 'great calamities that hath been brought upon this nation', while Bertrand Barère in 1793 told Louis Capet, 'Louis, the French nation accuses you'. Frankenstein's monster had destroyed its creator.

The extent to which national consciousness emerged in different parts of Europe depended, of course, upon a variety of factors and vicissitudes. In the south-east, the conquests of the Ottoman Turks retarded developments until the nineteenth century, since there were few autonomous or independent states to serve as a focus for national loyalty. In this case, resistance to assimilation was as much religious as national. In Italy, as Machiavelli argued, the Papacy was the great obstacle to national unity, 'not powerful enough to be able to master all Italy, nor having permitted any other power to do so'.[17] The Netherlands' national development was halted when the north failed to retain the southern provinces in 1648, and by the time they were reunited in 1814 they had grown apart. In Spain, the sustained attempt to recover the peninsula from the Moors promoted a sense of Christian purpose and ultimately led to the supremacy of Castile, but strong centrifugal tendencies remained. Portugal, united with Castile from time to time, turned towards Atlantic and world expansion; Catalonia retained its powerful economic and cultural links with the Mediterranean to the east, while the Basques were cut off from easy assimilation by a unique and difficult language. In Russia, the violent incursion of the Golden Horde between 1237 and 1240 and the subsequent establishment of the Tartar Khanates seems to have cut across the earlier development, which was not resumed until the Khanates began to disintegrate from the end of the fifteenth century onwards.

But in many other parts of Europe, there were clear signs of developing national consciousness throughout the medieval and early modern periods. It seems probable that the first European nation to develop a sense of identity was France. Provincial loyalties remained strong, and still do, and to the original area around the Isle de France were added, in the course of time, Normandy (1204), Anjou (1214), Toulouse (1271), Burgundy (1477) , Brittany (1488), Roussillon (1659), Franche Comté (1678), Lorraine (1738), and Corsica (1769). But working in favour of unity were geographical compactness and the powerful direction imposed by Capetian monarchs and their Valois and Bourbon successors. Marc

---

[17] *The Discourses*, bk. I, sect. 12.

Bloch's opinion was that, from their common origins in the Carolingian empire, French and German national consciousness, based upon divergent linguistic trends, was well established by 1100.[18] Dislike between French and Germans was already causing problems during the First Crusade in 1096, and in the Fourth Crusade, at the end of the twelfth century, Pope Innocent III was warned that it was essential to keep the French and German contingents apart.[19] The *Chanson de Roland*, dating from mid-twelfth century, insisted that there was not one coward in the armies of the Franks—all were brave as lions—and in 1200 a French knight improved upon the boast with the opinion that the Germans, even if armed, would not dare attack a solitary Frenchman, even if unarmed.[20] Suger's life of Louis VI, written in the 1150s, represented the king's victories as a national triumph: never had France achieved anything more illustrious.[21] Dislike of the Italians and their monopoly of the Papacy was a powerful factor behind the Babylonian captivity in the fourteenth century and the Great Schism which followed when, at one stage, three rival popes were in the field. French national pride was vigorous before Jeanne d'Arc appealed to it in 1431: 'I know not whether God loves the English or hates them, but I know they will be thrown out of the kingdom of France.'[22] To what extent knowledge of high politics or literary epic penetrated down the social scale we cannot know, but the fact that French monarchs thought it worthwhile to disseminate anti-English propaganda during the Hundred Years War suggests that they believed it could have considerable influence. One French writer assured his readers that in one hundred years the English had slaughtered more people than all other nations, while the author of *Ballade contre les Anglais* in 1429 revived the old story that the English had tails.[23]

The development of national consciousness in Germany was less straightforward than in France. The boundaries of the country were not as well defined and large movements of peoples and populations continued deep into the twentieth century. The Holy Roman Emperor

---

[18] *Feudal Society*, 2nd edn. (London, 1965), 436.   [19] Ibid. 436 n. 3.

[20] Quoted in Koht, 'Dawn of Nationalism in Europe', 269.

[21] Ibid. 266.

[22] Private examination, 17 Mar. 1431. T. D. Murray (ed.), *Jeanne d'Arc* (London, 1903), 88.

[23] Quoted in C. T. Allmand, *The Hundred Years War* (Cambridge, 1988), 140. French nationalism stimulated that of other nations, as it did during the eighteenth century. The Bretons thought that the French were effeminate and had forked beards. M. Jones, '"Mon pais et ma nation": Breton Identity in the Fourteenth Century', in C. T. Allmand (ed.), *War, Literature and Politics in the Late Middle Ages: Essays in Honour of G. W. Coopland* (Liverpool, 1976), 144–68.

was unable to play the role of the monarch as in France, partly because the long struggle with the Papacy was weakening, partly because so many of the interests of the empire lay outside Germany itself. Hence, loyalty grew up around the smaller German states such as the Palatinate, Saxony, Bavaria, Baden, and Prussia. It was well recognized by later German nationalists that the Holy Roman Empire, far from promoting unity, had become an obstacle to it.

Nevertheless, the concept of Germany did not disappear. The aggressiveness of the French—exemplified in Louis XIV's devastation of the Palatinate in 1689—was a constant reminder and reproach. But, in the absence of political advance, German nationalism remained for several centuries linguistic and historical. As early as the end of the twelfth century, Walther von der Vogelweide claimed that German civilization was superior to that of other countries and that Germans were better educated. Towards the end of the fifteenth century, humanist scholars helped to produce a remarkable reassertion of German pride, on which Luther was able to build in his defiance of the Papacy. The poet Konrad Celtis, in an address of 1492, demanded that the frontiers of Germany be gathered together and the Poles and Danes put in their places. In 1500 he published an edition of Tacitus' *Germania*, recently discovered, which paid tribute to the liberty of the Germans, their fighting qualities, and their purity of stock.[24] A less scholarly commentator, Joannes Becanus, argued that German must have been the original language of the Garden of Eden. Martin Luther himself gave a further stimulus to German pride and tradition in a series of direct national appeals. 'We have the title of Empire,' he told his readers, 'but the Pope has our goods, our honour, our bodies, lives, souls and all we possess. That is the way to cheat the Germans, and because they are Germans to go on cheating them.' For the first time he was able, he rejoiced, to find his God 'in the German language'. Though the Thirty Years War in the following century dealt a devastating blow to German prosperity and culture, by the eighteenth century interest in German history and tradition was once more reviving.[25]

English nationalism, it has been suggested, was by comparison a plant of slow growth. Koht argued that, unlike that of France, English national

---

[24] A. G. Dickens, *The German Nation and Martin Luther* (London, 1974), 33–6. See also H. A. McDougall, *Racial Myth in English History: Trojans, Teutons and Anglo-Saxons* (Montreal,1982), 42–4.

[25] Luther's remarks are in *An Appeal to the Ruling Class of German Nationality*, pub. 1520. Other regions in which early nationalist sentiments can be detected are Scotland, Scandina-

consciousness 'could not be stimulated by opposition to foreign enemies', and Kohn agreed that nationalism in England 'came later than on the continent'. Kenneth Minogue believed that England had had 'relatively little national experience'.[26]

This seems doubtful. It is true that the Anglo-French struggle was fought out mainly on French soil, and that England was spared many of the ravages of war, but there were domestic enemies to replace the foreign foe. The loathing which Frenchmen, Italians, Germans, and Poles felt for one another was easily matched by the contempt and scorn expressed between English, Scots, Welsh, and Irish, who frequently referred to one another as the dregs of humanity. Giraldus Cambrensis, in the late twelfth century, believed the Welsh to be valiant, intelligent, hospitable, and devoted to liberty, and to deem it an honour to die in battle; by contrast, the English were muddy and servile, fit only for herdsmen and labourers.[27] A riposte from an English cleric one hundred years later saw the Welsh as lewd and depraved, thievish, cowardly, and treacherous.[28] At the start of Edward I's campaign in 1296, Scots and English traded abuse. The Scots were said to have burned two hundred schoolboys at Corbridge on a border raid, and, at the siege of Dunbar, taunted the English with the threat to cut off their tails.[29] Hardly anyone had a good word for the Irish.

At one point it had looked as though an English nation-state would emerge in the tenth century, under the leadership of Alfred's Wessex. When his grandson Athelstan and his great-grandson Edgar established their supremacy, the way ahead seemed clear. But the chance of a smooth national development was halted by the Scandinavian resurgence under Sweyn and Cnut, and by the second-stage conquest by the Northmen in 1066. Norman French became the language of the official and political

via, and Bohemia. G. S. Barrow has written on the later twelfth century that 'contrary to a common belief, the concept of Scottish nationality and the fact that it was distinct from English nationality, was clearly understood.' *Robert Bruce and the Community of the Realm of Scotland* (Edinburgh, 1965), 97. The growing separatism of Sweden, Denmark, and Norway helped to defeat the Union of Kalmar (1397), with the Vasa dynasty emerging as the champions of Swedish nationhood against Danish domination. Bohemia, where the national cause became identified with that of the Hussites, has been described as one of the earliest nation-states in Europe: R. W. Seton-Watson, *History of the Czechs and Slovaks*, 2nd edn. (Hamden, Conn. 1965), 11.

[26] Koht, 'Dawn of Nationalism in Europe', 270; Kohn 'The Genesis and Character of English Nationalism', *Journal of the History of Ideas*, 1 (1940), 69; Minogue, *Nationalism*, 29.

[27] *The Journey through Wales and the Description of Wales*, tr. L. Thorpe (Harmondsworth, 1978), 233, 245.

[28] Report believed to have been composed for Archbishop Peckham c.1282, *HMC Various Collections*, i. 246.   [29] Quoted in Barrow, *Robert Bruce*, 100–1.

nation and the highest positions in Church and State were reserved for Normans.

It has been remarked that, with some few exceptions, there was little sustained resistance by the English to Norman domination after 1066. But, in the course of time, intermarriage and the ubiquity of the English language achieved what an English resistance movement would have attempted. In 1100 Henry I, younger son of the Conqueror, married Eadygyth, a princess in direct descent from the Wessex line under Edmund Ironside: though Norman knights are said to have jeered at the alliance, the English regarded the son of the marriage, William, as Aetheling and the rightful heir.[30] M. T. Clanchy, in a book of sustained brilliance, has traced how the English nation survived its ordeal after the Conquest to reassert itself in the thirteenth century.[31] Much of this was the work of English chroniclers and of English-speaking parish priests. After the battle of Lincoln in 1217, where the French-supported opponents of Henry III were defeated, Ralph of Coggeshal declared 'thus the Lord struck his enemies who had come to destroy the English people'. The *Song of Lewes*, in 1264, celebrated the discomfiture of the Poitevins, who had crowded round Henry III in his later reign:

Now England breathes again, hoping for liberty: the English were despised like dogs but now they have raised their heads over their vanquished foes . . . Read this, you Englishmen, about the battle of Lewes.

The constant struggles against French, Welsh, and Scots helped to fuse English and Norman. When Edward I wanted to arouse a national response for men and money, he appealed for help in preserving the English tongue.[32] In 1362, during the reign of Edward III, English was declared to be the language of Parliament and the law. Before the end of the fourteenth century, John Wycliffe and his associates had completed their task of translating the Bible into English, which helped to fuel cultural nationalism in England, as did the German humanists in their own country one hundred years later.

This impetus was sustained during the fifteenth century, despite the divisions caused by the Wars of the Roses. The great victory against the

---

[30] Eadygyth, or Matilda, was the daughter of Malcolm III of Scotland by Margaret, granddaughter of Edmund Ironside. The son of the marriage, William, was drowned in the *White Ship* in 1120 at the age of 17. Comments on Henry's marriage are in Orderic Vitalis, himself the son of a Norman priest and an English mother.

[31] *England and its Rulers, 1066–1272* (Totowa, NJ, 1983).

[32] Writ of summons to Parliament, *Stubbs' Select Charters*, 9th edn. (Oxford, 1913), 480. The writ was of course in Latin.

odds at Agincourt in 1415 gave a powerful boost to national pride, which the subsequent disasters in France did not totally erase. It was celebrated in a number of popular songs, including 'The Siege of Harfleur' and the famous 'Song of Agincourt', with its chorus 'Deo gracias Anglia redde pro victoria'.

A new note of commerical nationalism entered during the 1430s with the *Libelle of English Policy*, which offered the attractive aims of godliness and profit, advising:

> Keep then the sea, that is the wall of England
> And then is England kept by Goddes sonde (grace).

In his treatise on the governance of England, written in the 1470s, Sir John Fortescue praised the English constitution in contrast with that of the French, and Sir Thomas Malory, in the same period, brought together the growing number of tales of Arthur, weaving them into a heroic national past in *Morte d'Arthur*, published by Caxton in 1485. It has haunted the English imagination ever since, through Purcell's *King Arthur*, to Tennyson's *Idylls of the King*, published in 1859, and Elgar's sombre suite *King Arthur*, composed in 1923.

It is, of course, possible to dismiss this evidence as episodic, representing little more than individual enthusiasms. J. R. Hale comments that 'as for nationalism, where it existed in something like the modern sense, it was literary, the invention of the intellectuals . . . This jingoism of the intelligentsia evoked little public response.'[33] Perhaps it is necessary to be warned against seeing nationalists under the beds, but it is not easy to see what other forms of national sentiment were likely to have survived as evidence for historians to consider. Peasants are tiresomely reluctant to record their opinions for posterity. It is a little strange if monarchs and writers misjudged the situation by appealing to feelings which were unlikely to be appreciated or even understood. Wycliffe did not want for followers, nor did the Hussites in Bohemia. It is certainly true that we do not know how many read Walter von der Vogelweide, but we do know that Luther's pamphlets sold in thousands and that the results of his work were not venial.

Not even the most sceptical of historians, however, is likely to deny the fierce release of national feeling in sixteenth-century England, both in the political and in the cultural sphere. Henry VIII's breach with Rome both exploited and stimulated national feeling, and the Anglican Church,

---

[33] *Renaissance Europe* (London, 1981), 110–11. It is a curious and enduring tradition for intellectuals to despise other intellectuals.

after a shaky start, attracted to itself great national loyalty. The struggle against Spain during the reign of Elizabeth helped to promote literary nationalism. Poets and antiquarians, political scientists and theologians, combined to claim great things for the English tongue, the English character, the English constitution, and English valour. Shakespeare's history plays turned the national past into an epic, a pageant. John of Gaunt in *Richard II* spoke of 'this other Eden, demi-Paradise, this fortress built by nature for herself, against infection and the hand of war, this happy breed of men . . . this blessed plot, this earth, this realm, this England'. The Bastard of Fauconbridge, at the end of *King John*, boasted: 'come the three corners of the world in arms and we shall shock them'; and Henry V cheered his 'poor condemned English' with the thought that 'gentlemen in England now abed, shall think themselves accursed they were not here, and hold their manhoods cheap whiles any speak, That fought with us upon St Crispin's day'.

The genius of Shakespeare was supported by a number of other writers. One of the most influential was Richard Mulcaster, a London schoolmaster whose pupils included Edmund Spenser. Mulcaster defended his decision to publish *The First Part of the Elementarie*, an education treatise, in English:

I do write in my natural English tongue, because though I make the learned my judges, which understand Latin, yet I mean good to the unlearned, which understand but English . . . I love Rome, but London better; I favour Italy but England more; I honour the Latin, but I worship the English.

Spenser himself drew upon the Arthurian legend for *The Faerie Queen*, explaining his intentions in the preface to Ralegh. In the same year as Mulcaster's treatise appeared, Richard Hakluyt began his famous series. He had been irritated while on a visit to Paris at the patronizing tone adopted by the French towards English sailors and explorers, and the full title of his volume made the point explicitly: *Diverse Voyages Touching the Discovery of America . . . Made First of All by Our Englishmen and Afterwards by the Frenchmen and Bretons*. Another friend of Ralegh was the historian William Camden, whose *Britannia*, the first part of which was published in 1586, traced English liberty back to the Saxons and the German forests, commended the English language, and declared that England had produced more princes renowned for sanctity that any land whatever. In a later publication he improved on the description: Britain was well known to be the most flourishing and excellent, most renowned and famous Isle of the whole world; so rich in commodities, so beautiful in situation, so resplendent in all glory . . .[34]

A remarkable passage in Samuel Daniel's *Musophilus*, published in 1599, looked to the prospect of English surpassing all other languages:

> And who, in time, knows whither we may vent
> The treasure of our tongue, to what strange shores
> This gain of our best glory shall be sent
> T'inrich unknowing nations with our stores?
> What worlds in the yet unformed Occident
> May come refined with the accents that are ours?

Despite the damage to national unity caused by the Civil Wars, the seventeenth century saw little slackening in fervour. Indeed, the dissensions may have even heightened national awareness. The opposition to the early Stuarts drew freely upon history, particularly that of the Saxon period, to reinforce their notions of liberty, while the concept of the English as the chosen nation of God gathered impetus in the minds of Puritans. John Milton's *Areopagitica* in 1644 celebrated 'a noble and puissant nation rousing herself like a strong man after sleep, and shaking her invincible locks'. Why else had God chosen to reveal himself first of all 'to his Englishmen'. In *St. Edward's Ghost*, published in 1647 by John Hare, England was claimed as 'the chief and most honourable nation in Europe' and her people exhorted to throw off the Norman yoke. Cromwell himself saw in the English 'a people that have the stamp upon them from God . . . the apple of his eye'.[35] In 1658 Richard Hawkins published *A Discourse on the National Excellencies of England*, in which the country's advantages were spelled out:

What people live so happily under their Law? . . . What nation is so great as England? . . . Let us tremble and fear before our God for all that prosperity which he hath procured for us.

The three Anglo–Dutch wars revived the note of economic rivalry. Mercantilist policies were built on and encouraged national competition. Though the Dutch were fellow Protestants, pamphleteers frequently

---

[34] *Remains Concerning Britain* (1605). In this miscellaneous volume, Camden included Richard Carew's *An Epistle Concerning the Excellencie of the English Tongue*.

[35] S. C. Lomas (ed.), *The Letters and Speeches of Oliver Cromwell* (London, 1904), ii. 404.

called upon God to humble their pride and destroy their predominance.[36] During the reign of Charles II there was little for national pride to feed on. But one of the most moving confessions of national feeling came at the end of his reign, and from an unlikely source, the marquess of Halifax, known to posterity as the Trimmer. Written late in 1684, it was printed in 1688. Though Halifax advocated balance and moderation in party matters and in foreign diplomacy, in one respect he was categorical:

Our Trimmer is far from idolatry in other things, in one thing only he cometh near it; his country is in some degree his idol. He doth not worship the sun, because it is not peculiar to us, it rambleth about the world, and is less kind to us than it is to other countries; but for the earth of England, though perhaps inferior to that of many places abroad, to him there is divinity in it, and he would rather die than see a spire of English grass trampled down by a foreign trespasser.[37]

It is not surprising that in the eighteenth century—a period of increasing education and enlightenment—many of the manifestations of national sentiment took a cultural form. This is not to say that fiercer national passions were absent. The incessant warfare, and particularly the Seven Years War, ensured that plenty of national enemies remained. Colonial encounters stoked the fires with reports of massacres, deceits, and subterfuges, though most of these exchanges were between the French, Dutch, English, and Spaniards, who were already mistrustful of one another. Cultural assertion, though not a new element, was more prominent than in the past.

There were, of course, counter-currents. The eighteenth century has been claimed as a quintessentially cosmopolitan period, united by reason, scepticism, and humanity. French was spoken widely among the upper classes. Hume was at home in Paris; Gibbon retired to Lausanne to finish *Decline and Fall*; Voltaire visited Sans-Souci; and Diderot stayed at Catherine's court of St Petersburg. But we have to ask how deep this went and to how many it applied.

The argument of cosmopolitanism is developed very fully for England by Gerald Newman.[38] His main tenet is the domination of polite society of the period by French values and the reaction against this by the middle

---

[36] 'Too long have the Hollanders enriched themselves by feeding on the fat of this Commonwealth . . . but by God's Holy assistance and the Parliament's providence, they may easily be subdued and brought to obedience.' *The Seas Magazine Opened, or the Hollanders Dispossessed* (1653).

[37] *Complete Works*, ed. J. P. Kenyon (Harmondsworth, 1969), 96.

[38] *The Rise of English Nationalism: A Cultural History, 1740–1830* (London, 1987).

classes and the lower orders. But the case is rather badly overstated. We are told, for example, that some English peers had estates and even titles in France. In fact, the only two peerages with French counterparts were Portsmouth and Richmond, both stemming from the fact that Charles II had a French mistress. Two of the most zealous advocates of a common humanity were Bolingbroke and Voltaire: 'a wise man', wrote Bolingbroke, 'looks on himself as a citizen of the world.'[39] But circumstances do sometimes affect opinions and there is nothing like being driven out of your native land for making instant converts to international hospitality. Bolingbroke's opinions, in particular, suffered several sea-changes. A furious party man in Queen Anne's reign, he helped to wreck the Tories in 1715, only to discover that wise men were above party. His declaration as a citizen of the world came shortly after he had fled to France in the face of an attainder for treason; later he remembered how much he missed his native land and begged to be allowed to return. Voltaire fled from France in 1727 under threat of arrest, spent several years in England, and returned to France in 1734 only to have his book on the English burned. Their internationalism was, to many people, a little suspect.

Newman may have made rather too much of the predilections of Lord Chesterfield, of whom Johnson observed brutally that he taught 'the morals of a whore and the manners of a dancing-master'.[40] Let us take more important characters. Between 1722 and 1806, a period of eighty-four years, four men were first ministers for a total of sixty-one years. It is not easy to see Sir Robert Walpole, Henry Pelham, Lord North, and William Pitt as Frenchified dandies.

Newman also brought in the Grand Tour as an example of cosmopolitanism, observing that by the late 1750s it had become 'the one indispensable element' in the education of a gentleman.[41] But the reference he gave was to a book published at the time of the Great War.[42] More recent scholarship has modified the picture. John Brooke, in his introduction to *The House of Commons, 1754–90*, remarked that only ten per cent of members of Parliament seem to have made the Tour, that its popularity was declining after 1740, and that it was 'by no means customary'.[43] Nor should we presume that every traveller returned from

---

[39] 'Reflections upon Exile', in *Letters on the Study and Use of History, etc.* (London, 1870), 155.
[40] *Life*, i. 266.   [41] *Rise of English Nationalism*, 42.
[42] W. E. Mead, *The Grand Tour in the Eighteenth Century* (Boston, 1914).
[43] *House of Commons, 1754–90*, i. 112–13.

the continent full of enthusiasm for what he had seen. 'Every young man ought to go abroad', wrote John Charles Villiers from France in 1778, 'to make him more attached to his own country. I find everything here so extremely inferior, that I glow with pride and rapture, when I think I am an Englishman.'[44]

There is widespread evidence from many parts of Europe of a quickening of cultural nationalism before the French Revolution. First, we must not overlook France itself. Though Voltaire has been quoted as an example of cosmopolitanism, his *Henriade*, first performed in 1723, soon acquired national status as a celebration of Henri IV, a king who placed love of country first. Belloy's *The Siege of Calais*, in 1765, surveyed the rivalries of French and English in the fourteenth century and became extremely popular. The enthusiasm for the unity of the French nation, so evident in the spring of 1789, had been developing for years, with politicians striving to appeal to it. While more radical writers argued that the privileged orders did not form part of the nation, moderates countered with the argument that the *parlements* and particularly the Paris *parlement* protected the nation from royal despotism. The court found the *parlement*'s claims irritating and presumptuous, and at the famous *séance de la flagellation* in 1766 Louis XV, booted and spurred, warned the *parlementaires* to abandon this line of argument. It was, he insisted, false to assert that *parlement* was 'the organ of the nation, the protector of the nation's liberty, interests and right, that it is accountable in all matters of the public good not to the king only but to the nation'.[45]

In other countries we see the establishment of learned societies for the study of the national past, revived interest in legend and folk-song, and the foundation of national theatres. The Royal Danish Society, set up in 1745, was dedicated to printing national historical evidence in Danish. There was a fierce reassertion of Danish nationalism after the fall of the German Struensee in 1772, with Danish declared to be the official language of the country and legislation passed to forbid the employment of foreigners in public office. In Sweden, Olof von Dalin's *Den Svenska Argus* in the 1730s protested against foreign (and particularly French) influence, and a Swedish Royal Theatre was established in 1737. Though Gustav III was French-educated and at home with French culture, his

---

[44] J. C. Villiers, *A Tour Through Part of France* (1789), quoted in J. Black, *The British and the Grand Tour* (London, 1985), 239. Black also denied that many Englishmen returned as fops, remarking '*pace* contemporary critics, there was relatively little unthinking assumption of foreign customs, manners and mores'.

[45] Quoted in R. R. Palmer, 'The National Idea in France before the Revolution', *Journal of the History of Ideas*, 1 (1940).

reign saw further Swedish advance, especially in the 1780s when the king needed to appeal to Swedish patriotism during the war with Russia. One of the tasks of the Swedish Academy, founded in 1786, was to encourage the use of Swedish as a literary medium, and Gustav himself sketched out the opera *Gustav Vasa*, with music by J. G. Naumann, performed with great success the same year. The poems and music of Carl Michael Bellman, though using melodies that were mostly borrowed from German and French composers, created a brilliant and moving panorama of Stockholm life and helped to form a strong Swedish musical tradition. In Switzerland, divided by language and religion, the Helvetic Society, established in 1761, worked to promote national feeling, drawing on the heroic struggles of William Tell. In Scotland, John Home had a great success with his historical play *Douglas*, performed in Edinburgh in 1756 and received with cries from the gallery of 'Where's your Wully Shakespeare noo?'. Not surprisingly, Johnson did not think much of it.[46] William Wilkie, on the strength of his *Epigoniad*, published in nine books in 1757, was hailed as 'the Scottish Homer'. One of Home's close friends was James Macpherson, and an element in the controversy over *Fingal*, in which Johnson took a prominent part, was native pride in the distant Scottish past, dismissed by Johnson as mere 'Caledonian bigotry'.[47] In Germany, Herder and Klopstock argued the case for a German literature, and at Göttingen in 1773 the works of Wieland were ceremoniously burned as contaminated by French influence. Wales also shared in this awakening. Interest in Welsh antiquity was kindled by the work of Edward Lhuyd, keeper of the Ashmolean Museum at Oxford, whose study of the Celtic languages came out in 1707. The Society of Cymmrodorion, founded in 1751 to collect old Welsh manuscripts, was followed in 1771 by the Society of the Gwyneddigion to encourage Welsh literature. In 1789 the poet Thomas Jones was responsible for the revival of the institution of eisteddfods.

These developments were closely paralleled in Hanoverian England. Since the country was at war for almost half of the eighteenth century,

---

[46] He maintained that there were not ten good lines in the whole play. The success of Scots writers and authors he attributed to 'their spirit of nationality', observing that there was a claque of Scotsmen determined to puff the work of any of their fellow countrymen: 'no Scotsman publishes a book, or has a play brought upon the stage, but there are five hundred people ready to applaud him.' *Life*, v. 360; iv. 186.

[47] *Journey to the Western Islands*, 118. Hugh Blair claimed that Ossian had eclipsed Homer. For recent comment on Johnson's part in the controversy, see J. J. Carter and J. H. Pittock (eds.), *Aberdeen and the Enlightenment* (Aberdeen, 1987), esp. nos. 39–42.

they often took militaristic forms. Patriotic feelings were fed by 'The British Grenadiers', 'Rule Britannia', 'God Save the King', and 'Heart of Oak', which followed one another in quick succession between 1740 and 1759.[48] The taste for sturdy sentiment continued through the period and into the Napoleonic Wars, from Charles Dibdin's magnificent 'Tom Bowling' (1789) to John Braham's 'The Death of Nelson' (1811), with the hero dying for 'England, Home and Beauty'.

Revolt against the cultural domination of the French and Italians was a familiar theme in all the arts. In no. 414 of the *Spectator* (1712) Addison fired the first shots against the formal tradition of landscape gardening, with its gravel walks, clipped box hedges, and classical statues. A remarkable group of landscape artists—Charles Bridgeman, William Kent, and Lancelot Brown—developed a more relaxed and natural style, which they argued was better suited to the English genius for liberty. Their successor, Humphry Repton, made the connection explicit: they had achieved 'the happy medium betwixt the wildness of nature and the stiffness of art, in the same manner as the English constitution is the happy medium between the liberty of savages and the restraint of despotic government'.[49] John Hawkins, one of Johnson's closest friends, defended English music from the imputation that foreign must necessarily be superior. Alert for native genius, in 1741 he hailed the blind composer John Stanley with what seems rather excessive praise. Italy, it is clear, had been put in her place:

> Purcell at first their Empire did control
> With arts unknown to them he mov'd the Soul;
> Thine was the task the Victr'y to complete;
> He made them humble; Thou has made us Great.[50]

A persistent advocate of English culture was William Hogarth, cockney by birth. In one of his earliest engravings, 'Masquerades and Operas' (1724), the works of Shakespeare and other English authors were carted

---

[48] 'The British Grenadiers' is based upon an older tune, but the first extant copy of the words is c.1735–40; 'Rule Britannia' (1740) is by James Thomson with music by Arne; 'God save the King', again based on older melodies, became popular in 1745; 'Heart of Oak' (1759) was by David Garrick with music by Boyce. An interesting article, tracing the evolution of the concept of patriotism and its move from a libertarian to a nationalist flavour, is J. H. Shennan, 'The Rise of Patriotism in Eighteenth-century Europe', *History of European Ideas*, 13/6 (1991), 689–710.

[49] 'A Letter to Uvedale Price, Esq. of Foxley in Herefordshire, 1 July 1794', in J. C. Loudon, *The Landscape Gardening and Landscape Architecture of the Late Humphrey Repton, Esq.* (London, 1840), 104–9.

[50] *Daily Advertiser*, 21 Feb. 1741, and preface to Stanley's cantatas in 1742.

away as waste-paper. In 1748 he turned to advantage an unpleasant personal experience at Calais, with his highly popular engraving 'The Gate of Calais', in which starving Frenchmen gazed in astonishment at 'the roast beef of old England'.[51] David Garrick joined in the attack in 1752 with a Drury Lane prologue complaining that 'all artists are encouraged but our own'.[52] Four years later Hogarth and Garrick combined forces, Hogarth providing contrasting prints of France and England, and Garrick the verse commentary:

> With lantern jaws and croaking gut,
> See how the half-starved Frenchmen strut,
> And call us English dogs;
> But soon we'll teach these bragging foes
> That beef and beer give heavier blows
> Than soup and roasted frogs.[53]

This unsophisticated output, for popular consumption, should not distract attention from the substantial cultural and scholarly achievements of the period. In 1747 William Innys, a London bookseller, began the publication of *Biographia Britannica*, in direct imitation of Bayle's *Historical and Critical Dictionary* but the first publication of its kind before the *Dictionary of National Biography*, commissioned by George Smith in 1882.[54] Sir Hans Sloane's bequest to the nation of his collection of books and specimens became the basis for the British Museum, opened on its present site in 1759.[55] The Society of Antiquarians, which had eked out a rather spasmodic existence since Elizabethan days, was incorporated in 1751 and placed on a firm footing.[56] Two other societies whose fortunes were closely connected were the Society of Arts and the Royal Academy. The first, founded in 1754 by William Shipley, a successful drawing master, aimed at encouraging 'the arts, manufactures and commerce of

---

[51] The song 'The Roast Beef of Old England', to the tune of 'The king's Old Courtier', was sung in Henry Fielding's anti-Walpole piece *The Grub-Street Opera* at the Haymarket in 1731. The phrase 'Old England' was a powerful rallying-cry, calling to mind wooden walls, gamecocks, village greens, foaming ale, bulldogs, and hearty slaps on the back.

[52] Prologue to Samuel Foote's two-act comedy *Taste*.

[53] J. Hannay (ed.), *The Complete Works of William Hogarth* (London, 1890), iii. 131–2.

[54] Johnson thought highly of *Biographia Britannica*, though he declined to take charge of a rev. edn. in the 1770s, which was undertaken by Andrew Kippis and Joseph Towers, two dissenting ministers. They did not complete it and the dictionary ended abruptly in 1795 with 'Fastolf'.

[55] The existing building, by Sir Robert Smirke, was completed in 1847.

[56] A sketch of the early years of the society is in the first number of the society's journal *Archaeologia*.

this kingdom'.[57] In 1760 the society gave the use of one of its rooms for an exhibition of paintings by English artists, which developed eight years later into the Royal Academy. Other contemporary societies whose purposes seemed largely humanitarian had important national objectives. One of the aims of Captain Coram's Foundling Hospital, established in 1741, was to rescue abandoned children, thereby helping to redress the population advantage possessed by the French.[58] More directly utilitarian was the Marine Society, founded in 1756 to gather funds to clothe poor boys and send them into the navy. The prologue to one of its benefit performances at Drury Lane in 1760 drove home the national message:

> France shall look pale to see their glorious toil,
> And tremble at the gleanings of our isle.[59]

It is, of course, true that appeals to the public for funds were likely to sound a patriotic note, but they did so in the expectation that they would meet with a response.

The national feeling evinced in these activities was English rather than British. Though a good deal of effort was made after 1707 to persuade the inhabitants of the British Isles to abandon old animosities, the results were disappointing. Londoners demonstrated their dislike of the Scots in the Wilkite riots of 1768–70 and of the Irish in the Gordon riots of 1780. At his accession in 1760, George III tactfully gloried in the name of Briton, but he did not follow it up by paying a single visit to Scotland, Ireland, Wales, or even northern England.[60] It took more than rhetoric to overcome ancient enmities. Fashionable circles referred to Scotland as North Britain, but, since England was never referred to as South Britain, the effect was one-sided.

A recent volume which has greatly added to our understanding of the development of national feeling in this period is Linda Colley's *Britons: Forging the Nation, 1707–1837*. She identifies many factors after the Act of Union promoting a greater sense of British solidarity between England

---

[57] The society moved to its present premises at the Adelphi in 1774 and was reformed under the patronage of Prince Albert in 1847.

[58] For the utilitarian side of the philanthropy of this period, see Donna T. Andrew, *Philanthropy and Police: London Charity in the Eighteenth Century* (Princeton, NJ, 1989), 55–7. Hogarth was an enthusiastic supporter of the hospital and painted a memorable portrait of Coram; the annual charity concerts were supported by Handel and the annual artists' dinner and exhibition led to the establishment of the Royal Academy.

[59] *British Magazine*, 5 Dec. 1760.

[60] Since his main journeys were to Cheltenham and Weymouth, he might more appropriately have gloried in the name of Wessex, the heartland of his dynasty.

and Scotland: the continued feeling of a beleagured Protestantism, locked in combat with Catholic France and Spain; the spread of information; the improvements in travel; the removal of customs barriers and the sharing of a political, though not a legal or ecclesiastical, system. Some of these factors were, of course, also helping to draw closer together the shires of north and south, east and west England.

But, as recent difficulties in the European Community suggest, closer contacts do not invariably bring enhanced affection. The concept of Britain was a sickly plant, slow to grow and putting out modest blossoms. Side by side with the gradual growth of British loyalty went a rapid growth of English sentiment. After 1760 this is easily perceived, since it fed upon the elevation of Bute as first minister and the long tenure of Mansfield as Lord Chief Justice. Wilkes made attacks upon the Scots his stock-in-trade, protesting against the use of the term 'Great Britain'. He was echoed by his uncomfortable ally Junius, who warned his readers repeatedly against Scottish insincerity—'when they smile, I feel an involuntary emotion to guard myself against mischief'—and pointedly dedicated the collected edition of his letters in 1772 'to the *English* nation'.[61]

But strong English feeling may also be discerned before 1760, when it could focus upon Jacobitism. Gratifying though it was that a Scot, James Thomson, should have written 'Rule Britannia', he felt obliged to explain defensively to a fellow countryman, 'Britain includes our native kingdom of Scotland, too'.[62] We must also remember that when, on 28 September 1745, the audience rose at Drury Lane to sing 'God Save the King'— which became the first national anthem in the world—the enemies in verse 2 who were to be scattered and confounded were the Scots, who had just defeated Sir John Cope and were preparing once more to cross the border. Indeed, a later verse, subsequently dropped, made the point rather explicitly:

> Lord, grant that Marshal Wade
> May by thy mighty Aid
>   Victory bring.
> May he sedition hush,
> And like a Torrent rush,
> Rebellious Scots to crush,
>   God Save the King.

[61] *Junius*, Letter XLI.
[62] Quoted in J. L. Robertson (ed.), *The Complete Poetical works of James Thomson* (Oxford, 1908), p. xiv.

The point may be reinforced by referring to the evolution of the character of John Bull. He appeared in print in 1712 in John Arbuthnot's *Law Is a Bottomless Pit*, a plain, blunt man, easily taken in by foreigners, and contrasted with the wily Lewis Baboon.[63] In the course of the century John Bull established himself as a national archetype, and in the nineteenth century acquired the familiar Pickwickian appearance, complete with squat top hat and union-jack waistcoat. But he was always an Englishman, never a Briton, and, though pubs and taverns called themselves 'The Old English Gentleman', I know of none that was called 'The Old *British* Gentleman'. Consequently, English national feeling could accommodate, even flourish upon, fierce antipathy to the Scots, Welsh and Irish.

In this context, Johnson sits easily. His close friend Reynolds was first President of the Royal Academy, and, though Johnson's bad eyesight prevented him from having much appreciation of painting, he wrote the preface for the catalogue of the exhibition of the Society of Artists in 1762 and the dedication in 1778 for Reynolds's *Discourses*. Two of his other friends, John Hawkins and Charles Burney, produced histories of music in 1776. He was an early member of the Society of Arts and took an active part in its proceedings. What are sometimes seen as his personal idiosyncrasies take on a wider significance when they are seen to be shared by so many of his friends. In his detestation of the French as an insolent nation needing periodic chastisement, he was at one with most contemporaries. At the famous dinner party arranged by Boswell, he and John Wilkes quickly found a common bond, conservative and radical competing in anti-Scottish jokes.[64] 'It is not so much to be lamented that Old England is lost', remarked Johnson in reply to what Boswell calls 'patriotic groans', 'as that the Scotch have found it.' Johnson's lack of enthusiasm for the Americans, which has worried many scholars west of the Atlantic, was shared by the majority of his fellow countrymen.

But Johnson's connection with rising English nationalism goes much further than that. We should perhaps not read too much into the national sentiments expressed in 'London', his first important work. There are, of course, plenty of offensive references to France and Spain, and two sustained attacks upon the invasion of Britain by starving foreigners:

[63] Louis XIV, a Bourbon. The tradition of seeing the French as monkeys was perhaps some revenge for the insults suffered in medieval times about the English having tails.

[64] *Life*, iii. 64–79. Had he ever met his anonymous enemy Junius, dislike of Scots would have been another bond. Junius peppered his letters with references to Scottish cunning and treachery.

> LONDON! the needy Villain's gen'ral Home,
> The common shore of *Paris* and of *Rome*;
> With eager thirst, by Folly or by Fate,
> Sucks in the dregs of each corrupted state.
> Forgive my transports on a theme like this,
> I cannot bear a *French* metropolis.

It is followed by contempt for the rejects of France and Spain:

> All that at home no more can beg or steal,
> Or like a Gibbet better than a Wheel;
> Hiss'd from the stage, or hooted from the Court,
> Their air, their dress, their politicks import;
> Obsequious, artful, voluble and gay,
> On *Britain*'s fond credulity they prey.

But we cannot be certain to what extent Johnson was constrained by Juvenal's original and by the demands of patriot ideology. It is difficult to take at face value Johnson's exposition of the delights of the wilds of Scotland, and the anti-foreign stance may also contain synthetic elements.[65]

But in the *Dictionary*, on which Johnson began work in 1746, a national purpose was clear from the outset. Indeed, the whole enterprise seems to have been conceived—and was certainly publicized—in terms of national literary competition. The Accademia della Crusca of Florence had produced an Italian *Vocabolario* as early as 1623: the Académie française, established by Richelieu in 1635, had taken until 1694 to produce its *Grand dictionnaire*. There had been hopes that the newly-founded Royal Society might do something in the 1660s for the English language; Swift addressed a proposal to Harley in 1712 for some form of Academy; and Addison and Pope had thoughts of working on such a project. But nothing came of it, and Lord Chesterfield, in his ill-fated letters designed to give Johnson's enterprise a fair wind, declared that it was 'a disgrace to our nation that hitherto we have had no such standard of our language'.[66]

---

[65] 'The common shore of Paris and of Rome', for example, follows very closely John Oldham's version from 1682, which referred to 'the common shore, where France does all her filth and ordure pour'. He follows Oldham again in bringing Alfred in as a symbol of the golden days of the past. Other borrowings are from Dryden. Smith and MacAdam (eds.), *The Poems of Samuel Johnson*, 60–3. Johnson's intense feelings seem to refer to poverty rather than to politics. See Mary Lascelles, 'Johnson and Juvenal', in F. W. Hilles (ed.), *New Light on Dr. Johnson* (New Haven, Conn. 1959), where she compares Oldham's, Dryden's, and Johnson's treatment of the same Juvenal passage. See also Rudd, *Johnson's Juvenal*.

[66] J. H. Sledd and G. J. Kolb, *Dr. Johnson's Dictionary: Essays in the Biography of a Book* (Chicago, 1955), 5–7. Swift's work was entitled *A Proposal for Correcting, Improving and Ascertaining the English Tongue*. Chesterfield's letters were printed in *The World*, nos. 101 and 102, and repr. in *Gentleman's Magazine* (1754).

Johnson's *Plan* for the dictionary, issued to the public in 1747, envisaged a history of the language and an account of English grammar, as well as definitions and illustrations of words. At that stage, Johnson still believed that it might be possible to arrest the corruption of the English language by pronouncing against foreign and uncouth borrowings, a common indication of defensive nationalism. 'Whoever knows the English tongue in its present extent', he wrote in *Rambler*, no. 208, 'will be able to express his thoughts without further help from other nations.' When he surveyed the task he had undertaken, he confessed himself 'frighted at its extent', but took comfort from the thought that, should he fail, it would be no shame to have 'retired without a triumph from a contest with united academies and long successions of learned compilers'.

The *Dictionary* survived a number of crises in production and did not make its appearance until April 1755. Johnson's preface repeated the national moral: 'I have devoted this book, the labour of years, to the honour of my country, that we may no longer yield the palm of philology, without a contest, to the nations of the continent.' Though he had abandoned the idea of freezing the development of the language as inimical to the spirit of English liberty, he urged restraint in the adoption of words, lest we be reduced 'to babble a dialect of France'. England, he observed grandly, had long preserved its constitution: 'let us make some struggles for our language.'

The illustrations of usage were a major part of the enterprise and one which Johnson found most congenial, since it enabled him to browse through the literature of the nation:

The chief glory of every people arises from its authors . . . I shall not think my employment useless or ignoble . . . if my labours afford light to the repositories of science, and add celebrity to Bacon, to Hooker, to Milton and to Boyle.

Johnson was by no means averse to beating his own drum, though in muffled tones and dignified manner. He painted a vivid picture of the drudgery of dictionary makers, rightly compared by Scaliger with the labours of the anvil or the hardships of the mine:[67]

It is the fate of those who toil at the lower employments of life to be rather driven by the fear of evil than attracted by the prospect of good; to be exposed to censure, without hope of praise . . . among these unhappy mortals is the writer of dictionaries . . . doomed only to remove rubbish and clear obstructions from the paths through which Learning and Genius press forward to conquest and glory, without bestowing a smile on the humble drudge that facilitates their progress.

[67] J. J. Scaliger (1540–1609), historian and philologist.

Again he drew attention to the collective endeavours of France and Italy, and wove his own struggles and misfortunes into a sad elegy:

The English dictionary was written with little assistance of the learned, and without any patronage of the great; not in the soft obscurities of retirement or under the shelter of academic bowers, but amidst inconvenience and distraction, in sickness and in sorrow . . . I have protracted my work till most of those whom I wished to please have sunk into the grave, and success and miscarriage are empty sounds; I therefore dismiss it with frigid tranquillity, having little to fear or hope from censure or from praise.[68]

Johnson could scarcely have been disappointed, however, at its reception. It gave him solid recognition at home and abroad.[69] Though there were critics, most reviewers were respectful, if not fulsome. There was, inevitably, more comment on his feat than on his scholarship. The *Gentleman's Magazine*, in a five-page review, pointed to the 'honour due to him, who alone has effected in seven years, what the joint labour of forty academicians could not produce to a neighbouring country in less than half a century'.[70] Adam Smith, in the *Edinburgh Review*, drew attention to the Italian and French works, and added: 'when we compare this book with other dictionaries, the merit of its author appears very extraordinary.'[71] Garrick was less restrained and broke into verse to celebrate his friend's triumph over the French:

> Let 'em rally their heroes, send forth all their powers
> Their verse-men and prose-men, then match 'em with ours,
> First Milton and Shakespeare, like Gods in the fight,
> Have put their whole drama and epic to flight;
> In satires, epistles and odes would they cope,
> Their numbers retreat before Dryden and Pope;
> And Johnson, well arm'd, like a hero of yore
> Has beat forty French and will beat forty more.[72]

Johnson's next major work was his edition of the plays of Shakespeare. To some extent this grew naturally out of his labours on the *Dictionary*, in which he quoted from Shakespeare far more than from any other author. Johnson announced the project in June 1756 and solicited subscriptions,

---

[68] Gilbert Walmsley of Lichfield had died in 1751 and Johnson's wife in 1752.
[69] Oxford gave him an MA in Feb. 1755 just before publication; the Accademia della Crusca and the Académie française both exchanged volumes.
[70] *Gentleman's Magazine* (Apr. 1755), 150.
[71] *Edinburgh Review*, 1 (May 1755), 61–73; repr. in *Scots Magazine* (Nov. 1755).
[72] *Public Advertiser*, 22 Apr. 1755; repr. in *Gentleman's Magazine* (1755), 190. Boswell included it in *Life*, i. 300–1.

but the work languished, and it was not until October 1765 that the eight volumes finally appeared.

If Johnson was right that the 'chief glory' of a nation was to be found in its authors, the English already held an ace of trumps in William Shakespeare. But his reputation had not completely recovered from its comparative eclipse in the Restoration period, and outside England he was little known. One of the achievements of the Hanoverian era was to establish Shakespeare as the national bard. Rowe, Pope, Theobald, Hanmer, and Warburton had all produced editions of the plays before Johnson's, between 1709 and 1747. In 1741 a statue by Scheemakers had been placed in Westminster Abbey by public subscription, and Garrick's sensational triumph as Richard III the same year paved the way for a series of stage revivals.[73] Indeed, Johnson and Garrick worked so closely in promoting Shakespeare that the enterprise had something of the character of a Lichfield operation. When Garrick took over as manager of Drury Lane in 1747, Johnson wrote for him a celebrated verse prologue, praising 'Immortal Shakespeare'.[74] In 1784 when Johnson was himself buried in the Abbey, it was at the side of Garrick, and with his feet opposite to the monument to Shakespeare.[75]

It was inevitable that the preface to Johnson's edition would be more read and discussed than the detailed textual commentaries, and it has become a key document in Shakespearean criticism. Johnson did not make the vulgar error of disparaging previous editors, nor did he defend Shakespeare against all criticism. Though Kenrick, Colman, and other reviewers took him to task for want of respect towards Shakespeare, Johnson aimed at a balanced assessment of excellencies and faults. He defended Shakespeare against the charges of not respecting the unities, of writing neither pure tragedy nor pure comedy, and of undermining authority by showing drunken kings and foolish senators: 'these', declared Johnson grandly, 'are the petty cavils of petty minds.' His main reservation was that Shakespeare 'seems to write without any moral purpose', though he argued that, from the plays, 'a system of social duty' might be inferred. In his wish that the plays should have been more consciously

[73] The monument was designed by Kent and the statue carved by Scheemakers. It is said to have been the first time a public subscription had been raised to place a memorial in the Abbey. M. R. Bromnell, *Alexander Pope and the Arts of Georgian England* (Oxford, 1978), 354–6.

[74] When, in 1769, Garrick organized the Shakespeare jubilee at Stratford, rainbow ribbons made in Coventry were sported, with a quotation from the prologue, 'Each change of many-coloured life he drew'.

[75] *Gentleman's Magazine* (1784), ii. 947.

didactic, we catch a glimpse of Johnson the schoolmaster, as well as the earnest tone of Hanoverian evangelicalism.

Historically, Johnson placed Shakespeare at a critical moment in national linguistic and literary development. Of his genius, Johnson had no doubt. Shakespeare built so solidly on real life and real observation that 'the stream of time, which is continually washing the dissoluble fabricks of other poets, passes without injury by the adamant of Shakespeare'. But Johnson was embarrassed by the stage business with which Shakespeare filled his plays:

The English nation in the time of Shakespeare was yet struggling to emerge from barbarity . . . Literature was yet confined to professed scholars, or to men and women of high rank. The public was gross and dark; and to be able to read and write was an accomplishment still valued for its rarity . . . His plots whether historical or fabulous are always crowded with incidents . . . the shows and bustle with which his plays abound have the same original . . . He knew how he should most please.

Though to Johnson this seemed an undignified concession to the taste of the audience, it might have occurred to him that *Irene* would have had a longer run had it included a little more for the groundlings.

Johnson's edition of Shakespeare was in preparation while the Seven Years War was taking place. There was widespread recognition that this was the great crisis of Anglo-French rivalry and, since for a long time the issue remained in doubt, the public mood was volatile and tense. The loss of Minorca at the outset led to the demand for Byng's execution and cast a long shadow. 'Every person I converse with', wrote John Wilkes, not the most nervous of men, 'seems to be under the dread of something very terrible approaching.'[76] One form which the excitement took was a leap forward in national awareness.

Christopher Smart, Johnson's poet friend, spent the war years in private lunatic asylums, suffering from a form of religious mania. Johnson's remark that he would as lief pray with Kit Smart as anyone else is well known.[77] But we can go further and surmise what they might have prayed about. While in confinement, Smart wrote his *Jubilate Agno*, adding a verse or so each day. It is a strange, chaotic work, but certain themes emerge strongly, and within religious mania lurked a good deal of national pride. Smart praised the English as the seed of Abraham, condemned the Welsh, Irish, Scots, and French, decided that England was 'the head of Europe in the spirit', and looked forward to the time

---

[76] W. J. Smith (ed.), *Grenville Papers* (London, 1852), i. 223.   [77] *Life*, i. 397.

when the English tongue would be 'the language of the West'. More modestly, he insisted that 'English cats are the best in Europe'. I do not think Johnson would have quarrelled with him for that opinion, and Johnson seems to have visited him, for one of Smart's lines is 'God be gracious to Samuel Johnson'.[78]

Between finishing the edition of Shakespeare and beginning his last major work, Johnson paid three visits abroad, the first time he had been outside his native land. He had left it until well into his sixties. He found little to praise and nothing to shake his belief in the superiority of England. The first, and best-known, of the journeys was to the Western Islands with Boswell in the autumn of 1773. The publication of Johnson's account of their travels, in January 1775, gave yet another stir to the nationalist pot. Though he was at pains to acknowledge the hospitality they had received and his respect for the civilities of life in some of the lairds' dwellings, Johnson did not disguise the fact that he found the Hebrides, as he had expected, poor, desolate, and unremarkable: 'of these islands, it must be confessed, that they have not many allurements, but to the mere lover of naked nature.'[79] Indeed, the very idea of Johnson visiting Scotland to inspect some outlandish species was bound to rouse the pride of many Scots. He was attacked vigorously as ungrateful, ill-informed, and prejudiced. The author of *Remarks on a Voyage to the Hebrides* declared that 'the flame of national rancour and reproach has been for several years but too well fed—you too have added your faggot.' Donald McNicol, in a long and detailed refutation, insisted that 'the Doctor hated Scotland; that was the *master-passion*, and it scorned all restraints . . . every line is marked with prejudice.'[80] A less sophisticated revenge was taken by James MacIntyre in the form of a Gaelic song:

> You are a slimy, yellow-bellied frog.
> You are a toad crawling along the ditches.
> You are a lizard of the waste, crawling and creeping like a reptile.[81]

The second visit, to North Wales in 1774 with the Thrales and their young daughter Queenie, was a tamer business. Johnson was unwell for some of the time and since part of the purpose was to visit Mrs Thrale's property at Bach-y-Craig, Johnson could hardly be too disparaging.

---

[78] K. Williamson (ed.), *The Poetical Works of Christopher Smart* (Oxford, 1980), i. *Jubilate Agno*, B. 433, 435, 436, 437, 438; C. 102, B. 127, 731, 74.

[79] *Journey to the Western Islands*, 130.

[80] *Remarks on Dr S. Johnson's Journey to the Hebrides* (Edinburgh, 1779).

[81] The full version is printed in J. T. Boulton (ed.), *Samuel Johnson: The Critical Heritage* (London, 1971), 240–1.

'Wales, so far as I have yet seen of it, is a very beautiful and rich country, all enclosed and planted,' he wrote.[82] The castles of Carnarvon and Beaumaris particularly impressed him. Though he kept a brief record of the visits made, there was little temptation to publish. 'Cambria will complain', urged Boswell, if not honoured with some remarks, but Johnson was reluctant: 'Wales is so little different from England that it offers nothing to the speculation of the traveller.'[83]

Johnson's last trip abroad was also made with the Thrales, in the late autumn of 1775. They spent seven weeks at Paris and in northern France. It was a mixed success. Johnson commanded little French and, unwilling to appear at a disadvantage, insisted on speaking Latin to scholars. Though he kept a fairly full record of the journey, he had no wish to publish: 'I cannot pretend to tell the publick any thing of a place better known to many of my readers than to myself.' He was not greatly impressed with what he saw: 'France is worse than Scotland in every thing but the climate,' he told Boswell obligingly, and his conclusion was that the French were 'a gross, ill-bred, untaught people: what I gained by being in France was learning to be better satisfied with my own country.'[84]

Johnson's last great work, which he started at the age of 68, continued the tracing of the nation's literary history. This was *The Lives of the Most Eminent English Poets*, from Cowley to Gray. In one respect, Johnson was responding to a hint dropped by the king during their audience in the royal library in 1767. George III, leading the conversation, remarked—no doubt predictably enough—that Johnson ought to undertake 'the literary biography of this country'.[85] But the immediate occasion of the new enterprise was that a poor edition of the English poets was being printed by Martins of Edinburgh and was selling well. The group of London booksellers who approached Johnson in 1777 for a series of short biographical introductions were in the happy position of making a little money and striking a blow for their country's honour.[86]

Once again, Johnson was setting sail on a strong tide. An increased reading public, combined with awakening interest in the national past, made the moment propitious. In 1765 Thomas Percy, a close friend, had published his *Reliques of Ancient English Poetry*; it went into a second edition in 1767 and a third by 1775. Public interest in these ballads,

[82] *Life*, ii. 282.

[83] Ibid. 284. Boswell did not know that Johnson had made notes, but they are printed in the Hill–Powell edn. (ibid. v. 427–60).

[84] Ibid. ii. 384–404; iii. 352.   [85] Ibid. ii. 40.

[86] Ibid. iii. 110–11 prints Edward Dilly's letter of 26 Sept. 1777 explaining the details of the arrangement. See also *DNB*, under John Bell. Bell was agent for the Martins in London.

literally snatched from burning, was certainly in part a response to the acclaim given to Macpherson's work on Scottish verses. A less successful undertaking in 1770 was the young Thomas Chatterton's attempt to pass off his own writings as the work of Thomas Rowley, a medieval monk. In 1774 Thomas Warton, Johnson's main contact at Oxford, began the publication of his *History of English Poetry*.

Johnson's enterprise, as he confessed, grew in the writing. The first volumes appeared in 1779, the last in 1781. One of his beliefs was that, for an author, controversy was better than neglect and, since he rarely refrained from strong comment on the selected poets, reviewers had a good deal to discuss. The followers of George, Lord Lyttelton, were much aggrieved at Johnson's reference to 'poor Lyttelton', and Mrs Montagu cut off all acquaintance with him.[87] His lack of enthusiasm for Gray's poetry, except for the *Elegy*, brought more complaint. But most of the criticism was reserved for his treatment of Milton. Into his life of that poet, Johnson poured all his distaste for sectaries and rebels. Milton's republicanism, he insisted, was 'founded in an envious hatred of greatness and a sullen desire of independence; in petulance impatient of control, and pride disdainful of superiority . . . he hated all whom he was required to obey . . . and he felt not so much the love of liberty as repugnance to authority.' This was no way to treat an epic poet and, for good measure, Johnson painted an unflattering portrait of Milton as domestic tyrant. William Cowper, from his snug retreat at Olney, protested at Johnson's treatment: 'a pensioner is not likely to spare a republican; and the Doctor, in order I suppose, to convince his royal patron of the sincerity of his monarchical principles, has belaboured that great poet's character with the most industrious cruelty.'[88]

Other readers reverted to the national theme. The *Critical Review* for May–June 1779 thought that, in general, Johnson had erred on the side of severity. But the volumes were a matter of national concern:

As the general character of every polished nation depends in a great measure on its poetical productions, too much care cannot be taken, in works of this nature, to impress on foreigners a proper idea of their merit. This task was perhaps never so well executed as in the performance before us. Our poetical militia, clothed in the new uniform which the editors have here bestowed upon them, make a most respectable figure.

[87] *Life*, iv. 64–5.
[88] J. King and C. Ryskamp (eds.), *The Letters and Prose Writing of William Cowper* (Oxford, 1981), i. 306–8 (31 Oct. 1779).

Even poets were conscripts in the relentless struggle against the French.

By this time, the transformation of Johnson himself from Grub-Street hack into something approaching a national institution, and thence into the pantheon of national heroes, was nearly complete. Dublin had given him an honorary LL D in 1765 for his work on Shakespeare; Oxford, with maladroit timing, had added a DCL in March 1775.[89] Johnson's major works had dealt with England's language, with England's greatest dramatist, with England's most famous poets. He had defended the cause of his country against their rebellious American subjects; he had defended true Patriotism in *The Patriot* and the *False Alarm*. Friend and foe alike testified to his growing pre-eminence. Christopher Smart in 1756 regarded the *Dictionary* as a national monument: 'a work I look upon with equal pleasure and amazement, as I do upon St. Paul's cathedral: each the work of an Englishman.'[90] As early as 1759 Smollett could refer to him as 'that great Cham of literature'.[91] William Kenrick, in a waspish review of the Shakespeare edition of 1765, was both nonplussed and exasperated at the position Johnson enjoyed:

Is it, by the way, then to be wondered at, that a private individual, like Samuel Johnson, should be even preposterously elated at finding that homage paid to him, which has been in vain solicited by sovereigns, and is refused even to the King on his throne? Graduated by universities, pensioned by his prince, and surrounded by pedagogues and poetasters, he finds a grateful odour in the incense of adulation; while admiring booksellers stand at a distance and look up to him with awful reverence . . .[92]

By 1784 his place was beyond question. The newspapers reported with concern his last illness. At his interment in Westminster Abbey, Reynolds, Burney, William Scott (the future Lord Stowell), Paoli, Burke, Sir Joseph Banks, Sir Charles Bunbury, and William Windham were among the mourners. A university sermon was preached in St Mary's, Oxford. A public subscription raised 1,100 guineas for a memorial by John Bacon in St Paul's cathedral.

---

[89] It coincided with the appearance of his most contentious political pamphlet, *Taxation No Tyranny*, allowing Johnson's opponents to suggest that it was a reward for servility.

[90] 'Some Thoughts on the English Language', *Universal Visiter* (Jan. 1756), quoted in A. Reddick, *The Making of Johnson's Dictionary, 1746–1773* (Cambridge, 1990), 177.

[91] Smollett to Wilkes, 16 Mar. 1759, *Letters of Tobias Smollett*, ed. L. M. Knapp (Oxford, 1970), 75.

[92] *Review* (Nov. 1765), repr. in Boulton (ed.), *Johnson: The Critical Heritage*, 181–8.

Johnson died on 13 December 1784. Biographers and memoirists were off their marks with impressive speed. Within two days of his death, 'before he was shrouded', notice of a biography was given and a volume appeared within nine days.[93] The *Gentleman's Magazine* managed to include in its December 1784 number a thirteen-page biographical sketch by Thomas Tyers, together with a long account of the funeral, two commemorative poems, and a complete report of Johnson's last will and testament. William Shaw, the Gaelic scholar who supported Johnson in the Ossian affair, published his *Memoirs of the Life and Writing of the Late Samuel Johnson* in 1785. Boswell came up to London in the spring of 1785, refused to be rushed into publishing the *Life*, but offered in October 1785 his *Journal of a Tour to the Hebrides with Samuel Johnson*. The following year saw an *Essay on the Life, Character and Writings of Dr. Johnson* by Joseph Towers, and Hester Thrale's *Anecdotes*. In 1787 Sir John Hawkins published the collected works in eleven volumes, with a long biography as an introduction. Mrs Thrale was back in action in 1788 with her edition of the letters that had passed between her and Johnson. Boswell, partly to keep public interest alive, printed in 1790 the letter to Lord Chesterfield and the conversation with George III, at the inflated price of half a guinea each, and in May 1791 at last produced the *Life of Johnson*, published by Charles Dilly. 'My *magnum opus* sells wonderfully,' he told his friend Temple.[94]

By this time, Johnson's character was as important as his writings. In his *Tour of the Hebrides*, Boswell added a long and shrewd description of Johnson. He did not attempt to deny Johnson's prejudice against the Scots, but commented: 'he was indeed, if I may be allowed the phrase, at bottom much of a *John Bull*, much of a *true-born Englishman*.'[95] Boswell could not decide whether this was a compliment, adding, 'I am, I flatter myself, completely a citizen of the world'. As the decades slowly unfolded, Johnson became a national treasure, a period piece, a quaint old-fashioned figure, instantly recognizable, impossible not to parody. In May 1840 Thomas Carlyle gave his course of lectures on Hero-Worship, and brought in Johnson as 'the Hero as man-of-letters'. He was in strange company with Rousseau and Robert Burns, not to speak of Cromwell, Frederick the Great, and Napoleon Bonaparte. Carlyle managed to

---

[93] This I take to be the *Life of Samuel Johnson with Occasional Remarks on his Writings*, attributed to the barrister William Cooke. The fact that it included an account of Johnson's assistance to Dr Dodd makes it more probable. *Gentleman's Magazine* (Dec. 1784), 932, offered corrections to it.

[94] Boswell to W. Temple, 22 Aug. 1791 (*Letters*, ed. Tinker, ii. 439–40).

[95] *Tour*, 10.

patronize him as 'brave old Samuel'—heroic, staunch, but a bit dim, and always *old*.[96] With adulation came distortion and caricature. A man with little faith in colonies and a deep dislike of war seemed the very embodiment of assertive nationalism; a man with a ready and practical sympathy for the poor became the spokesman for authority; a shy and reluctant conversationalist who, like a ghost, spoke only when he was spoken to was transformed into the hectoring bully of the dinner table; a man who tried desperately to think clearly and systematically and who referred wryly to his 'obstinate rationality' became a favourite example of hopeless and ludicrous bigotry. It was the price paid for fame. But 'a *true-born Englishman*' Johnson would have worn as a badge of honour.

[96] It is remarkable that in his letters Carlyle almost invariably referred to him as 'Old Johnson'. In part this is a tedious rhetorical trick to claim easy acquaintance with people of the past, but it is also a reminder that the three people who produced the most vivid reminiscences of Johnson—Boswell, Mrs Thrale, and Fanny Burney—only met him when he was well over 50.

8

The Nature of Hanoverian Politics

JOHNSON had no doubt about the nature of Hanoverian politics. There had been a sorry decline since the days of Stuart England and all principle had been abandoned. 'Politicks', he told Boswell in 1775, 'are now nothing more than means of rising in the world. With this sole view do men engage in politicks, and their whole conduct proceeds upon it.'[1]

We do not often find the reign of Charles II held up as a pattern of integrity. We could dismiss Johnson's remark as the routine cynicism directed against politicians in all ages. But for many years the account of Hanoverian England offered by historians seemed to endorse Johnson's opinion. Hanoverian politics was seen as the politics of a landed oligarchy, the politics of Brooks's and the Cocoa Tree, of Newmarket and the Quarter Sessions, the politics of country houses like Moccas Court, Brocket Hall, and Weston Underwood. It reflected the economic and social domination established by the gentry and aristocracy. Political life was confined to a small and exclusive circle. Members of Parliament had so many relatives and friends in the House of Commons that the opening day of a new session was not unlike a family gathering or a school reunion. Many of those characteristics survived deep into the nineteenth century, when Trollope's novels treated politics as a game, the stakes high, enthralling to the players, of less consequence to the onlookers. In *The Prime Minister*, published in 1876, Lady Glencora explained her view of the contending parties to her friend Mrs Finn:

The country goes on its own way, either for better or for worse, whichever of them are in. I don't think it makes any difference as to what sort of laws are passed. But, among ourselves, in our set, it makes a deal of difference, who gets the garters, and the counties, who are made barons and then earls, and whose name stands at the head of everything.

In such a system there would be little room for heroism or self-sacrifice, and high principle would be regarded as tiresome, theatrical, and divisive.

---

[1] *Life*, ii. 369. The account entered by Boswell in his private journal was slightly different, using the phrase 'means of success in life'. Ryskamp and Pottle (eds.), *Boswell: The Ominous Years*, 152. The private account softens the remark, making it less self-seeking.

Enthusiasm would be looked upon with mistrust, whether in politics or religion, as the factor which had plunged the country into civil war, setting brother against brother, father against son. Lewis Namier, in the late 1920s, expressed this view of Hanoverian England in his own laconic way: 'Men no more dreamt of a seat in the House in order to benefit humanity than a child dreams of a birthday cake that others may eat it.'[2] Such a society appeared greedy, even gross, and Sir Robert Walpole— solid, earthy, cynical—a fitting representative. This image of the century, which held the field for decades, helps to explain why the study of eighteenth-century politics remained something of a minority taste. Schoolchildren were steered towards the heroic exploits of the Tudor period, the melodrama of Stuart England, or the advent of liberalism and democracy in the nineteenth century. The politics of Henry Pelham, George Grenville, Bute, North, and Rockingham seemed to have little to offer.

Support for Namier's interpretation came from unexpected quarters. Some Marxist historians were so anxious to hail the advent of class politics that they could muster little interest in anything else: to them, the Glorious Revolution was poor stuff, since it did not do much for either the bourgeoisie or the proletariat. Gentry politics was therefore little more than the division of the spoils, Namier's birthday cake. Since liberal historians also saw little to admire in Hanoverian England, regarding it as a backward society waiting to be rescued by Benthamite and Whig reform in the nineteenth century, it followed that for some decades the old order was distinctly short of defenders.

But Namier's *bon mot* may mislead us. It is true that, until the later decades of the eighteenth century, humanitarian endeavour did not often run in parliamentary channels. But Hanoverian society as a whole had its fair share of philanthropists: Thomas Guy, Captain Coram, James Oglethorpe, Jonas Hanway, John Howard, Elizabeth Fry, Thomas Gilbert, Granville Sharp, Thomas Clarkson, Thomas Day, and William Wilberforce. Its record of charitable and humanitarian achievement was impressive. Johnson himself paid tribute to the spirit of the age when he wrote in *The Idler*, no. 4, that 'no sooner is a new species of misery brought to view, and a design of relieving it professed, than every hand is open to contribute something, every tongue is busied in sollicitation, and every art of pleasure is employed for a time in the interest of virtue'. Even

---

[2] *The Structure of Politics at the Accession of George III* (London, 1929), i. 4. Though he warned against the concept of a close oligarchy (p. 12), much of Namier's work tended to reinforce that view.

in strict relationship to politics the remark needs to be glossed, since its burlesque character rather misrepresents the true position. True, few country gentlemen would have expressed their aspirations in terms of benefiting humanity—a concept which came in largely with the French Revolution and soon acquired the pejorative flavour Namier gave it—but many certainly felt it their duty to serve their families, their shires, and their country in Parliament. Many of them, particularly the knights of the shire, did not seek office, expect pensions, or hope to rise in the world. They were not, perhaps, much given to reflecting upon their own motives, but one who did, George Dempster, is a warning against easy generalizations. He had served in Parliament, he wrote in 1793, for nearly thirty years, which

neither suited to my fortune nor genius, where I never was metaphysician enough to settle to my own satisfaction the bounds of the several duties a member owes to his King, his country, to purity or Puritanism rather, and to party, to myself and those who depended upon my protection . . . but went on floundering like a blind horse in a deep road and a long journey.[3]

One of the first to question the unflattering and cynical view of Hanoverian politics was Herbert Butterfield.[4] Though many of his criticisms of Namier and his school were of a technical nature, and some were unduly alarmist, he protested passionately against a mechanistic view of motivation, insisting that human beings were the carriers of ideas as well as the repositories of vested interests.[5]

The rehabilitation that followed came from a number of different quarters: from historians who argued that there was much wider participation in politics under the old system than had been allowed; from others who pointed to the political and financial success of Hanoverian England and to its commercial vitality; and from those who insisted that, despite what seemed blemishes and defects to later generations, the political and constitutional arrangements commanded for decades widespread support. The counter-attack was long overdue and did much to restore a more balanced understanding. There is even some danger that revisionism might go too far and feel under an obligation, not merely to explain, but to defend the old order.

There are two other objections that have been increasingly levelled at a simple theory of aristocratic exclusiveness. The first is that very few societies can be totally closed, and Hanoverian society was not, socially or

---

[3] *House of Commons, 1754–90*, ii. 317.
[4] *George III and the Historians* (London, 1957).   [5] Ibid. 211.

politically. Though it can be argued that the openness of the upper crust was something of a myth, new men could move upwards, particularly into the gentry and the professional classes. Johnson's remark hinted at this mobility. Nor could political life be hermetically sealed, even if Parliament tried, for most of the century, to restrict the publication of debates. At the very least, some regard to the opinions of the electorate was prudent, especially in the eighteen months before a general election. In France, by comparison, there was no Parliament, and political discussion, though vigorous, was sterile, rarely engaging upon governmental decisions.[6]

Secondly, and perhaps of greater importance, Hanoverian England was changing throughout Johnson's lifetime. One recent historian has suggested that the pace of change was so rapid that Englishmen in the 1780s did not, in any fundamental sense, inhabit the same society as in the 1730s.[7] That is perhaps excessive, as is the later comment that Hanoverian society was 'in a state of turmoil'.[8] Nevertheless, the fact of change can hardly be disputed. Of course, the process was neither regular nor systematic. Society was almost certainly changing faster than the political system and, in the end, the adjustments which had to be made in the 1830s were left so late that there was doubt whether they could be made at all.

The ideological assumptions of a regime may usually be traced back to the circumstances which brought it to power. In the case of the Hanoverian regime, this is not totally straightforward. The gentry and nobility had held wealth and influence for centuries and the continuity of English history was very strong. But the events of 1688 enhanced their position by ruling out the possibility of an autocratic or absolutist monarchy. Certainly the politicians of Hanoverian England had little doubt that their system derived from 1688 and scarcely wearied of paying tribute to the immortal principles of the Glorious Revolution.

That revolution was primarily the work of the aristocracy and gentry, Whig and Tory momentarily united against popery and despotism. The mass of the people played little part and the organizers had no great desire that they should. The main purpose of the new regime was therefore to protect the interests of the landed class, which they identified chiefly

---

[6] The States-General, the equivalent of the British Parliament, was not summoned between 1614 and 1789. The *parlements* were courts of law, though they had important powers of registration and protest.

[7] P. Langford, *A Polite and Commercial People* (Oxford, 1989), 725.

[8] P. Langford, *Public Life and the Propertied Englishman, 1689–1789* (Oxford, 1991), p. v.

as the preservation of the rights of property. In his *Second Treatise on Government,* Locke gave that objective pride of place: 'the great and chief end of men's uniting into commonwealths, and putting themselves under government, is the preservation of their property.'[9] It followed, in his view, that government must therefore be limited, since 'property cannot be taken away without a man's consent—either given by himself or by his representatives'. The supporters of the regime were not apologetic: they accepted Harrington's argument that power must follow property, and that the security of the property of every man was the rock on which civilization was built.

Johnson was in complete agreement. In his *Journey to the Western Islands,* he remarked that civil society depended upon 'reverence for property'.[10] In practice there was hardly any man, however humble, who had not some property to be protected, and so all benefited to a certain extent. But the rich benefited most and it was right that they should. Adam Smith declared bluntly in *The Wealth of Nations,* in 1776, that civil government, in so far as it is instituted for the security of property, 'is in reality instituted for the defence of the rich against the poor, or of those who have some property against those who have none at all'.[11] There was, consequently, scant enthusiasm for extending the franchise to persons of little or no property, most of the capital offences added to the statute book were concerned with the defence of property,[12] and the citadel of power was buttressed by legislation which declared that local government must be in the hands of JPs of property and membership of Parliament reserved for men of substantial landed estates.[13] When the militia was reorganized in 1757, in order to meet the objection that it was imprudent to place arms in the hands of the 'poor and indigent' it was enacted that colonels of regiments must possess landed estates worth at least £400 p.a. or be heirs apparent to double that value.[14] The principle was maintained even in

---

[9] Ch. 9, sect. 124.   [10] *Journey to the Western Islands,* 45.

[11] *An Inquiry into the Nature and Causes of the Wealth of Nations,* bk. V, ch. 1, pt. ii: 'Of the Expense of Justice'.

[12] The statutes were particularly concerned with Luddite protests and with forgery. Radzinowicz, *History of English Criminal Law,* i. 148, noted that, of 97 executions in 1785, the great majority were for crimes against property. One execution was for murder; there were none for crimes against the state, but 74 for robbery or burglary.

[13] 5 George II c. 18; 9 Anne c. 5.

[14] Recruitment for the armed forces produced many constitutional and legal problems for Hanoverian England. The difficulty was how to maintain forces large enough to resist the French without beggaring the country or endangering its liberties. Manning the navy produced agonized debates on the propriety of the press gang. Members of Parliament were well aware of the critical role of the army and militia in 1641 and again in 1688 and of the way

1832 by the Reform Act, which took a long step towards dismantling the old system. The clause which introduced a uniform franchise based upon the £10 householder disqualified a considerable number of poorer voters in certain boroughs, and the instructions given to the committee which drafted the bill made it plain that it should be 'so based on property, and on existing franchises and territorial divisions, as to run no risk of overthrowing the [existing] form of government'.[15]

A number of secondary considerations flowed from the main one. The chief restraint on a despotic monarchy, which might claim the right to seize the subjects' property at will, was the existence of Parliament, since the Law had shown itself, in the reign of James II, dangerously vulnerable to royal pressure. It was therefore essential to sustain Parliament's independence and vitality, and to uphold its privileges. The support throughout the century for place bills and for economical reform had the double advantage of preserving the legislature from encroachment by the executive, while restraining the growth of an independent civil service, which could become a rival source of authority as it did in many continental states. Financial control must also be safeguarded. The frantic opposition to excise was not merely factious and opportunist politics, but an awareness that, on the Continent, the introduction of taxes not under parliamentary control had proved fatal to a number of representative institutions. Most landed men wished to see an unobtrusive executive and low levels of direct taxation: for much of the period they got their way, since successive ministers resorted to borrowing in order to raise revenue for war. The zeal of the Commons to see taxation reduced provoked severe political difficulties after the Seven Years War, an outcry against Pitt's proposals in 1798 for an incomes tax, and a revolt against Vansittart as chancellor of the Exchequer immediately after Napoleon had been defeated in 1814.[16]

---

in which continental rulers had used their armed forces to suppress estates. A large standing army in peacetime was too expensive. To rely upon Hanoverian and Hessian mercenaries was also expensive, mortifying to the national spirit, and possibly dangerous to liberty. An efficient militia was one possible way out of the dilemma, provided that it did not dabble in politics, as the army had done in the 1640s and the Irish Volunteers were to do in the 1780s. The first proposals in 1756 were rejected by the House of Lords, after Hardwicke had complained that they were 'too democratical' and Sandys had warned that officers would not be able to prevent their men from becoming 'riotous and seditious'. The 1757 Act cut the proposed numbers by half and imposed a high property qualification. There was general agreement that, as Lord Talbot put it, 'none but men of fortune should have the command of our militia'. *Parl. Hist.* xv. 704–69; 30 George II c. 25.

[15] Quoted in M. Brock, *The Great Reform Act* (London, 1973), 136.
[16] The deepest apprehensions were revealed by the debates on the Assessed taxes and the

An unambitious executive meant that much legislation was private or local in character. Perhaps the most obvious indication of the weight of emphasis placed upon property was the growing respect for the law, which has been identified as one of the prime characteristics of the period.[17] Yet this high regard for the law did not lead, as one might have expected, to enthusiasm for the establishment of an effective police force. Apart from the cost of such an establishment, which would have been not inconsiderable, there was deep mistrust of a police force as an engine of despotism, whether in the hands of the Crown or controlled by local corporations, many of them dominated by dissenters, over whom the gentry had very fitful command. The word 'police' was, as Johnson noted in his *Dictionary*, of French origin, made its way slowly into the English language, and retained for many years something of the original taint. But London and its suburbs, growing year by year, posed an almost impossible problem for the old system of government. In 1785 Archibald Macdonald tried to propose a police force for London, with stipendiary magistrates, and ran into a hornet's nest. Lord Beauchamp presumed that the idea must have come from Paris; Alderman Hammett declared that the suggestion could not have caused more alarm 'had a torch been applied to the buildings of London'; and Pitt, the first minister, gave lukewarm support, explaining that he had not studied the proposals in detail. Macdonald's bill was knocked on the head.[18] Not until after the French Revolution was Parliament ready to grasp the nettle and then with great reluctance. The opposition saw vast dangers in the bill introducing paid magistrates for Middlesex. Sheridan complained that more patronage would be placed at the disposal of government: 'it would become a job'. Fox went to the heart of the matter, protesting against 'a dangerous innovation in principle', the consequences of which no man could foresee: 'the police of this country was well administered by the ordinary mode by gentlemen who undertook

tax upon income. Fox, in 1797, led the way with a declaration that no human being could calculate the horrors to which the measure might give rise. George Tierney, the following year, denounced it as a 'monstrous proposition'; Sir John Sinclair declared that the whole property of the country would in future be at the mercy of the government; and M. A. Taylor insisted that, since the genius of the constitution was that a man's property was sacred, the sanctity of property and the English constitution would go down together. The House of Commons approved the measures only because they feared the French Revolution even more than the horrors of income tax. *Parl. Hist.* xxxiii. 1125; xxxiv. 22, 86, 90.

[17] See e.g. D. Hay, 'Property, Authority and the Criminal Law', in D. Hay (ed.), *Albion's Fatal Tree* (London, 1975); D. Hay (ed.), *Crime and Society in 18th Century England* (London, 1975); J. Brewer and J. Styles (eds.), *An Ungovernable People: The English and their Law in the 17th and 18th Centuries* (New Brunswick, 1980), esp. Introd.

[18] *Parl. Hist.* xxv. 888–914.

to discharge the duty without deriving any emolument from it.'[19] But he was defeated, and the Players had taken a vital wicket in their long match against the Gentlemen.

To what extent was this an effective system of government? Victorian reformers excoriated Hanoverian administration for its sloth, corruption, and inefficiency. A recent attempt to introduce the term *ancien régime* to describe the system is unfortunate, since it is whiggish, patronizing, and teleological.[20]

The system established in 1688 survived, struck roots, and proved remarkably stable. For the first sixty years it was handicapped by the existence of a rival dynasty which posed at times a considerable threat. In addition, any parliamentary regime within a balanced constitution must necessarily produce occasional crises and tensions. Throughout Johnson's life a series of episodes may have seemed menacing to anxious subjects: the Sacheverell riots of 1710, the '15 rising, the South Sea bubble, the Atterbury plot, the Excise crisis, the gin riots of 1736, the fall of Walpole, the '45, the political crisis of 1746, the Jew Bill agitation, Minorca, Byng and the fall of Newcastle, the hunger riots of the 1760s, Wilkes and Liberty, the American troubles, the Gordon riots, and the protracted constitutional crisis of 1782–4. A century which seemed tranquil to later observers did not always feel so to contemporaries.

This evidence has persuaded a number of historians to deny that stability was a feature of the period.[21] It is not a point that can be argued closely. Stability is a vague term and can only be assessed comparatively. Hanoverian Englishmen compared their situation either with the previous century or with that of contemporary Europe. The seventeenth century nearly started with the bang of the Gunpowder Plot and continued with a series of convulsions that were to make the troubles of the eighteenth century seem very small beer. A comparison with the continent in the eighteenth century shows three tsars murdered in fifty years, the king of Sweden shot dead, France engulfed by revolution, and Poland removed from the map completely.

The mood of Hanoverian politics was very different from that of Stuart England, when exile or the Tower had been a possibility for disgraced

---

[19] Debate on the Middlesex Justices Bill, *Parl. Hist.* xxix. 1182–3, 1464–5.
[20] J. C. D. Clark, *English Society, 1688–1832: Ideology, Social Structure and Political Practice during the Ancien Régime* (Cambridge, 1985), esp. Introd.
[21] A valuable historiographical summary is J. Black, 'Introduction: An Age of Political Stability?', in Black (ed.), *Britain in the Age of Walpole*, 1–22.

politicians. Though Edmund Burke, ever excitable, threatened Lord North with the block, one doubts whether the noble lord in the blue ribband slept any less soundly. The institutions of the country were generally admired, the religious settlement was acceptable to most men, and the supremacy of the landed gentry was not much resented. Ian Christie has reminded us recently that 'oligarchical government . . . stood foresquare on its foundations in the tacit consent of the people'.[22] We must not fall into the error of demanding a standard of stability that is unreasonably high. Paul Langford remarks that 'if stability means either tranquillity or unchanging government, it will not do to describe the experience of the eighteenth century'.[23] That is hardly a fair test. Tranquillity is scarcely to be expected in public affairs, while, since adaptation is the law of survival, an unchanging government is a recipe for disaster, not success.

We must not exaggerate the instability of Hanoverian life. Westminster mobs could be menacing and elections turbulent, and the Gordon riots, in particular, did vast damage to property. But no minister of the Crown or member of Parliament was ever seriously injured during the eighteenth century. As for political stability, the Hanoverian period witnessed five of the longest administrations in modern British history, with Walpole (21 years), Pelham (10 years), North (12 years), Pitt (17 years) and Liverpool (15 years) outclassing the great majority of their successors.[24]

For many years, Hanoverian history was studied largely for its constitutional interest. Since crises are more exciting than routine, the malfunctioning of the constitution is particularly well documented. But there is a risk of producing a distorted impression. Many of the remaining prerogatives of the Crown were hardly contentious at all. The veto fell into abeyance and was removed from the practical agenda. The right of dissolution was annexed by ministers, gave them a slight advantage on the timing of general elections, and annoyed the opposition, but was hardly a major issue. The granting of honours, though a source of persistent irritation and worry to monarchs and ministers, rarely produced serious crises.[25] The prerogative which caused most difficulty was choice of min-

---

[22] *Stress and Stability in Late-eighteenth-Century Britain* (Oxford, 1984), 35.

[23] *A Polite and Commercial People*, 684.

[24] Only Mrs Thatcher's twelve years in office can compare. Asquith's eight years at 10 Downing Street are misleading, since the Parliament Act was suspended at the outbreak of war in 1914 and he did not have to face another general election.

[25] George III's refusal to grant peerages to the Coalition in 1783 was of great importance, but it was really a symptom of the bad feeling which already existed between the king and North and Fox.

isters, since it was close to the heart of royal power, and it remained a source of dissension throughout the nineteenth century. But crises about the appointment of the first minister were relatively infrequent and were often the prelude to a long period of effective administration. The crisis of 1727, when the new monarch intended at first to dismiss Sir Robert Walpole, lasted only a few days and gave him, in the end, a further fifteen years of power. The confrontation of February 1746 lasted only four days and Henry Pelham continued in office until his death, eight years later, when George II remarked, 'Now I shall have no more peace'. The convulsions of 1756–7, which were protracted, set up the Newcastle–Pitt coalition, one of the most successful administrations of all time, while the great crisis of 1782–4 established William Pitt in office for seventeen years. It would be misleading to see monarchs and ministers as being at loggerheads for most of the time, or to judge the normal working of the constitution from the occasional grinding of gears.

The strength of the Hanoverian monarchy, which has been emphasized in much recent work, was itself a stabilizing factor in a changing society. Though the revolution settlement imposed restrictions on the Crown, it retained formidable powers. Ministers were, in a real sense, the king's ministers and had, at least, to be acceptable to him. Most monarchs retained a close watch on foreign affairs, where they were often dealing with relatives, and the possession of Hanover gave them an independent position and alternative sources of information. Their keen interest in the army was not mere prudence but reflected the traditional role of the monarch as leader in battle. Ecclesiastical appointments were of special concern to most monarchs, who took very seriously their coronation oath to protect the Church.

It followed that an important ingredient in political life was competition for court favour. Walpole established an inside track by his understanding with Queen Caroline and his position was weakened by her death. Carteret's strong influence with George II was based in part upon his command of German and his knowledge of the politics of the Holy Roman Empire. Bute's hold on George III depended upon the respect felt, in those days, by youth towards wise tutors and was bound to diminish as he grew up. Royal disfavour, on the other hand, was a severe handicap. William Pitt wrote in 1754 that he was crushed under the weight of royal displeasure; the collapse of George Grenville's ministry was, to a great extent, because the king found him boring beyond belief; while George's detestation of Charles Fox consigned that politician to the opposition benches for almost the whole of his life.

The monarch's attitude was therefore monitored with great attention. His most casual remarks at the levee were searched for deeper meanings, the people to whom he spoke noted carefully, and the tone and length of his observations assessed. In 1783, much depended on whether George's initial distaste for the Fox–North coalition would be maintained. Young William Pitt, an opponent of the coalition and a first minister in waiting, reported to his mother in May 1783 that 'the same *fixed aversion* still, I believe, continues . . . you will easily guess where'. On 19 December at the levee, Soame Jenyns inferred from the pains the king took to be agreeable to his ministers that they were about to be turned out. A few hours confirmed his cynical guess.[26]

However fascinating contemporaries found these efforts to evaluate court favour, to guess who was on the way up and who down, historians are apt to be impatient with such tittle-tattle. But to disregard it completely would be to construct a false impression of Hanoverian political life. 'To stand well in the closet', as the phrase went, was essential. Public opinion had a considerable and increasing effect upon Parliament but less on the Crown itself. The king did not, after all, have to stand for re-election or defend his conduct at a county meeting. We should therefore remember that there was a crucial area of political life which public opinion could do little to influence.

The time is fast approaching when a complete reassessment of Hanoverian administration may be possible and a number of recent studies have argued that it may have attained a higher level of competence than has usually been recognized. N. A. M. Rodger, writing on the Georgian navy, clears away many legends of life at sea as 'a floating concentration camp' and writes that it was an extremely efficient instrument of war: patronage did not ignore professional skill.[27] Tony Hayter, editing the papers of Lord Barrington, who held the post of Secretary at War for nearly twenty years, credits him with attempts to promote officers by merit and claims for him 'an impressive administrative achievement'.[28] John Brewer, in an extremely important volume, traces the way in which England was transformed from an ineffective and peripheral seventeenth-century country into a world power, praises many features of the administration, remarks that the excise was a byword for efficiency, and insists

---

[26] J. A. Cannon, *The Fox–North Coalition: Crisis of the Constitution, 1782–4* (Cambridge, 1969), 95, 144.

[27] *The Wooden World: An Anatomy of the Georgian Navy* (Annapolis, Md., 1986), 344–6.

[28] *An Eighteenth-century Secretary at War: The Papers of William, Viscount Barrington* (London, 1988), 18.

that financial and administrative success was built upon the political foundations laid by the Glorious Revolution.[29] Even the old electoral system, one of the best-known and least-admired aspects of Hanoverian government, has found its defenders of late, and Frank O'Gorman has argued, with a wealth of illustration, that its weaknesses and defects have been exaggerated and its merits overlooked.[30] One can hardly repeat too often that one can judge Hanoverian administration and politics only by comparison with rivals in its own period. In that comparison it comes out well. Autocracy, which had seemed so promising in the late seventeenth century, produced paralysis in France, excessive centralization in Prussia, and bizarre shifts of policy in Russia. Britain, by comparison, won its wars, established colonial supremacy, and laid the foundations of the first industrial breakthrough.

A very recent attempt to explain how an aristocratic regime came to preside over the commercial and industrial developments is by no means sentimental towards Hanoverian governments.[31] They were willing, it suggests, 'to deal viciously with the lower orders' and their predisposition to *laissez-faire* had less to do with principle than with the practical difficulties of enforcing policies. But it concludes that 'like the proverbial hedgehog of Aeschylus the Hanoverian governments knew some big things, namely that security, trade, Empire and military power really mattered'.

The question of the degree of exclusiveness in Hanoverian political life demands more detailed consideration, since it is complex and not uncontroversial. It is perhaps easier to deal with if broken down into different parts: the composition of the legislature and of the executive, the mechanics of representation, and the additional means whereby public opinion might be expressed.

The House of Lords, still in theory the senior house, represented hereditary landed wealth. The exceptions to this were few. Many of the sixteen Scottish representative peers were far from wealthy and had to be given a helping hand. The twenty-six bishops had little landed property

---

[29] *The Sinews of Power: War, Money and the English State*, 1688–1783 (London, 1989).

[30] 'The Unreformed Electorate of Hanoverian England: The Mid-eighteenth Century to the Reform Act of 1832', *Social History*, 11 (1986), 33–52. O'Gorman wrote that the purpose of his paper was 'to rescue the unreformed electorate from the Whig interpretation of English history'. The argument is followed up in his *Voters, Patrons and Parties*.

[31] P. K. O'Brien, *Power Without Profit: The State and the Economy, 1688–1815* (Inaugural lecture, University of London). A very valuable survey of recent writings on Britain's emergence as a great power is by H. M. Scott, 'The Second "Hundred Years War", 1689–1815', *Historical Journal*, 35/2 (1992), 443–69.

and those who sat for the poorer sees, such as Bristol, Bangor, or Oxford, had modest incomes. It was always necessary to have legal advice available in the Lords and newly ennobled lawyers were rarely men of broad acres. Lastly, there was always a small number of impoverished peers, particularly those whose estates had become alienated from the title. Members of the Commons promoted from time to time to strengthen the debating talent in the Lords were usually younger sons of the nobility, like Lord Hervey. Though many peers had financial, commercial, and industrial interests, these lobbies were not represented in the Lords as such. Until the expansion of the peerage at the end of the century, during Pitt's term of office, the Lords was a select body of fewer than two hundred members. Recruitment was slow and the newcomers were almost invariably from the same social class as the rest. Despite their loss of control of financial measures, the Lords retained considerable powers, though these were mainly held in reserve in the eighteenth century.

The House of Commons was throughout the period composed mainly of country gentlemen. This is not a particularly helpful description, since many people might aspire to that life-style, and the term covered very substantial differences in wealth and prestige. The only formal addition to membership during the century was the forty-five Scottish members added by the Act of Union. In different conditions one might have expected them to form an indigestible nationalist bloc, but they were easily incorporated and proved to be a factor making for stability, since they could normally be relied upon to support the government of the day.

The social composition of the House of Commons was not impervious to change, even if it was slow and undramatic. Three groups which appear to have increased their share of the legislature were sons of peers, merchants and industrialists, and professional men. Only one of these groups can be precisely identified. In the Tory-dominated houses at the end of Anne's reign, the sons of peers and Irish peers totalled 54 and 48, respectively.[32] By 1741 the number had risen to 100, by 1768 to 112, and by the end of the century it was up to 120. That group had more than doubled its share. The category of 'professional men' is less easy to establish, since it had no legal basis, but the evidence suggests that the aggregate of army and navy officers, together with lawyers, rose from about one-quarter of the House at the beginning of the eighteenth century to about one-third of the House by the beginning of the next.[33] The third category, that of merchants and industrialists, increased from about 7 per

[32] i.e. in the Parliaments elected 1710 and 1713. Cannon, *Aristocratic Century*, 112.
[33] O'Gorman, *Voters, Patrons and Parties*, 119–20.

cent in Anne's reign to about 15–20 per cent at the start of the nineteenth century.[34]

It follows that, if these prospering groups took an extra 30 per cent of the House, some group must have been doing badly.[35] The probability is that this was the lesser gentry. In the later seventeenth century, gentlemen of comparatively modest means had often come in for their neighbouring boroughs and had taken it in turns to represent the counties.[36] But the rising cost of electioneering meant that they were increasingly driven out by more affluent candidates. The counties fell to the greater gentry and the aristocracy, and the number of contests decreased markedly as the powerful interests made non-aggression pacts. The local boroughs were increasingly represented by strangers. At the beginning of Anne's reign, the choice of strangers was still sufficiently unusual to be remarked upon in the newsletters; fifty years later it was taken for granted. Indeed, when the young Lord Palmerston was returned for the borough of Newtown in the Isle of Wight in 1807, the patron insisted that he should never set foot in the place. Not surprisingly, Palmerston forgot for which constituency he had been first returned, and in his memoirs believed it to have been Newport, a bizarre mistake which misled a number of his biographers.

A loss of some 30 per cent meant a decrease of about 150 seats for the lesser gentry, which represented a considerable shift of power. But this may have helped the old electoral system to adapt to changing economic and social circumstances. Small closed boroughs gave opportunities for brewers, bankers, planters, merchants, nabobs, and industrialists to buy their way into the House.

The degree of flexibility which the anomalies of the system permitted was of some consequence. New men were not completely shut out from the citadel of power, nor, by and large, did they feel that Parliament was indifferent to their interests. The House did not divide up into disparate and hostile groupings, as had appeared possible during Anne's reign, and as was to occur briefly in the 1840s, when the dispute over the corn laws was widely interpreted as land versus trade.[37]

[34] O'Gorman, 120.

[35] It is unwise to try to be too precise. There is bound to be some overlap, since some army and navy officers were also Irish peers or sons of peers, and because the category of 'merchant' is a little vague.

[36] 'Most borough MPs lived nearby or in the same county'. B. D. Henning (ed.), *The House of Commons, 1660–1690* (London, 1983), i. 59.

[37] Prince Albert's memorandum of 25 Dec. 1845 quoted Peel's opinion that the dispute had got on to the dangerous ground of 'a war between the manufacturers, the hungry and the poor against the landed proprietors, the aristocracy, which can only end in the ruin of the latter'. A. C. Benson and Lord Esher (eds.), *Letters of Queen Victoria* (London, 1908), ii. 66.

A recent historian has referred to the Hanoverian bourgeoisie as increasingly 'dictatorial'.[38] It is not my impression that there was any sustained challenge to aristocratic domination during the eighteenth century. Many of the professional and business men were concerned mainly with their own careers or were content to play a part in the affairs of their own town. Others were dependent upon noble patronage and custom. Though intermarriage between the world of business and the aristocracy was not common, there was enough to blur some of the edges. The daughter of John Major, a Yorkshire iron-dealer, married the second duke of Chandos; Samuel Fludyer, a wealthy clothier, married a niece of the earl of Cardigan; three of the daughters of John Bristow, a Portuguese merchant, married into the nobility. As might have been predicted, bankers and their offspring did well. John Drummond married into the St Albans family in 1744; Robert Colebrooke's first wife was a daughter of Lord Harry Powlett. Thomas Coutts's matrimonial ventures were anything but social climbing: his first wife was a servant girl and his second an actress. But money smooths many difficulties: his three daughters married the earl of Guilford, the marquis of Bute, and Sir Francis Burdett, and his widow married the ninth duke of St Albans.

The Anglican landed interest kept a strong grip on what we would now call the executive part of government. There was little competition. Catholics were excluded from office. Though there were a number of dissenting members of Parliament, few of them were office-seekers. Merchants and bankers who entered the House did so more in pursuance of their professions, through contacts, than in search of parliamentary careers: they tended to enter Parliament later in life and few rose to high positions. Consequently, the theory that men of broad acres were the natural governors of the country seemed confirmed in practice. Only in the law, a profession of much drudgery, and in the navy, one of danger and hardship, were there many opportunities for boys of humble birth to rise to the top. The higher places in the civil service and the army were filled by patronage or purchase, and the reforms in the later nineteenth century to introduce competitive examinations and to abolish purchase were rightly seen as body-blows to aristocratic supremacy and were resisted with great tenacity.

[38] Langford, *Public Life and the Propertied Englishman*, 510: 'Generalizations about the aristocratic and elitist nature of Georgian society assume that the prominence of the nobility signifies its unchallengeable hegemony. A more subtle appreciation of its role suggests the extent to which it was made the tool of an increasingly dictatorial bourgeoisie.' With respect, the comment on generalizations is quite unsupported, and anything less subtle than the proffered alternative would be hard to imagine.

The cabinet itself was not merely a landed preserve, but an aristocratic one. In 1763 George Grenville had an inner cabinet of nine, in which he was the only commoner. But Grenville himself was not exactly badly connected, since his mother was a countess in her own right, his wife was the granddaughter of a duke, and his two brothers-in-law were earls.[39] There was little danger of the interests of the nobility being overlooked. Not until the second half of the nineteenth century did the peerage find itself in a minority in the cabinet.

All the great offices of state were firmly in the hands of the aristocracy. Of twenty-two First Lords of the Treasury in the eighteenth century, sixteen were peers and four more were sons of peers.[40] Seventy per cent of the Field Marshals were peers. Only two of the fourteen Lord Chancellors were not peers, and one of the two would have been had he lived a day longer.[41] The Lord-Lieutenants were responsible for the maintenance of law and order in their shires. Of more than two hundred Lord-Lieutenants in the English counties, only fourteen were not peers or peers' sons.[42] There was not much chance of subversives, malcontents, or dangerous radicals penetrating the higher reaches of the state.

The executive side of Hanoverian government may be described as tripartite. The nobility had preponderant strength in the great offices of state and commanded central power. In local government, however, which impinged more on ordinary subjects, there were hardly enough peers to play the most important roles, save as Lords-Lieutenant. Consequently, executive power in the shires was largely in the hands of the gentry. In London, the great ports, and trading towns, power was held by local oligarchies of merchants, shipowners, bankers, clothiers, coal-owners, and business and professional men. Though there were tensions between all three groups, their collaboration was sufficient to keep the system working.

Next we must ask to what extent opinion could express itself through the rusting mechanisms of the unreformed electoral system. Here again there

---

[39] Grenville's mother was Countess Temple; his wife was the daughter of Sir William Wyndham and the granddaughter of the sixth duke of Somerset; his wife's brother was the earl of Egremont; and his sister was married to the earl of Chatham.

[40] The remaining two were James Stanhope, grandson of a peer, and Walpole, created a peer.

[41] Charles Yorke died in 1770 while his patent as Lord Morden was in preparation; the odd man out was Sir Nathan Wright, who held the great seal between 1700 and 1706.

[42] Seven of them subsequently became peers; two more were bishops of Durham, acting in the Palatinate. For the others, see Cannon, *Aristocratic Century*, 121–2.

are formidable methodological and interpretative difficulties. The wide-spread evidence of bribery, treating, and intimidation, coupled with considerable evidence for a closing-up of boroughs and counties during the eighteenth century, suggests that there was little vitality left in the representative system and that it had become as much an obstacle to the expression of public opinion as a means to it. No fewer than seventy-five constituencies were contested only once or not at all during the seventy-six years between the beginning of the Seven Years War and the Reform Act of 1832—thirty-six of them were not contested at all.[43] There were boroughs like St Germans in Cornwall or Bere Alston in Devon which seem to have survived between the Glorious Revolution and the Reform Act, a period of nearly 150 years, without the rowdiness of a single contested election disturbing their streets. Only once did the market-place outside the Golden Fleece at Thirsk echo to the noise of rival candidates during all those years.[44] Many of the counties were just as quiet. Oxfordshire had a famous contest in 1754, when the Old Interest put up its last fight, but it was the only one between 1699 and 1826—generations of Oxfordshire electors lived and died without a chance of recording a vote. Dorset and Devon had only one contest each in a comparable period of more than one hundred years.[45]

A state of affairs which, to the modern mind, may seem a betrayal of the ideal of active citizenship was by no means unsatisfactory to many Hanoverians. Though Junius was considered by some to be very radical, his private advice to Wilkes in 1771 on the subject of reform of Parliament was moderate: 'I would not give representatives to those great trading towns, which have none at present . . . You will find the interruption of business in those towns, by the triennial riots and cabals of an election, too dear a price for the nugatory privilege of sending members to Parliament.'[46] Not until the nineteenth century did many of the middle class in large towns show much interest in obtaining representation, and the prospect of annual drunkenness and annual absenteeism was one reason why the proposal for annual elections, so dear to Granville Sharp and his friends, did not greatly appeal. To a number of electors, a vote at the

---

[43] The list is composed of 6 English counties, 45 English boroughs, 5 Welsh counties, 8 Welsh boroughs, and 11 Scottish counties. Because the Scottish burghs were arranged in groups of four or five, contests were much more common.

[44] There was a contest at the general election of 1695.

[45] Dorset had one contest between 1688 and 1806, in 1727; Devon had one contest between 1688 and 1812, in 1790.

[46] *Junius*, 411. For the changing attitude of middle-class employers, see J. A. Cannon (ed.), *The Whig Ascendancy* (London, 1981), 111–13.

hustings was no more than an embarrassment and a potential danger: Lord Egmont in a survey of Westminster in 1749 noted that the electorate included a number of tradesmen 'who out of policy will vote on no side to disoblige no party'.[47] In the counties, once the party zeal of Anne's reign had subsided, the disinclination to disturb the peace by unnecessary contests was even more marked. Many freeholders were anxious to avoid the bitterness of contested elections, to live on easy terms with their neighbours, and to shun the unpleasantness of taking sides and offending people. In many counties, a fierce contest every fifty years or so was enough to persuade the warring factions to get together.[48]

Even when there were contests it is unsafe to presume that the voters had much political choice. Namier was of the opinion that even in the counties, which were greatly admired for their purity of election and where the freeholders were by definition independent men, only one in twenty could freely exercise the vote. Though the arithmetic sounds a little pat and the suggestion has been criticized, social and economic pressures meant that for many voters the choice was probably between candidates of very similar views.[49]

If, however, we are trying to piece together the reality of Hanoverian political participation, it would be wrong to limit ourselves to the formal evidence of contests and voting. There was much activity, particularly canvassing, which did not, in the end, result in a contest. Many people living in towns which were not represented had votes in other towns, or in their neighbouring counties. Non-voters could take part in the excitement as messengers, clerks, canvassers, chairmen, bruisers, or merely as chorus. In towns with corporations, the elections of mayor and councillors were important and often highly controversial. In boroughs where the parliamentary representation seems unremarkable, local politics was frequently exciting.

The evidence for a marked decrease in the number of contests in mid-century has been known for some time and has not been challenged. Nevertheless, the interpretation needs care. A contest is not, in itself, a very precise guide to political activity. Candidates might carry out a very vigorous canvass, only to decline at the last minute; at the other extreme

[47] Quoted in *House of Commons, 1715–54*, i. 286.

[48] In Gloucestershire, for example, the Beaufort–Berkeley understanding was challenged at by-elections in 1776 and again in 1811. Otherwise, the county was uncontested between 1734 and 1832, save for a forlorn-hope candidate in 1784 who polled only twenty votes. Warwickshire was uncontested between 1695 and 1832, save for the general election of 1774.

[49] *Structure of Politics*, 2nd edn., 73. See comments by O'Gorman in *Voters, Patrons and Parties*, 3. It should be noted that Namier was specifically referring to county elections.

were candidates who insisted on going to the poll but retired after winning only a few votes. The bare record of a contest underestimates political activity in the first case, overestimates it in the second. Nor will the record of a contest tell us whether the persons casting their votes did so freely, deferentially, or under promise.

Yet the argument for mistrusting contests as evidence may be carried too far. There is little reason to believe that, taken in aggregate, they are not useful pointers to political excitement, the part of the iceberg that shows above the waves. There is, after all, a good deal of corroborative evidence. We find that contests were numerous during Anne's reign, when Whigs and Tories were engaged in a life-or-death struggle, only to falter in the period of the Pelhams, when the political waves were less steep. When we find that the borough of Thirsk, with its two members, was contested only once in 170 years, it does not seem perverse to conclude that the possession of the franchise did not mean much there, even if there is evidence of banners, bands, speeches, and jollity.

Recent commentators have warned against presuming that the decline in the number of contests meant a corresponding decrease in the number of votes cast, since the boroughs which were closed up were usually corporation or burgage boroughs, with small electorates in the first place. The boroughs with substantial electorates remained open and were contested.[50] This is certainly true. But the majority of voters were the freeholders in the counties.[51] There the decline in the number of contests was more dramatic and there is no doubt that there was a sharp decrease in the number of electors voting. The twenty contests in England and Wales in 1715 and the sixteen contests in 1734 gave opportunities to vote to well over 70,000 freeholders at each general election. By contrast, in 1747 only three counties went to a poll, producing fewer than 9,000 votes.[52]

The evidence from the boroughs is less decisive. Yet the number of contests in 1722 was certainly more than 113, while by 1761 it had fallen to 42. The corresponding total of votes cast fell from roughly 73,000 to

[50] J. A. Phillips, *Electoral Behaviour in Unreformed England* (Princeton, NJ, 1982), esp. ch. 2; H. T. Dickinson, 'Popular Politics in the Age of Walpole', in Black (ed.), *Britain in the Age of Walpole*, 48–51; O'Gorman, *Voters, Patrons and parties*, 106–11.

[51] *House of Commons, 1754–90*, i. 514–20, suggests some 177,000 freeholders in England and Wales in 1754 and 105,000 borough voters.

[52] The figures for Anne's reign would be even more significant, since the general election of 1705 produced 27 county contests and that of 1710 produced 26. The absence of a History of Parliament volume for Anne's reign makes it hard to assess the aggregate vote. If one presumes that most voters polled in 1705, the total may have exceeded 100,000. See W. A. Speck, *Tory and Whig: The Struggle in the Constituencies, 1701–1715* (London, 1970), app. E.

about 34,000.[53] There are then indications of a recovery in the 1760s as political excitement revived once more with the advent of Wilkes and America.

But the aggregate figures hide another point of substantial interest. Urban voting figures did not fall as dramatically as county figures partly because they were supported by some twenty or so boroughs which remained open, were contested frequently, and had large electorates.[54] At every general election, more than half the urban votes cast were in eight or nine of these boroughs.[55] Outside these turbulent areas, the political pulse beat sluggishly in mid-century.

This statistical evidence coincides with the impression one gains from newspapers that, at each general election, attention concentrated on one or two constituencies. In 1747 it was Staffordshire, and in 1754 the Oxfordshire election commanded attention. In 1768 the Middlesex election attracted much comment and in 1780 and 1784 it was the elections for Westminster. The spotlight turned on these constituencies may have helped to disguise how little was happening elsewhere and, to that extent, the system ran on vicarious excitement.

The existence of open voting meant that bribery was always a possibility, particularly in the small boroughs. It is doubtful whether the voters

---

[53] These figures are for England and Wales. It is scarcely worth making an analysis for Scotland, where the electorate after the Union was tiny. The History of Parliament computed the total electorate for the 33 Scottish counties in 1715 at about 1,300, comparable to that in Northumberland, one of the smallest English county electorates. The total for the groups of Scottish burghs was also about 1,300, about half the size of the electorate in Newcastle upon Tyne. The city of Bristol had nearly twice as many voters as the whole of Scotland.

'Roughly' is an important reservation. There are a number of contests for which the poll figures have not survived. Even when the figures are known, we cannot usually be certain of the total number of voters, except at by-elections, since at general elections most electors had two votes. No simple formula will allow one to compute exactly the total, which depends upon distribution, and particularly the number of plumpers. Speck, *Tory and Whig*, app. E, offers a useful and ingenious formula that works well in most cases. Occasionally the total number of voters is reported in the press, and sometimes non-voters are reported. Where poll books exist, there is no difficulty.

[54] In rough order of size of electorate, these were Westminster, London, Bristol, Norwich, Coventry, Worcester, York, Lancaster, Liverpool, Gloucester, Monmouth, Newcastle upon Tyne, Nottingham, Shrewsbury, Southwark, Colchester, Leicester, Carnarvon boroughs, Canterbury, Chester, Durham, Exeter, and Northampton.

[55] In fact, the trend towards narrowness shows up even in this analysis. The following list shows how many boroughs made up just over half the total vote at successive general elections: 1715: 11; 1722: 15; 1727: 14; 1734: 13; 1741: 7; 1747: 6; 1754: 6; 1761: 7; 1768: 8; 1774: 8; 1780: 6; 1784: 5. At the general election of 1784 the total urban vote was approximately 49,300. Westminster (11,000), London (5,100), Bristol (5,000), Norwich (2,500), and York (2,000) accounted for half that total.

in Wootton Bassett or Leominster spent much time on legal and moral issues. If the vote was essentially regarded as property, there was no reason why it should not be bought and sold. Irish borough-patrons were compensated for the loss of their electoral influence in 1801 and there were people who argued that English patrons should have been compensated in 1831.[56] Even today the word 'franchise' has an additional meaning as a right which may be sold off or bade for.

We have recently been warned not to exaggerate the extent of bribery by recycling picturesque examples.[57] It is a useful reminder. Bribery in the counties and the larger freeman boroughs was scarcely practicable, while in many of the corporation and burgage boroughs it was hardly necessary. It is also true that bribery continued well into the nineteenth century, and it is not daringly cynical to suggest that there is an element of mass bribery of the electorate today. Nevertheless, there are dozens of examples of direct bribery in Hanoverian England, to say nothing of heavy treating and payment over the odds for expenses. It was of consequence. Bribery worked against the development of a coherent public opinion. When John Wilkes went down to Cricklade in 1775 with his naïve friend Samuel Petrie, who was standing as a non-bribing candidate, it did not take him long to sum up the situation: 'Sam,' he is reported to have said, 'Wilkes and Liberty will not do here. I see it must be hard money.'[58] It meant the existence of groups of people determinedly opposed to reform: when Cobbett visited Honiton as a purity-of-election radical candidate, he was told that he ought to be ashamed of himself for taking bread out of the mouths of the poor.[59] Moreover, bribery helped to discredit the case for manhood suffrage by suggesting that the lower orders were hopelessly corrupt and incapable of independent and disinterested political conduct.

Nicholas Rogers, *Whigs and Cities: Popular Politics in the Age of Walpole and Pitt* (Oxford, 1989), rightly draws attention to the vitality of some of the large urban constituencies which defied control. This is of vast importance if we compare England, say, with Poland, where the towns were not even represented in the Sejm until the reform of 1791. It meant that the voice of trade, finance, and commerce was always heard. So much work has been done recently on boroughs like Norwich and Worcester that there is some danger of distorting the overall picture. If it is a valid criticism of Namier that he paid undue attention to the small boroughs, revisionism risks the opposite. One or two large boroughs are being hard pressed in the case for broader participation and perhaps are due for a rest.

[56] Pitt's third reform motion in 1785 had included the suggestion of compensation, and no less than £1,400,000 was set aside in 1801.
[57] O'Gorman, *Voters, Patrons and parties*, 158–64.
[58] *House of Commons, 1754–90*, i. 34.
[59] *Political Register* (7, 14, 28 June 1806), quoted in Cannon (ed.), *Whig Ascendancy*, 109.

It is natural enough for twentieth-century minds, when evaluating political participation, to think first of voting behaviour or of the formal membership of political parties. But, as we have seen, this is not necessarily appropriate for Hanoverian England. There were no mass parties. The great majority of men and all women did not have the vote. Those who did often had only occasional opportunities to make use of it. The limitations of a vote as a means of influencing policy were great. General elections came round only every six or seven years and might not be fought on public issues. The voter might be intimidated or bribed. He had little or no influence over the choice of candidate and little control once the candidate was elected. Voters did not make or unmake governments. Not until 1835 is there a clear example of a government losing a general election. The revulsion from the coalition in 1784 helped to swell Pitt's majority, but it did not create it. We must therefore consider what alternative means existed for expressing political opinions.

Of these, the most important was probably the right to submit petitions or addresses, either to Parliament or to the Crown.[60] The right of the subject to petition the monarch was specifically confirmed by clause five of the Bill of Rights in 1689. London had a traditional right to submit petitions to the monarch direct, which William Beckford, when Lord Mayor in 1770, used to embarrass George III on the Wilkes issue.[61]

Once oppositions began to realize the potential in coordinating petitions, governments were forced to mobilize counter-petitions, lest they appeared to be without support in the country. 'A general run of addresses just before the opening of Parliament', wrote Lord North to the king in September 1775, 'will be of great service.'[62]

Since there were no restrictions on the signing of petitions, they could reach much further into the general public than the electorate did.[63] In towns without any representation, or with a limited franchise, petitioning

[60] The convention was that petitions relating to legislation went to Parliament; those referring to executive action to the monarch. The device of offering freedoms of boroughs, used to good effect in 1757, was to avoid the accusation, which worried many Tories, that to demand Pitt's reinstatement trenched upon the royal prerogative.

[61] After delivering on 23 May a strongly-worded petition and receiving a curt answer, Beckford, against all precedent, made a reply, the substance of which was carved in gold on the statue erected in the Guildhall. Horne Tooke's later assertion that Beckford merely mumbled a retort, which Tooke worked up into a heroic speech, is disposed of in the article on Beckford in *DNB*.

[62] Fortescue, iii. 255.

[63] There was a law still on the statute book, 13 Car. II c. 5, limiting petitioning to county meetings or meetings of the Common Council of London, on the grounds that tumultuous petitioning had helped to bring about the civil wars, but it had fallen into abeyance.

was a valuable outlet for opinion. In 1775 important unrepresented towns, such as Birmingham, Manchester, Leeds, Wolverhampton, Wakefield, and Whitehaven, petitioned on the American issue.[64] In the spring of 1784, 209 persons at Penryn evaded the grip that the patron, Sir Francis Bassett, had upon the borough, and petitioned against the coalition, which he supported. Lord North, whose influence over the eighteen members of the corporation of Banbury was sufficient to secure for him twelve consecutive uncontested returns, was also obliged to explain away a hostile petition in 1784.[65] Petitions were, almost as a matter of course, derided by their opponents as unrepresentative, synthetic, and orchestrated, signed only by the factious and disreputable, and Johnson's account of the progress of a petition is one of his most famous and effective pieces of prose. But recent scholarship has demonstrated a good deal of political awareness and intellectual coherence amongst many of the petitioners in this period.[66]

The scale and size of petitioning increased greatly in the course of the eighteenth century, as oppositions began to master the techniques of coordinating a campaign. The Kentish petition at the beginning of the century, demanding war with France, produced a furious quarrel when the Tory majority in the House of Commons declared it 'scandalous, insolent and seditious' and clapped the persons presenting it into gaol.[67] During the Excise crisis of 1733 protest, for technical reasons, took the form of instructions to members rather than petitioning. The total number of instructions came to fifty-four, with towns like Bideford, Newbury, Towcester, and Whitehaven, which had no direct representation, making use of their county members. It has rightly been described as among 'the most massive demonstrations of extra-parliamentary opinion in the entire century'.[68] The agitation against the Jewish Naturalization Act of 1753 also produced great excitement, but the more modest number of twelve petitions.[69]

The beginning of George III's reign saw petitioning come into its own as a political weapon, and the later years of Johnson's life witnessed four

[64] *CJ*, xxxv. 77–8, 80–2, 89, 90, 124, 139.

[65] For Penryn, see *House of Commons, 1754–90*, i. 237; for Banbury, see *Parl. Hist.* xxiv. 683.

[66] Esp. Phillips, *Electoral Behaviour*, 28–35; Bradley, *Religion, Revolution and English Radicalism*, 326–8. They correlated petitioners with their voting pattern as given in poll books.   [67] *CJ*, xiii. 518.

[68] P. Langford, *The Excise Crisis* (Oxford, 1975), 47 and app. A. *Gentleman's Magazine* (1733) printed the St Albans instructions in full and referred to many of the others.

[69] T. W. Perry, *Public Opinion, Propaganda and Politics in Eighteenth-century England* (Cambridge, Mass., 1962), 111.

major petitioning campaigns, each one of which involved as many signatories as there were voters in a general election. Sir Francis Dashwood's tax upon cider in 1763 brought twenty-four petitions of protest, but they were almost all from the South and West, and the subject was a limited one.[70] But the election of John Wilkes and his subsequent expulsion led the Society of the Supporters of the Bill of Rights and their temporary Rockingham allies to organize a major campaign for the meeting of Parliament in January 1770. Eighteen counties and twelve boroughs sent in petitions demanding redress and the dissolution of Parliament. The petition from Yorkshire claimed ten thousand signatures and opposition insisted that, in all, 60,000 persons had signed.[71] Nor can it be presumed that they were without effect, since the first minister, the duke of Grafton, already smarting under attack from Junius, tendered his resignation in the course of the month.

The deterioration of relations with America in 1774–5 and its effect upon trade produced another campaign: in the spring of 1775, 11 counties and 47 boroughs sent in petitions, not all of them hostile to North's government; the total involvement has been estimated at some 60,000.[72] Next came the campaign started by Wyvill in Yorkshire in 1779 for economical reform: 29 English and Welsh counties were joined in the spring of 1780 by 12 boroughs; Rockingham's own estimate of 60,000 petitioners does not seem unreasonable.[73] The campaign burgeoned into a movement for reform of Parliament and Pitt's motion for an inquiry into the state of the representation in 1783 was supported by 12 counties and 23 boroughs—a respectable enough demonstration, though Thomas Powys, in the debate on Pitt's motion, was able to make great play with the fact that the large unrepresented towns had not been heard from.[74] Of considerable significance for the long-term prospects for reform was the fact that the inhabitants of eleven boroughs protested against the narrowness of their parliamentary franchise, an issue which Wyvill had not intended to raise: Bury St Edmunds complained that the franchise was exercised by thirty-seven people in a town of 6,000 persons, while

---

[70] From six counties and seventeen towns, Leominster petitioning twice.

[71] I. R. Christie, *Wilkes, Wyvill and Reform* (London, 1962), 39; G. Rudé, *Wilkes and Liberty*, chs. 7, 8, and app. VII.

[72] Bradley, *Religion, Revolution and English Radicalism*, 319. Bradley calculated the spring campaign at about 44,000 but added in the autumn campaign.

[73] Christie, *Wilkes, Wyvill and Reform*, 97. Dunning's rather exuberant estimate in the debate on his famous motion was that 100,000 persons had petitioned. *Parl. Hist.* xxi. 345.

[74] *Parl. Hist.* xxiii. 826–75; *CJ*, xxxix. 41–406; J. A. Cannon, *Parliamentary Reform, 1640–1832* (Cambridge, 1972), 88–90.

Portsmouth pointed out that fewer than one hundred had the vote in a town of 20,000, and begged for the restoration of the franchise to the inhabitants at large, as it had been before 1695.[75]

The most numerous, and possibly the most decisive, petitioning campaign came in the spring of 1784, when Pitt's fledgeling ministry was locked in mortal combat with the coalition majority in the House of Commons. The number of petitions submitted, most of them supporting Pitt, exceeded two hundred. Though it is not possible to ascertain the exact number of signatories, it was certainly well over the 60,000 claimed for previous campaigns. Petitions from more than 8,000 people came from Fox's own constituency of Westminster, and from 5,000 in Bristol, being strictly comparable with the turn-out in those boroughs at a contested election. Some 64,000 people voted in England and Wales at the subsequent general election and no more than 40,000 had voted at the general election of 1761.[76]

The weapon that had been so useful to Pitt was soon turned against him. His own motion for a reform of Parliament in 1785 was very poorly supported by petitions,[77] while his financial and economic policy ran into a massive fusillade. No fewer than 80,000 people petitioned from Lancashire against his tax on cotton, and won concessions, while Manchester alone claimed 55,000 signatures for a petition against his Irish commercial propositions, which he was forced to withdraw.[78]

It is clear that, by the end of Johnson's lifetime, petitioning had become a major means of expressing opinion. Campaigns on this scale represented a massive and novel organizational effort, and we see Wyvill and his Associators learning from the Supporters of the Bill of Rights, and passing on their own experience to nineteenth-century radicals like Cartwright, Burdett, and Hunt. We must, however, exercise caution in estimating size and effect. There was bound to be some truth in the objection by counter-petitioners that the campaigns were orchestrated rather than spontaneous. It was often difficult to whip up public interest, as the Rockinghams discovered in 1769 and Pitt and Wyvill in 1783 and 1785.[79] There was usually enough reduplication to give some impression of a stage army on

---

[75] The remaining nine boroughs were Great Yarmouth, Tiverton, Poole, Lyme Regis, Launceston, Lymington, Winchester, Hastings, and Scarborough. *CJ.* xxxix. 231, 363.

[76] Cannon, *Fox–North Coalition*, 185–90. *London Gazette* (1784) gave the numbers for 119 petitions—i.e. just over half. These came to 59,828. Many of the remaining petitions claimed considerable support, and the grand total can scarcely have been less than 70,000.

[77] Only two counties and ten boroughs sent in petitions. The issue had gone off the boil.

[78] The Lancashire petition is referred to in *Parl. Hist.* xxv. 362. Sixty petitions came in against the Irish propositions.

[79] Cannon, *Parliamentary Reform*, 63, 87–8.

the move. When Yorkshire, one of the Rockingham's strongholds, could be induced to take part, its vast numbers lent respectability to any campaign, as it did in 1769 with 11,000 petitioners and in 1780 with 8,000. In the towns, campaigners leaned heavily on the numbers which London, Westminster, Bristol, and Norwich could provide, with provincial towns like Nottingham, Newcastle, York, Gloucester, and Canterbury in support. Since these were also the boroughs which were most frequently contested at elections, there was considerable overlap. Nevertheless, the inclusion in petitioning campaigns of some unrepresented towns and the signatures in some places of persons who were not electors, added an extra dimension.[80]

In the political armoury, petitioning had its limitations, being a sapping weapon rather than one capable of direct assault. There was no method of forcing either the king or Parliament to give way and organizers found it hard to persuade their troops to charge and charge again. To have much effect, petitioners had to work closely with sympathizers in Parliament itself. The main effect of petitions was to weaken the enemy's resolve and shake his nerve. Bute was upset by the cider petitions but he was not, in any case, the most resolute of politicians; the king and Lord North spent much time in 1770 deciding how to deal with the Wilkite petitions; and there is some evidence that the campaign of 1784 dampened the spirits of the coalitionists. More immediate success was rare, save perhaps in economic matters. Even in the early nineteenth century when, once more, the size and number of petitions had greatly increased, successes were infrequent. In 1817 Cochrane is said to have waded among petitions for reform, but his cause did not prosper;[81] nor did the two million signatures for the Charter in 1848 carry it to victory.[82] By that time petitioning had begun to lose its effect. The vast campaigns on the Catholic issue and on the reform question drove home to members of Parliament what a monster had been released. Despite the bitter conflict between them, Whigs and Tories closed ranks in the face of ordeal by petition. The Whig government of Lord Grey took steps to curtail time spent on hearing petitions and their Tory opponents did not object.[83]

[80] Some organizers restricted signatures to freeholders and voters, in order to ensure respectability, while others allowed all inhabitants, including women, to sign.

[81] Cochrane's campaign is discussed in Cannon, *Parliamentary Reform*, 176–7; Cannon (ed.), *Whig Ascendancy*, 109–10. By 1830, petitions from single towns had more signatories than whole eighteenth century campaigns: an anti-Catholic petition from Kent in 1829 was said to have been signed by 81,000 persons.

[82] O'Connor claimed well over 5 million signatures for the petition, but the committee reported no more than 1,975,000, of which many were reduplications or facetious frauds.

[83] P. Fraser, 'Public Petitioning and Parliament before 1832', *History*, 46 (Oct. 1961), 195–211.

A famous campaign in which public opinion played an important part was that waged in support of William Pitt at the start of the Seven Years War. Pitt's patriot opposition during the 1730s and his insulting references to Hanover made him *persona non grata* with George II for many years. In 1746, after the collapse of the ill-advised Bath–Granville attempt, the Pelhams were able to force the king to appoint Pitt to junior office, though he was denied further promotion. But time of war often placed constitutional monarchs in an awkward position and the disastrous start of the Seven Years War played into Pitt's hands, shattering the Newcastle administration. Pitt's electoral base was of no significance at all. But he had considerable popularity in the country and, particularly, in the city of London, a remarkable domination of the House of Commons, and extraordinary self-confidence. Beckford, his wealthy ally in London, sponsored his cause in the *Monitor*, a newspaper started in 1755, and it was pushed in a number of influential pamphlets. Though the Pitt–Devonshire ministry was short-lived, Pitt returned in July 1757 to form the war-winning coalition with Newcastle.

At face value, it was a remarkable triumph for public opinion. Johnson declared that Pitt had been a minister given to the king by the nation, and the king himself is said to have told Pitt that he had taught him to look elsewhere than the House of Commons for the sense of the people.[84] Pitt's followers made the most of the 'rain of gold boxes' which he received when he left office in the spring of 1757. It seemed to be a singular example of how to mobilize public opinion and storm the closet.

But the truth is, as usual, more complex. Pitt's trump-card was not public opinion but his mastery of the Commons, which made it hard to find men to stand against him. It has been shown that the rain of gold boxes was far from spontaneous and was sedulously exaggerated in Pitt's newspapers. 'Every city is striving', wrote the *Monitor*, 'who shall first imitate the gratitude of London, with their freedom presented to the firm patriots.'[85] The reality was less ecstatic: a total of twelve boroughs, most of them places like Bath, Salisbury, and Chester, where Pitt had loyal supporters.[86] Above all, Pitt himself was forced to compromise, first by working with Newcastle, then by 'doing the King's German

---

[84] *Life*, ii. 195–6; Walpole, *Memoirs of George II*, ii. 223.

[85] Quoted in M. Peters, *Pitt and Popularity: The Patriot Minister and London Opinion during the Seven Years War* (Oxford, 1980), 76.

[86] The list given by Horace Walpole, *Memoirs of George II*, ii. 251, is very accurate. See P. Langford, 'William Pitt and Public Opinion, 1757', *English Historical Review*, 88 (1973), 54–80.

business'.[87] Within months he had abandoned the patriot distaste for continental connections, became a great advocate of the Prussian alliance, and boasted that he had conquered Canada on the banks of the Elbe.

Though public opinion could help him into office, it could do little to control him once there. Pitt's volte-face, growing disenchantment even with a victorious war, and indignation at his retirement honours in 1761 eroded his popularity quickly. But the example of the adroit use of the press was not wasted upon his erstwhile follower John Wilkes. Wilkes had none of Pitt's oratorical or debating talents, but when the exigencies of his demanding way of life necessitated raising a dust or dying in a gaol, he turned to popular journalism and set up as Patriot in the *North Briton*.[88] The odd alliance between Pitt and Wilkes succeeded in 1769 in launching the first campaign for reform of Parliament.

In assessing popular participation, it would be a mistake to concentrate too exclusively on high politics. In most societies there are many people who have no great desire or expectation of serving in Parliament, but who get satisfaction by contributing at other levels, as councillors, secretaries or treasurers of clubs, school governors, churchwardens and members of congregations, trustees of charities, organizers of pressure groups, and so on. In terms of real commitment, these activities often count for more than the transitory satisfaction of casting a vote. The point also applies to Hanoverian England, where the people whom historians describe, slightly condescendingly, as the excluded do not always seem conscious of or concerned by their exclusion. Johnson was, after all, in one sense 'excluded'. There is no evidence that he ever cast a vote. He does not appear to have resented it, remained a warm supporter of the constitution, and can hardly be described as a man devoid of political influence.

In addition to the national and parliamentary scene, there was a vast range of municipal organizations, very varied in structure and composition. To inward-looking communities, the politics of their shire, borough, riding, parish, or vestry might well be as absorbing as the Westminster scene. The elections for mayor and corporation usually took place in the autumn and could be hotly contested. Rival mayors and rival corporations were by no means unknown. It has been demonstrated that the turn-out in municipal elections could be very high, at times reaching

---

[87] P. C. Yorke, *The Life and Correspondence of Philip Yorke, Earl of Hardwicke* (Cambridge, 1913), ii. 221.
[88] Wilkes started his journalistic career on the *Monitor*.

90 per cent of the electorate.[89] The evidence of practical democracy is not always in favour of the twentieth century.

More people voted in 1781 at Norwich for the contest for aldermen than at the previous general election.[90] At Exeter, the contests for the mayoralty in 1735, 1736, 1738, and 1740 provoked so much interest that printed poll books were produced.[91] The struggle between the Lytteltons and Winningtons for control of the corporations of Bewdley provided generations of inhabitants with picturesque incident. In 1755 the Lytteltons seized control when a key voter, captured by the French but released on parole, arrived in time to turn the scales. Two years later they lost control again, regained it in 1767 with the creation of ten honorary freemen, lost it on the decision of the House of Commons, and recaptured it once more the following year. Of the 1768 parliamentary election in the borough Lyttelton wrote that 'our adversaries brought a madman to vote for Sir Edward, but he gave his vote for my son'.[92] The fact that all this was played out in public gave a dramatic quality sorely missing from modern municipal elections.

Since administration had not yet become professionalized, there were many offices to which ordinary men might aspire. By the later eighteenth century, there were some 25,000 land tax commissioners, who exercised considerable influence.[93] Much local work was done by improvement commissioners, acting under statute. An Act of 1769 to improve the paving and lighting in Gainsborough named as trustees fourteen individuals and all resident inhabitants rated to the Land Tax at £20 p.a.[94] A similar Act for Southwark named well over one hundred commissioners, including Henry Thrale as the member for the borough.[95] Even in those posts filled directly by patronage, a degree of popular participation could creep in, and Henry Fownes Luttrell, member and patron for the borough of Minehead, had to deal carefully with a petition in 1770 from forty-two voters to use his influence in the appointment of a tide-waiter.[96]

In addition, there were many posts filled by election, including coroners, masters of Houses of Correction, churchwardens and sextons, sheriffs, headmasters, lecturers, clerks and surveyors of turnpike trusts,

[89] Phillips, *Electoral Behaviour in Unreformed England*, 101–11.

[90] Ibid. 108. The total seems to have been 2,748. At the general election of 1780, 2,367 had voted. Phillips is, I think, mistaken in suggesting that the aldermanic total was greater than at any parliamentary election previous to 1802, since 3,306 voted at a by-election in 1735. He also seems to have transposed the aldermanic and shrieval votes (ibid. 109 n. 34).

[91] Colley, *In Defiance of Oligarchy*, 134.   [92] *House of Commons, 1754–90*, i. 423.

[93] Langford, *Public Life and the Propertied Englishman*, 423.

[94] 9 George III c. 21.   [95] 6 George III c. 24.

[96] O'Gorman, *Voters, Patrons and Parties*, 251.

Verderers of the Forest of Dean, and Registers for land transactions in the North Riding of Yorkshire.[97] In a contest for churchwarden at Newark in 1751, the vicar was said to have hired a band of French-horn players to drown out his opponents.[98] The results of these contests were frequently reported in local newspapers, helping to eke out thin parliamentary representation and perhaps to disguise it.

Lastly, we should remember the extent to which the Hanoverian period was a great age of clubs and societies. There were many reasons for this: the increasing size of towns; the improvement in living standards, which allowed a little more leisure and wealth; the emergence of recognized professions; the fact that knowledge had not yet fragmented and men of different professions could, with profit, exchange ideas.[99] The clubs were evidence of a more sophisticated and stable society. As early as 1739 one writer commented that, although many of the societies were composed of 'the meanest and rudest of citizens', yet they were kept in 'the best order and decorum' by rules and conventions.[100] Of course, some of the clubs were by no means cerebral in character. But, at the very least, they performed a socializing function and provided an experience of self-government. Johnson's own club was primarily for dining and good conversation, yet the conversation often explored moral, educational, legal, and constitutional questions, even if direct political argument seems to have been discouraged.

There was a considerable number of debating or self-improvement clubs. Others were founded for specifically political purposes or found it easy to adapt themselves for politics. Sir William Jones, in 1783, elevated clubbability into a high virtue and related it to political advance: 'A free state is only a more numerous and more powerful club, and that he only is a free man, who is a member of such a state.'[101]

---

[97] *Newcastle Courant* (20 Aug. 1774) reported the election of George Crowle as Register. This was a post established by 8 George II c. 6, which laid down the arrangements for voting and appointed all freeholders of £100 p.a. value as electors. There were similar Acts for Middlesex and for the other two ridings in Yorkshire (7 Anne c. 20, 2 Anne c. 4, and 6 Anne c. 35).

[98] 'An Impartial Relation of Some Late Parish Transactions at Newark' (Bodleian Library, Gough Coll. Notts. (II), 3), quoted in J. D. Chambers, *Nottinghamshire in the Eighteenth Century* (London, 1932), 61 n. 3.

[99] See esp. John Brewer, 'Commercialisation and politics', in McKehdrick *et al.* (eds.), *The Birth of a Consumer Society*.

[100] W. Maitland, *The History and Survey of London from its Foundation . . . to the Present Time* (London, 1739).

[101] *The Principles of Government: In a Dialogue between a Scholar and a Peasant*, subsequently reissued as *Dialogue between a Gentleman and a Farmer* (London, 1782). The dissemination of this tract by Jones's brother-in-law, the dean of St Asaph's, led to an important libel action.

Further evidence which tends to modify the exclusive character of the Hanoverian political system is the vast increase in newspapers throughout the period.[102] Foreign visitors often remarked on the number of quite humble men who frequented coffee-houses in London or the larger provincial towns in order to read the newspapers provided. One historian of the press has warned against presuming that such a development necessarily had radical implications.[103] It is true that the early newspapers carried little real news, filled their columns with items copied from their competitors, and offered few comments on events. But they soon began to change in character and composition. The *Craftsman* and *Mist's Weekly* were avowedly political papers, specializing in attacks upon Sir Robert Walpole, and they were followed by the *North Briton*, the *Middlesex Journal*, and later the *Political Register*, which were highly critical of government. Henry Sampson Woodfall, the enterprising printer of the *Public Advertiser*, realized early on the appeal of readers' letters and scored a great commercial success with his mysterious correspondent Junius. Above all, the printers waged a long and ultimately successful campaign for the right to print parliamentary debates, a strange misunderstanding of their own interests if few of their readers wished to have them. In that campaign Johnson had played a significant part.

The question of the reporting of parliamentary debates illustrates both the élitist character of early Hanoverian political life and the extent to which it became more liberal during Johnson's lifetime. In the seventeenth century, the secrecy of parliamentary proceedings afforded members some protection against the Crown. After 1688, that was of diminished importance, yet the growth of the newspaper press meant that there was danger on the other flank. News-letters and news-sheets soon came into collision with the House of Commons. As early as 1694 John Dyer was reprimanded for his 'great presumption' in referring to debates and a resolution carried warning news-letters not to intermeddle.[104] The message was repeated after the Hanoverian succession. In 1718 the printers of the *Exeter Mercury* and the *Exeter Post Boy* were taken to task for breach of privilege; another resolution was passed in 1723; and Robert Raikes, printer of the *Gloucester Journal*, established in 1722, was in trouble by 1728 and 1729.[105]

---

[102] See Ch. 6, 'Johnson and Enlightenment'.
[103] Black, *English Press in the Eighteenth Century*, esp. ch. 5.   [104] *CJ*, xi. 192, 193.
[105] Ibid. xix. 30, 42, 43, 44; xx. 99; xxi. 85, 104, 108, 119, 127, 238. Raikes explained that he received his news-letters through Edward Cave, then a clerk in the Post Office.

The two great pioneers of parliamentary reporting were Abel Boyer, a Huguenot refugee, and Edward Cave. In 1711 Boyer began the production of a monthly periodical, the *Political State of Great Britain*, which included regular reports of debates. When Boyer was threatened with prosecution in 1729 and died soon afterwards, Cave took the opportunity to launch his *Gentleman's Magazine*. The multiplication of newspapers during the previous decades, Cave explained, made it impossible to read them all, 'unless a man makes it a business'. In 1732 Cave began to include summaries of debates, telling his readers: 'we don't pretend to give the very words of every speech, but hope we have done justice to the arguments on each side.' The *Gentleman's Magazine* was an enormous success and was followed in April 1732 by the *London Magazine*, with an almost identical format. By the early 1730s, therefore, there were three journals printing reports of parliamentary speeches with some regularity.[106]

The competition between these journals was fierce, with the *Gentleman's Magazine* forging steadily ahead. In January 1738 Cave broke into verse to celebrate his success:

> Happy is this, that while his rivals fall,
> Ten thousand monthly for his labours call.

Two years later, he told his readers gleefully that there were 'seventy thousand *London Magazines* mouldering in their warehouses, returned from all parts of the kingdom, unsold, unread, and disregarded'.

Not least of the attractions of the new journal was its parliamentary reporting, which was expanded rapidly. Though one must take with a pinch of salt Cave's claim that his readers clamoured for more, he had clearly struck a rich vein. In the supplement for 1737, he reported that readers wanted to have the debates 'entire, with the names of the speakers', and pointed out that this would fill the whole magazine.[107] Starting with 33 pages in 1732, Cave increased it to 134 the following year, 190 by 1734, 156 in 1735 (a year beset by publication difficulties),[108] and 232 by the year 1737.

Members of Parliament were suspicious of this new development. A few were only too willing to see their names in print and sent copies of

---

[106] The *Political State* limped on after Boyer's death until 1740.

[107] Some confirmation of the interest comes from the Newcastle University library copy of the magazine for 1735, the owner of which added comments at the side, and painstakingly filled in the blanks in the speakers' names.

[108] Cave took his reports from the *Political State*, which unexpectedly postponed its summary for June 1735, leaving Cave to make an awkward apology and produce a *Gentleman's Magazine Extraordinary* for August.

their speeches to the papers. Others complained of misrepresentation or were alarmed that systematic reporting would destroy freedom of debate. On 13 April 1738, at the request of the Speaker, the House of Commons discussed the whole matter. The most remarkable feature was the near unanimity among members in deploring any reporting at all. Pulteney and Wyndham, from the opposition benches, joined with Walpole and Winnington from the Treasury bench in denouncing it. If the House did not take action, Sir William Yonge warned, 'you may soon expect to see your votes, your proceedings and your speeches printed and hawked about the streets'. The only point of disagreement was whether the prohibition should apply to the parliamentary recess as well as the session. Winnington called reporting 'a scandalous practice', insisting that 'you will have every word spoken here by gentlemen misrepresented by fellows who thrust themselves into our gallery'. Pulteney who, as leader of a formed opposition, might have been expected not to shun publicity, was as determined as the others to stamp out the practice: 'no appeals should be made to the public with regard to what is said in this assembly . . . It looks very like making them accountable without doors for what they say within.' Walpole did not think it worthwhile to argue a point 'wherein we are all agreed'. The stronger line, banning reports at all times, was adopted unanimously, and printers were warned that the House would proceed against them 'with the utmost severity'.[109]

It says much for the degree of public interest and the commercial potential that Cave and his competitors were not cowed by this stern resolution. Instead, they hit upon the idea of giving their reports some flimsy disguise by printing them as 'debates of the political club' or as 'proceedings in the Senate of Lilliput'. Speakers were given either a Roman *nom de plume* or transmogrified by anagrams.

This was the situation in 1738 when Cave hired Samuel Johnson as his parliamentary reporter. For five years Johnson's duty was to work up the speeches from lists and notes passed on to him.[110] Since this period saw the outbreak of war with Spain, the assault upon Maria Theresa's province of Silesia, and the protracted fall of Sir Robert Walpole, interest among the public ran high and continued publication was worth the risk. Accounts of the debates were printed at the beginning of each month's magazine, and after twelve of them in 1741, Cave added a further sup-

[109] *Parl. Hist.* x. 800–12.

[110] The specialist study is B. B. Hoover, *Samuel Johnson's Parliamentary Reporting* (Berkeley, Calif., 1953). See also C. L. Carlson, *The First Magazine: A History of the Gentleman's Magazine* (Providence, 1938).

plement. No less than 39 per cent of the *Gentleman's Magazine* for 1741 was given over to debates and parliamentary protests, and though it dropped in 1742 to 33 per cent, the following year it was back to 39 per cent once more.

For some years, Parliament seemed disinclined to take up the challenge to its position and authority, and no attempt was made to enforce the resolution of April 1738. The newspapers did not attempt to report debates in any systematic way, though in 1745 the printer of the *York Courant* was formally reprimanded for breach of privilege. But in 1747 the House of Lords reprimanded Cave and the printer of the *London Magazine* for including accounts of the trial of Lord Lovat. Cave abandoned his reporting, while the *London Magazine* made do with summaries until 1757, when it dropped them altogether. When certain papers printed odd reports in 1760 and 1762 they were stopped at once.[111]

After the excitement of the Middlesex election in March 1768, the situation changed rapidly. Wilkes's ally John Almon began printing reports in his *London Evening Post* and then set up the *London Museum* as a monthly with the avowed intention of carrying reports. Other papers followed suit at once and a bitter legal battle broke out between the government and the printers. By 1771 the administration was embroiled with no fewer than twelve London newspapers and their proprietors.[112] In February and March 1771 George Onslow, the member for Guildford, complained that eight London papers were in breach of privilege for publishing debates. Wilkes sprang a carefully prepared trap, engineering a theatrical confrontation between the House of Commons and the city of London. The Commons had the temporary satisfaction of sending the Lord Mayor, Brass Crosby, to the Tower of London for six weeks, but, although the many resolutions against reporting debates remained unrescinded, no further effort was made to enforce them.[113] Since, in the

---

[111] *CJ*, xxviii. 741; xxix. 109, 129, 206. In 1760 the printers of the *Public Advertiser*, *London Chronicle*, *Daily Advertiser*, and *The Gazetteer* were reprimanded; J. Wilkie of the *London Chronicle* was taken into custody again in 1762. *Gentleman's Magazine* resumed cautiously in 1752.

[112] *The Gazetteer*, *General Evening Post*, *Independent Chronicle*, *London Evening Post*, *London Packet*, *London Museum*, *Morning Chronicle*, *North Briton*, *Middlesex Journal*, *Public Advertiser*, *St James' Chronicle*, and *Whitehall Evening Post*.

[113] P. D. G. Thomas, 'The Beginings of Parliamentary Reporting in Newspapers, 1768–1774', *English Historical Review*, 74 (1959); 'John Wilkes and the Freedom of the Press, 1771', *Bulletin of the Institute of Historical Research*, 33 (1960). For the situation after 1771, when the restrictions on reporting were practical rather than legal, see A. Aspinall, 'The Reporting and Publishing of the House of Commons Debates, 1771–1834', in R. Pares and A. J. P. Taylor (eds.), *Essays Presented to Sir Lewis Namier* (London, 1956).

action against Henry Sampson Woodfall for publishing Junius's letter to the king, the jury brought in a verdict of 'guilty of printing and publishing only', which led to an important change in the law of libel, the printers had won two substantial victories for freedom of expression as a result of Wilkes's activities.[114]

It is hard to think of a more important step on the path towards liberalism and democracy than the right of ordinary subjects to know what is said in Parliament, and in this respect Johnson was on the side of liberty. Regular and systematic reporting of debates helped to shift the balance between public opinion and the legislature. In 1817, in the midst of the difficult post-war period, when Cartwright and Cochrane's campaign for reform of Parliament was at its height, Southey looked back to Dunning's motion of 1780:

At present it is the influence of the democracy which has increased, is increasing, and ought to be diminished. Whatever additional influence the Crown has obtained by increased establishments . . . is but a feather in the scale, compared to the weight which the popular branch of the constitution has acquired by the publication of the parliamentary debates.[115]

A further development which helped opinion to circumvent the limitations of the representative system was the spread of pressure groups, lobbies, and associations. It has been suggested that the potential for peaceful evolution depended upon the extent to which these groups could succeed in persuading Parliament to introduce changes.[116] It is certainly true that lobbies like the Catholic Association, the Political Unions, the Anti-Corn Law League, and the suffragettes played a crucial role in nineteenth- and early-twentieth-century political development, and in the later twentieth century citizens are as likely to belong to pressure groups as to be formal members of political parties. It was in the Hanoverian period that these organizations began to develop, even if they came of age later.

---

[114] Mansfield had directed that the function of the jury was merely to establish the fact of publication (which was rarely in dispute), leaving the judge to decide whether the words printed were libellous. Woodfall's jury, in effect, claimed the right to decide what was libellous. Their claim was eventually confirmed by Fox's Libel Act of 1792. Junius followed the proceedings with keen interest and commented on them at some length (*Junius*, 9–10, 14–20, 209–14, 476–8). See also T. B. Howell (ed.), *State Trials* (London, 1809), xx, and *Parl. Hist.* xvi. 1211–301. Lord Camden, who had obtained an acquittal in 1752 by arguing the more liberal line, was in the Lords in 1792 to support the Act which confirmed the matter.

[115] *Quarterly Review*, 16 (1816–17), 252.

[116] Hunt, *Two Early Political Associations*, pp. xiii–xvi.

Before 1688 there were few opportunities for such groups to influence Parliament. It was easier to lobby ministers or the court directly. Parliament was in existence for such short periods that the timing of campaigns was extremely difficult: between the dismissal of the Oxford Parliament in 1681 and the calling of the Convention in 1689, the Commons were sitting for only eight weeks in a period of nine years.[117] There were other practical and theoretical difficulties. Internal communications were very slow and Westminster and its concerns distant. Parliament itself had to be handled with great care. Governments were often reluctant to stir up a hornet's nest while the support of oppositions was usually a good way of losing. Members of all parties were on their guard against groups who might intimidate or challenge Parliament and the experience of the 1640s had shown how easily supporters might become masters.

First in the field were the religious groups, particularly the Protestant dissenters. The 1688 settlement was of Church as well as State, and the religious arrangements were a good deal less acceptable than the constitutional ones to the supporters of the new regime. The ecclesiastical organization of the sects gave them a framework which could easily be adapted for political purposes. While the Church of England had direct representation in Parliament through the bench of bishops, the dissenters had only individual members, and very few in the upper house.

The Quakers, whose organization and methods became a model for other pressure groups, began lobbying before the Glorious Revolution, though their efforts were not very successful. After the Revolution, though afforded a large measure of freedom of worship, they were left with two substantial grievances: their refusal to take oaths subjected them to severe legal disabilities, and they were obliged to pay tithes towards the upkeep of a Church from which they dissented. The national organization which developed was based upon their local meetings and rapidly acquired many of the attributes of a pressure group, systematically monitoring parliamentary activity, collecting funds, distributing pamphlets, lobbying members of Parliament, and even attempting to influence the election of friendly members. Their first major campaign, to persuade Parliament that they should be permitted to make a solemn affirmation instead of an oath, succeeded in 1696 with the support of William III;[118] their second, for an alteration in the method of collecting tithes, failed in 1736 when the House of Lords rejected their bill.

[117] The only Parliament of James II sat in the summer of 1685 for six weeks and for a further two weeks in November.
[118] 7 and 8 William III c. 34.

The example set by the Quakers was copied by others. In 1702 the Sephardic Jewish congregation at Bevis Marks established a committee to 'attend to the business of the nation which is before Parliament'.[119] Three Protestant dissenting groups—the Baptists, Presbyterians, and Independents—resolved in 1732 to join forces to seek the repeal of the Test and Corporation Acts.[120] After the Hanoverian succession, the Occasional Conformity Act and the Schism Act had been repealed, the first Indemnity Act passed, and the *regium donum* restored.[121] But N. C. Hunt pointed out that the Indemnity Acts were by no means annual, that they still required attendance at Anglican communion, and that, above all, they still did nothing for dissenters whose consciences would not allow them to stand for public office under these circumstances.[122] Their first campaign against the Test and Corporation Acts, frequently postponed at Walpole's suggestion, ended unsuccessfully in March 1736, the Commons voting against by 251 to 123.[123] Their second, though better organized, was no more successful, going down in 1739 by 188 votes to 89.[124] These were severe set-backs. But the dissenters' organization was sophisticated, with the retention of a paid solicitor to monitor their interests and at least some attempt to influence elections by identifying members of Parliament who had 'acted a friendly part'. The Protestant dissenting deputies continued in existence as a coordinating body, though their next effort to obtain repeal was not until 1787, three years after Johnson's death.

Catholic dissenters had the least chance of obtaining concessions since they had backed the wrong horse in 1688, and not until Jacobitism had been removed from the agenda did their chances improve. Though most of the penal laws were no longer enforced, they remained on the statute book, affording an opportunity for occasional, but spiteful, prosecutions. The more enlightened mood of the 1770s, coupled with the need for Catholic soldiers from Scotland and Ireland to serve in America, per-

---

[119] *Bevis Marks Records: being contributions to the history of the Spanish and Portuguese congregation of London; the early history of the congregation from the beginning until 1800* ed. L. D. Barnett (Oxford, 1940), 35.

[120] B. L. Manning, *The Protestant Dissenting Deputies* (Cambridge, 1952). James Winter's committee in 1734 specifically commended 'the conduct of the Quakers . . . they have deputies meet together annually . . . they have a fund to defray all charges . . . they watch all proper opportunities of carrying their points . . .'. Quoted in Hunt, *Two Early Political Associations*, 141.

[121] The *regium donum* was a small grant towards the stipends of Presbyterian ministers in Ireland, begun by Charles II, increased by William III, and suspended under Anne. It was restored by George I, increased, and a small amount made available for England also.

[122] *Two Early Political Associations*, 122–8.

[123] *Parl. Hist.* ix. 1046–59. Hunt, *Two Early Political Associations*, 146–53.

[124] Hunt, *Two Early Political Associations*, 156–9.

suaded leading Catholics that an initiative might be well received. A committee was established, and a petition from 10 peers and 163 gentlemen submitted to the king. In 1778 a Relief Act, repealing certain clauses of the 1700 Act, passed without difficulty, though Catholics who wished to take advantage of the legislation were still required to swear a long oath against papal jurisdiction.[125]

The sequel was more dramatic and demonstrated that popular participation was not always an unmixed blessing. Since the Act of 1700 was before the Act of Union, the Lord Advocate had explained that parallel legislation would be introduced for Scotland. This produced a furore. Opponents there began by appealing to the church synods. Next, a Committee for the Protestant Interest was formed, which inaugurated a network of correspondence and drew in the royal burghs. The propaganda campaign was massive, crude, and effective. People like the historian William Robertson, who stood out against the tide, were threatened and ostracized. Mob violence forced the ministry to give way within weeks and assure the protestors that no Scottish legislation would be introduced. Rarely has a pressure group met with more instant success.

Lurid though these events were, they were nothing compared with those which followed in London. Wilkes, of all people, pointed out in the Commons that 'an example of a fatal nature has been given by the mobs of Edinburgh and Glasgow to the mob of London to rise'.[126] An English committee, under the leadership of Lord George Gordon, took up the running from the Scots, but aimed at the repeal of the 1778 Act. Gordon's intention was, he explained, for 'a congress, or political presbytery'. This developed into the Protestant Association, whose plan was to present a monster petition to Parliament. Gordon demanded that at least 20,000 followers should accompany him to Westminster. In the event, on 29 May, he got more than twice that number, and claimed 120,000 signatures for his petition, which, if true, made it by far the biggest ever presented. A week of rioting and bloodshed followed. The duke of Richmond, a leading radical, had the misfortune to be moving a motion for reform of Parliament, including manhood suffrage on 2 June. While he was speaking, the supporters of Lord George Gordon, blue cockades in their hats, knocked off Lord Mansfield's wig, broke the bishop of Lincoln's carriage,

---

[125] *Parl. Hist.* xix. 1138–45. 18 George III c. 60 repealed some provisions of the Act for the further preventing the growth of popery. Priests were no longer to be subject to life imprisonment and Catholics were permitted to hold landed estates. The Test and Corporation Acts remained in force.

[126] *Parl. Hist.* xx. 280–1.

stole the duke of Northumberland's watch, tore off the archbishop of York's lawn sleeves, and manhandled Lord Boston. Richmond was unable to finish his speech. Their lordships, who had had their fill of popular participation, threw out his proposals without a division.

Economic pressure groups were also common, though local rivalries were so intense that national lobbies were slower to develop. Since turnpikes, canals, enclosures, and improvement schemes all needed special Acts of Parliament, which had to be prepared and steered through, the foundations were laid. The great trading companies had their links with Parliament, many directors of the South Sea or East India company sitting in the Commons, and most of the American colonies retained agents to monitor their interests. The older tradition of looking to government for protection had not totally given way to *laissez-faire*, and poor harvests, trade recessions, or privateering activity could call up petitions to Parliament for redress. One well-conducted lobby was that organized in 1766 by Barlow Trecothick, a London merchant, to assist the first Rockingham ministry by producing evidence of the havoc caused by the Stamp Act, which they wished to repeal. Trecothick summoned a meeting, raised funds, sent out a circular letter, organized a petitioning campaign, and orchestrated the testimony offered to a parliamentary inquiry on the subject.[127] Far more ambitious was the lobby organized in the 1780s by Samuel Garbett, a Birmingham iron-master. As early as 1766 he had expressed discontent at trying to work through the members for Warwickshire, who, however willing, did not really understand business: 'we sorely want somebody who is not only intelligent but hath enlarged views to take the lead in considering our commerce as a subject of politicks.'[128] In 1785 he succeeded, with Josiah Wedgwood the potter, in setting up the General Chamber of Manufactures to bring the voice of industry to bear: 'three hundred gentlemen who are connected with that association', he wrote proudly, 'have more property and more knowledge of the state of general commerce than 300 that might be named in the House of Commons.' Garbett intended the Chamber to be a permanent organization. He succeeded in defeating Pitt's Irish propositions, but the following year the Chamber split on the Eden commercial treaty with France and disintegrated into local and separate industrial lobbies.

The vigorous growth of extra-parliamentary political associations in the

---

[127] P. D. G. Thomas, *British Politics and the Stamp Act Crisis*, 144–50.
[128] To William Burke, quoted in J. M. Norris, 'Samuel Garbett and the Early Development of Industrial Lobbying in Great Britain', *Economic History Review*, 2nd ser., 10 (1957–8), 450–60.

later eighteenth century is itself a comment on the limited, parliamentary, and hierarchical nature of the political parties. There were, of course, flourishing constituency or borough societies, such as the Union Society at Bristol, the Rockingham Club at York, or the Deptford Club in Wiltshire. But not until the foundation of the Whig Clubs in the 1780s and the Pitt Clubs after 1806 was much done to seek a national following, and then there was little in the nature of a programme or policy.

The general explanation of this marked increase in political activity is, no doubt, the more widespread dissemination of information and knowledge, which we noted earlier as part of the Enlightenment. The more immediate cause was the activity of John Wilkes, who, whatever his personal motives, seemed to many of his fellow citizens to raise important legal and constitutional questions. 'You will not suspect me of setting up *Wilkes* for a perfect character,' wrote Junius to Horne Tooke; 'the question to the public is, where shall we find a man, who . . . will go the lengths and run the hazards that he has done.'[129] The first issue, that of general warrants, was complex and technical, yet it raised the rights of the individual against the executive, a matter on which the eighteenth century was particularly sensitive. The second issue, that of the Middlesex election, would not necessarily have been of vast general interest, save that the government's legal advisers decided on the logical but maladroit step of seating Luttrell. It then became a trial of strength between Parliament and the Middlesex voters and raised quite fundamental issues: where did sovereignty reside, what was the nature of representation, and, above all, who should be the judge? It was unfortunate for the government that the American question, coming on top of the Wilkes dispute, raised many of the same themes and on a grander scale. We should also note that Wilkes provided argument for the serious and entertainment for the light-hearted. He had the rare gift of making politics seem fun—an attribute that has almost vanished from the world.

The organizational side of the Wilkite movement was the Society for the Supporters of the Bill of Rights, established in February 1769. The driving force was Horne Tooke, who, quickly disenchanted with Wilkes's egotism, seceded to form a Constitutional Society. Each society then produced its programme of reform. Though the organization of the societies was not impressive, their programmes helped to establish the radical agenda for decades to come. The Society for the Bill of Rights did not long outlast the general election of 1774, in which its success was

---

[129] Letter LII, 24 July 1771 (*Junius*, 256)

limited, but a number of members of the Constitutional Society were associated with the Society for Constitutional Information, founded in the spring of 1780. Its object was to distribute reform propaganda, it had a paid secretary, and it succeeded in carrying on until crushed by the reaction to the French Revolution in 1794.

Although the membership of the Constitutional Society was professional and gentlemanly, a class note entered into the discussion, particularly in some of the more radical pamphlets sponsored: representation should be based on persons not property.[130] The Society envisaged a network of societies in provincial towns, forming, in the end, a national association.[131] Little of this actually developed and we must not exaggerate the resources available for the political education of the British people. At its height the membership was only 169, subscriptions were often in arrears, many meetings were inquorate, the first secretary was incompetent or fraudulent or both, and, as Burke later pointed out, 'whether the books so charitably circulated were ever as charitably read', one could not say.[132]

Christopher Wyvill's Yorkshire Association was on a very different scale. Previous Associations had been little more than demonstrations of loyalty at moments of crisis and had little in the way of elaborate organization. They were also semi-official in character. The Association formed after the assassination plot against William III in 1696 was proposed in the House of Commons, and that in 1745 at the time of the Jacobite invasion by the archbishop of York.[133] By contrast, the Yorkshire Association was a grass-roots affair, though it received powerful support from the Rockingham opposition. It had its origins in the American conflict, the cost of which by 1779 made taxpayers receptive to the idea of economical reform. Yorkshire's decision on 30 December 1779 to form a committee of correspondence met with a good response from other counties, though supporters of administration were quick to denounce all Associations as seditious and potentially revolutionary. The critics of the Association were certainly right in suggesting that Wyvill would have great difficulty

---

[130] e.g. Jeremiah Batley, *Address to the People of Great Britain of All Denominations, but Particularly Those who Subsist by Honest Industry* (London, 1782).

[131] The idea of a convention was further developed by the Corresponding Societies in the 1790s and by the Chartists. It is not surprising that moderate men viewed it as an anti-Parliament.

[132] *Reflections*, 3. This account of the SCI is based upon E. C. Black, *The Association* (Cambridge, Mass., 1963).

[133] For the first, see Horwitz, *Parliament, Policy and Politics*, 175–6; for the second, a good account is Speck, *The Butcher*, 55–8, 70–1.

in retaining control. Moderate parliamentary reform soon made its appearance in addition to the proposals for economical reform, and in the London area the Quintuple Alliance took the lead in advocating radical and democratic reform. A meeting of the counties and boroughs which had responded was called by Wyvill for the St Albans Tavern, London, in February and March 1780, but it served to show how difficult it was to hold together even his loose alliance. Of the fourteen counties that had formed committees, two gave up at once, four more would not associate, three would only go as far as economical reform, and only five went the full distance with Wyvill.[134] Economical reform made some progress when the Rockinghams took office in the spring of 1782, moderate parliamentary reform had to wait some fifty years, and some of the more radical proposals, like annual Parliaments, have yet to be accomplished.[135]

The framework of Wyvill's Association was in part an attempt to eradicate some of the weaknesses of previous petitioning movements. Burke wrote to a Bristol friend in January 1780 of the importance of establishing committees of correspondence and of pursuing political objectives over several sessions of Parliament: 'the great constitutional remedy of petition is fallen into discredit enough already, by being thrown into the House and neglected ever after'.[136] Wyvill was at least able to sustain his Association, though weakened, over a period of several years and to offer support for three motions for reform of Parliament.[137] In this respect, the Yorkshire Association had considerably more stamina than some previous lobbies.

Two other Associations founded during Johnson's lifetime must also be noted, one national in character, the other humanitarian. The significant character of the Irish Volunteer movement is that, uniquely, it had force at its disposal, which may well account for its spectacular success. Rarely has the adage that England's weakness is Ireland's opportunity been more clearly demonstrated. The suggestion in 1778 that the Irish should arm themselves to resist a French invasion was gratifying, difficult to dispute, and extremely alarming. By 1780 there were no less than forty thousand

[134] Ches. and Wilts. disbanded; Sussex, Hunts., Kent, and Glos. would not associate; Bucks., Dorset, and Herts. would only support economical reform; Yorks., Middx., Essex, Surrey, and Devon adopted the full programme.

[135] For the Association, see Christie, *Wilkes, Wyvill and Reform*; Black, *The Association*; Cannon, *Parliamentary Reform*, ch. 4.

[136] Burke to Richard Champion, 24 Jan. 1780 (*Correspondence of Burke*, iv, ed. J. A. Woods, 199–200).

[137] In May 1782, May 1783, and Apr. 1785. After Pitt's third defeat, Wyvill proposed that the Yorkshire Association be disbanded, but it was allowed to 'die away'. Wyvill, iv. 467–94.

men under arms and the government was in full retreat. Substantial commercial concessions made by North's administration were followed by the grant of Irish legislative independence in 1782. But the movement overplayed its hand when it went on to embrace parliamentary reform in Ireland. The end of the American war meant that the Castle government was in a stronger situation; the question of the franchise split the movement on the issue of Catholic emancipation; and the summoning in November 1783 of a national convention in Dublin raised the spectre of an anti-Parliament. The Irish House of Commons stood firm and rejected the proposal for reform by overwhelming majorities.

The humanitarian cause was the campaign against the slave trade. The question of slavery was brought to the public attention partly by the considerable number of negro servants in London—put by the *Gentleman's Magazine* in 1764 at nearly 20,000—and by advertisements placed in newspapers for the sale or recapture of slaves. In the earlier part of the century the legal view was that slaves were 'as much property as any other thing' and had no civil rights.[138] But by the beginning of George III's reign, a change in attitude was perceptible, Lord Chancellor Henley declaring that a slave in England was entitled to habeas corpus.[139] Granville Sharp took up the cause in the 1760s after a chance meeting with an ill-used slave and in 1769 published *The Injustice of Tolerating Slavery*. Sharp was also responsible for obtaining the freedom of James Somerset in 1772 on a famous ruling by Lord Mansfield.[140] John Wesley came out strongly in *Thoughts on the Slave Trade*, written in 1774. But the most dramatic stirring of the public conscience came in the 1780s when the facts became known of the voyage of the *Zong*, a Liverpool slaver, from which no fewer than 132 slaves were thrown overboard.

The initiative for an organized campaign came, once more, from the Quakers, responding to appeals from their American brethren. In 1782 they established a committee to lobby against the trade which, in 1787, developed into a national organization. The following year it was able to mobilize more than one hundred petitions in its first parliamentary campaign. Though abolition was not carried until 1807, it represented a remarkable triumph for public opinion since, as the *Edinburgh Review* remarked, 'the sense of the nation has pressed abolition on our rulers'.[141]

[138] Lord Hardwicke, quoted in H. T. Catterall, *Judicial Cases, Concerning American Slavery and the Negro* (Washington, 1926–37), i. 12–13.

[139] Ibid. 13.

[140] But see cautionary observations on the limited nature of Mansfield's ruling in Walvin, *England, Slaves and Freedom*, 41–2.

[141] *Edinburgh Review*, 10 (1807), 205–6. See also R. Anstey, *The Atlantic Slave Trade and*

The significance of these extensions of public opinion was not lost on contemporaries. Henry Dundas—who, as Home Secretary during the early 1790s, attempted to deal with mass meetings organized by the London Corresponding Society, an offshoot of the Society for Constitutional Information—blamed the associations of the 1780s for setting an example which had 'proved fatal in their consequences'.[142] Lansdowne, in the House of Lords, declared that the mode of proceeding by association was 'a discovery of as much moment in politics as any that the present century had produced in any other science'.[143] After the peace in 1815 James Mackintosh wrote that 'the number of those that take an interest in political affairs has increased with rapidity formerly unknown'.[144] Nor was it only the Whigs who acknowledged the process. In debate in December 1819 George Canning insisted that public opinion possessed tenfold force compared with former times:

Its power was accumulated and conveyed by appropriate organs, and made to bear upon legislation and government, upon the conduct of individuals, and upon the proceedings of both Houses of Parliament.[145]

Sir James Stephen, writing in the 1840s when the Anti-Corn Law League had triumphed, placed it in a long perspective:

In later days, agitation for the accomplishment of great political objects has taken a place among social arts. But sixty years since, it was among the inventions slumbering in the womb of time, taught by no professors, and illustrated by no examples.[146]

The picture of Hanoverian politics in Johnson's lifetime which has emerged is one of a society changing so rapidly that it was in danger of outgrowing its political institutions. The settlement of 1688 had dealt remarkably well with the challenges of that period, chief of which was seen as Catholic despotism. By banishing Catholics from public life and tying down the monarchy, that danger had been overcome. For many years, and particularly while the Jacobite challenge gave a somewhat false sense of continuing menace, it was sufficient to congratulate the country on its good fortune in escaping shipwreck. Critics, malcontents, and even mild

---

British Abolition, 1760–1810 (London, 1975). The dinner party at which William Wilberforce declared his intention to work for abolition was given by Benet Langton, Johnson's old friend.

[142] *Parl. Hist.* xxxii. 340.   [143] Ibid. 534.
[144] *Edinburgh Review*, 31 (1818).   [145] *Hansard's Parliamentary Debates*, xli. 1547.
[146] *Essays in Ecclesiastical Biography* (London, 1849), ii. 234.

reformers were at a disadvantage in that they were easily accused of rocking the boat and endangering the settlement. But by the 1760s issues began to arise—on personal and political liberty, on America—which were novel and to which the old and tried formulas seemed hardly relevant.

Not that the governmental system was static and unchanging. Important concessions were made to various religious groups—indeed, as the consequences of the Jew Bill and the Roman Catholic Relief Act showed, perhaps faster than public opinion was ready for. There were indications of legal and penal reforms. New standards were set in matters of financial probity,[147] new accountability to the electorate in matters of disputed elections. In a matter of thirty years, the House of Commons abandoned its attempt to restrict the publication of debates. Even the old electoral system was subject to change in the Acts to disqualify Shoreham and Cricklade for gross corruption, and in the attempts to do the same for Shaftesbury and Hindon.[148]

The question was whether reform would be fast enough to maintain confidence in the institutions of the country. The political parties, formed for different reasons, found some difficulty in coming to terms with the situation, but more subtle politicians, like Grey, Liverpool, and Peel, began to reflect on the mood of the country and the pace of change. Grey, in particular, prided himself on his sensitivity to public opinion, and in 1820, in the aftermath of Peterloo, Peel wrote his shrewd comment to J. W. Croker:

Do not you think that the tone of England is more liberal—to use an odious but intelligible phrase—than the policy of the government? . . . It seems to me a curious crisis, when public opinion never had such influence on public measures, and yet never was so dissatisfied with the share it possessed. It is growing too large for the channels it has been accustomed to run through.[149]

Historians have found some difficulty in assessing this state of affairs. This is a little surprising since 'change and continuity' and 'a period of transition' come easily to most hard-pressed analysts. There are several reasons for the hesitancy. The static and hierarchical view of Hanoverian

---

[147] One reason for Pitt's popularity in the 1750s was his well-publicized refusal to avail himself of the interest on the Paymaster's balances. The newly established commissioners for public accounts reported sharply on Richard Rigby in 1782 and the matter was dealt with in the Rockinghams' economical reform legislation.

[148] Shoreham in 1770 and Cricklade in 1782. Bills against Shaftesbury and Hindon were brought in after 1774 but lost.

[149] L. J. Jennings (ed.), *The Correspondence and Diaries of John Wilson Croker* (London, 1884), i. 170.

England was expressed so forcibly by Namier that, when at length his statue was pulled down, men stared aghast at their own handiwork. The image of the Hanoverian period as one of calm after the turbulence of the seventeenth century was so compelling, and had so much to commend it, that there was some reluctance to begin to register those forces undermining stability. Historians often work on specific and detailed questions, and an unfortunate tendency developed to divide up into a *parti de mouvement*, tracing opinion, party, the press, reform, economic growth, and radicalism, and stressing national concerns, against a *parti de résistance*, emphasizing local horizons, deference, Anglican values, and acceptance of aristocratic rule. The historian of Hanoverian England needs a foot in both camps. He is a trimmer, leaning one way and then the other as enthusiasts overstate their cases.

The pace of change was, as we have seen, different in particular areas of public and social life, and varied greatly from place to place. It is peculiarly difficult to generalize from local studies. A certain amount of the excellent work that has been done on psephological and electoral analysis has been weakened by insufficient reflection on the distortions that can be introduced, at the very first stage, by the choice of evidence to study.[150] Let us limit ourselves to one illustration. In an important and scholarly article, J. A. Phillips uses a variety of computer techniques to study political development in Maidstone, and concludes that the increasing interest in national politics reveals the vitality of the old system: 'unless electoral behaviour in Maidstone is a complete abberation, the orthodox view that stresses the grotesque inadequacies and shocking iniquities of the unreformed electoral system neglects a significant component of eighteenth-century English politics.'[151] We can set aside the rhetoric designed to discredit the 'orthodox view'. The fact is that Professor Phillips chose to examine, out of a total of 314 possible constituencies, the one which was, in the period 1701–1832, most con-

[150] It was, I think, unwise of Frank O'Gorman, in *Voters, Patrons and Parties*, to construct a sample for analysis including five freeman boroughs, having warned of the need to obtain a representative group. One understands that uncontested boroughs, with no poll books, or corporation boroughs like Buckingham or Malmesbury with only thirteen voters, offer little for the computer to work on. But, at a later stage, placing the particular work in its larger setting, the snug boroughs must be reintroduced into the argument. The concentration of analysis on boroughs at the expense of the counties, where most of the voters lived, has produced another distortion. A detailed commentary on O'Gorman's analyses is offered by D. Beales, 'The Electorate Before and After 1832: The Right to Vote, and the Opportunity', *Parliamentary History*, 2/1 (1992), 139–50.

[151] 'From Municipal Matters to Parliamentary Principles: Eighteenth-century Borough Politics in Maidstone', *Journal of British Studies*, 27 (1988), 327–51.

tested.[152] It is hardly surprising that he discovered considerable vitality. Had he made instead a computer analysis of voting behaviour in St Germans, the programming would have been easier, since not one vote was cast in that borough between 1660 and 1832, a matter of 172 years. To generalize the character of the Hanoverian electoral system from St Germans would be as absurd as to generalize it from Maidstone. Our explanation must include them both.

This forms part of a wider question which causes some difficulty: how to place urban growth in Hanoverian England in a correct perspective. At the start of the seventeenth century, England was less urbanized than many of her continental neighbours. By 1700 the situation had changed. London, with a population of more than half a million, dwarfed all other towns and accounted for more people than the rest of the English towns put together. Norwich and Bristol, the two great provincial capitals, had 30,000 and 20,000 people, respectively. Of the others, only Newcastle upon Tyne, Exeter, and York had more than 10,000 inhabitants.

One hundred years later London had doubled in size. But the rate of growth in the rest of the urban sector had been even greater. In 1700 there had been only five towns with more than 10,000 people; by 1800, there were more than twenty-seven. Bristol and Norwich had fallen back in relative terms, and in the top twenty had emerged a number of towns without parliamentary representation at all: Manchester, Birmingham, Leeds, Sheffield, Sunderland, Stoke, Chatham, Wolverhampton, and Bolton.[153] There were social as well as political implications. 'A great city', declared Johnson, 'is, to be sure, the school for studying life.'[154]

The proportion of English people living in towns had risen from about 17 per cent in 1700 to somewhere around 27 per cent in 1800. But this meant that nearly three-quarters of the English people still lived in hamlets, villages, or small market towns. The great connurbations were far in the future and many Victorian industrial towns were still villages. The farms and disused gravel pits of Middlesbrough could muster 25 persons; Swindon had 1,198 people and Cardiff fewer than 2,000.[155]

This is, perhaps, a salutary reminder not, for Johnson's lifetime, to

---

[152] Maidstone was contested at every general election between 1701 and 1832, save that of 1713, a total of 28 contests. It is followed by London (27), Coventry (25), Southwark and Liverpool (24), Norwich, Canterbury, and Colchester (23), and Nottingham (22).

[153] E. A. Wrigley, 'Urban Growth and Industrial Change: England and the Continent in the Early Modern Period', in P. Borsay (ed.), *The Eighteenth-century Town: A Reader in English Urban History, 1688–1820* (London, 1990). Slightly different figures, on a different baseline, are offered by P. J. Corfield, *The Impact of English Towns, 1700–1800* (Oxford, 1982), but the trend is not in dispute. In table XIII, Corfield prints a very useful summary of the position in relation to parliamentary representation.

[154] *Life*, iii. 253.   [155] Census of 1801.

concentrate exclusively on London and the big towns. London was no more England in 1769 than it is today. While discussing the vitality of Coventry, Bristol, and Manchester, we must not overlook Louth, Ledbury, Buntingford, Brigg, Pershore, Thornbury, Upton-on-Severn, Much Wenlock, and Pocklington. Not infrequently, this means the historian listening to silence but that is sometimes a useful exercise.

In 1769, at the height of the agitation over John Wilkes, one of the opposition, Sir William Meredith, claimed that 'the Middlesex election was a cause in which not only the freeholders of that county were interested, but every other freeholder in the kingdom'.[156] But the Rockinghams did not find it all that easy to organize petitions on the subject. Middlesex might be on fire with indignation at the treatment of its member of Parliament, but its neighbours in Buckinghamshire were said to be 'totally ignorant of the question'; Sussex was reported 'indolent'; in Worcestershire, people waited deferentially for a lead from their superiors; while the best that Rockingham himself could report of the freeholders of Lincolnshire was that they were not all supine.[157] Mary Yorke wrote from Lincoln in the spring of 1769 that

we have scarcely heard the names of Wilks, Lutterell, etc. three times since we came; for my own part I am convinced in general that the spirit is confined within a circle of 50 miles round London . . . indeed, to say the truth, the people in general of Lincoln have the least curiosity for anything out of their own circle that ever I met with.[158]

Though it is not easy to demonstrate much continuity in either Tory personnel or party organization between the 1760s and the revived Tory party of the early nineteenth century,[159] there is less doubt of the persistence of a Tory ideology, or, if that is too pretentious a word, a Tory disposition. In this, Johnson's influence was considerable, partly as edition after edition of Boswell's *Life* diffused his views to a wider audience, more specifically through the attitudes of his friends Burke and Windham. In a very recent and important work, James Sack has pointed out how much Johnson and Burke, despite their party differences, had in common, and has traced a 'Johnsonian Tory Anglican tradition'.[160]

---

[156] *The question stated* . . . (London, 1769).

[157] *Correspondence of Burke*, ii, ed. Woods, 76, 67, 70, 48. These were responses to Burke who was masterminding the campaign.

[158] Quoted in Sir Francis Hill, *Georgian Lincoln* (Cambridge, 1966), 8.

[159] See e.g. Ian Christie's criticisms of Brian Hill's attempt to demonstrate such continuity in his article 'Party in Politics in the Age of Lord North's Administration', *Parliamentary History*, 6/1 (1987), 47–68.

[160] J. J. Sack, *From Jacobite to Conservative: Reaction and Orthodoxy in Britain*, c.*1760–1832* (Cambridge, 1993).

It is clear that Boswell's account of Johnson's life plays down the importance of Burke, who is frequently referred to anonymously as 'an eminent public character', 'an eminent person', or 'a celebrated friend of ours', and so on.[161] To some extent this was prudence on Boswell's part, since Burke was one of the people who were agitated while the *Life* was in production, fearing that Boswell would betray the decencies of society and reveal private conversations.[162] It was also artistry, in that Boswell did not want his masterpiece to have two heroes. But it means that it is necessary to reconstitute Burke. He and Johnson had known each other since the 1750s, when Burke was a young man-of-letters seeking his fortune. The two spent Christmas together in 1758 and Burke was a founder member of the Club. To Johnson, Burke was 'a great man by nature', 'an extraordinary man', 'the first man everywhere'. Burke reciprocated. He was chief pallbearer at Johnson's funeral and in December 1792, in debate in the Commons, paid a characteristically extravagant tribute, telling the House that his friendship with Johnson had been 'the greatest consolation and happiness of his life'.[163] Sack points out that they shared not only a profound distrust of metaphysical speculation, but a dislike of colonialism and of slavery, and great sympathy for the Irish and for Catholicism. Above all, each saw life as a moral and humanitarian challenge, in which the priorities were the practice of Christianity and the defence of the Church of England.

The apostolic succession was carried on by Windham, Johnson's young friend and Burke's spiritual heir. Windham had been at University College, Oxford, where his tutor was Sir Robert Chambers, at exactly the time that Johnson and Chambers were collaborating closely on the Vinerian law lectures. He was elected to the Club at an early age and was also a member of the Essex Head Club. In the last summer of Johnson's life, Windham sought him out at Ashbourne for a long conversation, visited him on his death bed, and received from his hands a copy of the New Testament. In turn, Windham became pallbearer for Burke in 1797. Brougham wrote of Windham that 'first Johnson in private, and afterwards Burke on political matters, were the two deities whom he adored'.[164]

---

[161] Commented on by T. W. Copeland, *Edmund Burke: Six Essays* (London, 1950), 11–35.

[162] See the exchange between Burke and Boswell in *Correspondence of Burke*, v, ed. H. Furber (Cambridge, 1965), 257–9; vi, ed. A. Cobban and R. A. Smith (Cambridge, 1967), 299–300.

[163] *Parl. Hist.* xxx. 109. The debate was on Fox's motion for further negotiations with revolutionary France. Erskine had quoted at length from Johnson's pamphlet on the Falkland Islands, against hasty and irresponsible war. Burke replied.

[164] *Historical Sketches* (London, 1839–43), i. 210.

Burke has often been hailed as the founding father of modern conservatism and it has been suggested that the decisive moment was in 1794, when the Portland Whigs joined with Pitt in order to prosecute more effectively the war against revolutionary France.[165] Burke was the fugleman of that campaign and Windham, by taking office as Secretary at War, placed himself in the front line of the struggle against the new order. In their furious warnings of the peril in which Britain stood and the heartlessness of metaphysicians, one hears echoes of Johnson's denunciations in the 1760s of Rousseau and his acolytes.

Though Johnson was often excitable and belligerent, he was not rancorous. In the last analysis, friendship meant more to him than politics. Even of the American war, which called forth strong passions in Johnson and many other Englishmen, it was said that, once it was over, 'he spoke without the heat and prejudice of a partisan'.[166] He was, at the end, on civil terms with Soame Jenyns and with John Wilkes, to whom he sent a set of the *Lives of the Poets*. In the crisis of 1784 he told a somewhat surprised Boswell that, though he was for the king against Fox, he was for Fox against Pitt: 'the king is my master; but I do not know Pitt; and Fox is my friend.'[167]

It is not, I hope, fanciful to suggest that in the life of Samuel Johnson one sees some of the ambiguities, contradictions, and uncertainties of Hanoverian England. He had one foot in Lichfield, a quiet cathedral city of less than five thousand people, and the other in London, fashionable, cosmopolitan, teeming, argumentative. He loved the poor and hated the rabble. Towards the aristocracy his attitude was, formally, respectful, but in practice prickly. He disliked the savagery of the penal code while worrying about the growing irreverence of the populace. He was unsentimental about the past, disturbed by the present, and apprehensive for the future. He was a gregarious loner—'a kind of solitary wanderer in the wild of life' was his own elegiac phrase[168]—and a ferocious moderate.

By the end of Johnson's life could be discerned the shape of the great crisis of early-nineteenth-century England. Party was established on the political scene and it was idle to dream any longer of eradicating it. The concept of a permanent and systematic opposition had been long recognized and widely accepted. Radical proposals and aspirations were dis-

---

[165] F. O'Gorman, *British Conservatism: Conservative Thought from Burke to Thatcher* (London, 1986), 12; R. Pares, *King George III and the Politicians* (Oxford, 1953), 194–5.

[166] Testimony of William Bowles to Boswell, in Waingrow (ed.), *Correspondence Relating to the Making of the Life of Johnson*, 245–50.

[167] *Life*, iv. 292.   [168] To Thomas Warton, 21 Dec. 1754 (*Letters*, ed. Redford, i. 90).

cussed and supported by a vigorous and expanding press. A less deferential attitude meant that the aristocracy, Parliament, and the Crown were criticized in ways that would have been almost unthinkable one hundred years before. The contrast between the living and dead parts of the electoral system was more apparent than ever.

Within thirty years of his death, great developments had taken place in areas in which Johnson had been much concerned: popular education,[169] public information,[170] negro emancipation,[171] and penal reform.[172] It was a long way from the world of Queen Anne into which Johnson had been born. Politically, it was no longer a question of whether reform would come but, as Peel said, how and when. To these changes Johnson had made, perhaps unwittingly, a significant contribution.

[169] The foundation of Joseph Lancaster's Royal Lancastrian Society and, in 1811, Andrew Bell's National Society.

[170] T. C. Hansard, son of Luke Hansard, whom Johnson admired as a printer, took over the publication of parliamentary debates from 1803 onwards.

[171] Wilberforce carried the abolition of the slave trade in Mar. 1807.

[172] Romilly's first success in his campaign to reduce capital offences came in 1808, when an Act, 48 George III c. 129, was passed to abolish the death penalty for stealing from the person.

Select Bibliography

The bibliography is divided into four sections: 1. works by Johnson; 2. contemporary accounts of Johnson; 3. recent works relating to Johnson; 4. recent works on Hanoverian politics and society.

Works by Johnson

A Course of Lectures on the English Law, Delivered in the University of Oxford by Sir Robert Chambers . . . in Association with Samuel Johnson, ed. T. M. Curley, 2 vols. (Oxford, 1986). (Sir Robert Chambers succeeded Blackstone as Vinerian Professor of English Law in the University of Oxford and delivered his course of lectures from 1767 onwards. Johnson gave substantial assistance.)

Adventurer, The, ed. W. J. Bate, J. M. Bullitt, and L. F. Powell, in *Yale Edition of the Works of Samuel Johnson*, ii (New Haven, Conn., 1963). (29 contributions to *The Adventurer* by Johnson between Mar. 1753 and Mar. 1754.)

Diaries, Prayers and Annals, ed. E. L. MacAdam, Jr., with D. and M. Hyde, in *Yale Edition of the Works of Samuel Johnson*, i (New Haven, Conn., 1958).

Dictionary of the English Language (London, 1979). (Facsimile of 1st edn. of 15 Apr. 1755.)

Early Biographical Writings of Dr. Johnson, ed. J. D. Fleeman (Farnborough, 1973). (A collection of short biographies.)

History of Rasselas, Prince of Abissinia, The (1759), ed. R. W. Chapman (Oxford, 1927).

Idler, The, ed. W. J. Bate, J. M. Bullitt, and L. F. Powell, in *Yale Edition of the Works of Samuel Johnson*, ii (New Haven, Conn., 1963). (104 contributions to *The Idler* by Johnson between Apr. 1758 and Apr. 1760.)

Irene, a Tragedy, ed. E. L. MacAdam, Jr., with G. Milne, in *Yale Edition of the Works of Samuel Johnson*, vi (New Haven, Conn., 1964). (D. Nichol Smith and E. L. MacAdam, Jr. (eds.), *The Poems of Samuel Johnson* (Oxford, 1941), reproduce the original capitalization and also Johnson's first draft of the play.)

Johnson on Shakespeare, ed. A. Sherbo, in *Yale Edition of the Works of Samuel Johnson*, vii–viii (New Haven, Conn., 1968).

Journey into North Wales in the Year 1774, in James Boswell, *The Life of Samuel Johnson*, ed. G. B. Hill (Oxford, 1887), rev. L. F. Powell (Oxford, 1934–50), v. 427–61. (This diary was unknown to Boswell.)

Journey to the Western Islands of Scotland, ed. M. Lascelles, in *Yale Edition of the Works of Samuel Johnson*, ix (New Haven, Conn., 1971); ed. J. D. Fleeman (Oxford, 1985).

Letters of Samuel Johnson, The, ed. R. W. Chapman, 3 vols. (Oxford, 1952); rev. B. Redford, 5 vols. (Oxford, 1992–4).

Lives of the English Poets, ed. G. B. Hill, 3 vols. (Oxford, 1905); ed. with introd. by Arthur Waugh, 2 vols. (World's Classics ser.; Oxford, 1906).

Parliamentary Debates, ed. John Stockdale, 2 vols. (London, 1787); repr. in Arthur Murphy (ed.), *Works of Samuel Johnson* (London, 1811). (Johnson had responsibility for the parliamentary reports in the *Gentleman's Magazine* between 1741 and 1744. For a modern commentary, see B. B. Hoover, *Samuel Johnson's Parliamentary Reporting: Debates in the Senate of Lilliput* (Berkeley, Calif., 1953).)

Poems, ed. E. L. MacAdam with G. Milne, in *Yale Edition of the Works of Samuel Johnson*, vi (Yale, 1964). (Includes 'London', 'The Vanity of Human Wishes', and 'On the Death of Dr. Robert Levett'.)

Political Writings, ed. D. J. Greene, in *Yale Edition of the Works of Samuel Johnson*, x (New Haven, Conn., 1977). (Includes the four pamphlets of 1770–5.)

Rambler, The, ed. W. J. Bate and A. B. Strauss, in *Yale Edition of the Works of Samuel Johnson*, iii–v (New Haven, Conn., 1969). (Johnson's 208 essays for *The Rambler* between Mar. 1750 and Mar. 1752.)

'Review of Soame Jenyns, *A Free Inquiry into the Nature and Origin of Evil*', in D. J. Greene (ed.), *Samuel Johnson* (Oxford, 1984), 522–43. (This important review was first pub. in the *Literary Magazine* (1757).)

Samuel Johnson, ed. D. J. Greene (Oxford Authors ser.; Oxford, 1984).

Sermons, ed. J. Hagstrum and J. Gray, in *Yale Edition of the Works of Samuel Johnson*, xiv (New Haven, Conn., 1978). (28 sermons written for John Taylor and other clergymen.)

Voyage to Abyssinia (1735), ed. J. J. Gold, in *Yale Edition of the Works of Samuel Johnson*, xv (Yale, 1985). (Johnson's trans. of Father Lobo's 17th-cent. French work.)

Works, ed. J. Buckland, 11 vols. (London, 1787; incl. Hawkins's *Life*); 12 vols. (London, 1792; incl. Murphy's *Essay*); ed. A. Chalmers, 12 vols. (London, 1806); 12 vols. (London, 1824). (First coll. edns.)

Contemporary Accounts of Johnson

BOSWELL, JAMES, *The Letters of James Boswell*, ed. C. B. Tinker, 2 vols. (Oxford, 1924).

——*Journal of a Tour to the Hebrides with Samuel Johnson, LL.D.* (1785), ed. F. A. Pottle and C. H. Bennett (London, 1936). (This edn. follows the orig. MS.)

—— *The Life of Samuel Johnson, LL.D.* (1791), ed. G. B. Hill (Oxford 1887), rev. L. F. Powell, 6 vols. (Oxford, 1934–50). (This standard edn. is a vast repository of information, but fast becoming outdated in the light of modern scholarship.)

—— *Journals*, in *Yale Edition of the Private Papers of James Boswell* (New Haven, Conn., 1950–••).

BURNEY, FANNY, *Journal and Letters of Fanny Burney*, ed. J. Henlow *et al.*, 12 vols. (Oxford, 1972–84).

HAWKINS, SIR JOHN, *The Life of Samuel Johnson, LL.D.* (1792), abr. and ed. B. H. Davis (London, 1962).

HILL, G. B. (ed.), *Johnsonian Miscellanies* (Oxford, 1897), ii. (Contains a number of shorter memoirs.)

MAXWELL, WILLIAM, 'Collectanea', in James Boswell, *The Life of Samuel Johnson, LL.D.*, ed. G. B. Hill (Oxford, 1887), ii. 116–33. (Boswell used evidence furnished by Maxwell to fill a gap in his *Life of Johnson*.)

MURPHY, ARTHUR, *An Essay on the Life and Genius of Samuel Johnson, LL.D.* (1792), in G. B. Hill (ed.), *Johnsonian Miscellanies* (Oxford, 1897), i. 355–488.

PIOZZI, MRS HESTER, *Anecdotes of the Late Samuel Johnson, LL.D., During the Last Twenty Years of His Life* (1786), in G. B. Hill (ed.), *Johnsonian Miscellanies* (Oxford, 1897), i. 141–351.

—— *Thraliana: The Diary of Mrs. Hester Lynch Thrale (later Mrs. Piozzi), 1776–1809*, ed. K. C. Balderston (Oxford, 1942).

REYNOLDS, SIR JOSHUA and MISS FRANCES, 'Recollections', in G. B. Hill (ed.), *Johnsonian Miscellanies* (Oxford, 1897), ii. 219–300.

SHAW, WILLIAM, *Memoirs of the Life and Writings of the Late Dr. Samuel Johnson* (London, 1785).

TOWERS, JOSEPH, *An Essay on the Life, Character, and Writings of Dr. Samuel Johnson* (London, 1786).

TYERS, THOMAS, *A Biographical Sketch of Dr. Samuel Johnson* (1784), in G. B. Hill (ed.), *Johnsonian Miscellanies* (Oxford, 1897), ii. 335–81. (This was rushed out on Johnson's death and appeared in *Gentleman's Magazine* (Dec. 1784). It was subsequently reprinted in pamphlet form.)

WAINGROW, M. (ed.), *Correspondence and Other Papers of James Boswell Relating to the Making of the Life of Johnson* (New Haven, Conn., 1969). (Anecdotes and evidence assiduously collected by Boswell after Johnson's death.)

Recent Works Relating to Johnson

ALKON, P. K., *Samuel Johnson and Moral Discipline* (Evanston, Ill., 1967).

BATE, W. J., *The Achievement of Samuel Johnson* (Oxford, 1955).

—— *Samuel Johnson* (London, 1978).

BOULTON, J. T. (ed.), *Samuel Johnson: The Critical Heritage* (London, 1971).

BRACK, O. M., Jr., and R. B. KELLEY (eds.), *The Early Biographies of Samuel Johnson* (Iowa City, Ia., 1974).

BRADY, F., *Boswell's Political Career* (New Haven, Conn., 1965).

CHAPIN, C. F., *The Religious Thought of Samuel Johnson* (Ann Arbor, Mich., 1968).

CLIFFORD, J. L., *Hester Lynch Piozzi* (Oxford, 1941).

CLIFFORD, J. L., *Young Samuel Johnson* (London, 1955).

—— *Dictionary Johnson* (London, 1980).

CLIFFORD, J. L., and D. J. GREENE, (eds.), *Samuel Johnson, a Survey and Bibliography of Critical Studies* (Minneapolis, 1970).

CLINGHAM, G. (ed.), *New Light on Boswell: Critical and Historical Essays on the Occasion of the Bicentenary of the Life of Johnson* (Cambridge, 1991).

DAVIS, P., *In Mind of Johnson: A Study of Johnson the Rambler* (London, 1989).

GREENE, D. J., *The Politics of Samuel Johnson* (New Haven, Conn., 1960).

—— (ed.), *Samuel Johnson: A Collection of Critical Essays* (Englewood Cliffs, NJ, 1965).

GRUNDY, I., *Samuel Johnson and the Scale of Greatness* (Leicester, 1986).

—— (ed.), *Samuel Johnson: New Critical Essays* (London, 1984).

HARDY, J. P., *Samuel Johnson, a Critical Study* (London, 1979).

HIBBERT, C., *The Personal History of Samuel Johnson* (London, 1971).

HILLES, F. W., *New Light on Dr. Johnson* (New Haven, Conn., 1959).

HINNANT, C. H., *Samuel Johnson: An Analysis* (Basingstoke, 1988).

HOLMES, R., *Dr. Johnson and Mr. Savage* (London, 1993).

HOOVER, B. B., *Samuel Johnson's Parliamentary Reporting: Debates in the Senate of Lilliput* (Berkeley, Calif., 1953).

HUDSON, N., *Samuel Johnson and Eighteenth-century Thought* (Oxford, 1988).

HYDE, D., *Eighteenth-century Studies in Honour of Douglas Hyde* (New York, 1970).

KAMINSKI, T., *The Early Career of Samuel Johnson* (Oxford, 1987).

KERNAN, A., *Printing Technology, Letters and Samuel Johnson* (Princeton, 1987).

—— *Samuel Johnson and the Impact of Print* (Princeton, NJ, 1989).

KORSHIN, P. J. (ed.), *Johnson After Two Hundred Years* (Philadelphia, 1986).

KRUTCH, J. W., *Samuel Johnson* (London, 1948).

LASCELLES, MARY, JOHN HARDY, JAMES L. CLIFFORD, and J. D. FLEEMAN (eds.), *Johnson, Boswell and their Circle: Essays Presented to L. F. Powell* (Oxford, 1965).

MCINTOSH, C., *The Choice of Life: Samuel Johnson and the World of Fiction* (New Haven, Conn., 1973).

PIERCE, C. E., *The Religious Life of Samuel Johnson* (London, 1983).

QUINLAN, M. J., *Samuel Johnson, a Layman's Religion* (Madison, Wis., 1964).

REDDICK, A., *The Making of Johnson's Dictionary, 1746–73* (Cambridge, 1990).

SCHWARTZ, R. B., *Samuel Johnson and the New Science* (Madison, Wis., 1971).

—— *Samuel Johnson and the Problem of Evil* (Madison, Wis., 1976).

SLEDD, J. H., and G. J. KOLB (eds.), *Dr. Johnson's Dictionary: Essays in the Biography of a Book* (Chicago, 1955).

TEMMER, M., *Samuel Johnson and Three Infidels: Rousseau, Voltaire, Diderot* (Athens, Ga., 1988).

VANCE, J. A., *Samuel Johnson and the Sense of History* (Athens, Ga., 1984).

VOITLE, R., *Samuel Johnson the Moralist* (Cambridge, Mass., 1961).

WAIN, J., *Samuel Johnson* (London, 1974).

WHARTON, T. F., *Samuel Johnson and the Theme of Hope* (London, 1984).

WILTSHIRE, J., *Samuel Johnson in the Medical World: The Doctor and the Patient* (Cambridge, 1991).

Recent Works Relating to Hanoverian Politics and Society

BECKETT, J. V., *The Aristocracy in England, 1660–1914* (Oxford, 1986).

BLACK, E. C., *The Association: British Extra-parliamentary Political Organization* (Cambridge, Mass., 1963).

BLACK, J., *The English Press in the Eighteenth Century* (London, 1987).

—— (ed.), *Britain in the Age of Walpole* (London, 1984).

—— (ed.), *British Politics and Society from Walpole to Pitt* (London, 1990).

BRADLEY, J. E., *Religion, Revolution and English Radicalism: Non-conformity in Eighteenth-century Politics and Society* (Cambridge, 1990).

BREWER, J., *Party Ideology and Popular Politics at the Accession of George III* (Cambridge, 1976).

—— *The Sinews of Power: War, Money and the English State, 1688–1783* (London, 1989).

—— and J. STYLES (eds.), *An Ungovernable People: The English and their Law in the Seventeenth and Eighteenth Centuries* (London, 1980).

BUTTERFIELD, H., *George III and the Historians* (London, 1957).

CANNON, J. A., *The Fox–North Coalition: Crisis of the Constitution, 1782–4* (Cambridge, 1969).

—— *Parliamentary Reform, 1640–1832* (Cambridge, 1972).

—— *Aristocratic Century: The Peerage of Eighteenth-century England* (Cambridge, 1984).

—— (ed.) *The Letters of Junius* (Oxford, 1978).

—— (ed.) *The Whig Ascendancy: Colloquies on Hanoverian England* (London, 1981).

CHALKIN, C. W., *The Provincial Towns of Georgian England* (London, 1974).

CHRISTIE, I. R., *The End of North's Ministry, 1780–1782* (London, 1958).

—— *Wilkes, Wyvill and Reform* (London, 1962).

—— *Myth and Reality in Late-eighteenth-century British Politics and Other Papers* (London, 1970).

—— *Stress and Stability in Late-eighteenth-century Britain* (Oxford, 1984).

CLARK, J. C. D., *English Society, 1688–1832: Ideology, Social Structure and Political Practice during the Ancien Régime* (Cambridge, 1985).

COLLEY, L., *In Defiance of Oligarchy: The Tory Party, 1714–60* (Cambridge, 1982).

—— *Britons: Forging the Nation, 1707–1837* (New Haven, Conn., 1992).

CORFIELD, P. J., *The Impact of English Towns, 1700–1800* (Oxford, 1982).

CRANFIELD, G., *The Development of the Provincial Newspaper, 1700–1760* (Oxford, 1962).

—— *The Press and Society: From Caxton to Northcliffe* (London, 1978).

CRUICKSHANKS, E., *Political Untouchables: The Tories and the 1745* (London, 1979).

—— (ed.), *Ideology and Conspiracy: Aspects of Jacobitism, 1689–1759* (Edinburgh, 1982).

—— and J. BLACK (eds.), *The Jacobite Challenge* (Edinburgh, 1981).

DICKINSON, H. T., *Liberty and Property: Political Ideology in Eighteenth-century Britain* (London, 1977).

—— (ed.), *Politics and Literature in the Eighteenth Century* (London, 1974).

EARLE, P., *The Making of the English Middle Classes: Business, Society and Family Life in London, 1660–1730* (London, 1989).

FORTESCUE, SIR JOHN (ed.), *The Correspondence of King George the Third from 1760 to December 1783* (London, 1927–8).

GUNN, J. W., *Beyond Liberty and Property* (Ontario, 1983).

HAY, D. (ed.), *Albion's Fatal Tree: Crime and Society in Eighteenth Century England* (London, 1975).

HILL, B. W., *The Growth of Parliamentary Parties, 1689–1742* (London, 1976).

—— *British Parliamentary Parties, 1742–1832* (London, 1985).

HOLMES, G. S., *British Politics in the Age of Anne* (London, 1967).

—— *The Trial of Doctor Sacheverell* (London, 1973).

—— *Augustan England: Professions, State and Society, 1680–1730* (London, 1982).

—— *The Making of a Great Power: Late Stuart and Early Georgian England, 1660–1722* (London, 1993).

—— and W. A. SPECK (eds.), *The Divided Society: Party Conflict in England 1694–1716* (London, 1967).

—— and D. SZECHI, *The Age of Oligarchy: Pre-industrial Britain, 1722–83* (London, 1993).

HORWITZ, H., *Parliament, Policy and Politics in the Reign of William III* (Manchester, 1977).

HUGHES, E., *North Country Life in the Eighteenth Century*, i: *The North-East, 1700–1750* (London, 1952); ii: *Cumberland and Westmorland, 1700–1830* (London, 1965).

HUNT, N. C., *Two Early Political Associations: The Quakers and the Dissenting Deputies in the Age of Sir Robert Walpole* (Oxford, 1961).

JONES, C. (ed.), *Britain in the First Age of Party: Essays Presented to Geoffrey Holmes* (London, 1987).

JONES, J. R., *The Revolution of 1688 in England* (London, 1972).

—— (ed.), *Liberty Secured?: Britain Before and After 1688* (Stanford, Calif., 1992).

LANDAU, N., *The Justices of the Peace, 1679–1760* (Berkeley, Calif., 1984).

LANGFORD, P., *The First Rockingham Administration, 1765–66* (London, 1973).

—— *The Excise Crisis* (Oxford, 1975).

—— *A Polite and Commercial People: England, 1727–1783* (Oxford, 1989).

—— *Public Life and the Propertied Englishman, 1689–1789* (Oxford, 1991).

MACHIN, G. I. T., *The Catholic Question in English Politics, 1820–1830* (London, 1964).

MCKENDRICK, N., J. BREWER, and J. H. PLUMB (eds.), *The Birth of a Consumer Society* (London, 1982).

MIDDLETON, R., *The Bells of Victory: The Pitt–Newcastle Ministry and the Conduct of the Seven Years War, 1757–1762* (Cambridge, 1985).

MINGAY, G. E., *English Landed Society in the Eighteenth Century* (London, 1963).

—— *The Gentry: Rise and Fall of a Ruling Class* (London, 1976).

MITCHELL, L. G., *Charles James Fox and the Disintegration of the Whig Party, 1782–94* (Oxford, 1971).

MONEY, J., *Experience and Identity: Birmingham and the West Midlands, 1760–1800* (Manchester, 1977).

MONOD, P., *Jacobitism and the English People, 1688–1788* (Cambridge, 1985).

MUNSCHE, P. B., *Gentlemen and Poachers: The English Game Laws 1671–1831* (Cambridge, 1981).

NAMIER, SIR LEWIS, *The Structure of Politics at the Accession of George III* (London, 1929).

—— *England in the Age of the American Revolution* (London, 1930).

—— and J. BROOKE (eds.), *The History of Parliament: The House of Commons, 1754–90* (London, 1964).

NEWMAN, G., *The Rise of English Nationalism: A Cultural History, 1740–1830* (London, 1987).

NORRIS, J., *Shelburne and Reform* (London, 1963).

O'GORMAN, F., *The Whig Party and the French Revolution* (London, 1967).

—— *The Rise of Party in England: The Rockingham Whigs, 1760–1782* (London, 1975).

—— *The Emergence of the British Two-party System, 1760–1832* (London, 1982).

—— *Voters, Patrons and Parties: The Unreformed Electorate of Hanoverian England, 1734–1832* (Oxford, 1989).

OWEN, J. B., *The Eighteenth Century: 1741–1815* (London, 1974).

PERKIN, H., *The Origins of Modern English Society, 1780–1880* (London, 1969).

PERRY, T. W., *Public Opinion, Propaganda and Politics in Eighteenth-century England* (Cambridge, Mass., 1962).

PETERS, M., *Pitt and Popularity: The Patriot Minister and London Opinion during the Seven Years War* (Oxford, 1980).

PETRIE, SIR CHARLES, *The Jacobite Movement* (London, 1959).

PHILLIPS, J. A., *Electoral Behaviour in Unreformed England: Plumpers, Splitters and Straights* (Princeton, NJ, 1982).

PLUMB, SIR JOHN, *The Growth of Political Stability in England, 1675–1725* (London, 1967).

ROGERS, N., *Whigs and Cities: Popular Politics in the Age of Walpole and Pitt* (Oxford, 1989).

RUDÉ, G., *Wilkes and Liberty: A Social Study of 1763 to 1774* (Oxford, 1962).

SACK, J. J., *From Jacobite to Conservative: Reaction and Orthodoxy in Britain, c.1760–1832* (Cambridge, 1993).

SEDGWICK, R. R. (ed.), *The History of Parliament: The House of Commons, 1715–54* (London, 1970).

SMITH, E. A., *Whig Principles and Party Politics: Earl Fitzwilliam and the Whig Party 1748–1833* (Manchester, 1975).

SPECK, W. A., *Tory and Whig: The Struggle in the Constituencies, 1701–1715* (London, 1970).

—— *Stability and Strife: England, 1714–1760* (London, 1977).

—— *Society and Literature in England, 1700–60* (Dublin, 1983).

—— *Reluctant Revolutionaries: Englishmen and the Revolution of 1688* (Oxford, 1988).

SZECHI, D., *Jacobitism and Tory Politics, 1710–1714* (Edinburgh, 1984).

THOMAS, P. D. G., *British Politics and the Stamp Act Crisis: The First Phase of the American Revolution, 1763–1767* (Oxford, 1975).

—— *The House of Commons in the Eighteenth Century* (Oxford, 1981).

THOMPSON, E. P., *Whigs and Hunters: The Origin of the Black Act* (London, 1975).

WARD, W. R., *Georgian Oxford: University Politics in the Eighteenth Century* (Oxford, 1958).

WHITEMAN, A. (ed.), *Statesmen, Scholars and Merchants: Essays in Eighteenth-century History Presented to Dame Lucy Sutherland* (Oxford, 1973).

WILES, R. M., *Freshest Advices: Early Provincial Newspapers in England* (Columbus, Oh., 1965).

WILLIAMS, E. N. (ed.), *The Eighteenth-century Constitution, 1688–1815* (Cambridge, 1960).

Index

Johnson's writings are indexed under Johnson IV